Government policy towards industry in the United States and Japan

Government policy towards industry in the United States and Japan

Proceedings of a conference co-organized by Chikashi Moriguchi and John B. Shoven and sponsored by the Center for Economic Policy Research of Stanford University and the Suntory Foundation of Japan.

Edited by
JOHN B. SHOVEN
Stanford University
and
National Bureau of Economic Research

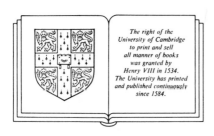

The right of the
University of Cambridge
to print and sell
all manner of books
was granted by
Henry VIII in 1534.
The University has printed
and published continuously
since 1584.

CAMBRIDGE UNIVERSITY PRESS
Cambridge
New York   New Rochelle   Melbourne   Sydney

Published by the Press Syndicate of the University of Cambridge
The Pitt Building, Trumpington Street, Cambridge CB2 1RP
32 East 57th Street, New York, NY 10022, USA
10 Stamford Road, Oakleigh, Melbourne 3166, Australia

First published 1988

Printed in the United States of America

Library of Congress Cataloging-in-Publication Data
Government policy towards industry in the United States and Japan /
edited by John B. Shoven.
p. cm.
ISBN 0-521-33325-3
1. Industry and state – United States.   2. Industry and state –
Japan.   3. Corporations – Taxation – United States.   4. Corporations –
Taxation – Japan.   I. Shoven, John B.
HD3616.U47G7145   1988
338.952 – dc19   87–29490
                                                                            CIP

British Library Cataloguing in Publication Data
Government policy towards industry in the
United States and Japan.
1. Japan. Industries. Policies of
government   2. United States. Industries.
Policies of government
I. Shoven, John B.
338.952

ISBN 0 521 33325 3

Contents

v

Contributors

Albert Ando
Department of Economics
University of Pennsylvania
Philadelphia, PA 19104

Masahiko Aoki
Department of Economics
Stanford University
Stanford, CA 94305

Alan Auerbach
Department of Economics
University of Pennsylvania
Philadelphia, PA 19104

Michael J. Boskin
Department of Economics
Stanford University
Stanford, CA 94305

Akira Goto
Economics Department
Seikei University
Musahino-Shi, Tokyo 180
Japan

James E. Hodder
Industrial Engineering and
   Engineering Management
Stanford University
Stanford, CA 94305

Hiromitsu Ishi
Department of Economics
Hitosubashi University
Kumitachi, Tokyo 186
Japan

Richard C. Levin
Department of Economics
Yale University
New Haven, CT 06520

Chikashi Moriguchi
Institute of Social and Economic
   Research
Osaka University
Ibaraki, Osaka 567
Japan

Iwao Nakatani
Faculty of Economics
Osaka University
Toyonaka, Osaka 567
Japan

Merton J. Peck
Department of Economics
Yale University
New Haven, CT 06520

John M. Roberts
National Bureau of Economic Research
204 Junipero Serra Boulevard
Stanford, CA 94305

John B. Shoven
Department of Economics
Stanford University
Stanford, CA 94305

W. Edward Steinmueller
Center for Economic Policy Research
Stanford University
Stanford, CA 94305

Toshiaki Tachibanaki
Institute of Economic Research
Kyoto University
Sakyo-ku, Kyoto 606
Japan

Kazuo Ueda
Institute of Monetary and Fiscal Policy
Ministry of Finance
Chiyoda-ku, Tokyo 100
Japan

Acknowledgments

The chapters in this volume offer many insights into government policies toward industry in the United States and Japan. I believe that they provide essential material to gain a better understanding of the economic interactions and performances of these two great economies. The conference and this book would not have been feasible without the financial support of Stanford's Center for Economic Policy Research and Japan's Suntory Foundation. It also would not have been possible without the planning of the conference co-organizer, Chikashi Moriguchi, the editorial assistance of John Karl Scholz, and the secretarial and administrative support provided by Karen Prindle.

John B. Shoven

Editor's summary

John B. Shoven

1   Introduction

The United States and Japan are the two largest economies in the world. Both countries experienced the inflationary consequences of the oil price shocks of the 1970s, both national governments have large deficits, and both have been considering or enacting major tax reforms. The growth rate of the Japanese economy continues to be the envy of the rest of the developed world, despite the fact that Japan has suffered many of the same external economic shocks as the other countries.

There are numerous important economic issues that involve the United States and Japan and their interaction. Considerable trade friction has developed between the two countries as a consequence of the large current-account deficit of the United States, the trade surplus of Japan, and, most directly, the bilateral trade surplus of Japan. A widely debated issue is whether the trade imbalance is due to Japanese trade restrictions or due to the imbalance of U.S. fiscal policy.

The trade frictions between the United States and Japan have perhaps been most severe in the microelectronics industry. One issue regarding that industry is whether Japan has been dumping integrated circuits on world markets or is simply more cost-efficient in producing them. Certainly, Japan has proved to be a tough competitor in that market, as in so many others.

There are many important economic issues that concern government policies toward industry in the United States and Japan. For instance, how have the two countries handled their declining industries, such as steel? These industries exist in both countries, and the number of such situations probably has grown because of the rapid increase in the relative price of energy. Whereas considerable attention has been paid to the

1

Japanese success stories (as in their microelectronics industry), little notice has been taken of how resources have been redeployed away from shrinking industries in Japan.

Japan, of course, has very limited domestic energy supplies, and it is remarkable that the economy weathered the oil price shocks as well as it did. An issue worth examining is the government policy that accompanied that success. Another factor alleged to be important in Japan's rapid growth rate is its low cost of capital. The issue is whether or not the cost of capital in Japan is really lower than in the United States and, if so, what government policies have accomplished this. In particular, does the Japanese tax system create a smaller wedge between the earnings of Japanese investments and the return to investors than the American system imposes between U.S. investments and investors? Has the use of targeted tax incentives in Japan been a major aspect of industrial policy, and how extensive is the practice? How are Japanese firms and banks, with their traditional close working relationship, reacting to the deregulation of world and domestic capital markets?

With these sorts of issues framing the agenda, Stanford University's Center for Economic Policy Research and the Suntory Foundation of Japan jointly funded a conference held on the Stanford campus in May of 1985. The conference was co-organized by Chikashi Moriguchi and myself. Our goal was to facilitate an exchange of economic research on the effects of government policy toward industry in Japan and the United States. The conference provided lively discussion, and 11 of those presentations have been revised to form the chapters of this volume. They represent state-of-the-art thinking on many important issues relating to government policy in the Japanese and American economies.

The chapters in this book have been grouped into three broad topic areas. Chapters 2–5 concern the cost of capital, capital-income taxation, and saving/investment in the two economies. Saving and capital formation are widely regarded as primary determinants of economic growth, and tax policy clearly affects saving and investment in both countries. Chapters 6 and 7 concern bilateral and international trade and the effects of tax policy on the persistent current-account imbalance between the two countries. The international trade issue is one of great current interest, and the link between that issue and taxation has previously not been carefully examined in the literature. Finally, Chapters 8–12 deal with industrial organization and bureaucratic structure in Japan and the United States. Separate studies are presented concerning declining industries, energy conservation, the finance industry, and policies affecting semiconductor companies in the two countries.

The chapters are quickly summarized in the next three sections of this introductory chapter.

2   Taxation of income from capital

The first section of this book contains four chapters that examine the taxation of income from capital in Japan and the United States. In Chapter 2, Albert Ando and Alan Auerbach investigate a proposition that is frequently made in business and policy circles: that Japan's economic success over the past two decades has been a consequence of Japanese firms' ability to raise funds in capital markets at a lower cost than American firms. Ando and Auerbach empirically examine this proposition using a sample of 19 American firms and 21 Japanese firms, including major companies in 10 different industries in each country.

Ando and Auerbach start their analysis by examining earnings–price ratios and total return to debt plus equity averaged over the 1966–81 period for both the Japanese and American companies. When the data are aggregated over time in this manner, there is no evidence that Japanese firms have had a lower rate of return to capital than American firms; in fact, the median values for all firms in the Japanese and American samples are identical when a correction is made for Japanese pension accounting.

Ando and Auerbach recognize the difficulties posed by drawing conclusions from using book-value earnings data to measure the cost of capital. They spend the next section of their chapter modifying the aggregate earnings–price ratios and figures on total return to capital to account for the different inflationary experiences of Japan and the United States. They first estimate the difference between the book measure of depreciation and economic depreciation for each company in each year of the sample. This difference is added to earnings.

Inflation will also undervalue inventories and exaggerate earnings under all inventory accounting systems other than an indexed first-in, first-out (FIFO) system. Thus, Ando and Auerbach estimate the fraction of inventories carried under each accounting method for each year. They then reduce measured returns to capital accordingly. It is well known that the nominal interest cost (without indexed liabilities) exceeds the real debt burden in an inflationary environment. Thus, it is important to add the "capital gains" (reduced cost of debt due to inflation) on nominal liabilities to book earnings. One would expect firms with higher debt-to-equity ratios to have larger gains on nominal liabilities – these gains increase as inflation increases.

These adjustments lower the overall return to capital in both countries, as measured by inflation-corrected earnings and interest payments divided by the sum of equity and the book value of financial liabilities. The reduction in Japanese value is larger, however, so that the corrected median average before-tax return to capital in the United States is 9.4%.

In Japan it is 7.5%. These differences are more evident in some industries than in others, but this suggests that the return to capital (and hence the cost of capital) may in fact be systematically lower in Japan than in the United States.

The final section of the Ando–Auerbach chapter considers potential sources of differences in returns to capital and raises some cautionary issues concerning interpretation of the results they present. They first ask whether or not business taxation forces the before-tax return to capital to be higher in the United States than in Japan. After calculating the effects taxes have on the corrected before-tax earnings–price ratios and return to capital, Ando and Auerbach find that it is Japanese firms, not American firms, that are taxed more heavily on their real equity income at the corporate level. More than 75% of the Japanese firms have their average before-tax return to capital cut in half after taxes, whereas that is the case for fewer than half of the American firms. These authors point out that this conclusion would be strengthened even further if the government business tax provisions of the U.S. 1981 tax act were incorporated into their analysis. Ando and Auerbach also provide upper-bound estimates of the tax advantage to leveraging firms (the corporate deductibility of interest payments). Even adopting the extreme assumption implicit in their upper-bound calculations, these authors conclude that features of the corporate tax system would not lower the cost of capital to Japanese firms.

Ando and Auerbach raise and dismiss the possibility that Japanese firms take fewer risks (and consequently have lower earnings), and they entertain the possibility that Japanese firms possess greater "exceptional growth opportunities," and thus the price appreciation of equity exceeds corporate retained earnings. These authors calculate a market rate of return on equity that is defined as the sum of capital gains and dividends divided by the market value of the shares outstanding at the beginning of each year. These authors find an enormous difference in the experienced rate of return on equity between 1971 and 1981 (and, by assumption, the required real rate of return on equity). The difference is on the order of 6 to 1 (the median Japanese value is 13.6%, and the median U.S. value is 2.2%). These authors again urge great care in interpreting these results. However, the results indicate a higher rather than lower cost of equity capital in Japan. Overall, these authors conclude that there is not much evidence to suggest that the cost of capital in Japan is significantly lower than that in the United States.

Chapter 3 is written by John Shoven and Toshiaki Tachibanaki. This chapter fits nicely with the Ando–Auerbach chapter as it examines in considerable detail one of the conclusions of the Ando–Auerbach work. Ando and Auerbach state that they are able to rule out business taxation as a reason for the lower Japanese cost of capital. They find, in fact, that Japanese real investment is more, rather than less, heavily taxed than real investment undertaken in the United States. The Shoven–Tachibanaki chapter computes effective marginal tax rates on capital income in Japan, including personal as well as business-level taxes, and compares the results with those found for the United States.

The analysis found in the Shoven–Tachibanaki chapter follows that of King (1977) and King and Fullerton (1984). In this chapter they compute the wedge between the gross earnings of a marginal new investment and the net return that the investor earns. The result is then compared to the gross earnings of the investment to yield an effective rate of taxation. Two features of this calculation are critical for reconciling the Shoven–Tachibanaki results with those presented in the Ando–Auerbach chapter. First, Shoven and Tachibanaki calculate a marginal tax rate on an incremental new investment. Ando and Auerbach compute average tax rates on existing capital. Second, Shoven and Tachibanaki examine other taxes besides the corporate income tax that contribute to the taxation of income from corporate capital. These taxes include the personal income tax and wealth taxes. That is, they look at all taxes levied on capital income, rather than just the corporate-level tax.

The methodology adopted in this chapter allows Shoven and Tachibanaki to calculate marginal tax rates for 81 classes of investments. The classes include three industries, three assets, three types of investors, and three types of financing. By using the King–Fullerton approach, the results presented in this chapter can be compared directly with those found earlier for the United States, the United Kingdom, Sweden, and West Germany. The final sections of the chapter present a brief summary of the approach used and the results of the authors' analysis.

Shoven and Tachibanaki find that the marginal tax rate on capital falls as inflation rises in Japan. This is because of the advantage of being able to deduct high nominal interest payments from the corporation tax base, while paying relatively low rates on the same income at the level of individual income taxes. Because Japan had higher inflation rates than the United States over the 1970s, inflation has led to lower tax rates on capital in Japan than in the United States, all other things being equal. Of course, other features of the U.S. and Japanese tax systems are not the same. Japanese firms have a greater likelihood of financing their new projects with debt finance than do their U.S. counterparts. Debt finance is heavily subsidized in Japan. This subsidy arises because nominal interest rates are deductible from the corporation tax, there is a low rate of taxation of interest at the personal level, and depreciation and special tax incentives apply to debt-financed as well as equity-financed investments. Because inflation provides its greatest subsidy to projects financed with debt finance, this enhances the tendency for Japanese firms to have lower marginal tax rates on capital income.

An interesting result emerges when Japanese average marginal tax rates are compared with those found in the United States, the United Kingdom, Sweden, and West Germany. In their study of these four countries, King and Fullerton found that the ranking of these countries from highest to lowest in regard to growth rate is exactly the same as their ranking on the basis of effective tax rate on capital income. That is, the higher-growth-rate countries had higher capital tax rates. Addition of Japan to the group alters this result. Japan has the highest growth rate of the five countries, but it has a relatively low rate of taxation on corporate investment. This result differs from that found by Ando and Auerbach and other earlier authors. There is indeed a high rate of taxation on corporate income, as Ando and Auerbach point out. However, the financing of an investment project is also influenced by the personal taxes faced by the saver who supplies the project's finance. Because Japan has a light burden of interest and dividend taxation at the personal level, the effective tax rate on corporate investment income is accordingly low.

The first portion of the Shoven–Tachibanaki chapter presents a detailed description of the institutional characteristics of the Japanese tax system. In their discussion of the personal income tax system, these authors describe the mechanism through which dividend and interest income is lightly taxed. There is a dual rate structure that allows high-income taxpayers to pay a lower tax rate on interest and dividend income. Furthermore, a large amount of this income is simply exempted from tax. Shoven and Tachibanaki also provide details on the corporation income tax, the tax allowances for inventory and depreciation, investment grants and incentives, local taxes, wealth taxes, tax-exempt institutions, and the taxation of insurance companies.

Chapter 4, by Hiromitsu Ishi, describes the evolution of special tax-incentive measures in Japan since the 1950s. After describing what comprises a special tax-incentive measure in the Japanese tax law, Ishi presents tables and graphs to demonstrate that there has been a declining trend in the use of tax-incentive measures over the last 30 years. This decline has primarily been due to reductions in incentive measures aimed at the corporate sector. Ishi also documents a shift in the type of tax-incentive measures employed, from exemptions and credits, in the 1950s and early 1960s, to tax deferrals, such as accelerated depreciation and tax-free reserves. Ishi provides a great deal of interesting historical and current detail about these incentive measures.

In order to more fully understand the objectives of tax-incentive policy, Ishi classifies Japanese tax incentives into five categories. He then outlines the historical evolution of those five categories. The largest category of special tax incentives since 1958 has included those going toward the promotion of individual saving and housing. Interestingly, the share of special tax incentives directed at the protection of export and foreign investment has fallen from 18% of all special tax incentives in 1958 to 2.2% in 1985.

In the third section of Chapter 4, Ishi reviews earlier studies of the corporate tax burden in Japan. He draws out the distinction between the statutory structure of the corporate income tax that the Ministry of Finance commonly uses to assess tax burdens and the effective tax rate calculated by the *Keidanren* that takes into account special tax-incentive measures. Making the distinction between these two approaches barely alters the results of measuring the corporate tax burden in Japan. It does, however, dramatically alter international comparisons of Japanese corporate tax rates. Under the statutory-rate approach, Japanese corporate tax rates are about the average of those for the United States, the United Kingdom, West Germany, and France. Using the measure of effective tax rate, Japanese corporations face the highest tax rate. This is essentially the basis of the debate surrounding corporate taxation in Japan. Over time, the trend has been for both statutory and effective tax rates to rise. Also, medium-size corporations (defined as those having 0.1–10 billion yen of paid-in capital) face the highest rate of tax (measured statutorily or as an effective rate).

The final section of Chapter 4 presents a new set of calculations of the corporate tax burden that Ishi calls the ultimate tax rate calculations. This measure of tax burden amends the *Keidanren* measure of effective tax rates to include the effects of special tax-incentive instruments of tax-free reserves and accelerated depreciation. Ishi presents calculations disaggregated by 18 industries over the time series 1970–82 that show the effective tax rate in each industry and thus the change in effective tax rate due to the availability of tax-free reserves and due to accelerated-depreciation provisions. The benefits from tax-free reserves have appeared to decline over the time series covered. However, for public transportation and utilities, the financial sector, and the textile industry, the benefits remain reasonably high (on the order of 5%). The benefits from accelerated-depreciation provisions have also declined over the time series, and the highest rates are only 40% of the levels of tax-free reserves.

A tremendous amount of attention has been paid to the savings rates in the United States and Japan. The conventional view holds that the Japanese savings rate is several times that of the United States. Recently, a somewhat different view has appeared. Advocates of this view argue that several important components of savings, including consumer durables and education, are treated as consumption in the national accounts. When these items are treated as savings, the gap between Japanese and U.S. savings rates narrows. Chapter 5, by Michael Boskin and John Roberts, examines the measurement and policy issues that arise when discussing savings behavior in the United States and Japan.

The first major section of Chapter 5 examines the methodology involved in measuring savings. For example, should stock data or flow data be used to measure savings? Should net or gross savings figures be computed, and if the answer is net, how should depreciation be measured? Are individual savers affected by whether a corporation or the government is saving on their behalf? These authors discuss these and a variety of other issues before surveying previous empirical studies of U.S. and Japanese savings.

The estimates of Boskin and Roberts adjust national savings rates to include consumer-durables expenditures and government investment as savings. These items, in contrast to education and research and development, have more easily estimable rates of depreciation and greater differences in levels between the United States and Japan. In their estimates, these authors choose to use flow-based net measures of savings. They take the position that the distinction between household savings and corporate savings does not matter, but that the distinction between public savings and private savings does matter.

These authors' estimates of U.S. and Japanese savings rates are presented in a series of tables. The first table highlights measurement differences in gross savings between U.S. national income and product accounts (NIPA), OECD definitions, and a definition of savings that includes government investment and expenditures on consumer durables. The final measure, when computed on a gross savings basis, suggests that U.S. savings are only 30% less than those of Japan.

These authors then present a table containing net savings rates and a variety of adjustments to these rates. The table begins with a standard NIPA definition of net savings. Adjustments are first made to include government nonmilitary investment. Similar adjustments are then made to include net expenditures on consumer durables. The net result of the first adjustment is to widen the U.S.–Japanese savings differential; the second narrows the differential. The final two adjustments incorporate government net expenditures on military capital as investment and then add the rental flow from the nonmilitary government capital stock to national product.

The third of the Boskin–Roberts tables separates savings into the public and private components. A striking feature of this table is the high rate of Japanese government savings. When compared with government savings, the disparity in private savings between the two countries is much smaller. The final table of the series shows various consumption and investment rates. The chapter concludes with a summary of findings and a suggestive discussion of factors that might combine to generate higher Japanese savings rates. Assessing the relative importance of these factors undoubtedly will be a promising area for future research.

3   The Japanese current account

The two chapters that compose the second section of this volume focus on the economic policies in Japan and the United States that have contributed to the Japanese current-account surplus. Chapter 6, by Kazuo Ueda, focuses on the role played by U.S. fiscal policy is causing the large Japanese current-account surplus. Ueda constructs a two-country model in which two endogenous variables, the real interest rate and the real exchange rate, determine savings and investment. The model is static and thus does not consider economic growth and feedback effects, such as the effect of the capital stock on investment, the effect of a change in wealth on savings, and the effect of a change in net foreign assets on the exchange rate. Because of this, Ueda frames his study as a short- or medium-term analysis.

In the Ueda model, net savings in each country are determined by the interest rate, which is equalized across countries, and by an exogenous component. The current account is also decribed by an exogenous component and a real-exchange-rate term. Including a goods market equilibrium condition, the system can be solved for the interest rate, real exchange rate, and current account in terms of autonomous levels of private and net government savings. In the model, an increase in private or government savings in either country will lower the equilibrium interest rate. This will disequilibrate the balance of domestic savings and domestic investment, which in turn will lead to a capital inflow or outflow. The exchange rate is determined such that the current-account deficit is equal to the negative of the capital-account surplus.

To implement the model, Ueda estimates private-sector savings and investment functions and equations for the full-employment government budget deficit. After doing this, regressions are run on the current account using the previously estimated variables to decompose the evolution of the current account into structural and cyclical components.

The proposed fixed-investment equations are Jorgensonian in that investment depends on production, the capital stock, and the user cost of capital. Housing investment is thought to depend on the interest rate and income relative to housing prices. The savings functions depend on the current year's net national product [real gross national product (GNP) less government expenditures], last year's net national product, budget deficits, and, for the Japanese case, bonus payments. Series are also constructed to represent full-employment GNP for both the United States and Japan. These variables are then used to calculate what Ueda considers the autonomous or exogenous parts of private and government net savings. Ueda suggests that large parts of the movements in U.S. net savings are cyclical, that U.S. savings are not explained by his exogenous factors. For Japan, the author suggests that the exogenous or structural determinants of savings also do not explain the variations in national savings rates over the past few years.

The final estimation presented in Chapter 6 is for the current account. These equations are used to decompose movements in the current account into structural and cyclical components. The structural components are considered to be the exogenous determinants of the savings-less-government-deficits variable. The cyclical components include the constant term and the real GNP divided by full-employment GNP for the United States and Japan. Ueda finds that a major part of the Japanese surplus is structural. Of this structural surplus, Ueda finds that the increase in the U.S. budget deficit and the decrease in the Japanese budget deficit have been the major causes of the increase in the Japanese current-account surplus. Although differences in the country's net savings base also played a role, Ueda suggests that this effect is smaller than that of fiscal policy.

Based on the coefficient estimates of his empirical work, Ueda presents some simulations of policy actions that may lead to a decrease in the structural component of the Japanese current-account surplus. Here he finds that complete elimination of the U.S. budget deficit would eliminate the structural component of the Japanese current-account deficit. Alternatively, raising the Japanese deficit to 6% or 7% of GNP would eliminate the surplus. Ueda also discusses the implications of his analysis for exchange-rate policies. The final section focuses on the sustainability of the budget deficits modeled in Chapter 6. The most relevant conclusion of the chapter for current trade-policy debate, however, remains that a primary determinant of the trade deficit faced by the United States is its own federal-government budget deficit.

Chapter 7, by Iwao Nakatani, focuses on the roles of the Japanese and U.S. tax systems in exacerbating the large and growing current-account imbalance. The chapter begins by presenting figures documenting the large private-sector savings surpluses, fiscal deficits, and current-account surpluses that developed following the first oil price shock in 1973. After reviewing these figures, Nakatani presents an argument that the effectiveness of market-opening policies is limited. This argument has several features. First, market-opening policies attack a symptom of the problem, the current-account surplus, rather than the cause of the problem, the savings surplus. This alone is not a critical indictment. Nakatani argues that much of the activity that market-opening policies are directed toward is governed by implicit, unwritten rules. These rules arise through cultural and social values and are very difficult to alter through government policy. Furthermore, Nakatani suggests that some of the corporate structure that market-opening rules would try to alter may have sound economic rationality behind it. For these reasons, Nakatani sees some danger in adopting market-opening rules, but recognizes the need to make explicit the implicit and unwritten rules that govern certain Japanese business behavior.

Nakatani then presents figures showing the changes in the savings–investment balance in the United States since 1970. This balance has fluctuated widely over this period and has a tendency to exhibit surpluses during troughs in the economic cycle. One of the differences Nakatani highlights between the two countries concerns the structure of corporate taxation. Prior to 1972, Japanese corporate tax rates were appreciably lower than those in the United States (the difference was as high as 18 percentage points in 1970). Since 1973, there has been a reversal in corporate rates, so that at present, Japanese corporate rates are almost twice those faced by U.S. corporations. Furthermore, depreciation schedules for American investment are uniformly more generous than those for Japanese investment. To highlight the differences, Nakatani calculates the corporate tax liability that would be incurred by several Japanese firms if they were faced with the U.S. corporate tax laws. Depending on the company and the year, Japanese corporate tax liabilities would fall by 5% to 100%, with most of the figures falling in the higher range. Nakatani points out that investment decisions are governed by marginal, rather than average, tax burdens; nevertheless, Nakatani presents calculations showing that marginal tax rates are lower in the United States, especially for machinery and equipment. Nakatani finds that even the cost of capital is lower in the United States, despite the lower interest rates and higher firm debt–equity ratios found in Japan. The analysis seems contrary to the Shoven–Tachibanaki results. The reconciliation may lie in the fact that Nakatani does not consider the effects of inflation in the manner of Shoven and Tachibanaki.

Nakatani interprets his results by saying that the United States has a strongly pro-investment tax policy relative to Japan. However, he finds the tax policies directed toward savings to be even more different in the two countries. The *Maruyū* system in Japan shelters roughly two-thirds of Japanese total personal financial assets. In the United States, interest income is taxed as ordinary income [except for individual retirement accounts (IRAs)], and interest paid by borrowers can be deducted from taxable income. Nakatani suggests that this has at least something to do with the fact that the personal savings rate in Japan is 17% to 18%, whereas it is only around 5% in the United States.

Having made the case that U.S. tax policy is strongly pro-investment and Japanese tax policy is strongly pro-savings, Nakatani develops the implications of these propositions using graphic analysis. This analysis suggests that interest rates in the pro-investment country should be expected to exceed those in the pro-savings country if capital markets are restricted. If those restrictions are liberalized, interest rates will be equalized, but at a rate lower than the equilibrium rate in the absence of taxation, because of capital flows from the higher-savings country to the high-investment country. The movement of capital described is not induced by efficiency considerations, but by differences in the tax systems of the two countries. The result is that there is too little investment in the high-savings country, and too much in the high-investment country. Nakatani argues that this is a reasonable characterization of the Japan–United States current-account imbalance.

Nakatani suggests that the consequences of such tax policies are serious. By exporting so much of its domestic savings, Japan may be reducing its growth potential by having insufficient investment. The United States will be faced with harmful, inefficient investment decisions. The solution, Nakatani argues, lies not with unilateral adjustments of one country's tax policy but rather with international coordination of tax policies. Nakatani concludes by proposing an international summit conference to discuss the international coordination of tax policies. Alternatively, Nakatani suggests that the problems associated with external-accounts imbalance could be mitigated if the United States would raise its savings rate a few percentage points relative to the U.S. GNP. This position is consistent with Ueda's finding that reduced U.S. government dissavings would balance the U.S. current accounts.

4   Organization of Japan's industry and government

The final section of this book consists of five chapters that deal with various aspects of the industrial organization of Japan and the organization of the Japanese political system. Chapter 8, by Merton Peck, Richard Levin, and Akira Goto, describes the public policy toward declining industries in Japan. While describing the Japanese policy for dealing with declining industries, the chapter comments on several related topics. How well has the Japanese policy stayed within the OECD guidelines specifying that industrial policy should be temporary, transparent, directed at absolute capacity, and free of protectionism? How successful has the Japanese policy been, and how responsive is this policy to market forces?

Their study is valuable in two other respects. A great deal of attention has been paid to Japanese industrial policy, but this attention has been almost exclusively devoted to its winners. Chapter 8 redresses this imbalance. Furthermore, all the OECD countries have structural-adjustment problems, but Japan has treated its problems differently. The countries of Western Europe and the United States have generally relied on subsidies and overt protection as policies for their depressed industries. Japan has attempted to increase the resources of firms in depressed industries by encouraging the firms in an industry to form cartels to reduce capacity and raise prices. Higher prices then permit firms to assume a greater share of the costs of phasing out an industry than would otherwise be possible. In Japan, these costs are considerable. Large firms have union agreements or established practices that have created a system of permanent employment. These labor costs are not variable in the sense that they can be avoided by laying off or firing workers. In addition, the highly levered positions of Japanese firms make the externalities associated with bankruptcy particularly severe.

The first section of Chapter 8 describes the legal structure that has provided the cornerstone for the Japanese policy toward depressed industries. Peck, Levin, and Goto describe the process by which industries become designated as distressed. For this designation and the subsequent right to form cartels, the responsible government agency and firms within an industry must agree on the designation. The 14 industries identified in the 1978 law had all been adversely affected by the 1973 oil price shock and were facing depressed prices, decreased profitability, and substantial excess capacity. After the depressed-industry status has been granted (usually after a long period of consultation), the firms in the industry will discuss and agree on plans for capacity restriction. The formal designation is important, as it guarantees that the government will not prosecute firms under Japanese antimonopoly statutes. Furthermore, explicit collusion avoids many of the strategic problems associated with price and capacity changes. The resulting arrangement is monitored by the government, and modest fines can be imposed on firms that violate the agreement.

Peck, Levin, and Goto make a very useful distinction between firms characterized as existing in competitive and less competitive industries. The capacity-reduction targets for firms in competitive industries are little more than industry-wide forecasts of the capacity reduction that would be likely to be achieved if the industry were left to market forces. Thus, the targets have the tendency to be quite modest. The setting of targets in uncompetitive industries necessarily involves fewer players. The targets are set through direct bargaining between company executives, Ministry of International Trade and Industry (MITI) officials, and trade-association representatives. The resulting capacity-restriction agreement is therefore far more substantial. Targets for both types of industries have, for the most part, been met, but the methods by which targets have been achieved and the consequences of the reductions have differed. In the unconcentrated industries, capacity reductions have been met by exit of firms, whereas in the concentrated industries, firms have reduced their capacities.

Peck, Levin, and Goto state that the 1978 law had little impact on firms in competitive industries. However, for uncompetitive industries, capacity reductions did exceed those that would have occurred in the absence of the law, and the resulting prices in those industries were higher (the decline in prices was stabilized). In all of the OECD countries, banks and workers share some of the burdens of structural adjustments. In Japan, consumers of an industry's products, rather than taxpayers, shoulder an additional, perhaps primary, burden.

These authors also comment on efficiency considerations, such as whether or not high-cost plants are the first plants to be closed, and the degree to which resources leave the structurally depressed industries. They describe the types of financial support given to three industries: shipbuilding, aluminum smelting, and textiles. Whereas the amounts of government financial support granted to most depressed industries have been small, these three industries have been exceptions to that rule.

A question immediately arises from the analysis of Peck, Levin, and Goto: If policy is designed to artificially raise prices in Japan's distressed industries, why does import competition not undermine the entire process? This is the sticky policy issue associated with Japan's approach to declining industries. These authors examine seven industries to see whether or not hidden trade barriers may also have been erected with passage of the 1978 law. The chapter concludes with a description of the new law adopted in 1983, the year the 1978 law expired, and related legislation.

The second in the series of chapters on industrial structure, Chapter 9, is by James Hodder. It compares the corporate capital structure in Japan and that found in the United States. There are substantial differences in borrowing practices in the two countries. Average debt-to-equity ratios are much higher for Japanese corporations, and for some Japanese firms they are extraordinarily high by U.S. standards. The maturity composition and roles played by financial intermediaries have also been different for Japanese borrowers.

The first section of Chapter 9 summarizes developments in the theory of corporate capital structure. Hodder suggests that there are two dominant theories as to why corporations have optimal interior debt–equity ratios. The first is based on a modified Miller-type equilibrium in which firms have an optimal capital structure that may lead to firm borrowing. Optimal interior debt–equity ratios are achieved by considering agency costs and the probability of losing noninterest tax shields (e.g., depreciation) as a function of firm debt levels. The alternative theory described by Hodder is characterized as the "pecking-order theory." Firms are thought to initially finance new asset acquisition from internal sources. They then prefer additional debt as long as debt remains approximately default-free. When debt becomes sufficiently risky, new equity may be issued.

These two theories are then used as a framework from which the author examines the capital structures found in the United States and Japan. In addition to having higher average debt-to-equity ratios, some individual Japanese firms operate with 80% to 90% debt financing. Japanese firms maintain large cash and receivables positions, and Japanese debt tends to be shorter-term debt, though Japanese banks tend to routinely roll over their loans.

Hodder presents tables for Japan and the United States showing that in Japan, half of a firm's net investment has been generated internally, and of the remainder, 80% has been borrowed from private financial intermediaries. The United States, on the other hand, has generated three-quarters of its net industrial funds from internal sources. In addition, bonds are used much more extensively (and financial institutions correspondingly less) in the United States. In both countries, new equity issues are infrequently used. The remainder of the second section of Hodder's chapter relates changes in the Japanese capital structure over the 1970s and 1980s to implications of the modified Miller equilibrium theory and the pecking-order model.

The third section of Chapter 9 describes how the expected cost of financial distress has been controlled by the financial intermediation process. This intermediation process may be the single most important factor in explaining the high debt-to-equity ratio of certain Japanese firms. Hodder suggests that the relationship between a firm and its major lending bank (called the main-bank relationship) reduces in two ways the probability that highly levered firms will fail. The main bank is able to monitor and control management's risk-taking behavior, which reduces both bankruptcy costs and agency costs associated with management actions to benefit shareholders at the expense of lenders. The main bank also has the capacity to quickly reorganize a firm in difficulty while maintaining the confidence and support of customers, suppliers, and employees. This type of main-bank relationship can exist in Japan because relatively few (10 or so) Japanese banks account for a very large percentage of the banking done with Japanese corporations.

An interesting question then arises concerning the opening of Japanese financial markets: Given that the main-bank–corporate relationship has had such a profound influence on the Japanese corporate capital structure, what are the implications of opening Japanese financial markets? Hodder suggests that the main-bank system will weaken and that the aggregate equity-to-asset ratio for Japanese firms will continue to rise. Furthermore, slower-growing firms or more profitable firms, those with less need for bank funds, presumably will become more independent of the main bank as alternative sources of capital become available. Thus, one might expect to see a two-tier structure in which some firms will maintain a traditional main-bank relationship, whereas other firms will evolve into the capital structure more common to American firms.

Chapter 10, by Masahiko Aoki, examines the role of the bureaucracy in Japan. Aoki defines a concept, "administered pluralism," that he feels characterizes the Japanese bureaucracy. Aoki describes similarities between the administered pluralism of the Japanese bureaucracy and the coordinating process of the Japanese firm. These similarities, which Aoki calls isomorphisms, suggest that certain common features of the two systems may be deeply seated in the Japanese social system. To the extent that these features influence the evolution of economic policy in Japan, understanding these features is essential for understanding Japanese policy.

The second section of Chapter 10 describes two different aspects of the Japanese bureaucracy: the role of regulator and the role of advocate. Many of the theories of bureaucracy found in political science and economics focus on the former, the bureaucrat as a regulator. However, in the Japanese context, these theories miss an important characteristic of the bureaucracy. Because of the evolution of a bureaucrat's career, specifically the *amakudari* (descent from heaven), there are strong links between the private sector and public sector. The strength of these links dictates that different ministries act as advocates for their particular constituencies in budgetary and legislative negotiations within the bureaucracy.

This advocacy process ensures that conflicts between diverse interests are arbitrated through intrabureaucratic coordination, rather than being resolved by open and direct bargaining by interest groups. After reviewing the Japanese budgetary process, Aoki characterizes one of the features of this process as quasi-social bargaining. Without developing a fully articulated model, Aoki suggests that the conflict resolution generated by the quasi-social bargaining process may be both efficient and stable.

The fourth section of Chapter 10 discusses similarities between the Japanese firm and the bureaucracy. The similarities extend beyond the fact that management and bureaucrats both arbitrate conflict. Because the bureaucrat and manager are rotated through different bureaus or divisions, they absorb various interests and bodies of knowledge that facilitate problem solving. Thus, the internal informational structures of the Japanese firm and bureaucracy share important characteristics. Aoki ends this section by asking how the structure described affects the strategy (Aoki makes the further distinction between entrepreneurial and managerial strategies) of the firm.

Aoki goes on to describe the evolution of administered pluralism since the 1950s. This historical background provides an interesting context for examining the likely impacts of two recent developments on the structure of the Japanese bureaucracy. The first development is the increasing scarcity of resources the bureaucracy can command to administer pluralist interests. The second is the increase in jurisdictional disputes, brought on by the increasing complexity of the Japanese economy, faced by the ministries. As a result of these developments, the Liberal Democratic Party is taking a greater role in interministerial coordination. Although this does not yet signal a fundamental change in the nature of the bureaucracy, it may portend one. That is the subject of the final section of Chapter 10.

Chapter 11, by Chikashi Moriguchi, describes developments in Japan's energy policy during the 1970s. Japan was quite successful in dealing with the effects of the two OPEC oil price shocks, perhaps more successful than any other industrialized economy. Moriguchi first describes the evolution of government policy on the demand and supply sides of the energy industry. He then attempts to decompose the effects of energy-demand policy and autonomous adjustment through the market mechanism.

Prior to the first oil price shock, the Japanese economy was almost entirely dependent on oil as its source of energy. Even before the first price shock hit, inflation was already high, and therefore the first shock created an extremely difficult situation. The administration responded to this situation with a series of regulations and guidance to the suppliers of energy and imposed price controls to stabilize inflation.

In addition to these shorter-run policies, the Japanese government attempted to develop alternative sources of energy. Moriguchi suggests that the policy toward coal, including subsidies and other measures, created a divergence between foreign and domestic prices for coal that has persisted until today. Japanese policymakers also saw great promise in the possibilities for overseas oil development. As this development has evolved, it has proved less and less successful. The foreign oil that Japanese producers have found has been inferior in quality, and they have had difficulty processing this oil because of the control exercised by the major oil companies over the production process.

Japan's nuclear eneigy program is quite large, though its rate of expansion has been slowed. Nuclear energy did contribute to the fact that Japan did not increase its relative share of demand for oil after the first OPEC oil shock. Japan was extremely successful in reducing its energy consumption over the 1970s. That was achieved through the transformation of Japanese industry to more energy-efficient microelectronic technology and through vigorous conservation programs. Modest amounts of financial support have been granted for research into alternative energy sources. The final section of Chapter 11 discusses the effects of policy on the consumption of energy.

Chapter 12, by W. Edward Steinmueller, discusses industrial structure and government policies directed toward the U.S. and Japanese integrated-circuit (IC) industries. This industry provides a particularly interesting focus, because competition within the IC industry has received an enormous amount of attention in the popular press. Furthermore, developments in the IC industry serve almost to provide a prototype for American complaints against Japanese industrial practices. The chapter begins by examining three issues that arise from Japan's success in the IC market: the significance of Japanese industrial "targeting," the structural differences between the U.S. and Japanese economies and their roles in contributing to Japan's commercial success, and the existence of barriers to U.S. penetration of Japanese IC markets.

In the second section of Chapter 12, Steinmueller discusses the areas of concern that have been expressed by U.S. firms engaged in competition with the Japanese. The first concerns whether or not actions by Japanese firms and the Japanese government reveal a coordinated strategic plan to dominate the competition in IC markets. The second focuses on the structural differences between the U.S. and Japanese economies and can be characterized as "level-playing-field" concerns. The third area of concern has to do with nontariff trade barriers. American firms insist that they are not being treated the same as domestic Japanese firms when they try to penetrate Japanese markets. To the extent that this is true, it is a significant and previously unrecognized barrier to free trade.

Steinmueller goes on to describe the U.S. IC trade association's suggested remedies for the alleged unfair competition. The policy prescriptions the trade association offers involve a significant government presence in the operations of the IC industry. Specifically, the trade association proposes to create a regulatory body for ongoing monitoring of international IC markets, actions of the Japanese government and firms, and performance of U.S. firms operating in Japan.

The central section of Chapter 12 describes the industrial structure and evolution of the Japanese semiconductor industry and then does the same for the United States. The production of ICs in Japan has been highly concentrated in the hands of five large electronics companies. These companies devote a significant share of their IC production to external markets, whereas most of the other Japanese IC manufacturers produce for internal consumption. The largest producers of American ICs are International Business Machines Corporation (IBM) and American Telephone and Telegraph (AT&T), which produce almost exclusively for internal consumption. None of the largest U.S. electronics companies produces for external consumption; rather, the companies producing ICs for external sales tend to be smaller than their Japanese counterparts and are devoted primarily to that task.

Steinmueller describes four recent developments that may alter the shape of the U.S. IC industry. The first is the acquisition and merger of independent semiconductor producers by more diversified companies. If these trends continue, the U.S. IC industry will begin to look more like its Japanese counterpart. The second development surrounds the settlement of antitrust suits filed against AT&T and IBM. At a minimum, this will allow firms to form strategic alliances with existing component and equipment suppliers. The third development is the declining relative importance of captive IC production in the United States. Captive producers generally build specialized ICs for electronics companies and, together with the primary company, have served as a means to vertical integration. The final development is the recent establishment and growth of specialized IC producers. The aim of these companies is to provide an alternative to captive production facilities.

After a section that describes developments in the technological competition in international IC markets, Steinmueller concludes his chapter with a discussion of the influence of the military in the U.S. IC industry. One of the most interesting items in this section is that the benefits from the large amount of military production that takes place in the IC industry are quite small for the civilian production of ICs. Military specifications for IC production are far more demanding than those for civilian production – for instance, military circuits must hold up for long periods of time exposed to very high temperatures and radiation. In addition, the ultimate purposes and uses of ICs by the military often are vastly different than those of ICs made for civilian production. This has led some people to urge the military to develop greater reliance on the

civilian IC industry to enhance the spillover effects from military pro-
curements.

REFERENCES

King, M. A. (1977). *Public Policy and the Corporation*. London: Chapman &
Hall.
King, M. A., and Fullerton, D. (1984). *The Taxation of Income from Capital: A
Comparative Study of the United States, the United Kingdom, Sweden, and
West Germany*. University of Chicago Press.

CHAPTER 2

The corporate cost of capital in Japan and the United States: a comparison

Albert Ando and Alan Auerbach

1 Introduction

Very high real interest rates and a trade deficit that exceeded $100 billion in 1984 have caused much concern over the ability of American firms to keep up with their foreign competitors. A great deal of the discussion of this topic has focused particularly on Japan, because Japan alone accounted for a large fraction of this enormous overall 1984 trade deficit through its success in exporting to the United States goods once supplied primarily by domestic producers.

Attempts to explain this favorable Japanese performance have taken many forms. Some have suggested that Japan may have imposed barriers to American firms' attempts at establishing markets – through explicit policy actions, or by means of collusion among government, producers, distributors, and banks, or because of lack of faith in the quality of U.S.-produced goods. Others have argued that the U.S. trade imbalance is the inevitable result of our elevated real exchange rate, which makes American goods more expensive than those of our trading partners. This high real exchange rate is, in turn, attributed by many to the unprecedented peacetime fiscal deficits currently being experienced.

Although each of these potential explanations may be important, there is a third on which we focus in this chapter: the cost of capital. Some have suggested[1] that Japanese firms enjoy a lower before-tax cost of raising funds in capital markets that allows them to gain a competitive advantage in the capital-intensive industries in which they have made particularly striking progress during the past two decades, such as automobiles and steel.

This explanation is not entirely independent of those already mentioned. The mechanism through which the high real exchange rate is supposed to

21

have occurred is the strong foreign demand for U.S. assets brought on by high domestic real interest rates; one of the forms of Japanese industrial policy is said to work through the direction of funds to promising enterprises. There are, however, many additional factors that could contribute to a cost-of-capital differential between the two countries. The purpose of this chapter is to state clearly what these factors might be and adduce evidence that will shed light on their validity. Something more than claims of unfair competition should be required as evidence before such a complex proposition as a major difference in capital cost is accepted as a "fact." Hence, we begin with some basic calculations for our sample of Japanese and American firms to see if there is convincing prima facie evidence of a lower cost of capital in Japan.

Our approach involves the use of market and financial-statement data for a representative but nonrandom sample of 19 American and 21 Japanese firms to answer first the question whether or not the cost of capital really has been systematically lower in Japan.

In the case of an affirmative answer, our next step is to test predictions based on different theories of why these costs differ. Because we consider only a small sample of firms, our results must be regarded with caution in extrapolating to economy-wide conclusions. Nevertheless, we consider this to be an important first step in determining where further research should be directed.

2   Is the cost of capital lower in Japan?

For several reasons, one cannot simply look at the real interest rates in the United States and Japan to determine what the cost of capital is in each country. Because of differences in tax treatment, financial policies, and legal and financial institutions, to cite just some of the complicating factors, there is no simple way to translate an interest rate into a relevant measure of the cost of capital without additional information.

One alternative approach is to look at total before-tax returns to debt and equity over a period of several years. A still simpler approach is to look exclusively at equity alone by examining earnings–price ratios. In each case, one assumes that over a sufficiently long period of time, these ex post measures reflect their ex ante expectations. There are several problems with such measures of which we are well aware, but they are frequently used and cited and easy to calculate, making their presentation a good place to begin our empirical analysis.

Listed in the first column in Tables 2.1 and 2.2 are the names of the American and Japanese firms used in our study. The second column of

Table 2.1. *Sample companies, United States*

Company	1981 market value (million $)	E/P (1966–81) before tax	R/K (1966–81) before tax
AT&T	97,680.5	17.8	12.5
Chrysler	3,912.5	−15.1	5.2
CDC	1,889.5	9.3	9.2
Delta	1,228.2	15.1	13.4
DEC	4,798.9	6.1	6.0
Dow	9,435.6	13.7	11.7
Kodak	11,851.8	10.3	10.9
Exxon	35,322.3	31.4	26.7
Ford	6,903.0	15.3	18.0
GE	15,297.8	12.3	11.9
GM	17,744.9	18.4	18.3
IBM	37,128.7	9.5	9.4
Macy's	1,128.1	20.4	18.8
Merck	6,787.1	7.3	7.3
Nat. Semi.	561.2	7.1	7.4
Pfizer	5,155.9	9.1	8.9
P&G	7,668.8	10.6	10.3
Sears	16,244.9	10.4	9.5
USS	5,228.3	18.0	13.1

each table lists total market value of debt plus equity at the end of the company's 1981 fiscal year.

Our selection criteria included availability of data, firm size, and coverage of important industries. For each country, we have one representative of the airline industry (Delta Airlines and All Nippon Airways) and two retailers (Sears and Macy's, Mitsukoshi and Takashimaya). In steel, cameras and film, and consumer products, we have one Americn and two Japanese firms (U.S. Steel, Kawasaki Steel and Nippon Steel; Kodak, Fuji Film and Konishiroku Photo; Procter & Gamble, Kao Soap and Lion). In the automobile industry, we include all three major American companies (General Motors, Ford, and Chrysler) because of differences in their recent performances. We include only Nissan from Japan, because the largest producer, Toyota, underwent a major merger during the sample period, making its data difficult to use.

In the consumer and business electronics area, we include General Electric for the United States and Sony, National (Matsushita), and Toshiba for Japan. Companies in the computer and semiconductor industries

Table 2.2. *Sample companies, Japan*

Company	1981 market value (billion yen)	Pension reserve	E/P (1966–81) (without adjustment for pension reserve)	E/P (1966–81) (with adjustment for pension reserve)	R/K (1966–81) before tax (without adjustment for pension reserve)	R/K (1966–81) before tax (with adjustment for pension reserve)
Fuji	466.1	46.3	14.4	16.7	11.9	14.7
Fujitsu	744.1	13.9	8.0	8.5	7.4	7.8
Kao	179.2	2.4	15.0	15.4	10.0	10.6
Kawasaki	1,585.2	46.6	12.9	14.3	9.2	9.8
Konishiroku	190.1	15.6	9.3	12.6	7.8	10.0
Lion	117.3	6.5	27.2	28.9	15.7	17.4
Mitsubishi	831.8	13.8	9.3	10.0	7.1	7.4
Mitsukoshi	234.4	19.9	10.4	11.2	10.0	11.4
National	1,999.1	67.3	15.4	16.3	14.7	16.6
NEC	1,093.4	20.4	6.8	7.4	6.6	7.0
Nippon Air	555.2	12.8	2.6	3.2	4.5	4.8
Nippon Steel	2,969.4	154.7	14.2	15.7	9.5	10.3
Nissan	1,638.4	69.5	17.0	17.6	11.4	12.0
Oki	237.6	7.5	6.3	7.4	6.6	7.3
Shionogi	193.2	12.4	21.1	23.2	15.4	18.2
Sony	1,113.6	19.1	8.0	8.4	7.6	8.0
Sumitomo	641.0	15.8	6.8	7.5	7.0	7.5
Taisho	179.9	2.5	14.3	14.5	13.5	13.8
Takashimaya	139.1	6.9	13.1	14.2	9.7	10.5
Takeda	662.0	55.5	16.6	19.1	11.6	14.7
Toshiba	1,238.8	25.0	10.4	11.0	7.9	8.2

include IBM, Control Data, Digital Equipment (DEC), and National Semiconductor for the United States and Fujitsu, NEC, and Oki Electric for Japan. There is a substantial amount of overlap in the areas of business of these two groups of companies.

Drug and pharmaceutical companies included in the sample from the United States are Merck and Pfizer, and Shionogi and Taisho are included for Japan. In the related chemical industry, we have Dow Chemical and Mitsubishi Chemical, Sumitomo Chemical, and Takeda Chemical. Finally, although we do not have any suitable Japanese counterparts, we include AT&T and Exxon in the sample of U.S. firms because of their importance.

Data for the Japanese companies come primarily from the NEEDS – Nikkei Financial Tape. This data file is based on public balance-sheet and income-statement information provided by the companies on an annual basis. Our version of the file extends from 1964 to 1983, with individual companies having data either for 1964–82 or for 1965–83, depending on their fiscal years.

For the United States, we use Standard & Poor's Compustat file, which has comparable data for the American companies from 1963 to 1982, with most companies having data from 1963–81 or 1963–82, depending on their fiscal years. The two exceptions are DEC and National Semiconductor, for which data are not available before 1966.

In Tables 2.1 and 2.2 we show average rates of return for each company for the period 1966–81, including the before-tax earnings–price ratio and the total before-tax return to debt plus equity. For purposes of computing the latter statistic, we add interest payments to earnings to obtain the total return to capital. "Debt" is defined for each country to be the sum of long-term debt and short-term financial liabilities. Thus, although we include financial trade credit, we exclude from debt the general category of accounts payable. One exception to this rule is "accrued employees' severance indemnities," which we do exclude from debt.[2] In the third column of Table 2.2 we report the size of this account, which we shall hereafter refer to as "pension reserves." Columns 4 and 5 and 6 and 7 in Table 2.2 show how much difference the exclusion of this item makes in the earnings–price ratio (E/P) and the total return on capital (R/K). In the remainder of this chapter, we exclude this account from debt unless otherwise noted.

From these tables there is only mixed evidence in support of the proposition that Japanese firms enjoy a lower cost of capital. If one concentrates on total returns to capital, there are some industries in which Japanese firms have a substantially lower return (e.g., airlines, steel, and, excluding Chrysler, which should be considered a special case because of its near bankruptcy, autos), but others in which the reverse is true (e.g., pharmaceuticals) and many in which there is no clear pattern. For the U.S. sample of companies, the median average return to capital for the period was 10.3%, whereas it was 9.5% for the Japanese sample, and 10.3% with the correction made for pension-reserve accounting. Given the size of our sample, this does not constitute very strong evidence that returns are systematically lower in Japan.

3   Corrected measures of the return to capital

There are many problems with the use of book-value earnings data to measure the cost of capital. Perhaps the most serious is the distortion that inflation imparts to book-value measures of income.[3] Because of the general lack of inflation-adjusted financial data, we must make such corrections ourselves to the book-value information. This is especially important for a cross-country comparison, because historical patterns for the rates of inflation in the two countries are substantially different, and accounting practices, debt–equity ratios, and tax structures, three factors that affect the relationships among inflation, profitability, and accounting biases, are also markedly different. The most critical distortions to remove are the misstatement of depreciation and the cost of goods sold and the absence of any accounting for real gains and losses on nominal liabilities and assets. Given the nature of the data for each country, certain assumptions must be made in order to carry out each of these three corrections. These are described as we discuss how the corrections were performed.

3.1   Depreciation

We assume that depreciation would be properly measured in the absence of inflation. This reflects our fervent belief less than our inability to assume otherwise. To restate depreciation based on original cost in current-dollar terms requires information on the vintage structure of each year's overall depreciation, because the price factor by which book depreciation must be inflated depends on the age of the asset to which the depreciation applies. We produce an estimated vintage structure in the following manner.[4] We first assume that the net (of depreciation) capital stock listed in the first year requires no correction. This is reasonable, given the low rates of inflation in both countries in the years immediately preceding the mid-1960s. We then assume that each corporation's depreciable assets are written off using the declining-balance method at a single rate. Finally, using the perpetual-inventory method, we solve for the value of this rate that will yield the listed book value for net capital in the last year for which data are available. That is, the declining-balance rate, δ, is defined implicitly by

$$K_t = K_0(1-\delta)^t + I_1(1-\delta)^{t-1} + \cdots + I_t \tag{1}$$

where K_t is the book value of net capital at the end of year t, and I_t is the book value of gross investment during year t. Because all these values of I and K are positive, the solution for δ is unique. There are additional problems presented by each country's data set. For Japan, there are no separate figures listed for gross investment. We impute an investment series from the sum of depreciation and the first difference of the net capital stock. For the United States, there are no separate figures for land and depreciable assets, only the sum. This should lower the estimate of the average depreciation rate, because land is nondepreciable. In addition, the treatment of assets acquired through merger rather than direct investment is inconsistent; they appear in the capital stock, but are not in reported investment.[5] We performed calculations for the United States using both reported investment and, as was necessary for Japan, imputed investment. Estimated values of δ were generally lower and more reasonable (given previous estimates) when imputed investment was used. Because of this, as well as to be as consistent as possible in our methods for the two countries, we present calculations based on imputed rather than actual investment. This generally leads to a somewhat higher estimate of the overall return to capital (in the neighborhood of 1 percentage point before tax) than when actual investment is used. The depreciation rates are interesting in their own right and are given in the second column in Tables 2.3 and 2.4. The variation across companies is consistent with general expectations. Firms in the computer industry, for example, evidence very rapid rates when compared with retailers, whose capital is largely in the form of buildings.

It is difficult to know how much the generally more rapid depreciation rates for Japan are due to the omission of land from the calculations.[6] To the extent that this does not completely explain the difference, one might hypothesize that some of the gap between rates of return in the two countries is due to different procedures for measuring depreciation.

With these estimated rates of economic depreciation, we went back and estimated current-dollar capital stocks using the expression

$$K_t^c = P_t[K_0(1-\delta)^t/P_0 + I_1(1-\delta)^{t-1}/P_1 + \cdots + I_t/P_t] \tag{2}$$

where P_t is a price index (the gross-national-expenditure deflator for Japan and the gross-domestic-business-product deflator for the United States). Depreciation in year t is estimated to be δK_{t-1}^c, and the difference between this measure and the listed book measure is subtracted from earnings.

Table 2.3. *Depreciation rates and average adjusted rates of return, United States*

Company	Depre-ciation rate	D/D+E (1966–81)	E/P (1966–81) Before tax	E/P (1966–81) After tax	R/K (1966–81) Before tax	R/K (1966–81) After tax
AT&T	6.7	44.3	12.9	7.5	9.3	4.5
Chrysler	14.0	51.4	−9.6	−14.4	3.2	−2.5
CDC	35.1	38.5	10.9	8.9	7.2	4.0
Delta	13.2	22.2	14.7	8.6	11.6	6.1
DEC	18.4	4.3	4.9	2.5	4.6	2.2
Dow	14.1	30.8	15.1	9.8	10.7	5.9
Kodak	12.8	1.1	9.3	4.6	9.7	4.8
Exxon	9.0	18.2	30.9	12.0	25.2	9.3
Ford	20.8	29.3	15.5	6.8	15.5	6.9
GE	15.9	13.3	13.0	8.0	11.6	6.7
GM	32.2	9.4	17.3	8.8	16.4	7.9
IBM	21.3	2.8	8.6	4.2	8.4	4.0
Macy's	8.3	32.1	22.4	12.7	18.1	9.1
Merck	9.7	3.0	6.8	3.8	6.5	3.6
Nat. Semi.	31.1	9.9	8.3	4.3	7.7	3.7
Pfizer	10.7	15.0	8.8	5.4	7.5	4.1
P&G	6.8	6.5	10.2	5.3	9.4	4.7
Sears	8.7	31.1	9.7	6.1	6.9	3.4
USS	8.0	44.9	17.8	13.1	10.3	6.1

3.2   Inventories

Companies can use any one of several accounting methods for all or part of their inventories and can shift from one method or combination of methods to another. Japanese firms list all methods used in each year for each stage of fabrication (materials, work in process, and finished goods). U.S. firms also include information on which method is the most common, but information is not broken down by stages of fabrication.

In the presence of inflation, only a system of indexed FIFO (first-in, first-out) inventory accounting would correctly state the cost of goods sold in current dollars. Though this system is not in use, the same outcome occurs under the LIFO (last-in, first-out) method in the absence of relative price changes or decumulation of inventories. All other major methods systematically understate the cost of goods sold in the presence of inflation. Hence, this correction will reduce measured returns to

Table 2.4. *Depreciation rates and average adjusted rates of return, Japan*

Company	Depreciation rate	D/D+E ·(1966-81)	E/P (1966-81) Before tax	E/P (1966-81) After tax	R/K (1966-81) Before tax	R/K (1966-81) After tax
Fuji	24.4	28.2	15.8	9.2	12.0	6.1
Fujitsu	34.1	38.3	8.8	5.5	5.2	2.2
Kao	28.0	40.0	17.7	10.4	9.1	4.2
Kawasaki	13.2	73.0	22.0	16.8	7.2	3.5
Konishiroku	22.1	50.3	12.6	7.6	6.5	2.5
Lion	20.4	52.6	28.4	15.1	13.5	5.8
Mitsubishi	18.3	76.2	17.0	14.1	4.0	1.4
Mitsukoshi	15.9	9.8	11.4	6.6	10.8	5.9
National	44.0	11.0	16.0	8.8	15.5	8.4
NEC	34.6	52.4	8.6	6.1	4.0	1.5
Nippon Air	19.8	48.2	12.5	11.3	5.1	3.3
Nippon Steel	15.0	72.5	23.1	17.9	7.5	3.7
Nissan	30.3	48.5	18.4	11.8	8.9	4.3
Oki	30.2	54.8	7.2	4.6	3.8	1.1
Shionogi	20.2	30.5	20.0	10.2	13.8	6.2
Sony	30.1	15.0	7.5	3.9	6.3	2.9
Sumitomo	19.8	67.3	12.5	10.9	4.6	2.1
Taisho	18.1	7.7	12.1	6.1	11.0	5.4
Takashimaya	13.5	54.2	18.5	12.7	8.8	4.5
Takeda	24.0	31.5	15.6	7.1	10.2	3.8
Toshiba	31.8	65.2	10.0	6.3	3.6	0.6

capital, potentially more for the United States, which has experienced more inflation than Japan in the past two decades.

The algorithm used to restate the cost of goods sold proceeds as follows. First, we assume that firms use a combination of FIFO, LIFO, and average-cost accounting in each year. Other methods listed (such as specific cost) are assigned to whichever of these three major methods they most closely resemble, in our judgment.

Based on stated methods, we estimate, for Japan, the fraction of inventories carried under each method in each year. We then average these fractions over the sample period to obtain for each firm a single fraction corresponding to each of the three methods. Finally, we divide book inventories into three categories based on these fractions and adjust each separately in a manner appropriate for the accounting method.

Our approach for the United States differs slightly, because there was a much more pronounced trend (toward the use of LIFO) over the sample period. To accommodate this fact, we calculate average fractions as for Japanese firms, but allow one break during the sample period where the fractions may change. Thus, a firm switching from FIFO to LIFO in 1973 will have a FIFO fraction of 1.0 through 1972 and a LIFO fraction of 1.0 thereafter.

To perform the inventory corrections, once these separate stocks have been estimated, we begin by assuming that all goods purchased in a given year had a price equal to that year's price index and that the initial year's inventories are correctly stated. We then use book information on the cost of goods sold and the change in inventories to estimate a time series of the cost of goods sold in current dollars. The method by which this is done is different for each of the three methods. For LIFO, no change in cost of goods sold is made unless book inventories declined, in which case the last previous year of accumulation not already run down in the intervening years is determined, and an appropriate price correction made. For FIFO, a one-year price adjustment is necessary for those goods sold in the current year attributable to initial-inventory stocks. For average-cost accounting, our correction is based on the assumption that goods purchased in the current year are added to stocks and that the price corresponding to the cost of goods sold is the average price at which this pool of goods in inventory is carried.

Once a current-dollar measure of the cost of goods sold has been calculated for each of the inventory-method categories, the difference between their sum and book cost of goods sold is subtracted from book earnings.

3.3   Nominal assets and liabilities

This correction to earnings is simple. We take the book value of nominal liabilities net of nominal assets, multiply by the concurrent annual inflation rate, and add the resulting estimate of the capital gain on nominal liabilities to book earnings. Because we are studying nonfinancial companies, this is always a positive correction.

Nominal assets and liabilities include not only financial assets but also accounts payable and receivable. The major balance-sheet items not included are real assets: inventories, depreciable assets, and land.

Because of generally higher Japanese debt–equity ratios, one might expect this correction to increase estimated Japanese earnings (as applied to the *total* return to capital) by a greater fraction. However, Japan's more favorable inflation experience works in the opposite direction.

We have made no attempt, at this stage of research, to correct for deviations of the market values of long-term liabilities from their book values resulting from changes in long-term interest rates.

3.4   Results of the corrections

Tables 2.5 and 2.6 report the results of these three corrections to before-tax book earnings–price ratios. Average (1966–81) values for these series are presented in Tables 2.3 and 2.4, column 4. For the United States, these corrections increase estimated earnings–price ratios for many firms, and decrease them for slightly more. This may be seen by comparing the averages in Tables 2.1 and 2.2. The direction of the effect depends on whether or not increases due to accounting for gains on liabilities offset decreases that result from correct statement of inventory and depreciation costs.

For Japanese firms, the effects of the corrections are much clearer, increasing estimated earnings for virtually all firms. This is probably because of the generally higher debt–equity ratios found in Japan. Average percentages of debt in total market value (debt plus equity) are shown for U.S. and Japanese firms in column 3 of Tables 2.3 and 2.4, respectively. The median value of this statistic is 48.5% for Japanese firms, but only 18.2% for American firms.

Tables 2.7 and 2.8 present corresponding corrected measures of the total returns to debt plus equity.[7] Average (1966–81) values for these series are presented in the sixth column in Tables 2.3 and 2.4. As before, the denominator of this measure is the sum of equity and the book value of financial liabilities, and the numerator is the sum of corrected earnings and corrected interest payments, equal to interest payments less the inflation rate multiplied by the book value of financial liabilities. Because the addition of interest payments offsets most of the inflation gain on nominal liabilities included in corrected earnings, the effect of inflation corrections on the overall return to capital (R/K) is clearly negative for firms in both countries. For the United States, the reduction in the average value of R/K ranges between -0.4% and 3.2%. For Japan, the average reduction is typically somewhat larger, ranging from -0.3% to 4.6%.

The median average before-tax return to capital in the United States falls from 10.3% without correction to 9.4%. The median value for Japan falls substantially more, from 10.3% to 7.5%. These larger reductions strengthen the case that the return to capital is systematically lower in Japan.

This is evident in several industries. Consider, for example, computers, where the inflation corrections are much larger for Japanese firms than for U.S. firms. Here, average rates of return for the three Japanese

Table 2.5. Earnings-price ratios, United States (corrected)

Year	AT&T	Chrysler	CDC	Delta	DEC	Dow	Kodak	Exxon	Ford
1963	–	–	–	–	–	–	–	–	–
1964	8.76	16.87	5.77	17.36	–	8.15	6.62	8.43	13.43
1965	10.44	17.85	5.95	9.86	–	9.16	4.94	9.78	18.73
1966	12.91	24.09	−2.23	9.06	–	12.11	5.88	13.68	23.32
1967	14.50	13.19	1.62	14.07	2.01	8.99	5.86	14.72	−1.01
1968	15.25	23.00	3.57	9.60	2.51	11.71	6.36	13.96	18.48
1969	18.43	21.92	5.18	14.52	1.73	13.32	5.83	15.27	30.15
1970	17.02	−4.99	−4.75	12.49	4.41	10.84	5.98	16.24	17.14
1971	17.08	10.80	0.90	4.38	1.59	7.92	4.73	19.36	17.13
1972	15.10	19.68	5.66	4.94	2.31	7.21	3.99	19.14	20.56
1973	19.41	58.76	15.69	14.18	2.66	10.12	5.87	28.92	40.48
1974	29.96	−14.43	3.68	31.06	7.94	24.45	9.88	76.98	15.69
1975	22.88	−46.21	24.24	11.41	3.10	14.13	5.28	50.35	5.81
1976	16.54	51.66	15.77	12.13	4.71	12.82	7.41	31.69	27.23
1977	19.91	34.95	19.35	17.87	8.55	19.06	13.19	35.86	54.38
1978	24.31	−54.71	28.32	24.61	8.79	22.51	16.16	37.65	56.23
1979	28.97	−138.99	22.03	26.62	7.82	24.40	19.58	52.64	43.43
1980	31.36	−135.31	18.89	8.03	7.34	23.81	15.67	31.26	−75.23
1981	26.18	−17.74	16.90	19.97	8.51	18.80	17.10	35.40	−45.84
1982	–	–	–	−3.74	9.90	–	–	–	–

Table 2.6. Earnings-price ratios, Japan (corrected)

Year	All Nippon Air.	Fuji Photo	Fujitsu	Kao Soap	Kawa-saki Steel	Koni-shiroku Photo	Lion	Mitsu-bishi Chem-ical	Mitsu-koshi	National
1964	–	–	–	–	–	–	–	–	–	–
1965	–	15.12	–	–	–	–	29.46	–	–	10.83
1966	42.45	11.46	12.77	13.54	19.21	11.91	30.50	16.81	11.05	14.61
1967	9.21	17.64	13.34	22.24	19.33	11.87	28.10	9.66	10.49	21.94
1968	32.37	15.12	14.46	20.96	27.55	0.07	33.02	20.53	11.38	16.29
1969	16.48	16.43	6.58	19.23	17.32	−14.49	52.07	20.84	13.77	11.15
1970	19.76	15.00	7.27	16.49	22.81	6.66	49.79	36.10	13.32	23.91
1971	19.35	15.26	9.70	23.50	30.08	15.17	42.51	23.89	13.24	16.98
1972	8.66	13.90	7.86	15.70	21.62	9.94	31.74	16.86	9.90	14.98
1973	14.57	18.92	8.49	19.92	19.22	15.24	44.51	13.42	7.85	20.93
1974	16.72	28.44	13.04	50.00	62.49	38.10	53.87	31.09	13.40	24.55
1975	7.10	8.60	2.92	13.56	18.92	25.45	7.92	43.94	11.06	9.66
1976	7.09	11.25	2.01	9.58	9.90	16.50	20.36	11.15	11.16	14.65
1977	1.87	12.76	7.36	5.62	11.78	13.86	17.73	5.95	12.02	16.40
1978	0.87	13.98	–	10.37	9.47	12.67	13.64	8.26	11.10	13.93
1979	2.36	13.67	–	16.26	10.16	13.62	13.53	2.87	10.35	13.61
1980	0.17	20.21	–	17.94	32.21	13.63	4.99	5.00	11.78	11.86
1981	1.04	20.57	–	7.84	19.37	10.56	9.40	5.69	10.39	9.83
1982	0.35	15.77	–	7.03	21.85	16.99	10.44	0.58	8.16	8.08
1983	0.01	–	–	7.51	7.59	13.24	–	−5.12	−4.08	–

GE	GM	IBM	Macy's	Merck	Nat. Semi.	Pfizer	P&G	Sears	USS
–	–	–	–	–	–	–	–	–	–
5.69	9.86	8.11	8.26	5.49	–	8.02	7.39	5.64	17.93
7.22	12.22	5.97	10.88	4.82	–	6.40	8.21	5.83	18.16
9.31	14.53	5.52	15.89	5.75	–	7.96	8.56	8.87	27.66
8.65	10.67	4.18	10.72	5.49	2.81	6.51	8.23	7.44	15.36
8.65	13.44	5.49	11.62	5.58	3.93	7.60	9.70	7.73	14.40
8.83	19.77	4.78	14.01	4.84	4.96	5.90	7.94	7.43	15.73
7.13	3.04	5.35	11.51	5.98	2.80	5.96	8.67	6.43	7.33
6.96	15.35	4.72	8.99	5.32	5.55	5.35	6.52	5.44	7.31
6.61	17.45	4.81	10.44	4.00	5.95	5.55	5.39	5.26	9.86
9.22	33.26	7.82	27.34	5.02	12.44	6.01	6.85	7.91	22.69
19.00	12.97	12.59	47.52	6.96	23.98	8.92	8.76	10.83	51.25
12.18	10.20	9.20	23.12	6.65	4.63	11.70	8.17	8.64	22.77
13.38	23.02	9.27	23.96	7.31	3.95	10.57	9.05	9.20	9.99
16.38	34.08	11.26	25.34	9.99	13.04	13.23	11.68	13.06	0.44
20.45	32.69	11.81	32.88	8.81	20.98	13.48	12.51	19.40	13.20
21.32	32.30	12.80	31.76	9.78	19.08	12.93	16.30	18.11	-27.16
18.59	-7.01	12.70	32.85	8.93	8.92	10.50	18.55	–	31.55
21.39	0.84	15.14	30.21	7.84	-8.29	9.37	15.86	–	63.02
–	–	–	13.22	–	–	–	13.54	–	–

NEC	Nippon Steel	Nissan Motor	Oki Elec.	Shio-nogi	Sony	Sumitomo Chemical	Taisho	Taka-shimaya	Takeda Chemical	Toshiba
–	–	–	–	–	–	–	–	–	–	–
–	–	–	–	–	4.97	13.49	–	–	–	–
4.53	26.31	18.48	2.94	26.74	10.34	18.53	10.39	20.27	23.43	-8.34
6.70	33.22	12.46	4.05	29.49	10.32	19.27	1.23	19.06	23.07	0.10
11.11	52.97	22.78	10.01	27.84	6.49	21.29	16.36	23.84	26.05	14.93
5.42	41.73	20.22	5.64	19.40	2.67	16.62	14.52	24.39	19.49	15.19
9.70	30.43	26.50	8.56	18.73	4.20	27.79	13.17	20.97	17.12	19.67
11.47	29.43	30.32	10.31	31.62	4.57	18.78	18.01	22.47	22.68	12.74
8.70	20.54	14.06	12.63	28.15	4.19	5.50	16.47	15.39		3.40
10.04	14.52	17.57	11.01	17.52	5.75	14.38	13.50	14.75	8.91	6.50
22.07	42.47	28.92	21.88	22.64	10.67	33.45	14.18	33.99	8.48	23.51
8.18	13.63	8.40	5.03	28.72	3.39	13.31	10.18	18.24	19.85	5.36
5.55	5.83	17.19	4.16	14.51	7.17	0.69	9.47	14.12	10.45	1.48
7.48	11.72	20.16	2.76	9.95	9.06	1.27	9.85	15.51	10.21	11.24
6.24	1.11	13.03	4.25	8.57	10.32	-1.69	10.18	12.63	9.32	8.48
5.77	4.76	12.20	-3.08	11.04	12.24	5.66	9.53	11.57	11.66	12.32
7.96	23.12	17.60	7.70	14.40	8.90	5.77	12.87	12.62	16.84	21.89
6.46	27.51	14.76	6.91	10.56	8.95	-0.32	13.44	14.79	7.34	12.09
7.38	13.98	15.34	7.54	7.46	8.69	-6.09	14.10	15.64	7.94	13.95
5.51	3.51	11.09	3.01	10.18	–	–	15.42	12.96	8.31	10.80

Table 2.7. *Return to capital, United States (corrected)*

Year	AT&T	Chrysler	CDC	Delta	DEC	Dow	Kodak	Exxon	Ford
1963	–	–	–	–	–	–	–	–	–
1964	7.61	15.17	5.43	14.87	–	7.34	6.62	8.14	12.64
1965	8.54	16.09	5.18	9.16	–	7.96	4.94	9.33	17.00
1966	9.76	19.75	–1.15	8.22	–	9.50	–	12.43	19.58
1967	10.49	10.89	1.70	12.73	2.02	7.50	–	12.89	–0.33
1968	10.53	18.19	3.64	8.20	2.49	8.90	6.29	12.12	16.92
1969	11.42	12.36	4.28	10.75	1.70	9.16	5.79	12.60	26.27
1970	9.83	–2.95	–1.53	10.33	4.23	7.39	5.94	13.54	15.25
1971	9.65	6.48	1.78	3.93	1.73	6.00	4.73	16.14	15.11
1972	9.27	13.49	5.25	4.65	2.28	6.15	3.99	16.64	18.44
1973	10.41	21.24	8.72	11.49	2.67	8.31	5.85	24.86	29.18
1974	10.99	–2.32	0.71	18.48	7.75	18.25	9.78	27.54	8.79
1975	9.81	–10.35	9.08	6.76	2.73	11.27	5.25	40.03	4.92
1976	9.91	29.94	10.26	9.26	4.74	10.63	7.36	26.50	21.69
1977	11.25	16.05	12.22	14.45	8.28	12.87	13.08	29.41	40.54
1978	12.57	–17.13	17.07	21.16	7.39	13.23	15.89	30.60	40.81
1979	13.16	–32.62	14.57	21.94	6.71	15.33	19.18	41.83	26.89
1980	13.75	–29.64	15.18	7.18	6.19	14.62	15.57	26.98	–26.04
1981	13.10	–2.61	12.96	15.73	8.75	11.77	16.97	28.61	–10.41
1982	–	–	–	–1.71	9.87	–	–	–	–

Table 2.8. *Return to capital, Japan (corrected)*

Year	All Nippon Air.	Fuji Photo	Fujitsu	Kao Soap	Kawa- saki Steel	Koni- shiroku Photo	Lion	Mitsu- bishi Chem- ical	Mitsu- koshi	National
1964	–	–	–	–	–	–	–	–	–	–
1965	–	11.45	–	–	–	–	15.21	–	–	11.24
1966	10.69	8.76	7.88	10.12	9.25	7.80	16.29	6.04	10.36	12.63
1967	2.30	13.02	7.48	16.09	8.90	5.47	16.32	3.82	10.40	19.19
1968	10.98	11.37	9.12	13.20	9.28	2.08	16.48	6.40	11.51	15.00
1969	8.11	12.73	5.42	12.51	6.68	–2.52	25.96	5.76	13.48	10.80
1970	9.73	10.94	5.33	9.08	5.46	3.15	23.28	5.39	11.35	21.08
1971	8.86	10.52	7.11	13.03	8.75	6.06	26.83	4.97	10.94	16.04
1972	5.02	10.77	6.17	9.81	5.69	5.10	22.96	3.30	8.25	14.87
1973	6.75	11.78	3.74	11.88	2.96	5.05	18.86	0.36	6.14	19.86
1974	3.28	10.34	2.43	11.36	6.69	6.31	8.59	–2.49	8.32	22.59
1975	2.74	7.29	1.69	3.46	7.73	8.66	1.41	6.71	10.25	11.23
1976	3.69	10.09	1.72	4.08	4.46	10.92	9.33	2.83	11.56	15.37
1977	1.89	10.86	4.53	3.66	4.51	10.20	6.18	3.16	12.87	17.47
1978	1.36	11.79	–	5.77	4.25	8.97	7.98	3.90	11.88	15.14
1979	2.38	12.42	–	9.22	6.25	9.56	6.81	3.79	11.07	13.96
1980	1.46	18.76	–	6.49	11.98	8.50	3.07	4.23	12.38	12.55
1981	2.22	20.12	–	5.34	11.84	8.55	5.12	5.54	11.49	10.64
1982	2.99	15.76	–	5.31	12.08	13.21	6.39	3.64	8.23	9.00
1983	3.24	–	–	5.71	7.95	10.40	–	2.84	–1.24	–

GE	GM	IBM	Macy's	Merck	Nat. Semi.	Pfizer	P&G	Sears	USS
–	–	–	–	–	–	–	–	–	–
5.63	9.80	8.02	8.37	5.49	–	7.86	7.26	5.33	15.08
7.07	12.11	5.89	10.27	4.82	–	6.36	8.00	5.33	15.23
8.70	14.13	5.43	13.19	5.75	–	7.79	8.31	7.49	17.38
8.13	10.52	4.14	10.44	5.47	2.81	6.50	8.04	6.46	10.50
8.04	13.19	5.45	9.84	5.57	3.99	7.43	9.36	6.62	8.69
8.08	–	4.72	11.77	4.83	4.64	5.83	7.72	6.51	8.75
6.70	3.05	5.26	9.93	5.96	3.42	5.81	8.47	5.70	4.10
6.51	14.76	4.69	8.48	5.25	5.31	5.06	8.43	4.80	4.09
6.39	16.85	4.82	9.87	3.98	5.92	5.25	5.27	4.71	6.03
8.41	30.83	7.77	19.70	4.98	12.03	5.77	6.64	6.73	13.83
14.73	11.03	12.36	27.29	6.87	21.21	7.27	8.31	6.98	30.01
10.25	9.64	9.10	16.74	6.17	4.67	8.48	7.26	5.50	14.48
12.16	22.26	9.25	20.22	7.10	3.78	8.90	8.62	6.83	6.72
14.50	31.81	11.19	21.35	9.52	12.08	10.23	10.90	8.22	0.44
17.91	38.76	11.71	28.02	8.42	17.48	10.04	11.51	11.21	5.32
19.14	29.68	11.78	25.73	9.12	15.98	9.95	14.38	9.44	−11.47
17.05	−4.22	12.08	28.35	8.63	8.51	8.62	15.33	–	13.53
19.64	3.05	14.14	28.34	7.04	−6.36	7.81	13.93	–	31.65
–	–	–	15.37	–	–	–	12.66	–	–

NEC	Nippon Steel	Nissan Motor	Oki Elec.	Shio-nogi	Sony	Sumi-tomo Chem-ical	Taisho	Taka-shimaya	Takeda Chem-ical	Toshiba
–	–	–	–	–	5.10	9.53	–	–	–	–
3.75	9.16	9.11	2.63	13.68	6.72	8.29	8.96	9.09	14.09	−1.41
4.25	11.37	6.78	2.73	13.56	7.65	6.81	1.24	8.78	13.73	1.00
5.82	12.05	10.56	4.33	13.04	4.92	7.85	14.05	10.55	16.02	5.58
4.16	8.66	8.02	4.18	12.30	2.25	6.82	13.49	10.56	14.64	6.99
5.42	7.61	7.29	5.15	14.52	3.35	7.35	12.38	7.49	13.08	5.42
6.19	7.67	8.64	6.56	20.79	4.35	5.90	16.54	9.55	15.40	3.25
4.69	5.23	8.42	6.81	21.41	3.97	3.51	15.03	8.47	10.35	1.79
2.13	4.16	7.76	3.04	13.10	4.76	2.67	11.92	6.06	4.56	−0.96
0.06	7.37	4.50	2.67	14.33	6.60	3.92	10.53	6.91	0.14	−2.19
2.88	6.60	3.00	1.81	20.66	3.41	3.13	9.29	7.93	12.26	0.91
2.43	3.53	9.68	2.35	11.50	6.68	2.24	8.95	7.49	6.20	1.30
3.41	5.43	13.11	1.91	9.13	8.49	1.74	9.37	8.65	6.44	4.30
3.47	2.85	9.81	3.25	8.12	8.78	0.74	9.75	8.58	6.97	4.66
4.09	4.96	9.61	0.50	10.62	11.05	4.45	9.36	8.95	9.77	6.66
5.89	11.40	13.85	6.19	13.64	8.99	5.40	12.41	9.36	13.18	11.67
5.76	11.18	12.49	6.13	10.47	8.76	2.55	12.89	11.88	6.73	9.00
6.34	9.98	12.30	6.75	7.60	8.62	0.96	13.78	10.69	7.31	10.59
5.70	6.38	9.37	4.50	10.22	–	–	14.95	10.64	7.82	8.98

companies range between 3.8% and 5.2%, whereas the range is 4.6–8.4% for U.S. firms. In chemicals, the range is 4.0–10.2% in Japan, compared with Dow's 10.7% for the United States. There remain exceptions to this rule – in the drug industry, for example – but the result is clearer when corrected measures are used. In our sample, there are clear differences in rates of return (with Japan having a lower rate) in airlines, film and photographic equipment, steel, autos, computers, and chemicals. Although we would emphasize again that caution is necessary regarding results from such a small sample, there seems to be some evidence that a difference in returns to capital exists. The remainder of this chapter is devoted to considering the potential sources of this difference and whether or not it reflects a true difference in underlying capital costs.

4   Explaining differences in the rate of return

In this section, we explore two types of explanations for the apparent rate-of-return differential between the United States and Japan. One approach is to try to explain why the costs of capital differ; another is to show why the rate-of-return calculations of the preceding section may need further adjustment before they can be identified with costs of capital. Explanations of these two types would obviously have different policy implications.

4.1   *Taxation*

Although we know of no scholarly sources to cite, there is certainly a common perception in the United States that business taxes are at the root of our problems of competition with Japan. This argument is difficult to substantiate using our data.

Tables 2.9 and 2.10 present corrected after-tax earnings–price ratios for U.S. and Japanese firms, respectively, calculated by subtracting income taxes paid from the corrected before-tax earnings used to produce Tables 2.5 and 2.6. In similar fashion, we produce after-tax returns to capital, presented in Tables 2.11 and 2.12, by adding to after-tax corrected earnings corrected interest payments less the imputed tax deduction for such payments defined to be equal to nominal interest payments multiplied by the relevant corporate tax rate. These correspond to the financial concept of earnings before interest, after taxes. One may think of them as the after-tax returns the firms would earn if they were unlevered. Averages for these two measures for the period 1966–81 are provided in columns 5 and 7 of Tables 2.3 and 2.4.

By comparing before-tax and after-tax returns to capital, one can assess the impact of the corporate tax system, holding financial policy constant. Both returns are those the firm would earn if unlevered, and the difference thus represents the tax burden on the firm's real, rather than financial, activity.

Even a cursory comparison of before-tax and after-tax rates of return shows that it is Japanese firms, not American firms, that are taxed more heavily on their real income. All but 5 of the 21 Japanese firms have average after-tax rates of return to capital that are less than half of their before-tax rates of return. This is true for only 10 of the 19 American firms. Moreover, because of the substantial tax reduction introduced by the 1981 tax act, the trend beyond the 1966–81 period over which these averages were taken should be toward even more favorable comparative tax treatment in the United States.[8]

There are well-known pitfalls involved in using average rates of return to infer marginal effective rates relevant to the cost of capital for new investment. It would be preferable to use such measures[9] in the current discussion, but they are not yet available for Japan.

There is a second channel through which corporate taxes could affect the cost of capital. The preceding calculations of before-tax and after-tax returns to capital are based on costs to the unlevered firm: earnings before interest and taxes (EBIT) and earnings before interest, after taxes. To the extent that there are no differences in the after-tax costs of debt and equity finance, these are the appropriate statistics to use. If such differences do exist because of the corporate deductibility of interest payments, the extent to which this tax advantage is available in the two countries will also affect the cost of capital.

An extreme upper bound on the size of this advantage is the firm's annual tax deduction for interest payments. For example, if a firm had a 50% debt–value ratio, a nominal interest rate of 8%, and a tax rate of 40%, this would represent a maximum gain of 1.6 percentage points in its cost of capital. Even this would require that there be no offsetting costs to leverage, such as increased taxation at the individual level. Because equity income is taxed less heavily than interest income in both countries (capital gains are not taxed at all in Japan), one would not expect this to be the case, even if a full tax offset (as hypothesized by Miller 1977) is absent.

We have calculated these upper bounds for each company in each year. Averages for each company for the period 1966–81 are given in Table 2.13 for the United States and Table 2.14 for Japan. The U.S. averages range from 0.07% for Kodak to 2.55% for Macy's, with a median value of

Table 2.9. *After-tax earnings-price ratios, United States (corrected)*

Year	AT&T	Chrysler	CDC	Delta	DEC	Dow	Kodak	Exxon	Ford
1963	–	–	–	–	–	–	–	–	–
1964	4.70	8.96	3.31	8.97	–	5.13	3.31	5.46	5.44
1965	5.98	9.01	3.08	5.46	–	6.00	2.55	6.06	8.88
1966	7.51	12.47	-1.91	5.06	–	7.80	2.99	8.25	10.56
1967	8.40	6.73	0.64	7.69	1.11	5.72	2.96	8.76	-1.72
1968	8.54	10.79	1.67	5.47	1.32	7.80	2.85	7.89	7.15
1969	10.56	17.05	3.63	8.65	0.90	9.39	2.61	7.57	17.70
1970	10.68	-3.45	-1.56	7.24	2.41	6.88	2.80	9.14	9.24
1971	10.93	6.80	2.76	3.08	0.65	5.38	2.20	10.04	8.54
1972	9.26	10.99	4.69	2.84	1.27	4.48	1.97	7.18	10.92
1973	12.47	35.98	11.62	7.85	1.45	6.30	2.94	11.11	22.94
1974	18.70	5.68	16.91	18.91	4.34	14.05	4.71	22.86	9.21
1975	15.55	-50.54	18.66	8.03	1.42	8.53	2.40	13.69	2.13
1976	9.39	34.26	12.57	6.99	2.51	7.58	3.67	10.10	14.62
1977	12.05	22.67	14.31	9.99	4.81	11.43	6.43	9.71	29.91
1978	15.25	-44.11	20.06	13.33	4.80	13.99	7.93	11.22	32.90
1979	19.44	-138.25	15.53	15.66	3.66	15.55	10.48	17.71	34.84
1980	21.43	-139.58	12.94	5.34	3.65	16.58	8.49	15.68	-57.13
1981	17.57	-18.71	10.53	12.13	3.74	15.26	8.93	20.89	-42.45
1982	–	–	–	-1.69	5.25	–	–	–	–

Table 2.10. *After-tax earnings-price ratios, Japan (corrected)*

Year	All Nippon Air.	Fuji Photo	Fujitsu	Kao Soap	Kawa-saki Steel	Koni-shiroku Photo	Lion	Mitsu-bishi Chem-ical	Mitsu-koshi	National
1964	–	–	–	–	–	–	–	–	–	–
1965	–	9.07	–	–	–	–	14.80	–	–	4.74
1966	42.31	6.71	7.64	6.97	14.37	7.20	15.79	14.42	6.74	7.35
1967	9.21	9.86	7.54	13.73	14.87	7.88	15.42	5.92	6.20	12.51
1968	32.37	9.74	10.02	13.09	21.80	-0.57	18.93	16.21	6.59	8.94
1969	14.70	11.18	4.49	11.69	13.39	-14.99	30.85	17.02	8.62	6.38
1970	16.89	10.34	4.65	7.62	18.91	6.66	27.66	32.49	8.62	13.50
1971	15.95	10.52	5.51	15.21	22.96	12.84	23.77	19.57	8.24	9.62
1972	8.52	8.67	4.25	8.66	18.36	7.19	16.91	14.24	6.38	8.59
1973	12.02	11.10	4.69	12.43	18.55	8.84	23.63	12.50	5.34	12.60
1974	15.21	19.97	10.57	38.71	55.69	26.30	34.95	29.11	9.55	13.54
1975	6.77	4.50	2.03	7.95	14.63	19.46	-0.59	37.75	5.59	5.90
1976	6.27	4.80	0.71	3.39	9.90	7.87	8.37	10.28	5.25	6.94
1977	0.23	6.54	4.29	1.34	9.97	7.27	6.60	1.85	5.73	8.29
1978	-0.07	7.21	–	4.92	7.24	7.20	4.37	6.78	5.29	7.95
1979	1.16	6.89	–	8.57	0.84	7.22	7.94	2.62	5.09	7.33
1980	0.01	9.32	–	10.17	16.14	6.02	2.38	2.70	6.09	6.71
1981	-0.60	9.71	–	2.07	11.04	4.61	4.47	2.71	5.41	4.85
1982	0.34	7.69	–	1.31	13.54	8.49	4.89	0.45	3.95	4.42
1983	-0.06	–	–	2.41	6.39	7.20	–	-4.74	-4.01	–

38

GE	GM	IBM	Macy's	Merck	Nat. Semi.	Pfizer	P&G	Sears	USS
−	−	−	−	−	−	−	−	−	−
3.05	4.37	4.86	3.33	3.00	−	4.60	3.61	3.13	10.81
3.93	5.63	3.23	5.48	2.71	−	3.51	4.23	3.22	10.50
4.98	6.79	2.91	8.50	3.10	−	4.25	4.47	4.89	17.40
4.96	4.83	2.34	5.55	3.07	1.93	3.51	4.22	4.24	11.91
4.98	5.61	2.70	5.89	2.80	2.61	3.81	5.06	3.95	10.10
5.53	11.07	2.26	7.26	2.33	3.64	2.89	3.71	3.64	12.02
4.54	2.31	2.62	6.04	3.07	0.58	3.08	3.96	3.33	6.43
4.18	7.70	2.21	4.83	2.78	3.19	2.90	3.26	2.94	7.31
3.87	8.68	2.36	5.38	2.19	3.55	3.03	2.74	2.97	7.20
5.57	17.55	4.04	14.05	2.82	7.44	3.54	3.46	4.47	13.96
12.73	4.98	6.17	30.64	3.96	13.15	5.75	4.68	6.83	31.47
7.97	3.55	4.05	14.53	3.82	1.88	8.27	4.25	4.80	15.28
8.07	11.73	4.23	13.07	4.22	1.74	7.03	4.69	5.73	7.35
9.59	18.00	5.38	13.98	5.86	5.99	9.10	5.96	9.11	1.80
12.13	22.91	5.64	18.96	4.93	11.00	9.07	6.45	14.02	12.76
13.05	17.50	6.03	18.63	5.66	10.19	8.72	8.92	14.28	−7.86
11.73	−4.18	6.81	19.02	5.17	4.29	6.69	10.82	−	24.77
14.02	1.87	7.18	17.31	4.85	−6.81	5.42	8.07	−	38.41
−	−	−	6.92	−	−	−	7.18	−	−

NEC	Nippon Steel	Nissan Motor	Oki Elec.	Shio-nogi	Sony	Sumi-tomo Chem-ical	Taisho	Taka-shimaya	Takeda Chem-ical	Toshiba
−	−	−	−	−	1.34	11.33	−	−	−	−
2.91	21.21	13.37	0.34	16.43	4.95	15.89	6.80	15.57	13.86	−8.34
4.26	25.28	7.61	1.34	18.62	6.11	16.20	0.41	14.15	13.26	−2.19
7.47	44.13	16.06	6.03	17.28	4.29	19.23	9.38	16.79	13.18	9.92
3.47	33.67	14.71	3.29	11.28	1.62	13.17	8.64	16.87	9.87	9.94
7.09	25.87	18.19	6.01	10.54	2.62	24.56	7.53	16.26	9.34	14.11
7.80	25.18	20.02	7.07	17.86	2.11	16.80	10.02	15.00	12.67	10.31
6.22	18.64	8.50	8.91	16.43	2.03	5.00	8.87	11.47	9.40	1.63
7.64	13.54	11.37	7.21	8.90	3.23	12.27	6.20	0.91	3.02	4.73
17.62	36.05	22.42	17.68	9.16	4.58	30.80	4.57	27.02	0.15	19.37
6.33	10.10	5.48	3.48	13.28	1.13	13.31	4.09	13.24	9.36	3.48
4.16	5.83	7.79	2.40	3.95	3.16	1.24	3.97	10.46	2.21	−0.35
5.08	8.65	10.93	2.17	3.05	4.91	1.27	4.72	9.66	2.34	6.37
4.52	0.56	7.35	2.91	2.81	5.58	−1.69	5.00	7.43	1.36	6.16
3.94	−1.38	6.76	−3.48	4.65	6.74	1.95	4.72	5.81	4.11	6.62
4.92	11.87	8.98	3.91	6.05	4.35	4.07	6.40	5.30	6.68	12.65
4.02	7.49	8.67	4.37	4.31	4.92	−0.32	6.68	7.52	3.27	7.00
4.05	7.48	8.59	6.15	2.47	5.01	−6.09	6.85	6.34	3.45	8.08
3.17	2.73	6.85	1.08	2.96	−	−	7.55	4.46	3.76	6.26

Table 2.11. *After-tax return to capital, United States (corrected)*

Year	AT&T	Chrysler	CDC	Delta	DEC	Dow	Kodak	Exxon	Ford
1963	–	–	–	–	–	–	–	–	–
1964	3.96	7.99	3.05	7.57	–	4.52	3.31	5.20	5.09
1965	4.66	8.03	2.50	4.97	–	5.00	2.55	5.68	7.98
1966	5.30	9.97	-1.57	4.44	–	5.71	–	7.31	8.64
1967	5.65	5.33	0.52	6.79	1.12	4.43	–	7.46	-1.38
1968	5.25	8.11	1.47	4.33	1.28	5.25	2.80	6.51	6.36
1969	5.62	8.83	2.52	5.68	0.88	5.41	2.57	5.74	14.99
1970	5.19	-3.02	-1.02	5.32	2.23	3.83	2.76	7.19	7.88
1971	5.11	3.05	1.34	2.24	0.72	3.42	2.18	7.97	7.21
1972	4.83	6.95	3.39	2.42	1.23	3.38	1.96	6.06	9.53
1973	5.39	11.59	4.92	5.79	1.44	4.56	2.91	9.20	15.65
1974	5.52	-2.23	0.26	9.59	4.10	9.47	4.60	15.93	3.05
1975	4.57	-16.26	3.79	3.14	1.01	5.99	2.35	9.93	0.35
1976	4.53	18.05	6.08	4.47	2.42	5.71	3.62	8.16	11.02
1977	5.51	7.97	7.29	7.36	4.48	6.63	6.33	7.58	21.53
1978	6.20	-17.06	10.35	10.81	3.53	6.63	7.73	8.46	22.80
1979	6.81	-37.39	8.83	12.16	2.66	8.15	10.17	13.21	19.86
1980	7.16	-35.70	9.12	4.14	2.62	8.31	8.34	12.91	-22.60
1981	6.65	-7.79	6.65	8.65	3.80	6.95	8.76	15.37	-13.92
1982	–	–	–	-1.37	5.19	–	–	–	–

Table 2.12. *After-tax return to capital, Japan (corrected)*

Year	All Nippon Air.	Fuji Photo	Fujitsu	Kao Soap	Kawasaki Steel	Konishiroku Photo	Lion	Mitsubishi Chemical	Mitsukoshi	National
1964	–	–	–	–	–	–	–	–	–	–
1965	–	6.95	–	–	–	–	8.20	–	–	5.55
1966	9.42	4.56	3.96	4.76	5.72	3.91	7.69	3.88	6.13	6.14
1967	0.85	6.73	3.32	9.41	5.55	2.34	8.17	1.01	6.03	10.68
1968	9.37	6.83	5.49	7.63	5.96	0.13	8.59	3.66	6.61	8.09
1969	6.21	8.18	3.30	7.04	3.88	-4.50	14.63	3.31	8.33	6.08
1970	7.12	6.81	2.78	2.99	2.71	1.77	11.55	3.08	6.97	11.55
1971	6.16	6.50	3.47	7.68	4.92	3.74	14.37	2.32	6.39	8.92
1972	3.87	6.16	2.79	4.74	2.86	2.55	11.85	1.05	4.90	8.43
1973	4.27	5.49	0.37	6.22	0.78	0.69	7.51	-1.57	3.60	11.53
1974	1.56	4.26	-0.05	6.03	2.70	0.30	0.65	-4.83	4.68	11.60
1975	1.40	2.83	-0.16	0.10	3.41	4.68	-3.14	3.20	4.77	6.61
1976	1.78	3.98	-0.30	0.01	1.74	4.34	2.47	0.23	5.42	7.30
1977	-0.26	5.15	1.57	0.09	1.36	4.71	0.79	-0.27	6.23	8.86
1978	-0.05	5.74	–	1.97	1.24	4.54	1.94	1.25	5.76	8.58
1979	0.94	6.19	–	4.39	1.81	4.74	3.40	1.59	5.52	7.52
1980	0.44	8.80	–	2.96	5.60	3.40	1.05	1.63	6.44	7.08
1981	0.10	9.57	–	1.25	6.03	3.56	1.91	2.26	6.03	5.32
1982	1.46	7.74	–	1.61	6.71	6.46	2.73	1.68	3.99	4.93
1983	1.72	–	–	2.01	4.96	5.62	–	0.89	-2.10	–

GE	GM	IBM	Macy's	Merck	Nat. Semi.	Pfizer	P&G	Sears	USS
—	—	—	—	—	—	—	—	—	—
3.01	4.34	4.78	3.46	3.00	—	4.46	3.53	2.88	8.93
3.81	5.57	3.16	4.94	2.71	—	3.44	4.08	2.81	8.62
4.53	6.56	2.83	6.51	3.10	—	4.07	4.28	3.82	10.31
4.51	4.74	2.29	5.06	3.06	1.88	3.42	4.08	3.42	7.52
4.37	5.46	2.64	4.36	2.79	2.59	3.60	4.80	3.01	5.23
4.68	—	2.19	5.31	2.32	3.16	2.75	3.53	2.74	5.55
3.93	2.23	2.53	4.44	3.05	0.70	2.86	3.80	2.57	2.58
3.66	7.32	2.15	3.99	2.71	2.87	2.59	3.16	2.29	2.95
3.56	8.31	2.34	4.68	2.17	3.45	2.71	2.64	2.42	3.41
4.74	16.05	3.95	9.05	2.77	7.07	3.13	3.25	3.21	7.37
8.82	3.55	5.97	14.62	3.83	11.05	4.04	4.24	2.84	16.77
5.94	2.96	3.84	8.44	3.31	1.86	4.96	3.42	1.80	8.52
6.99	11.20	4.20	10.11	3.96	1.51	5.20	4.29	3.56	4.11
8.03	16.54	5.32	10.77	5.39	5.32	6.10	5.34	4.64	−0.29
10.03	20.36	5.55	14.73	4.52	8.51	5.75	5.63	6.23	3.22
11.11	15.60	5.28	13.63	5.03	7.77	5.70	7.40	5.14	−6.22
10.12	−3.50	6.20	15.10	4.79	3.78	4.57	8.24	—	8.61
12.08	1.16	6.32	15.12	4.04	−6.21	3.49	6.51	—	17.22
—	—	—	7.85	—	—	—	6.47	—	—

NEC	Nippon Steel	Nissan Motor	Oki Elec.	Shio-nogi	Sony	Sumi-tomo Chem-ical	Taisho	Taka-shimaya	Takeda Chem-ical	Toshiba
—	—	—	—	—	2.25	6.94	—	—	—	—
1.76	5.56	5.52	0.00	7.48	2.59	5.48	5.63	5.58	7.61	−3.11
1.77	6.87	3.19	0.02	7.42	4.02	4.13	0.20	5.14	7.09	−1.43
2.88	8.17	6.39	1.38	7.08	2.84	5.36	7.80	6.20	7.47	2.48
2.04	5.19	4.71	1.73	6.49	1.19	3.94	7.90	6.14	7.00	3.54
2.95	4.28	3.16	2.57	7.48	1.67	4.46	6.94	4.23	6.53	2.22
3.25	4.56	4.20	3.62	11.08	1.82	3.36	9.05	5.08	7.98	1.07
2.42	2.66	4.21	3.65	12.02	1.81	1.86	7.93	4.52	5.68	−0.42
−0.74	1.94	3.21	−0.18	5.63	2.25	0.16	5.04	2.84	−0.20	−3.02
−3.06	2.83	0.37	−0.68	3.32	0.97	1.06	1.88	2.51	−5.92	−5.01
0.22	2.60	0.04	−0.62	8.07	0.95	0.82	3.46	3.90	4.57	−1.61
0.10	1.21	3.29	−0.03	2.85	2.73	−0.26	3.61	3.97	0.29	−1.35
0.82	1.94	6.27	−0.03	2.68	4.38	−0.48	4.38	4.14	0.66	0.84
1.22	0.31	5.02	0.89	2.61	4.42	−0.95	4.70	4.24	0.64	1.96
1.99	0.93	5.06	−1.04	4.48	5.95	1.45	4.61	4.25	3.35	3.02
3.03	5.44	6.86	2.83	5.76	4.39	2.78	6.14	3.81	5.06	6.15
3.03	4.74	7.02	3.21	4.31	4.71	0.75	6.36	5.79	2.90	4.70
3.22	5.08	6.70	4.34	2.61	4.86	−0.84	6.68	4.47	3.14	5.81
3.20	3.78	5.63	2.12	3.17	—	—	7.32	4.43	3.57	5.10

41

Table 2.13. *Maximum tax advantage from debt, United States (average, 1966–81)*

Company	Percentage
AT&T	1.33
Chrysler	2.49
CDC	1.67
Delta	0.86
DEC	0.15
Dow	1.18
Exxon	0.70
Ford	1.42
GE	0.64
GM	0.65
IBM	0.13
Macy's	2.55
Merck	0.12
Nat. Semi.	0.44
Pfizer	0.63
P&G	0.24
Sears	1.36
USS	1.26

0.70% (Exxon). For Japan, the maximum, minimum, and median are 2.34% for Nippon Steel, 0.16% for Taisho, and 1.24% for Nissan Motors, respectively.

These measures indicate only a very small difference in the maximum potential gains from leverage in Japan and the United States. Given that these upper bounds may greatly overstate the gains from leverage in both countries, we would argue that greater Japanese ability to finance with tax-deductible debt is of negligible importance in explaining before-tax cost-of-capital differences between the two countries.

We conclude, provisionally, that corporate taxes cannot explain why Japanese firms would enjoy a lower cost of capital than those in the United States.

4.2   Differences in national savings rates

It appears, from calculations of after-tax rates of return, that Japanese corporations earn substantially less for the holders of their securities than do U.S. corporations. Some have been tempted to ascribe this result to the higher personal savings rate in Japan. There are two problems with

Table 2.14. *Maximum tax*
advantage from debt, Japan
(average, 1966-81)

Company	Percentage
Fuji	1.04
Fujitsu	1.01
Kao	0.46
Kawasaki	2.26
Konishiroku	1.29
Lion	1.53
Mitsubishi	1.95
Mitsukoshi	0.49
National	0.83
NEC	1.34
Nippon Air	1.11
Nippon Steel	2.34
Nissan	1.24
Oki	1.51
Shionogi	1.07
Sony	0.40
Sumitomo	1.93
Taisho	0.16
Takashimaya	1.59
Takeda	0.69
Toshiba	1.64

this conclusion. First, savings rates do not necessarily translate into rates of capital accumulation in a world of open capital markets, because capital will flow abroad to gain higher rates of return.

There is some controversy about the openness of the Japanese capital market. However, there is a second factor that must be considered. The Japanese economy, including, of course, its capital stock, has been growing much more rapidly than the U.S. economy over the past two decades. A greater rate of investment out of GNP has been required for Japan simply to maintain any given capital-output ratio. A comparison suggests that the capital-output ratios for productive sectors in Japan are no higher than comparable figures for the United States.[10]

4.3   Differences in growth and risk

One is accustomed to seeing some firms in the United States have higher price-earnings "multiples" than others. Systematic differences of this sort can be due to one of two factors. One is differences in risk. Riskier firms have higher rates of return to capital, on average, because investors are risk-averse. It is a matter of semantics whether or not the riskier firm has a higher cost of capital, because it must earn the same *risk-adjusted* rate of return as the less risky firm. A second reason for variation in earnings–price ratios is related to growth – not simply growth itself, but the unusual investment opportunities that one normally associates with rapidly growing enterprises. Firms with access to projects with high-marginal products will be expected to grow more quickly, and the excess returns on these future projects should be capitalized into the current stock price.[11]

This certainly will *not* represent a cost-of-capital difference, only a difference in the composition of economic earnings: A greater fraction will be accounted for by capital gains (in excess of retained earnings), which are not included in our calculations thus far.

If Japanese firms are less risky than U.S. firms, or possess greater "exceptional growth opportunities," these could help explain why the observed before-tax return to capital appears to be somewhat lower in Japan. To assess these possibilities, one must use data on total market returns to investors instead of the reported earnings of firms. For the United States, this calculation is straightforward. To compute the annual return to equity, we add common and preferred dividends to the change in the value of the firm (net of new share issues), and divide this by the beginning-of-year value of the firm. This yields a measure of the rate at which the firm's equity is capitalized.[12]

Deriving similar statistics for Japan presents some difficulties involving the growth in equity. In Japan, there have been many more new issues of equity shares than in the United States, and to complicate matters, some are given at no cost to current shareholders (stock dividends), some are sold in the market at the market price, and still others are sold to existing stockholders at face value (more frequently 50 yen per share, a fraction of the market price). Fortunately, we have been able to obtain, for each of the companies in our sample, the complete histories of new issues, including the prices at which they were issued. We therefore define the rate of capital gain on shares as the increase in the market value of outstanding shares less capital paid in the form of new share purchases divided by the market value of shares outstanding at the beginning of the period. The market rate of return on equity then is defined as the sum of the rate of capital gain so defined plus the dividends paid divided by the market value of shares outstanding at the beginning of the period.

The results of our calculations are presented in Tables 2.15 and 2.16. In these tables, we first list earnings–price ratio after tax, both unadjusted for inflation and adjusted for inflation, averaged over the period of 1971–81, in columns 2 and 3. Column 3 would have been the same as

Table 2.15. *Earnings-price ratio after tax and
market return on equity (1971-81)*

Company	E/P (after tax) Unadjusted	Adjusted	Mkt. ret./equity
AT&T	11.6	14.7	2.9
Chrysler	−32.3	−25.0	0.9
CDC	10.2	12.8	4.2
Delta	10.4	9.5	2.2
DEC	4.6	2.9	16.8
Dow	9.4	10.8	7.6
Kodak	6.7	5.5	2.1
Exxon	14.4	13.7	6.5
Ford	5.3	6.0	−4.5
GE	8.7	9.4	4.2
GM	11.2	10.0	−1.5
IBM	6.3	4.9	−2.3
Macy's	12.6	15.5	12.8
Merck	5.0	4.2	2.2
Nat. Semi.	6.3	5.1	43.6
Pfizer	6.6	6.3	1.8
P&G	6.2	5.8	0.7
Sears	8.4	7.2	−6.6
USS	14.6	13.9	5.8

column 5 in Tables 2.3 and 2.4, except that in Tables 2.15 and 2.16 it is averaged over the shorter period of 1971-81 rather than over 1966-81, because some detailed information on new-issues records was missing on the Compustat tape before 1971.

The results are quite dramatic. On an inflation-adjusted basis, the median earnings-price ratio for the United States is 7.2 (Sears), whereas it is 8.1 (Shionogi) for Japan. Looking at the third columns in Tables 2.15 and 2.16, we may conclude that there is little to distinguish between the distribution of the earnings-price ratio for the United States (excluding Chrysler, which is a special case) and that for Japan. In terms of the market rate of return shown in the fourth column, however, the difference is enormous. The median for the United States is 2.2% (Delta Airlines and Merck), whereas it is 13.6% (Toshiba) for Japan.[13]

There may be any number of reasons not to take these figures too seriously. Among them, we may note that during the period covered, the capitalization rate in general in the United States may have risen significantly, and figures for the United States may include a large one-time

Table 2.16. *Earnings-price ratio after tax and market return on equity (1971-81)*

| Company | E/P (after tax) | | Mkt. ret./equity |
	Pension adjusted only	Adjusted	
Fuji	10.3	9.0	9.2
Fujitsu	4.5	4.6	2.7
Kao	7.3	10.3	15.1
Kawasaki	8.5	16.9	16.5
Konishiroku	9.3	10.4	24.3
Lion	13.6	12.1	19.7
Mitsubishi	6.0	12.7	16.9
Mitsukoshi	5.9	6.2	5.9
National	8.4	8.4	12.2
NEC	4.7	6.6	7.3
Nippon Air	2.3	6.0	16.9
Nippon Steel	7.4	12.4	20.2
Nissan	10.4	10.8	22.9
Oki	4.4	5.2	5.2
Shionogi	12.3	8.1	11.8
Sony	5.0	3.9	19.6
Sumitomo	4.3	7.7	18.5
Taisho	8.8	5.9	8.2
Takashimaya	7.1	11.3	9.1
Takeda	9.3	5.0	12.6
Toshiba	6.9	7.1	13.6

capital loss that may be distorting our results. Japan may still have been on the postwar declining trend of the general capitalization rate during this period, which appears to have ended in the early 1960s for the United States.

We do not wish to assert here, on the basis of information presented in Tables 2.15 and 2.16, that the required rate of return on equity has been this much higher in Japan than in the United States. On the other hand, even a much smaller revision in this direction of the after-tax costs of equity reported earlier would be sufficient to nullify any apparent difference in overall returns to capital in the two countries. Given all the evidence presented in this chapter, therefore, there do not seem to be any grounds to conclude that the cost of capital in Japan was significantly lower than that in the United States for the period covered.

5 Conclusions

We have not yet reached any firm conclusions whether or not the Japanese cost of capital is lower than that in the United States, but we have made some progress. There appears some evidence of lower before-tax rates of return in Japan, though given our sample size and selection method, this result is by no means definitive.

In searching for potential explanations, we have been able to rule out one that is among the most frequently cited: business taxation. Japanese real investments appear to be more, rather than less, heavily taxed than those undertaken in the United States, and the maximum potential gain from the greater use of leverage is very small. It also appears that the understatement of capital gains by book-value data is sufficient to explain any apparent gap in returns between the two countries.

We have based our analysis on samples of firms from the United States and from Japan, but we have chosen these firms very informally on the basis of their size, industry to which they belong, comparability, and availability of data. It would be quite useful to work with a somewhat larger and more systematically chosen sample. It would also be very useful to estimate ex ante cost-of-capital measures, rather than working with purely ex post realization data. Finally, we hope to make parallel computations using data for industries and the whole economy, in order to supplement the results based on individual-firm data reported here. Ultimately, one wishes to understand variations in the rate of return in the context of the savings and investment patterns of the countries involved, and how two or more countries may adjust to each other when their savings and investment behaviors differ substantially.

ACKNOWLEDGMENTS

We are grateful to Professors N. Atoda and M. Homma of Osaka University and Mr. N. Kato of Daiwa Research Institute for their assistance in analysis of Japanese data and to Laurie Dicker for excellent research assistance. Partial financial support was provided by the Wharton School's Reginald H. Jones Center and the NBER. The second author also received support through a Sloan Research Fellowship.

NOTES

1. See, especially, Hatsopoulos (1983).
2. "Accrued employees' severance indemnities" is a special reserve account in Japanese corporations set up to meet a requirement of the tax law. To begin with, it must be understood that most employees of Japanese corporations are not given retirement annuities, but a large cash payment at the time of retirement,

three to four times the annual salary for the last year of employment. The corporate tax law of Japan says that (1) corporations must estimate the total amount of the severance payments that would have to be undertaken if the company were to cease operations immediately and pay all employees the severance pay to which they were entitled, (2) "accrued employees' severance imdemnities" should be 40% of the amount calculated under (1), (3) the retirement benefits actually paid during the fiscal year should be charged against this account, and (4) the difference between the amount defined under (2) and the remaining balance at the end of the fiscal year can be charged as current expenses, and it is deductible for corporate income tax purposes. In other words, this liability item is a book entry, a device to maintain the account for the retirement benefits on an accrual basis, and it is not an actual liability against which interest is paid. Indeed, there is no interest payment on this item in the income statement of a company. The entire contribution into this reserve account is treated as labor cost in the income statement. Thus, it is not appropriate to include this item in liabilities of corporations in Japan.

To bring the accounting with respect to this item to a cash basis, as in the case of U.S. corporations, we have subtracted the net change in this account from the current costs of Japanese companies.

3. See, for example, Shoven and Bulow (1975, 1976) for an evaluation of the effects on American corporations.

4. This procedure was also used by Auerbach (1984), where it is described and evaluated more fully.

5. We are grateful to Bronwyn Hall for calling this problem to our attention.

6. In principle, one could get a rough estimate by redoing the estimates for Japan with land included.

7. The use of such corrected estimates of the return to corporate capital to infer the required return is familiar in the literature. See, for example, Feldstein and Summers (1977) or Feldstein, Dicks-Mireaux, and Poterba (1983).

8. For a discussion, see Auerbach (1983a).

9. As found in Auerbach (1983a) or the international comparison volume edited by King and Fullerton (1984).

10. For the United States, for 1979, gross national product originating in the nonfinancial corporate sector divided by the stock of reproducible tangible assets excluding inventories at the replacement cost is approximately 1.10 (*Survey of Current Business,* July 1983, p. 30, and Board of Governors of the Federal Reserve System, *Balance Sheets of the United States, 1945-1982,* p. 44). For Japan, one needs to make some approximations in terms of the sectors included to come as close as possible to the one used for the United States. We have taken fixed reproducible assets other than inventories for nonfinancial incorporated enterprises (*Annual Report of National Accounts,* 1985, p. 309) less estimated residential structures owned by this sector as the capital stock, and we have used GNP originating in the private producer sector less agriculture, finance and insurance, real estate, and service industries as output. The corresponding figure for Japan is 1.14.

11. This can be rigorously shown using, for instance, the "q" theory of investment. Suppose there is the anticipation that an outward shift will occur in the production frontier in the future, increasing the marginal product of capital. This will increase investment, and market value, immediately, *decreasing* measured earnings in the short run because of capital deepening. Hence, one

will observe a low earnings–price ratio in the short run. The capitalized value of higher-future-marginal products rises as their date of appearance nears, giving investors a sufficient overall return to equity.

12. If the marginal source of equity funds is retained earnings, rather than new shares, then one should adjust dividends in this calculation, multiplying them by a factor less than 1 that represents the relative cost to the firm of delivering an after-tax dollar to the investor in the form of capital gains as opposed to dividends. This is the ratio $(1-\theta)/(1-c)$, where θ is the dividend tax rate, and c is the accrual equivalent of the capital-gains tax. See Auerbach (1979, 1983b). This correction is important in the current context to the extent that dividend yields differ between the United States and Japan.

13. This set of results is broadly consistent with those reported by Baldwin (1986), who found Japanese market returns to equity to be higher in the aggregate than those in the United States (but also riskier).

REFERENCES

Auerbach, A. J. (1979). "Wealth Maximization and the Cost of Capital." *Quarterly Journal of Economics,* Vol. 93, August, pp. 433–46.
    (1983a). "Corporate Taxation in the U.S." *Brookings Papers on Economic Activity,* No. 2, pp. 451–505.
    (1983b). "Taxation, Corporate Financial Policy and the Cost of Capital." *Journal of Economic Literature,* Vol. 21, September, pp. 905–40.
    (1984). "Taxation, Firm Financial Policy and the Cost of Capital: An Empirical Analysis." *Journal of Public Economics,* Vol. 23, February, pp. 27–57.
Baldwin, C. Y. (1986). "The Capital Factor: Competing for Capital in a Global Environment." In M. Porter (ed.), *Competition in Global Industries.* Boston: Harvard Business School Press.
Feldstein, M., and L. H. Summers (1977). "Is the Rate of Profit Falling?" *Brookings Papers on Economic Activity,* No. 1, pp. 211–27.
Feldstein, M., L. Dicks-Mireaux, and J. Poterba (1983). "The Effective Tax Rate and the Pretax Rate of Return." *Journal of Public Economics,* Vol. 2, July, pp. 124–158.
Hatsopoulos, G. (1983). *High Cost of Capital: America's Industrial Handicap.* American Business Conference and Thermo Electron Corporation.
King, M., and D. Fullerton (eds.) (1984). *The Taxation of Income from Capital.* University of Chicago Press.
Miller, M. (1977). "Debt and Taxes." *Journal of Finance,* Vol. 32, May, pp. 261–75.
Shoven, J., and J. Bulow (1975). "Inflation Accounting and Nonfinancial Corporate Profits: Physical Assets." *Brookings Papers on Economic Activity,* No. 3, pp. 557–98.
    (1976). "Inflation, Accounting and Nonfinancial Corporate Profits: Financial Assets and Liabilities." *Brookings Papers on Economic Activity,* No. 1, pp. 15–57.

CHAPTER 3

The taxation of income from capital in Japan

John B. Shoven and Toshiaki Tachibanaki

1 Introduction

The purpose of this chapter is to compute the effective marginal rate of taxation of capital income in Japan and to compare the result with the U.S. tax treatment of capital income. It is well known that the personal savings rate and the investment rate are quite high in Japan by international standards. This chapter attempts to investigate whether or not tax policies at both the personal level and the corporate level could be responsible for this high rate of capital accumulation.

In order to do this, we need to define precisely what we mean by the effective marginal rate of taxation of capital income. We follow the conventions of King (1977) and King and Fullerton (1984). We compute the wedge between the gross earnings of a marginal new investment and the net return that the investor earns. This wedge is then compared to the gross earnings of the investment to give us an effective rate of taxation. The result is a marginal rate, because it refers to the taxation of an incremental new investment. This marginal tax rate is to be contrasted with the frequently computed average tax rate, which is simply the ratio of taxes paid to gross earnings for all existing capital. Although we limit our analysis to capital in the corporate sector, we do not limit the analysis to the corporate tax. In fact, we include in the tax-wedge computation personal income taxes and wealth taxes, as well as the corporate income tax.

One result that King and Fullerton generated in their study of the effective marginal tax rate in the United States, the United Kingdom, Sweden, and West Germany is that these rates differ by industry, asset, type of investor, and type of financing. To enhance the comparability between our results for Japan and their results for the other four countries, we have disaggregated our results into the same categories and have utilized the same base year, 1980. This means that we look at three asset types (machinery, buildings, and inventories), three industries (manufacturing, "other," and commerce), three sources of finance or financial instruments (debt, new share issues, and retained earnings), and three ownership or investor categories (households, tax-exempt institutions, and insurance companies). This results in a total of 81 different combinations of assets, industries, financial instruments, and investors. We compute an effective marginal tax rate for each of these 81 combinations and calculate an average marginal tax rate by taking a weighted average of the 81 results. The computations can be presented in aggregated, subaggregated, or disaggregated form. They permit us to gain an impression of the tax disincentives faced by Japanese domestic investors and to compare their situation with those for investors in the United States, the United Kingdom, Sweden, and West Germany.

The next part of this chapter presents several institutional characteristics of the tax system in Japan and explains the data that we use to calculate the effective marginal tax rates. It also discusses the economic implications of the tax system for savings and investment. The third part of this chapter briefly reviews the methodology and presents the estimated results of our calculations of the effective tax rates on income from capital in Japan. We directly compare our calculations with similar estimates of rates of taxation of capital income for the United Kingdom, Sweden, West Germany, and the United States. We complete the chapter with an overall assessment of the results and make some policy suggestions.

2   Institutional characteristics of the Japanese tax system

2.1   Personal income tax

The personal income tax is the most important source of revenue at the national level in Japan (Table 3.1), as in the United States. Individual income taxes amounted to roughly 40% of total national tax receipts in Japan in 1982. Although there has been some discussion in academic circles whether income or expenditure is the more desirable personal tax base, the government and politicians in Japan do not seem inclined to change to an expenditure basis. Thus, it appears that the personal income tax will continue to be the most important component of the Japanese tax system at the national level for the foreseeable future. However, because of tax-sheltered savings accounts, zero taxation of capital gains, and so forth, it is possible that what is termed "income tax" in fact functions in a manner clearly resembling an expenditure tax.

Table 3.1. *Sources of tax revenue in Japan (%)*
(national level)

Source	1973	1976	1979	1982
Direct taxes				
Total	72.3	67.5	68.4	70.4
Income tax	37.9	37.0	37.1	39.9
Corporation tax	32.0	28.5	29.6	28.3
Inheritance tax	2.2	1.9	1.7	2.2
Others	0.0	0.2	0.0	–
Indirect taxes				
Total	25.4	29.6	29.1	27.2
Liquor tax	5.9	6.1	5.9	5.5
Gasoline tax	4.7	5.9	5.9	5.1
Petroleum tax	–	–	1.2	3.9
Commodity tax	4.1	4.4	4.4	2.3
Motor vehicle tonnage tax	0.8	1.7	1.5	1.4
Customs duty	3.3	3.0	2.8	2.3
Stamp revenues	2.8	3.1	3.4	3.9
Monopoly profits	2.5	3.9	2.4	2.4
Others	1.3	1.5	1.6	0.4
Special account				
Total	2.3	2.9	2.5	2.4
	100.0	100.0	100.0	100.0

Source: *An Outline of Japanese Taxes* (Ministry of Finance, 1983).

The Japanese personal income tax was originally based on the famous Shoup (1949) recommendations for a comprehensive income tax system. The Shoup Commission suggestions were embodied in the 1950 tax reform in Japan. However, several subsequent tax reforms have gradually eroded this system away from the principle of a comprehensive income tax. Examples include the adoption of a withholding system on interest income and dividend income, which can be taxed separate from other income, and the elimination of taxes on capital gains. This erosion of the tax base, plus evidence of considerable tax evasion, has resulted in a rather small base for taxation. Pechman and Kaizuka (1976), for example, found that only 33% of national income was reported as taxable income in 1970. This compares with a 59% figure for the United States. Moreover, the extent of and variation in tax evasion by occupation are quite evident in Table 3.2, which was extracted from Ishi (1981). The results of Homma et al. (1984a) were consistent with these figures. There is

Table 3.2A. *Ratio of number of taxpayers to number of income-earners by occupation (%)*

Taxpayers	1973	1975	1977
Wage-earners	77.6	71.9	74.2
Farmers	20.7	15.4	17.2
Self-employed (other than farmers)	36.6	32.3	33.4

Source: Sato (1979).

Table 3.2B. *Ratio of reported taxable income to total taxable income by income source (%)*

Income source	1973	1975	1977	1978
Wage and salary income	88.1	100.3	91.3	96.1
Enterprise income				
Case I	59.0	67.5	71.0	72.8
Case II	55.8	72.7	80.7	
Farm income	29.5	22.3	20.9	22.5

Source: Ishi (1981).

general agreement that farmers and self-employed workers vastly under-report their income. Table 3.2 indicates that only 17% of farmers pay taxes, and only about 22.5% of total taxable farm income is actually reported. This cheating gives the impression to ordinary employees that the Japanese personal income tax system is unfair.[1] Public reporting of tax evasion and erosion has brought the current personal income tax under considerable attack.

The progressivity of the Japanese individual income tax on a statutory basis is quite high. For low incomes, this is partially due to the fact that the initial amount of income that is exempt from tax (after various deductions) is also fairly high.[2] The progressivity of the rate structure is shown in Table 3.3. The marginal income tax rate begins at 10% and rises to 75% for the highest taxable incomes. Itaba and Tachibanaki (1987) found that the effective progressivity of the Japanese system, taking into account both the statutory rates of the income tax and the distribution of income, is greater than that in the United States. Several groups of people are demanding that this progressivity be lowered in order to reduce

Table 3.3. *Rates of individual income tax and distribution of taxpayers by income class*

Taxable income (million yen) (A)		Tax rate (%)	Cumulative tax for each bracket (million yen)
More than	But not more than	(B)	(C)
–	0.6	10	–
0.6	1.2	12	0.60
1.2	1.8	14	1.32
1.8	2.4	16	2.16
2.4	3.0	18	3.12
3.0	4.0	21	4.20
4.0	5.0	24	6.30
5.0	6.0	27	8.70
6.0	7.0	30	11.40
7.0	8.0	34	14.40
8.0	10.0	38	17.80
10.0	12.0	42	25.40
12.0	15.0	46	33.80
15.0	20.0	50	47.60
20.0	30.0	55	72.60
30.0	40.0	60	127.60
40.0	60.0	65	187.60
60.0	80.0	70	317.60
80.0		75	457.60

Note: Tax liability is computed by multiplying the taxable income in excess of the amount (A) by the rate (B) and adding the amount (C). For example, income tax due on taxable income of 25 million yen: (25 million − 20 million)(0.55) + 7.26 million = 10.01 million.
Source: An Outline of Japanese Taxes (Ministry of Finance, 1983).

the alleged negative effect of the income tax on the labor supply. However, there have been no quantitative studies to investigate the impact of the income tax on the total labor supply in Japan. There have been studies regarding the labor-supply elasticity of married women who work as part-time employees, but the general case for lowering the top marginal rate does not yet have solid empirical backing. It should be added, of course, that there is an opposite position, namely, that the income tax should provide an even stronger redistribution of income; see, for example, Wada (1980). Incidentally, Atoda and Tachibanaki (1987) found that the current income tax law provided the nearly optimal degree of progressivity under some reasonable assumptions in a model that considered the trade-off between efficiency and equity. In any case, the issue of the proper degree of progressivity will be one of the most controversial topics when tax reforms are implemented or discussed in Japan.

Under the current "Income Tax Law," taxable income is classified into the following 10 categories: (1) interest income, (2) dividend income, (3) real estate income, (4) business income, (5) employment income, (6) retirement income, (7) timber income, (8) capital gains, (9) occasional income, and (10) miscellaneous income. Among them, retirement income and timber income are taxed separate from other incomes. Interest, dividends, and capital gains also may be taxed separately under the Special Taxation Measures Law. Because we are interested in the taxation of income from corporate capital, we shall discuss the treatment of these sources in some detail.

Interest and dividends are subject to several important features of the tax law. Most important, these types of income may be taxed separately or aggregately with other income, at the taxpayer's option. For interest received on time deposits and deposits of a similar nature, a 20% tax is withheld at the source, and the income may be excluded from taxable income in filing a return. For other forms of interest income, the tax rate is 35% when separate taxation at the source is elected. In the case of dividends, there is a limit on the amount of dividends paid to a recipient by each corporation that is eligible for the separate 35% taxation. This limit is 500,000 yen per year (roughly $3,000). There is yet another limit. If the amount of dividends paid to a stockholder by a corporation is not more than 100,000 yen per year ($600), these dividends may be entirely excluded from taxable income in filing a return and are subject to 20% taxation at the source. This treatment, then, is similar to that for interest income. Taxpayers also receive a tax credit of 10% of dividends received if their total taxable income is below 10 million yen. The credit is reduced to 5% for those whose income is above this limit. The rationale for the credit is as an offset against the double taxation of dividends at the corporate and personal levels. Gains from original-issue discount on debentures issued from 1980 through 1986 are subject to withholding at the source at the rate of 16%. The provisions for separate taxation of interest and dividends were introduced to encourage savings. However, these provisions have frequently been criticized as unfair because they help only high-income households. Over time, the rate of separate taxation on this type of income has increased, as Table 3.4 shows, in response to such criticism.

There is another important provision that affects the taxation of interest and dividend income: the existence of nontaxable forms of capital income. These forms include the following as of 1980:

Table 3.4A. *Historical development of taxation of interest income*

Year	Report and payment	Rate with with-holding	Rate under separate tax	Small-savings tax exemption	Limit in postal savings
1965	Withholding	10%		1.0 million yen (deposit)	1.0 million yen
1966	↓	↓			
1967		15%		(1) Several savings and banks are possible	
1968				(2) Government bond is not taxable (limit: 0.5 million yen)	
1969					
1970	↓				
1971	(1) Time deposit (separate taxation		20%		↓
1972	may be elected) (2) Demand deposit		↓	1.5 million yen (deposit) 1.0 million yen (government	1.5 million yen
1973	(no report is required)		25%	bond) 1.0 million yen (asset formation)	↓
1974				3.0 million yen (deposit) 3.0 million yen (government bond)	3.0 million yen
1975			↓	5.0 million yen (asset formation)	
1976		↓	30% ↓		
1977		20%	35%		
1978					
1979					
1980					
1981					
1982					
1983	↓	↓	↓		↓

1. Interest accruing from postal savings when the principal does not exceed 3 million yen.
2. Interest income or distribution of profits from deposits, bonds, and debentures, open-end bond investment trusts, or specific stock investment trusts if the amount of principal in total does not exceed 3 million yen. This provision is called the "Small Saving Tax Exemption" (*Maruyū* in common Japanese).

Table 3.4B. *Historical development of taxation of dividend income*

Year	Report and payment	Rate with with-holding	Rate under separate tax	Redemption premium on debentures
1965	(1) Separate taxation may be elected for dividend	10%	15%	
1966	not exceeding 0.5 million yen per corporation	↓	↓	
1967	(2) No report is required for dividend not	15%	20%	Withholding and
	exceeding 0.05 million yen			separate taxation
1968				
1969				5%
1970				↓
1971	(1) Separate taxation and withholding may be			8%
1972	elected			
1973		↓	25%	10%
1974	(1) No report is required for dividend not			
	exceeding 0.1 million yen per corporation			
1975			↓	↓
1976			30%	12%
1977		↓	↓	↓
1978		20%	35%	16%
1979				
1980				
1981				
1982				
1983		↓	↓	↓

3. Interest on central-government and local-government bonds, not exceeding 3 million yen in total face value.

4. Interest income or distribution of profits received in accounts set up for the formation of employees' assets, particularly for housing and pensions. Various forms of monetary assets are eligible for this exemption. It requires, however, that the employees commit to savings contracts that are withheld from their wages and that the total amount of principle does not exceed 5 million yen.

Summing up these four items, an individual could have up to 14 million yen ($82,500) in nontaxable forms. If the household has several members, the amount of nontaxable savings can be increased accordingly. Further, there is widespread evidence of abuse of this system, with accounts being held in fictitious names.

To summarize, the "Individual Income Tax Law" features two main provisions to reduce the burden of tax on interest and dividends. First, it gives high-income taxpayers an option to have interest and dividends taxed separately at a rate lower than their rate on earnings and other income. Second, limits for the nontaxation of certain kinds of capital income, considerably higher than the average monetary assets per head, have been enacted. We take account of these features in calculating the tax wedge on capital income in Japan.

One can conceive of two channels by which these two provisions could encourage savings. The first is an income effect, in that the provisions may increase the resources of households with considerable savings and wealth. The second is a substitution effect in that the effective after-tax rate of return to savings is raised relative to the before-tax rate of return. We examine the second channel more carefully, partly because the second channel is more direct than the first, and partly because the first requires consideration of how the tax schedule would be modified if these provisions were dropped.

Japanese economists in general doubt that the interest rate greatly affects the amount of savings. There have been no serious empirical studies in Japan that have altered the understanding that the interest rate is not an important determinant of the level of savings at the macro level since the classical article by Komiya (1966) reached that conclusion. Fujita (1972) confirmed the findings of Komiya, although he found that the provisions for savings were effective in changing the composition of individual financial assets. Studies in the United States have come up with conflicting estimates of savings elasticity, although the consensus is that the elasticity is in the modest range of zero to 0.5. With these empirical estimates, we are somewhat doubtful that the Income Tax Law, which was aimed at raising the savings rate, should be given credit for the high rate of savings in Japan. It is our belief that there are other reasons that are equally important. These would include the low average income tax burden and the relatively low scale of the social security system.

It must be added, moreover, that the Income Tax Law in Japan, which aims at raising the savings rate, is often criticized on equity grounds. Rich people who desire to minimize tax payments on interest and dividend income abuse the law by using legal and illegal tax shelters. Although such intricate devices are not described in detail in this chapter, many people believe that the tax law does not work justly in these respects. It works as an instrument that may lead to more inequity in the income distribution. Atoda and Tachibanaki (1985), for instance, found that property income was one of the most important factors in explaining total-income inequality. Also, it is important to add the fact that the existence of the special provisions for promoting personal savings (even without the abuses) lower the tax burden of rich people, because those in higher-income classes have higher savings rates than those in the lower-income ranges. In other words, the progressivity of the tax system in terms of income is weakened by these special provisions. This has been demonstrated by Fujita (1972), Ishi (1979), and Wada (1980). Most economists in Japan believe that the provisions for dividends and interest harm the vertical equity of the Japanese tax system. These issues are discussed by Tachibanaki and Atoda (1984).

Finally, we come to the capital-gains tax. The gains on securities are not treated as taxable income, and, symmetrically, losses are not deductible. This practice has been in effect since 1953. Although a securities transaction tax was introduced in 1953 as a substitute for capital-gains taxation, its effective rate is virtually negligible, being well under 1%. Unlike securities, land, buildings, and the right to use land are subject to capital-gains taxation on a realization basis. This tax is important in Japanese society in light of the limited land area and extremely high land and housing prices. Because land is excluded from our calculation of the effective tax rates in this study, however, this tax is not discussed here.

2.2   Corporate income tax

The corporate income tax generates the second highest share of tax revenues, as shown in Table 3.1. It is not an exaggeration to assert that the most significant difference between Japan and the United States concerns the importance of this tax, because the corporate tax has been sharply declining as a revenue source in the United States. Whereas the share of corporate income tax in 1982 federal revenues in the United States was about 8% (down from 16% in 1978), it was about 28% in Japan in 1982.[3] Auerbach (1983) explained the decline in revenue from the U.S. corporate tax by citing several factors. First, more of the return to corporate capital has been paid out in the form of interest. Second, the before-tax total return to corporate capital has declined. Third, the acceleration of depreciation deductions has been increased, and the investment tax credit has become more generous.

In Japan, there is a dispute concerning the burden of the corporate income tax between the Ministry of Finance (MOF) and the *Keidanren* (Federation for Economic Organization). The *Keidanren* claim that the real rate of corporate tax in Japan is the highest in the world. They put the average tax rate at 51.57%. The MOF dispute this and contend that the effective corporate tax rate is equally high in other industrialized countries. Their numbers are shown in Table 3.5. The two organizations use

Table 3.5. *Comparison of estimated results on corporate tax between Ministry of Finance and* Keidanren

Country	Ministry of Finance (effective tax rate)	*Keidanren* (real rate of tax burden)
Japan (1984)	52.92%	51.57%
U.S. (1985)	51.18%	32.28%
U.K. (1982)	52.00%	18.06%
W. Germany (1984)	56.52%	49.84%
France (1984)	50.00%	42.20%

Sources: Ministry of Finance, *Zaisei-kinyu Tokei Geppo,* annual tax issues; Keidanren, *Corporate Tax Systems and Tax Burdens in Industrial Nations,* 1984.

different concepts and methodologies for their calculations, and so the figures are difficult to reconcile. However, their dispute makes the measurement of the real tax burden on capital income, which is the purpose of this study, important, both for Japan and for the other countries.

As in many industrialized countries, the corporation income tax in Japan is subject to a number of controversies. One example of such controversial issues concerns the "double" taxation of dividend income by the personal income tax and the corporate tax. Another concerns the proposition that the effective corporate income tax is regressive from smaller firms to larger firms, rather than progressive. Before those issues are examined, some basic characteristics of the corporate tax system are explained.

The taxable income of the Japanese corporation is the excess of gross revenue over the total of its costs and expenses. One important item excluded from gross revenue for tax purposes is dividends received from domestic corporations. This is to avoid double taxation, and it is worth noting in view of the large shareholdings of many Japanese corporations. Intercorporate dividends are also favorably treated in the United States, although 15% of them are taxed at the corporate level. The other important costs deductible in Japan are interest paid and depreciation, which will be described in detail later.

Corporate income tax rates are, in principle, proportional. A minor amount of graduation is provided in the rate structure, however. Because our calculations of effective marginal tax rates (see Section 3) are based on 1980, we report those rates here. Tax rates for ordinary corporations with capital of more than 100 million yen in 1980 are 40% for retained earnings and 30% for dividends paid out. For ordinary corporations with capital of not more than 100 million yen, tax rates are separated by annual incomes. If the year's income exceeds 7 million yen, then the tax rate is again 40% (and 30% for dividends paid out), whereas if this income is under 7 million yen, then the tax rate is 28% (and 22% for dividends paid out). Special corporations, such as those in the public interest, cooperative asociations, and so forth, are taxed at a rate of 23% (and 19% for dividends paid out). Two reasons are given for the split rates between retained earnings and dividends. The first is to increase the attractiveness of equity capital for the corporation vis-à-vis debt capital. The second reason is to further alleviate the double taxation of dividends. The historical changes in corporate tax rates are shown in Table 3.6. It documents the minor changes in the rates that have occurred and the beginning of the split rates.

On the issue of double taxation of dividends, Japan adopts a unique but complicated system that is somewhere between a classical system, such as that in the United States, and an imputation system, such as that in the United Kingdom, West Germany, and France. A lower rate is applied to dividends paid out than to retained earnings, and several special measures are also applicable on dividends at the personal level, such as separate taxation and a tax credit. The choice between a classical system and an imputation system depends on many factors, such as (1) debt–equity financing ratios, (2) equity (or equality) considerations between stockholders with large shares and stockholders with small shares, (3) the statutory rates for corporate tax and personal income taxes, and (4) the retention rate for corporate profits. Because there is a lot of intercorporate holding of shares in Japan, a simple integration between corporate tax and income tax may not effectively solve the problem.

There are several types of tax-free reserves allowed that tend to reduce the tax on corporations. They are classified into two categories, namely, *Hikiate-kin* and *Junbi-kin*. The *Hikiate-kin* are roughly those reserves that are justified by generally accepted accounting principles. Thus, the methodology of the calculations is provided in the "Corporation Tax Law." On the other hand, the *Junbi-kin* are those reserves that are not duly accepted by accounting principles. Thus, there are special stipulations in the Special Taxation Measures Law for *Junbi-kin* categories. Among six *Hikiate-kin* currently operative, the most important are (1) reserves for bad debts, (2) reserves for retirement allowances, and (3) reserves for bonus payments. Among a large number of *Junbi-kin*, reserves for price fluctuations are the most important. There are significant differences in the rates of utilization of these *Junbi-kin* and *Hikiate-kin* by firm size, as Figure 3.1 shows.

Table 3.6. Corporate tax rates since 1955

Year	Ordinary corporations					Corporative associations		Public
	Basic rates		Income class (million yen)	Reduced rates		Retained earnings	Dividend	
	Retained earnings	Dividend		Retained earnings	Dividend			
1955.7–1955.10	40%		—	—	—	35%	35%	35%
1955.10–			0.5 or less	35%		30%	30%	30%
1957.4–	38%		1.0 or less					
1958.4–			2.0 or less	33%		28%	28%	28%
1963.4–	38%	28%	3.0 or less	33%	24%	28%	20%	
1964.4–		26%			22%		19%	
1965.4–	37%		3.0 or less and capital value 0.1 billion yen or less	31%		26%		26%
1966.1–	35%			28%		23%		23%
1970.5–	36.75%							
1974.5–	40%	28%	6.0 or less					
1980.5–		30%	7.0 or less					
1981.5–	42%	32%	8.0 or less	30%	24%	25%	21%	25%

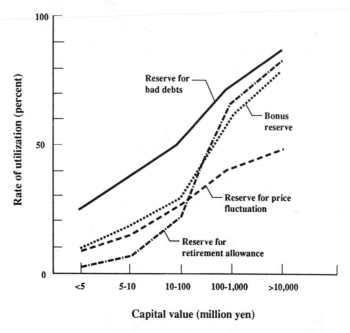

Figure 3.1. Rates of utilization in several reserves and allowances for tax purposes by corporation size. *Source: Survey of Corporate Firms* (Ministry of Finance, 1984).

Tajika and Yui (1984) found that the reduction in corporate income tax due to these reserves was 7.1% on average between 1963 and 1980. The largest reduction was in public enterprises in transportation and communication (13.7%) and in banking and insurance (11.6%). Agriculture (9.1%), iron and steel industries (8.9%), printing (7.6%), and chemical industries (7.4%) follow in order of importance. Tajika and Yui, however, found that these reserves were not effective in promoting investment activities during the postwar period.

Our calculation of the effective tax rate on capital income does not take these reserves into account, primarily because their use is not related to marginal investments. Thus, although they may lower average corporate tax rates, they do not lower the effective marginal rate on incremental investments. Of course, there has also been a substantial decrease in the reduction in corporate income tax due to these reserves in recent years. The Kansai Economic Center (1984) found that the effect of tax deferrals due to these reserves tends to be cancelled by the deferred charges in later years. Tajika and Yui (1984) also claimed that the rate

Table 3.7. *Corporations with positive profits and negative profits*

| Year | Number of corporations with | | | |
	Positive profits (A)	Negative profits (B)	Total	(A)/(B) (%)
1972	658,763	369,507	1,028,270	35.9
1973	736,571	348,899	1,085,470	32.1
1974	775,675	372,933	1,148,608	32.5
1975	690,861	520,139	1,211,000	43.0
1976	676,402	583,369	1,259,771	46.3
1977	667,744	644,480	1,312,224	49.1
1978	690,845	658,490	1,349,335	48.8
1979	734,222	667,838	1,402,060	47.6
1980	750,637	698,912	1,449,549	48.2
1981	750,537	748,351	1,498,888	49.9
1982	724,300	816,999	1,541,299	53.0

Sources: *Survey of Corporate Firms* (Ministry of Finance, 1984); Tax Bureau.

of reduction in corporate income tax due to these reserves in 1980 was almost negligible (about 0.3%). Thus, because they do not operate on the investment margin, and because they are of declining importance, we believe that errors due to our taking them as zero are negligible.

For corporation tax purposes, a corporation filing a return may carry back losses to the previous year or carry forward losses to five subsequent years. Accordingly, corporations with losses may claim refunds of previous taxes paid. In fact, one of the most important features in Japanese corporate taxation is the fact that a significant number of corporations do not pay any corporate taxes, because of losses. Table 3.7 shows that in 1980 the percentage of corporations with losses was 48%. This increased to 51% in 1981, 53% in 1982, and 55% in 1983 (920,000 corporations reporting losses, among 1.68 million companies). These rates seem quite high.

The proportion of corporations with losses is higher for smaller firms than for larger firms. There are a couple of reasons for this. First, the profits of smaller firms are more strongly affected by business cycles. They are more likely to lose money during downturns. Second, there seems to be an increasing trend for small family enterprises to incorporate in order

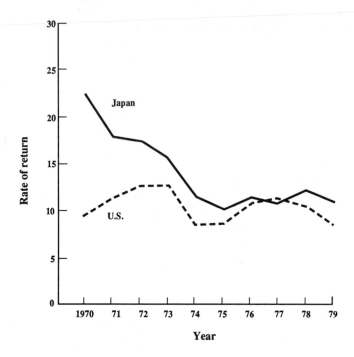

Figure 3.2. Comparison of rates of return to capital between Japan and the United States. *Source:* Nishina (1982).

to take advantage of the zero corporate income tax that can be claimed under the corporate status. With so many firms with negative taxable income, small numbers of larger firms with large positive profits are paying very high amounts of corporate income tax in view of the high share of corporate tax in the total government tax revenue. The fact that a large amount of tax revenue is produced by a small number of larger firms may arise because they enjoy extraordinary profits or because their share of the corporate tax burden may be quite high. It is important to distinguish between these two possibilities. Figure 3.2 presents a comparison between the real rates of return to capital in Japan and the United States. The numbers are taken from Nishina (1982). According to this figure, the rate of return for Japanese firms had been quite high in an absolute sense and was considerably higher than that for their American counterparts before, say, 1973. For this period, it may be valid to say that Japanese companies with positive profits paid lots of taxes because of their high profits. However, the rate of return for Japanese companies declined markedly from 1970 to 1975, and the gap between Japan and the United States has

Table 3.8. *Corporate income taxes by firm size, 1982*

Parameter	Small firms	Large firms
Number of firms	1,523,000 (98.25%)	17,731 (1.15%)
Profits	6,679 billion yen (30.6%)	15,125 billion yen (69.4%)
Corporate taxes	1,773 billion yen (32.9%)	3,612 billion yen (67.1%)

Notes: (1) Smaller firms are defined by their capital value less than 0.1 billion yen, with large firms being over 0.1 billion yen. (2) The numbers in parentheses are the shares of the total.
Source: Survey of Corporate Firms (Ministry of Finance, 1984).

been almost eliminated. Thus, it can be concluded that a few larger firms in Japan produce very large profits and pay most of the corporate tax, whereas the majority of firms produce modest profits or even losses. According to the *Survey of Corporate Firms* (Ministry of Finance, 1984), the largest 1.15% of Japanese firms had roughly two-thirds of all corporate income and paid about two-thirds of corporate taxes. These figures are shown in Table 3.8. This concentration of profits and taxes is similar to that in the United States.

2.3   Tax allowance for inventory and depreciation

The eligible methods for inventory valuations for tax purposes are the cost basis and "the lesser of the cost or the market price" basis. As for the cost basis, the taxpayer may choose between the following eight methods for inventories other than securities: (1) the actual-cost method, (2) the FIFO (first-in, first-out) method, (3) the LIFO (last-in, first-out) method, (4) the weighted-average method, (5) the moving-average method, (6) the straight-average method, (7) the most-recent-purchase method, and (8) the retail method. For securities, only the weighted-average method or moving-average method is allowed. The most popular methods for inventories are the three average methods; the actual-cost methods follow. About 80% of corporations listed are covered by these methods. There are few corporations that choose LIFO, and the FIFO method is chosen by only about 10% of corporations.

Depreciation for tax purposes for tangible fixed assets, such as machinery, equipment, and buildings (excluding land), and intangible fixed assets, such as patents, copyrights, and deferred assets, is allowed on the basis of acquisition cost. The residual value (or salvage value) is 10% of the acquisition cost in the case of tangible assets and zero in the case of intangible assets and deferred assets. The statutory useful life, or the number of years during which such assets are deemed to be serviceable, is given by the law. In general, these lifetimes are significantly longer than those used for depreciation calculations in the United States. For example, office buildings in Japan are depreciated over 65 years, office furniture over 15 years, and computers over 6 years. In the United States, the figures are 18, 5, and 5 years, respectively.

Corporations may elect either the straight-line method or a declining-balance method of depreciation calculation, with 80% of corporations electing declining-balance depreciation. Although there exist more accelerated depreciation techniques in the United States, such as double-declining-balance (DDB) or sum-of-the-year's-digits (SYD), they are not allowed in Japan.

This does not necessarily imply, however, that there are no measures to accelerate depreciation in Japan. In fact, there are two measures, called "increased initial depreciation" and "accelerated depreciation," that are provided by the law as special depreciation allowances. The increased-initial-depreciation measure allows deduction of an extra portion of the acquisition cost of an asset for the first accounting period in which such an asset is used; the accelerated-depreciation measure permits a corporation to deduct more than 100% of the ordinary depreciation allowance for an allowable asset for certain consecutive accounting periods. Typical examples of these special depreciation allowances are machinery and equipment used for prevention of environmental pollution (25% of the acquisition cost in the first year) or for saving energy (18%) and investments in underdeveloped areas or industrial development areas in farm villages (18%). There are about 30 special depreciation measures in Japan.

Historically, these special-allowance measures were introduced in 1961 and were modified in 1967 in accordance with the shortening of the statutory lives of tangible assets. In 1973 there was a reduction in the depreciation rate, and thus the special measures were also modified.

The purpose of these special-allowance measures is obvious. They help to reduce the amount of taxable income in earlier periods and possibly encourage more investment in the qualifying categories. Tajika and Yui (1984) found that the special-allowance measures were effective in promoting investment in two industries, namely, (1) chemical industries and (2) iron, steel, and machine industries, which were the leading industries during the period of rapid economic growth, although they suggested that the reduction in the effective corporate income tax rate due to these special measures was not particularly large. We take account of these measures in our calculation of effective tax rates.

2.4   Estimates of economic depreciation

Kuroda and Yoshioka (1984) published their estimates of economic depreciation in Japan for 30 industries and for 10 asset categories. We used the preceding method (4) for our purpose. By taking their weighted average of capital stock, it was possible to calculate the economic depreciation rates for two types of assets in our three industries. However, the rate of economic depreciation for buildings in "other industries" turned out to be implausibly high. This may be due to the inclusion of electricity, gas, and water industries in our "other industries." What we did was to assume that the economic depreciation rate for buildings in "other industries" was equal to the rate for buildings in the commerce sector.

2.5   Investment grants and incentives

An investment tax credit was first introduced in 1978 as a temporary measure to encourage investments of specific types, such as energy-saving or antipollution facilities. Tax reform in 1979 specified particular corporations to be eligible for the new investment tax credit in 1979 and 1980, namely, corporations engaged in "permanently depressed industries" and certain other small and medium-size corporations. Eligible corporations could take a credit against their corporate income tax liability of 10% of the acquisition cost of new machinery and equipment, with a credit ceiling of 20% of tax due. The carryforward of unused credits was allowed for three years.

A new tax measure to encourage investment in energy-saving facilities was introduced in 1981. A special depreciation (30% of the acquisition cost) or a tax credit (7% of the acquisition cost, with a credit ceiling of 20% of a tax liability) was allowed for certain energy-saving facilities and certain machinery exclusively for energy-saving uses or for use of alternative energy sources. An unused credit could be carried over in the following year. The provision was effective for only three years.

Another kind of investment tax credit was introduced recently. If research and development expenses exceed the largest amount of such expenses for any year since 1966, 20% of the excess amount can be deducted from the corporation tax, with a maximum of 10% of the tax liability.

As is obvious from the foregoing explanation, the investment tax credit is very limited in scope and coverage in Japan, applying only to energy-saving facilities and to the amount that research and development exceed previous record levels. The result is that the amount of the tax credit is very minor. Some countries provide generous credits to encourage investment. For example, in the United States, the 1980 statutory rate of credit was 10% for all qualifying equipment and special-purpose structures, and Jorgenson and Sullivan (1981) estimated that the effective 1980 tax-credit rates for equipment and structures were 0.078 and 0.045, respectively. Because it appears that the effective rates of credit in Japan are nearly zero, our calculations of the taxation of capital income ignore the role of the investment tax credit. Errors due to this omission should be negligible. This does not necessarily imply, however, that investment tax credits will not be introduced in the future. Although there was no need to stimulate investment in the past, at the present time some economists and government officials advocate the expansion of investment tax credits in Japan in order to stimulate the economy. Simulation studies by Homma et al. (1984b) suggest that an investment tax credit could be quite effective for promoting investment.

Another dispute related to investment concerns the durability of capital in the two countries. There is an argument, notably advocated by the Ministry of International Trade and Industry (MITI), that the lifetime of tangible assets in the United States is shorter than that in Japan. Actually, the MITI estimated that the average vintage in Japan was about 8.35 years in 1984, whereas it was about 8.2 years in the United States in the same year. Because it had been believed that the vintage of tangible assets in Japan was considerably younger than the American vintage, this finding was a surprise and was greeted with alarm. The main reason for this change, according to the MITI, which were supported by the *Keidanren*, is as follows: Whereas U.S. industries showed increasing rates of new investment, the total rate of investment in Japanese industries was falling. The Japanese, however, still devoted a far higher fraction of their GNP to capital formation. Whereas Japan's gross domestic capital formation fell from 35.53% of GNP in 1970 to 31.84% in 1980, in the United States gross domestic capital formation rose from 14.53% of GNP in 1970 to 15.27% in 1980 (and to 17.41% in 1984). Thus, we see that the trends are in opposite directions, but the level of investment relative to GNP is still about twice as high in Japan as in the United States. The composition of investment also varies, making the comparability of average durability figures questionable. Japanese investment is more intensive in terms of repair and replacement and, perhaps, less intensive in regard to new machines and buildings. Because the methods used to estimate the average duration of assets are considerably different for the two countries, as shown, for example, by Kuninori (1984), it is somewhat misleading to compare them. It is noted, however, that Kuninori (1984) concluded tentatively that the average vintage for Japanese tangible assets (about 6–7 years in 1982) was slightly younger than that in the United

States (about 9–10 years in 1982) when the methodology of the U.S. Bureau of Economic Analysis was applied to the Japanese data. More important, it was found that whereas the U.S. vintage was on a declining trend, the Japanese vintage was on an increasing trend. This result is one of the arguments used by those who want the tax system to offer more incentives for new investment. This position is mainly advocated by industries and by MITI.

2.6   Local taxes

Local taxes and finance are very complicated in Japan. There are numerous intergovernmental grant programs involving the national government, the prefectures (states), and the municipalities. We shall not deal with them here. There also are numerous local taxes. The "inhabitant tax" is levied on individuals at both the prefectural level and the municipal level. This is the local version of the personal income tax. The prefectural inhabitant tax applies a tax rate of 2% for the first 1.5 million yen of annual income and 4% for income above 1.5 million yen. The tax rate for the municipal inhabitant tax is more complicated and depends on the municipality. In general, the tax rates are progressive.

The important taxes for corporations at the local level are the inhabitant tax, the enterprise tax, and the property tax. Inhabitant taxes are levied on a per capita basis as well as on income. At the prefectural level, the per capita tax rates for corporations are determined by the capital-plus-reserve-fund value. The rate increases with this value. The standard corporation tax rate is 5.0% of the national corporation tax. At the municipal level, the per capita tax rates are determined by the size of the municipality where the corporation is located and the capital-plus-reserve value of the firm. The standard tax rate is 12.3% of the national corporation tax.

The enterprise tax is the main prefecture tax levied on corporations and individuals engaged in certain types of businesses or professions. The standard tax rates applicable to corporations are 6% for taxable income of not more than 3.5 million yen, 9% for taxable income over 3.5 million yen but not more than 7.0 million yen, and 12% for taxable income of over 7.0 million yen. One important fact is that the amount of enterprise tax in one year is deductible as expenses for tax purposes the next year. Also, individuals engaged in fishing or agriculture are exempt, as are corporations in newspaper publishing, forestry, and mining.

2.7   Wealth taxes

Wealth taxes, which are called property taxes, are levied at local levels. The person listed as the owner of fixed assets must pay the property tax to the municipality. Taxable assets for property tax purposes are land, houses, and tangible business assets that are depreciable. Automobiles and light vehicles are exempt from the tax because there is a separate automobile tax. The property tax base is, in principle, the market price of land, houses, and depreciable assets. In practice, however, the value registered by the tax assessor is used for the taxation of land and houses. As is well known, it is a difficult task to evaluate the market value of tangible assets. Because the yearbook of Japanese taxation reports assessed valuations, we have used these to estimate the effective tax rate for this project.

The standard tax rate is 1.4% of assessed valuation, and the ceiling rate is 2.1%. Depreciable assets whose value is less than 1.0 million yen are exempt from the tax.

2.8   Household tax rates

We have already discussed the taxation of interest income and dividend income at the household level. This section discusses the parameter values that we use in our calculation of the effective tax rate on corporate capital income.

One important but difficult problem is how to treat the various tax-free savings opportunities. Although the preceding section presented the statutory tax rates and the limits on nontaxable accounts, it is extremely difficult to estimate the effective tax rates on interest and dividend income. The reason is that neither the tax authorities nor the banks (and postal savings offices) know the exact amount of nontaxable interest and dividends, because abuse of the system is so common. It is extremely difficult to estimate this amount by income class, also. Thus, we are forced to abandon estimation of a marginal tax rate for interest and dividends at the household level and simply assume that the effective marginal tax rate is equal to the average tax rate. Furthermore, even estimation of the average tax rate for interest and dividend income is controversial, because the data may not be reliable. Bearing these cautions in mind, the effective average tax rate for interest income at the household level is calculated as 12.43%, and for dividend income, 18.09%. When postal savings, which normally are used to finance government activity, are included, the effective rate on interest becomes 9.59%. Table 3.9 presents detailed information on how these rates were calculated. Flath (1984) performed a valuable study of debt financing in Japan. As a by-product, he attempted to estimate the schedule of marginal tax rates on dividend income, taking account of several complicated provisions. His estimated average marginal tax rate for households was 16.08%, which is quite similar to our estimated figure, 18.09%.

Table 3.9. *Estimation of effective average tax rates for interest income and dividend income (billion yen), 1980*

Income	Interest or dividend paid	Tax revenues	Tax rate (%)
Interest income			
(1) Comprehensive income tax	4,733	949	20.06
(2) Nontaxable income of small-amount savings	4,702	–	0.00
(3) Separate tax with withholding system	1,610	424	26.35
(debentures)	(711)	(110)	(15.42)
(4) Postal savings	3,274	–	0.00
Total	14,318	1,374	9.59
Excluding postal savings	(−)3,274		12.43
Dividend income			
(1) Comprehensive income tax	2,285	457	20.00
(2) Nontaxable	148	–	0.00
(3) Separate tax with withholding system	77	27	34.46
(4) Dividend allowance	(473)	(−)30	(−)6.24
Total	2,510	454	18.09

Sources: Tax Bureau, *Annual Yearbook of Federal Tax,* and many other documents on banking and security.

Our treatment of banks requires explanation. In general, we assume that banks are financial intermediaries through which households hold part of their ownership of corporate capital. Because it is assumed that bank holdings of corporate equities are small enough to be safely ignored, we are able to use the personal tax rates for interest payments that companies pay to banks. We assume, then, that banks flow this interest income through to depositors. This is the assumption that King and Fullerton (1984) used in their study. It certainly is appropriate if the banking sector is competitive. In that case, the wedge between the return of investments and the return to bank depositors (that is, the difference between the interest rate received by the bank and that which it pays out) is not an effective tax, but is the price of the intermediation services the bank provides. In fact, this service, because it is paid for with forgone interest, is a kind of tax-free return. So the banking sector, rather than imposing an implicit tax on savers, offers them a portion of their return in the form of tax-free services. Of course, the banking sector is far from perfectly competitive in Japan. The role of banks in Japanese corporate finance and the differences between their borrowing and lending rates were explored by Aoki (1984b). He found that the interest-rate differential was very large in the 1960s because of regulation of banking activity, the use of compensating balances, and the monopoly power of the banks. However, by 1980, this wedge was very small (less than 0.5%), indicating that financial deregulation had eroded the banks' monopoly power, and making our "interest-pass-through" modeling reasonable.

2.9   Tax-exempt institutions

The growth of pension funds and the pension business of life-insurance companies is quite significant in contemporary Japan, as in many other industrial nations. Because trust banks also are engaged in pension business, these funds must be added to the funds operated by life-insurance companies. Thus, the main bodies of the tax-exempt institutions are pension funds of both life-insurance companies and trust banks. Other nonprofit institutions such as hospitals and universities may be regarded as tax-exempt institutions in several countries. However, this would not be appropriate for Japan, because these institutions normally have to pay taxes on their interest or dividend income. Further, the share of nonprofit institutions' equity holding is very minor. Finally, nonprofit institutions are included in the household sector in many data sources. In sum, many institutions that are tax-exempt in other countries are not in Japan. It is necessary and sufficient for us to consider the pension funds separately.

In fact, the tax rate on pension funds is not zero. Insurance companies and trust banks have to pay a tax, called the "special corporate tax," at a rate of 1.0% on their pension funds. This is different from the usual corporate tax levied on corporate profits. This tax is justified on the following grounds. Companies contribute some funds to their employees' retirement plans that are later paid out as a lump-sum payment to the employee or as a pension payment. These contributions normally are not taxed at either the household or corporate level. The deferral of the income taxation on such amounts until the pension payment is allowed by the law. However, the special corporate tax on insurance companies and trust banks may be considered as a tax on capital earnings during the period of tax deferrals, paid by these two institutions as agencies for the employees. That is, it offsets to some extent the deferral advantage.

Calculation of the effective rate for this tax is extremely difficult, because there are several special rules that make this tax complicated. In reality, the amount of revenue generated by this tax is very small in comparison with the amounts from other taxes, both because of the low statutory rate and because of several special measures. Thus, we feel safe in assuming that the effective tax rate is zero for the pension business of life-insurance companies and trust banks.

2.10 *Insurance companies*

Households receive investment income indirectly through insurance companies, and this income is taxed through a complicated set of provisions. Three categories must be considered in order to deal with insurance companies: (1) corporate taxes on life-insurance companies, (2) corporate taxes on non-life-insurance companies, and (3) personal taxes on amounts paid out by insurance companies.

We discuss first the personal taxes on individual savings through life insurance. Individuals pay insurance premiums by using after-tax income, although a part of the amount may be tax-deductible. Moreover, the accruals of interest on the reserves or on benefits paid at death of the insured are not taxed. Thus, it is possible to assume that the personal tax on insurance savings is zero.

Insurance companies, however, pay a corporate income tax. In 1984 there were 23 life-insurance companies and 22 non-life-insurance (automobile and fire casualties) companies in Japan. Of the 23 life-insurance companies, 16 are mutual companies, and 7 are stock companies. These companies are subject to local taxes like other corporations. An important fact is that the statutory tax rates are exactly the same as for ordinary corporations. Thus, it is possible to assume that the marginal tax rate for non-life-insurance interest income is equal to the corporate rate.

Calculating the tax base for life-insurance companies is complicated. For example, the base depends on whether the total amount of taxable income is equal to or less than 7.0% of the reserves. If it is, then 7.0% of the reserve is regarded as taxable income. This measure becomes complicated when group life insurance rather than individual life insurance or reinsurance is taken into account. Also, the treatment of dividends received is slightly different between stock companies and mutual companies. Because these special measures and many others are so complicated in the case of life-insurance companies, we do not estimate the exact tax rate on interest and dividend income flowing through this channel. To keep our task manageable, we use the following indirect method. Taxes paid by life-insurance companies are divided by before-tax current surplus (including the reserves for the next period's dividends). Then the weighted average of these rates, with weights being net debts, is calculated. Similar calculations were also made for non-life-insurance companies. Again, the weighted average is calculated. We regard this calculated rate as the effective tax rate.

3   Calculations of effective marginal tax rates

This part of this chapter presents the estimation procedure for the effective marginal tax rates on capital income in Japan and discusses the empirical results in comparison with other countries.

3.1   *Estimation procedure*

The essential concept we use in the estimation of the tax rate on capital income is the tax "wedge" between the rate of return on investment and the rate of return on savings for a series of hypothetical marginal projects. Because King and Fullerton (1984) presented a detailed analysis of this tax-wedge formulation, our discussion of methodology is very brief.

The effective tax rate, t, is estimated as

$$t = \frac{p-s}{p} \tag{1}$$

where p is the pretax real rate of return on the investment-project net of depreciation, and s is the posttax real rate of return to the saver who supplied the finance for the investment.

The posttax real rate of return to the saver is given by

$$s = (1-m)(r+\pi) - \pi - w_p \tag{2}$$

where m is the marginal personal tax rate on interest income, r is the real interest rate, π is the rate of inflation, and w_p is the marginal personal tax rate on wealth. Equation (2) reflects the fact that it is nominal income, not real income, that is subject to personal taxation.

The minimum pretax real rate of return that an investment must earn in order to give an investor a competitive or equilibrium posttax return is termed the cost of capital. The relationship between the cost of capital and the interest rate may be represented as

$$p = c(r) \tag{3}$$

The cost-of-capital function, $c(r)$, depends on the specifics of the tax code. For a general situation with a corporate tax, an investment credit, and a wealth tax, the expression for the cost of capital is given by

$$p = \frac{1}{(1-\tau)}[(1-A)(\rho+\delta-\pi)+(1-d_1\tau)w_c+d_2\tau\nu\pi]-\delta \tag{4}$$

where the notation is as follows: τ, corporate tax rate; A, present value of any grants, credits, or allowances; ρ, nominal discount rate; δ, economic depreciation rate; d_1, dummy equal to unity if corporate wealth taxes are deductible from corporate income tax base (equal to zero otherwise); w_c, rate of corporate wealth tax; d_2, dummy equal to unity if asset is inventory (equal to zero otherwise); v, proportion of inventory taxed on a FIFO basis.

Equation (4) is obtained by using equation (5), the rate of return on an investment net of depreciation, and equation (6), the present value of profits:

$$p = \text{MRR} - \delta \tag{5}$$

where MRR is the gross marginal rate of return for one unit of investment, and

$$V = \int_0^\infty [(1-\tau)\text{MRR} - (1-d_1\tau)w_c - d_2\tau v\pi] e^{-(\rho+\delta-\pi)u}\, du$$

$$= \frac{[(1-\tau)\text{MRR} - (1-d_1\tau)w_c - d_2\tau v\pi]}{\rho+\delta-\pi} \tag{6}$$

where V is the present discounted value of profits for a project. To obtain equation (4), we use the equality between V and C [the cost of the project, which is equal to $(1-A)$] and also use equation (5).

Next, we have to consider A, the present value of tax savings from depreciation allowances and other grants associated with a unit investment. This is given by

$$A = f_1 A_d + f_2 \tau + f_3 g \tag{7}$$

where f_1 is the proportion of the cost of the asset that is entitled to a standard depreciation allowance, A_d is the present discounted value of tax savings from standard depreciation allowances associated with a unit investment, f_2 is the proportion of the cost of an asset entitled to immediate expensing, f_3 is the proportion of the cost of an asset entitled to a cash grant, and g is the rate of cash investment grant. A_d is defined by either the declining-balance method or the straight-line method. The equations are nonlinear and thus need iteration to determine the discount rate.

The final step is to relate the firm's discount rate to the market interest rate, because with distortionary taxes those values are different. The difference depends on the source of finance. For debt finance, because nominal interest income is taxed and nominal interest payments are tax-deductible, the relationship is simple. For the other two sources of finance, the discount rates are influenced by both the personal tax system and the corporate tax system. Also, the degree of discrimination between retentions and distributions (dividends) in allocating profits plays an important role. See King (1977, chap. 3) and King and Fullerton (1984, chap. 2) for detailed discussion of these issues.

3.2   *Combinations of hypothetical projects*

There are four characteristics that define a hypothetical marginal project: (1) the asset in which the funds are invested, (2) the industry of the project, (3) the way the project is financed, and (4) the owner of the returns. Each characteristic has three alternatives: The three assets are (1) machinery, (2) buildings, and (3) inventories; the industries are (1) manufacturing, (2) other industries, and (3) commerce; the sources of finance are (1) debt, (2) new share issues, and (3) retained earnings; the ownership categories are (1) households, (2) tax-exempt institutions, and (3) insurance companies. Thus, there are 81 combinations. The mean tax wedge, $\bar{w}$, is calculated by

$$\bar{w} = \sum_{k=1}^{81} (p_k - s_k)\alpha_k \tag{8}$$

where α_k is the capital-stock weight of the kth combination ($\sum \alpha_k = 1$). By using equation (8), we can estimate not only the overall mean marginal tax rate but also the conditional mean marginal tax rates on investments in particular alternatives. One example is that we can estimate the conditional mean tax rate in machinery by summing over all combinations that involve machinery. There are 27 such combinations. Empirical results will be discussed later, mainly on the basis of these 27 combinations.

3.3   *Data requirement*

We need two sets of data: first, the statutory tax rates and the various parameter values, as discussed in detail earlier; second, the α weights for the proportion of total net capital stock and the data on financing and ownership. In this section we present and discuss the capital-stock weights and also the data on sources of finance and ownership of equity and debt.

3.4   *Capital-stock weights*

Capital-stock data are available from several sources. The government has performed national surveys of wealth every five years since 1955. The latest survey available was 1970. Thus, it was necessary to use the 1970 figures on wealth as a benchmark to estimate the allocation capital stock in 1980 in order to facilitate calculation of the taxation of income from capital.

Kuroda and Yoshioka (1984) and Homma et al. (1984b) estimated capital stock by industry and asset category (equipment, structure, and inventory). Although their estimation methods were slightly different, they

Table 3.10. *Allocation of corporate capital stock by asset and industry (fractions of units)*

Industry	Machinery	Buildings	Inventories	Total
Manufacturing	0.2345	0.1544	0.1185	0.5074
Other industries	0.1188	0.0789	0.0751	0.2728
Commerce	0.0376	0.0518	0.1304	0.2198
Total	0.3909	0.2851	0.3240	1.0000

Sources: (1) We used unpublished figures for machinery and buildings that were kindly supplied by Kuroda and Yoshioka, as well as their published figures up to 1977 (Kuroda and Yoshioka, 1984). (2) We used the inventory figures in Homma et al. (1984b, pp. 114–23). (3) We calculated the final weights by assembling and aggregating consistently the figures given by Kuroda and Yoshioka and Homma et al.

produced similar results. Kuroda and Yoshioka (1984) published their results up to 1977; however, they very kindly provided us with unpublished figures for 1979. Thus, we were able to obtain the capital-allocation weights in 1979 by industry (manufacturing, other industries, and commerce) and by asset category (machinery, buildings, and inventories) by aggregating their figures.

Table 3.10 presents the capital-stock weights for 1979. According to this table, about 51% of the total capital is owned by manufacturing industries, 27% by other industries, and 22% by commerce. With respect to asset types, about 39% of the total capital stock is machinery, 29% buildings, and 32% inventories.

3.5   Source of financial capital

The proportions of corporate investment financed through (1) retained earnings, (2) new equity, and (3) debt are available in the *Flow of Funds Statistics* published by the Bank of Japan. Table 3.11 shows those numbers. The first column gives gross internal funds, and the second column provides new equity issues. The third column is the net increase in liabilities from debt instruments. Table 3.11 shows that the role of internal funds has been increasing, while the role of debt financing has been declining. There was a common understanding that corporate finance in Japan had been relying mainly on debt rather than on internal funds. Table 3.11 shows clearly, however, that that feature has been gradually changing. Although inflation affects the validity of the debt–equity breakdown in Table 3.11, it does not affect the relationship between retained

Table 3.11. *Sources of finance for nonfinancial corporate business (unit 0.1 billion yen)*

Year	Gross internal funds	New equity issues	Debt plus debentures
1975	98,045 (0.368)	12,996 (0.049)	155,557 (0.583)
1976	125,876 (0.423)	10,682 (0.036)	160,956 (0.541)
1977	142,353 (0.518)	9,223 (0.034)	123,372 (0.449)
1978	185,929 (0.590)	13,253 (0.042)	116,080 (0.368)
1979	184,234 (0.575)	12,892 (0.040)	123,068 (0.384)
1980	162,772 (0.514)	15,577 (0.049)	138,410 (0.437)

Notes: Numbers in parentheses are shares.
Sources: Bank of Japan, *Flow of Funds Statistics;* Ministry of Finance, *Zaisei-kinyu Tokei Geppo* (various years).

earnings and new share issues. Thus, Table 3.11 is used only to determine the allocation between retained earnings and new share issues.

Homma et al. (1984b) estimated debt–capital ratios for a large number of industries. We aggregated their figures into our three sectors. Combining these figures with those of Table 3.11, we were able to estimate the 3 × 3 matrix (Table 3.12) for source of finance by industry. The debt–capital ratios are 0.3983 for manufacturing, 0.5983 for other industries, and 0.4368 for commerce. The corresponding American figures of King and Fullerton (1984) are 0.1981, 0.4847, and 0.3994, respectively. Although the role of debt is still more important in Japan than in the United States, the difference may not be as great as is generally believed.

Aoki (1984a) offered four explanations for the higher debt ratios in Japan. First, accounts receivable form a high proportion of assets and typically are debt-financed. Second, Japanese corporations do not perform inflation accounting. Third, there is the widespread practice of so-called *buzumi-ryodate* deposits (compensating balances). Finally, Japanese firms have been allowed to accumulate various nontaxable reserves and to include them under long-term debt. In fact, Aoki obtained considerably lower values for debt–equity ratios than the usually believed figures for nonfinancial corporations listed on the Tokyo Securities, after

Table 3.12. *Sources of finance by industry*

Source	Debt	New share	Retained earnings	Total
Manufacturing	0.3983	0.0492	0.5525	1.0
Other industries	0.5983	0.0329	0.3688	1.0
Commerce	0.4368	0.0461	0.5171	1.0

Sources: (1) The figures on debts were extracted from Tables 2-1 to 2-19 in Homma et al. (1984b). (2) Allocation between retained earnings and new share issues was performed by using *Flow of Funds Statistics* (Bank of Japan). (3) The final weights were obtained by assembling these two sources consistently.

making some relevant adjustments. Although Aoki's coverage of corporations and choice of methods were different than ours, both studies conclude that the real debt–equity ratio (or debt–capital ratio) is considerably lower than is usually believed. This does not deny that debt financing is still a major source of investment funds in Japan. Our study indicates that tax incentives can be added to his list of explanations for the high use of debt in Japan.

3.6   The ownership of equity

Table 3.13 presents proportions for equity ownership that are estimated from Bank of Japan data and others: *Flow of Funds Statistics, Report on Pension Funds,* and *Yearbook of Insurance.* The most difficult task was to divide insurance-company equity into the part attributable to the insurance business and the part attributable to the pension business, which must be moved into tax-exempt institutions. Of course, the pension business of trust-bank companies also was included in tax-exempt institutions. The final equity ownership proportions are 0.762 for households, 0.033 for tax-exempt institutions, and 0.205 for insurance companies. The share of tax-exempt institutions in 1980 in Japan is small compared with those for other industrial nations. However, their share has been increasing rapidly because pension funds are growing very rapidly in Japan.

3.7   The ownership of debt

The *Flow of Funds* data provide us with the figures for ownership of corporate debt. The difficult task, again, is to divide the ownership among

Table 3.13. *Ownership of corporate equity*
(billion yen)

Household	21,309	(0.7615)
Individuals	6,449	
Commercial banks	13,341	
Trust banks	1,392	
Security companies	126	
Tax-exempt	933	(0.0333)
Trust-bank pension fund	500	
Insurance-company pension fund	433	
Insurance companies	5,739	(0.2051)
Life	4,087	
Other	1,652	
Total	27,981	(1.0000)

Sources: (1) Bank of Japan, *Flow of Funds Statistics.*
(2) Koseinenkin Kikin, *Report on Pension Funds.* (3)
Ministry of Finance, *Yearbook of Insurance.*

three categories: households, tax-exempt institutions, and insurance companies. Table 3.14 shows the estimated results. An impressively high figure, 0.859, is obtained for households. Most of this debt is attributable to banks and finance companies, and this is quite understandable on the basis of Japanese banks' role in the financial market. The share of debt held by tax-exempt institutions is very small, as with equity holdings.

3.8   Empirical results

Table 3.15 presents the estimated results for the effective marginal tax rates, where each hypothetical investment project is assumed to earn a pretax real rate of return of 10% per year. The percentage of inventories that result in FIFO-type inventory profits with inflation is taken as zero, because we are computing the tax wedge when the firm uses a tax-minimizing inventory policy. This is consistent with the King–Fullerton approach for the United States, which also makes this assumption, despite the fact that in reality 70% of inventories use FIFO accounting. Table 3.15 shows that the overall marginal tax rate on new investments in Japan depends on the rate of inflation. The higher inflation is, the lower is the overall marginal tax rate on new investments. This is because of the advantage of being able to deduct high nominal interest payments from the corporation tax base, while paying only relatively low rates on the same

Table 3.14. *Ownership of nonfinancial corporate net debt (billion yen)*

Household	89,864	(0.8586)
Individuals	2,184	
Commercial banks	80,887	
Trust banks	6,574	
Security companies	241	
Tax-exempt	2,048	(0.0196)
Trust-bank pension fund	1,004	
Insurance-company pension fund	1,044	
Insurance companies	12,728	(0.1216)
Life	9,859	
Other	2,869	
Total	104,662	(1.0000)

Sources: (1) Bank of Japan, *Flow of Funds Statistics.* (2) Koseinenkin Kikin, *Report on Pension Funds.* (3) Ministry of Finance, *Yearbook of Insurance.*

income at the individual level. Interest income pays a net negative tax when the corporation and personal tax systems are examined as a whole.

There seems to be a misimpression in the United States about the Japanese experience with inflation in the 1970s. In fact, the average rate of growth of consumer prices between 1970 and 1980 was 9.0%, compared with the United States average of 6.67%. The impact of the oil price shocks led to higher inflation in Japan than in the United States. With the decade-long average inflation rate of 9%, the overall marginal tax rate on new investments in Japan amounted to only 9.4%. In fact, if we use the inflation rate for 1980 alone, which we calculate as 12.89%,[4] the overall effective marginal tax rate for 1980 was negative. That is, the investor in an incremental project was subsidized rather than taxed. Our bottom-line number, though, for the average marginal effective tax rate on new investments in Japan in 1980 is 4.4%. This means that the investor gets 95.6% of the return offered by the investment, and the government gets 4.4%.

The key advantage of this method, however, lies in the disaggregated results. Table 3.15 indicates that there are significant differences in effective tax rates for different sources of finance. The tax rate on projects financed by retained earnings is slightly lower than that on projects financed by new share issues. This reflects the fact that the tax system in Japan fails to completely offset the double taxation on dividends. Debt

Table 3.15. *Effective marginal tax rates (%), Japan, 1980*[a]

Parameter	Inflation rate			
	Zero	5%	10%	Actual (9%)
Asset				
Machinery	19.3	14.8	6.3	8.3
Buildings	23.4	15.0	1.5	4.4
Inventories	34.1	15.0	−4.3	−0.4
Industry				
Manufacturing	25.9	18.8	8.3	10.6
Other industries	20.4	6.3	−11.5	−7.7
Commerce	30.0	16.8	1.8	4.9
Source of finance				
Debt	−0.9	−32.0	−67.0	−59.7
New share issues	48.6	57.5	64.4	63.1
Retained earnings	47.6	54.9	59.7	58.9
Ownership				
Households	23.1	11.5	−3.2	−0.0
Tax-exempt institutions	24.9	14.7	1.6	4.4
Insurance companies	35.8	31.7	23.8	25.6
Overall	25.3	15.0	1.5	4.4

[a]Fixed-*p* case.

finance is subsidized very heavily at substantial rates of inflation. The subsidization of debt-financed projects is certainly a reason behind the relatively high use of this form of financing in Japan. The subsidization comes from the fact that nominal interest rates are deductible from the corporate tax (even though the inflationary component represents a return of capital). When this treatment is combined with the depreciation rules and the low taxation of interest at the personal level, a net subsidy results.

In the breakdown by ownership category, households enjoy extremely low tax rates. In fact, at the decade-long average inflation rate of 9%, households are, on average, not taxed at all on their marginal-investment returns. This means that the combined corporate and personal taxes on individual-investor-financed investments are zero. This implies that Japan's personal income tax, at least at the margin, is essentially a labor income tax. Tax-exempt institutions do face some taxes in Japan, but their effective marginal tax rate is also very low. The slightly higher effective tax rate on projects financed by tax-exempt institutions than on those financed by households may seem surprising. The reason for this is straightforward, however. Households supply proportionately more debt-financed capital, which is lightly taxed or subsidized, whereas tax-exempt institutions provide proportionately more equity-financed investments. The effective tax rate on insurance companies is about 25%.

The asset breakdown does not show a marked difference in tax rates. The effective tax rates decline with inflation for all asset categories. The industry breakdown also shows fairly small differences. We do find that the tax rate for "other industry" becomes negative if inflation is 8% or more. This is because of the relatively large use of debt financing in this category.

We can elaborate on the reasons that the effective tax rates decline with inflation. King and Fullerton (1984, chap. 7) list four separate effects of inflation. First, the effect of inflation on historical cost depreciation works to increase the effective tax rate, although depreciation becomes less and less important with higher inflation rates. Second, inflation tends to decrease overall taxes where nominal interest payments are deductible from the corporate income tax because it tends to increase these deductions. Third, because inflation tends to increase taxable nominal profits under FIFO inventory accounting, this effect could tend to increase the effective tax rate. This effect has been eliminated in Table 3.15 because of the assumption regarding inventory accounting. Fourth, the taxation of insurance companies may be affected by inflation. In Japan, it appears to be primarily the second effect that contributes to the effect of inflation in decreasing the effective tax rates. The Kansai Economic Center (1984) published similar evidence with respect to the effect of inflation, although their estimation procedure was considerably different.

Table 3.16 shows that the assumption about inventory accounting greatly affects the impact of inflation on the taxation of investment. The defense of the earlier assumption was that in order to calculate the effective tax rate, one should assume tax-minimizing behavior on the part of firms. This would imply zero use of the FIFO and similar techniques. This was assumed in Table 3.15. The calculations shown in Table 3.16 are based on the actual use of FIFO accounting and equivalent techniques. At zero inflation, this makes no difference, but at 9.0% inflation, the 4.4% overall tax rate shown in Table 3.15 becomes 17.3% in Table 3.16.

Tables 3.17 and 3.18 show some summary statistics for the United States, the United Kingdom, Sweden, and West Germany for comparison purposes at the actual decade-average inflation rate for each country and at zero inflation. Because the comparison among the four countries was made in very great detail by King and Fullerton (1984), we shall

Table 3.16. *Effective marginal tax rates (%), Japan, 1980^a*

Parameter	Inflation rate			
	Zero	5%	10%	Actual (9%)
Asset				
Machinery	19.3	14.8	6.3	8.3
Buildings	23.4	15.0	1.5	4.4
Inventories	34.1	37.2	40.2	39.6
Industry				
Manufacturing	25.9	23.7	18.2	19.6
Other industries	20.4	13.1	2.0	4.5
Commerce	30.0	29.7	27.6	28.1
Source of finance				
Debt	−0.9	−22.3	−47.7	−42.3
New share issues	48.6	62.3	74.1	71.8
Retained earnings	47.6	60.0	69.9	68.1
Ownership				
Households	23.1	18.8	11.5	13.2
Tax-exempt institutions	24.9	21.8	15.9	17.3
Insurance companies	35.8	38.1	37.0	37.4
Overall	25.3	22.1	15.9	17.3

^{a}Fixed-p case. Japanese depreciation data, percentage using FIFO equivalent = 60%.

attempt to compare the results only between Japan and the other countries. Also, a particular emphasis is placed on comparisons between Japan and the United States.

One of the interesting findings of the King and Fullerton study is that the ranking of the countries from highest to lowest growth rates is exactly the same as their ranking by effective tax rates. That is, the higher-growth-rate countries also had higher tax rates. The extreme examples are West Germany, with the highest overall tax rate on capital and the highest growth rate, and the United Kingdom, with the lowest rates for both. Although this may be surprising at first, two things should be noted. First, the long-run growth rate of a country depends on the growth of its labor force; it is the capital intensity of the steady-state growth path that should be related to the taxation of investments, not the growth rate itself. Unfortunately, comparable figures for capital intensities are difficult to obtain and would require a separate study. Second, poor levels of

Table 3.17. *Effective tax rates for five countries, 1980ᵃ, actual inflation*

Parameter	U.K.	Sweden	West Germany	U.S.	Japan
Asset					
Machinery	−36.8	0.2	44.5	17.6	8.3
Buildings	39.3	36.6	42.9	41.1	4.4
Inventories	39.5	68.8	59.0	47.0	−0.4
Industry					
Manufacturing	−9.6	27.1	48.1	52.7	10.6
Other industries	−5.4	60.5	57.0	14.6	−7.7
Commerce	36.2	39.2	44.4	38.2	4.9
Source of finance					
Debt	−100.8	5.0	−3.1	−16.3	−59.7
New share issues	−4.2	90.4	62.6	91.2	63.1
Retained earnings	30.6	68.2	90.2	62.4	58.9
Ownership					
Households	42.0	105.1	71.2	57.5	−0.0
Tax-exempt institutions	−44.6	−51.8	6.3	−21.5	4.4
Insurance companies	−6.7	18.9	−3.8	23.4	25.6
Overall	3.7	35.6	48.1	37.2	4.4

ᵃFixed-p case (actual depreciation, actual weights).
Sources: For Japan, our own calculations; for other countries, King and Fullerton (1984).

investment and growth may "cause" investment tax breaks through political pressure. That is, there is a direction of causation going from low growth to low taxes that may dominate the empirical observations.

Japan turns out to destroy the perfect rank correlation. Japan has enjoyed the highest growth rate of all of the countries investigated, but has one of the lower tax rates on new investment. Its precise ranking depends on the rate of inflation, as can be seen by comparing Tables 3.17 and 3.18. Japan, even more than the other countries, of course, has not been on a steady-state growth path. Instead, it went through a period of extremely rapid capital deepening and economic growth in the 1950s and 1960s. This capital formation may have been encouraged somewhat by the relatively light taxation of new investment. In view of a high tax rate on corporate income, it appears that the low effective personal tax rates on interest and dividend income are the main reasons for the relatively low tax rates on capital income together with the favorable tax treatment on debt financing. Of course, it is probably mistaken to raise only tax policy

Table 3.18. *Effective tax rates for five countries, 1980[a], zero inflation*

Parameter	U.K.	Sweden	West Germany	U.S.	Japan
Asset					
Machinery	−24.2	−18.1	38.1	3.9	19.3
Buildings	41.5	28.9	42.7	35.4	23.4
Inventories	50.5	26.5	57.7	50.9	34.1
Industry					
Manufacturing	−1.7	8.1	44.7	44.2	25.9
Other industries	4.6	29.6	50.8	10.0	20.4
Commerce	46.8	12.1	44.6	37.9	30.0
Source of finance					
Debt	−29.6	−12.9	12.1	−2.0	−0.9
New share issues	7.6	44.2	56.1	61.0	48.6
Retained earnings	23.5	40.9	72.0	48.4	47.6
Ownership					
Households	26.6	57.1	59.7	44.1	23.1
Tax-exempt institutions	−5.1	−39.2	17.6	4.0	24.9
Insurance companies	8.7	−16.0	14.6	4.0	35.8
Overall	12.6	12.9	45.1	32.0	25.3

[a] Fixed-p case (actual depreciation, actual weights).
Sources: For Japan, our own calculations; for other countries, King and Fullerton (1984).

as an important policy instrument for economic growth. The Japanese example, however, does seem to imply that tax policy can be valuable in promoting a transition to a more capital-intensive economy.

Several investigations have attempted to compare corporate tax burdens between Japan and the United States. We have already mentioned the studies by the *Keidanren* and the Ministry of Finance. Table 3.19 presents a summary of results from the various studies. Because estimation methods differed from study to study, exact comparisons are impossible. In fact, recall that we have been examining the total taxation on a new investment, not simply the corporation income tax. All the past studies, except for that by Horst (1977), showed that the corporate tax burden in Japan was higher than that in the United States. See Gravelle (1983) for an explanation why Horst (1977) obtained a different result. This higher rate of taxation in Japan has frequently been presented as evidence that the Japanese corporate income tax should be lowered, as noted previously. Our current study, however, does not support such a view. In fact,

Table 3.19. *Summary of estimated results on corporate tax burden for Japan and the United States*

Sources	Japan		U.S.	
	Year	Tax burden (%)	Year	Tax burden (%)
Keidanren	1984	51.57	1985	32.28
Ministry of Finance	1984	52.92	1985	51.18
Horst (1977)[a]	1977	29.2	1977	36.7
Gravelle (1983)[a]				
Without local taxes	1983	35.8		35.3
With local taxes	1983	50.5		27.7
Japan Development Bank (1984)[b]			1982	29.6
Kansai Economic Center (1984)[b]	1982	50.0		
This study (1985)[c]	1980	4.4		37.2

[a]Only the manufacturing industry is considered.
[b]Local taxes are excluded, but the effect of inflation is taken into account. The methods for estimation are common for the two sources.
[c]Our study and the King–Fullerton study (1984) calculate the combined personal and corporate tax burden on investments.

we find that corporate investment is more lightly taxed in Japan than in the United States. The most important reason that our results differ from those of other studies is that we incorporate the personal income tax, in particular the light taxation of interest and dividend income. Financing an investment project is influenced not only by corporate income tax but also by the personal tax for the saver who supplies the finance. One should not be surprised that our result is so different from those of the previous studies. When tax provisions for savings are introduced in estimating the effective rate of taxation of capital income, it is likely to change the outcome of the analysis considerably. We believe that the popular measurement of the corporate tax burden (or average effective corporate tax rate) may lead to erroneous conclusions. The results in Table 3.19 for Japan and the United States tend to indicate this.

Several noteworthy differences can be observed between Japan and the United States on the basis of Tables 3.17 and 3.18. First, inflation distorts the effective tax rates dramatically. In other words, the difference in effective rates between Japan and the United States in Table 3.17 is very significant. However, the difference in effective tax rates with a zero inflation rate is not so dramatic. If we examine the zero-inflation case shown in Table 3.18, we see that machinery in the United States is taxed very lightly because of the investment tax credit, whereas machinery in Japan is taxed in a way similar to that for the other assets. The effective tax rates for buildings and inventories are somewhat higher in the United States than those in Japan. As for the industry breakdown, manufacturing in the United States faces considerably higher taxes than in Japan, whereas the other-industry category has the inverse relation. The two countries have similar provisions in the case of source of finance, namely, debt is treated much more favorably than new share issues or retained earnings. It must be emphasized here that different weights on debt financing in the total capital stock in the two countries produce different overall effective tax rates. The most prominent difference appears in the treatment by ownership category. Although the effective tax rate is much lower for households in Japan than in the United States, it is much higher for tax-exempt institutions and insurance companies in Japan than in the United States. Not only different tax rates but also weights in the total capital stock again are responsible for the difference in the overall effective rates.

The earlier discussion of our assumptions regarding inventory accounting techniques does not greatly affect the relative comparison of the United States and Japan. With our assumption (and that of King and Fullerton) of tax-minimizing behavior with respect to this issue, the United States' overall marginal tax rate on capital investments is 37.2% of the actual inflation rate, whereas Japan's rate is 4.4%. If we did all the calculations using actual inventory accounting practices, the figures would be 43.2% for the United States and 17.3% for Japan. Thus, although the levels of marginal rates are raised in both countries and the gap is closed somewhat, Japan still has a tax rate on investment that is less than half that in the United States.

We have examined our calculations in order to determine why they indicate that Japanese investments are so much more lightly taxed than American investments. One possibility relates to the Kuroda and Yoshioka economic-depreciation data indicating that Japanese capital is far longer-lived than American capital. However, rates of economic depreciation are particularly difficult to measure, and so we wondered whether or not this apparent difference in useful lifetime for capital is real and whether or not it greatly affects our results. Rather than engage in an extensive study of Japanese economic depreciation, we simply used the U.S. depreciation rates from King and Fullerton and applied them to our model of the Japanese tax system. The results are shown in Tables 3.20 and 3.21. Table 3.20 shows that this causes the overall rate to increase to 12.7% at

Table 3.20. *Effective marginal tax rates (%), Japan, 1980[a]*

Parameter	Inflation rate			
	Zero	5%	10%	Actual (9%)
Asset				
Machinery	28.9	29.5	25.3	26.5
Buildings	26.1	18.7	5.8	8.6
Inventories	34.1	15.0	−4.3	−0.4
Industry				
Manufacturing	32.0	27.9	19.8	21.7
Other industries	24.1	12.2	−4.1	−0.6
Commerce	31.8	19.6	5.5	8.4
Source of finance				
Debt	4.9	−23.1	−55.7	−48.9
New share issues	51.8	62.2	70.4	68.9
Retained earnings	51.0	60.0	66.2	65.1
Ownership				
Households	27.7	18.4	5.7	8.4
Tax-exempt institutions	29.4	21.5	10.2	12.7
Insurance companies	39.8	37.9	31.8	33.3
Overall	29.8	21.8	10.2	12.7

[a] Using U.S. data for economic depreciation rate.

the actual inflation rate (versus 37.2% for the United States). Table 3.21 gives the figures when the FIFO inventory technique is used 60% of the time. This brings the overall tax rate to 25.6%, still well below the number for the United States of 43.2%.

We believe that the fact that Japan taxes capital income significantly less than the United States is quite robust to our assumptions. This lower tax regime is accomplished by light taxation of capital income at the personal level and by greater reliance on debt finance in Japan.

4   Concluding remarks

The findings presented in this chapter have shown that the effective marginal tax rate on income from capital in Japan is relatively low by international standards and is very low when the rate of inflation is high. This low rate stems mainly from the fact that interest income and dividend income are relatively lightly taxed. Our calculation of the effective tax

Table 3.21. *Effective marginal tax rates (%), Japan, 1980*[a]

Parameter	Inflation rate			
	Zero	5%	10%	Actual (9%)
Asset				
Machinery	28.9	29.5	25.3	26.5
Buildings	26.1	18.7	5.8	8.6
Inventories	34.1	37.2	40.2	39.6
Industry				
Manufacturing	32.0	32.8	29.8	30.6
Other industries	24.1	18.9	9.4	11.5
Commerce	31.8	32.5	31.3	31.6
Source of finance				
Debt	4.9	−13.4	−36.3	−31.5
New share issues	51.8	67.0	80.1	77.6
Retained earnings	51.0	65.1	76.4	74.3
Ownership				
Households	27.7	25.8	20.3	21.6
Tax-exempt institutions	29.4	28.6	24.6	25.6
Insurance companies	39.8	44.4	45.0	45.1
Overall	29.8	28.9	24.6	25.6

[a]Using U.S. data for economic depreciation rates, percentage using FIFO equivalent = 60%.

rate on income from capital enables us to reveal the interactions between the personal income tax and the corporate tax. Despite the relatively high rate of corporate income tax in Japan, this low tax rate on interest and dividend income lowered the burden of taxation on income from new investments. There has been a consensus in Japan that the personal tax system has not been responsible for the high rate of savings. This study, however, shows that it is responsible for lowering the overall effective tax rate on income from capital. A second factor that lowers the taxation on new investments in Japan is heavy reliance on debt financing. This result is hardly surprising in view of the Japanese financial market. It may be misleading, however, to predict that this effect will continue in the long run, because the degree of reliance on debt has been declining in Japan.

As for the comparison between Japan and the United States, it is possible to summarize the results as follows. First, both countries have quite high rates for their corporate income taxes. However, in both countries the effective rate of taxation on new investments is lower than the corporate income tax rate. The reasons for lowering the effective tax rates on capital income are different for the two countries. In Japan, it is the personal income tax, in particular the favorable treatment on interest and dividend income, whereas in the United States it is the investment tax credit and the accelerated depreciation deductions that have lowered the tax burden of the corporate sector recently. Overall, the tax wedge on new corporate investments is significantly lower in Japan than in the United States.

Appendix: Standard parameter values for Japan

Specific tax and inventory parameters

τ	Rate of corporation tax	0.5261
θ	Opportunity cost of retained earnings	1.117
π	Inflation rate	Zero, 10, and 8.25
ν	Proportion of inventories taxed on historical cost principle	0.1
w_c	Wealth tax rates	Machinery 0.0059
		Buildings 0.0032
		Inventories 0.0

Tax parameters by source of finance

w_p Personal-wealth tax rates   All zero

		Debt	New shares	Retained earnings
m	Tax rates on interest			
	household	0.1244	0.1809	0.1809
	tax-exempt	0.0	0.0	0.0
	insurance companies	0.0973	0.0973	0.0973

Z_s Tax rates on capital gains   All zero

Parameters for each asset by industry

		Manu-facturing	Other industries	Commerce
δ	Depreciation rate			
	Machinery	0.0666	0.0900	0.0910
	Buildings	0.0222	0.0248	0.0248
	Inventories	0.0	0.0	0.0
f_2	Proportion with immediate depreciation			
	Machinery	0.0110	0.0124	0.0047
	Buildings	0.0110	0.0124	0.0047
	Inventories	0.0	0.0	0.0
f_1	Proportion with later depreciation			
	Machinery	0.9890	0.9890	0.9953
	Buildings	0.9890	0.9890	0.9953
	Inventories	—	—	—

L_1 Lifetimes	Manu-facturing	Other industries	Commerce
Machinery	9.53	11.29	6.62
Buildings	32.60	37.16	33.44
Inventories	0.0	0.0	0.0

Type of depreciation
Machinery		
Buildings	Weights $\begin{cases} 0.8 \text{ declining-balance} \\ 0.2 \text{ straight-line} \end{cases}$	
Inventories		

Exponential tax depreciation rate
	Manu-facturing	Other industries	Commerce
Machinery	0.2697	0.2331	0.3640
Buildings	0.0878	0.0775	0.0857
Inventories	0.0	0.0	0.0

f_3 Proportion with investment grant	All zero
g Rate of investment grant	All zero

Weights

Proportion of capital stock	Manu-facturing	Other industries	Commerce
Machinery	0.2345	0.1188	0.0376
Buildings	0.1544	0.0789	0.0518
Inventories	0.1185	0.0751	0.1304
Proportion by source of finance			
Debt	0.3983	0.5983	0.4368
New share issues	0.0492	0.0329	0.0461
Retained earnings	0.5525	0.3688	0.5171
Ownership shares			
Debt			
Household	0.8586	0.8586	0.8586
Tax-exempt	0.0196	0.0196	0.0196
Insurance co.	0.1216	0.1216	0.1216
New shares			
Household	0.7615	0.7615	0.7615
Tax-exempt	0.0333	0.0333	0.0333
Insurance co.	0.2051	0.2051	0.2051
Retained earnings			
Household	0.7615	0.7615	0.7615
Tax-exempt	0.0333	0.0333	0.0333
Insurance co.	0.2051	0.2051	0.2051

ACKNOWLEDGMENTS

This work was supported by Stanford University's Center for Economic Policy Research (CEPR). A preliminary draft of this chapter was presented at the "U.S.-Japan Productivity Conference" of the NBER's "Conference on Research in Income and Wealth," Cambridge, Massachusetts, August 26–28, 1985. We benefited greatly from the able research assistance of Mr. Tatsuya Kikutani. We would like to thank Albert Ando, Masahiko Aoki, Alan Auerbach, Chuck Hulton, Don Fullerton, and Mervyn King for their helpful suggestions. We are grateful to M. Kuroda and K. Yoshioka, who provided us with unpublished data regarding Japan's capital stock.

NOTES

1. Ishi (1979) also proposed that the amount of tax erosion was quite large.
2. The basic exemption for the tax filer, spouse, and each dependent is 290,000 yen ($1,700) each. There are additional exemptions for specific people, such as those who are physically handicapped, aged, widowed, or students. Further, the first 1.5 million yen from employment income is 40% deductible, with a minimum deduction of 500,000 yen. After that, 30% of the next 1.5 million yen can be deducted, 20% for the next 3 million yen, and 10% for the next 4 million yen. Finally, 5% of earnings in excess of 10 million yen are deductible.
3. Many more small businesses are incorporated in Japan and for profit partnerships and sole proprietorships are subject to the corporation income tax.
4. The 12.89% is a simple average of the change in the consumer price index of 7.99% and the extraordinary rise in wholesale prices as 17.78%.

REFERENCES

Aoki, M. (1984a). "Aspects of the Japanese Firm." In M. Aoki (ed.), *The Economic Analysis of the Japanese Firm* (pp. 3–46). Amsterdam: North Holland.
  (1984b). "Shareholder's Non-Unanimity on Investment Finance: Banks vs. Individual Investors." In M. Aoki (ed.), *The Economic Analysis of the Japanese Firm* (pp. 193–226). Amsterdam: North Holland.
Atoda, N., and T. Tachibanaki (1985). "Income Inequality by Income Sources." *Quarterly of Social Security Research,* Vol. 21, Summer, pp. 330–40 (in Japanese).
  (1987). "Optimum Non-Linear Taxation and Heterogenous Preference." Discussion paper, Kyoto University.
Auerbach, A. J. (1983). "Corporate Taxation in the United States." *Brookings Papers on Economic Activity,* No. 2, pp. 451–512.
Bank of Japan. *Flow of Funds Statistics* (annual statistics).
Feldstein, M., and L. Summers (1979). "Inflation and Taxation of Capital in the Corporate Sector." *National Tax Journal,* Vol. 32, pp. 445–70.
Flath, D. (1984). "Debt and Taxes: Japan Compared with the United States." *International Journal of Industrial Organization,* Vol. 2, pp. 311–26.
Fujita, S. (1972). *Theory of Japanese Public Finance.* Keisoshobo (in Japanese).
Gravelle, J. (1983). "Comparative Corporate Tax Burdens in the United States and Japan and Implications for Relative Economic Growth." Washington, D.C.: Congresssional Research Service, Library of Congress.
Hayashi, M. (1982). "Principle of Corporate Behavior and Corporate Taxation." *Keizai to Boeki,* No. 134, March (in Japanese).
Homma, M., N. Atoda, F. Hayashi, and K. Hata (1984b). *Fixed Asset Investment and Corporate Tax.* Economic Planning Agency, Series No. 41 (in Japanese).
Homma, M., T. Ihori, N. Atoda, and J. Murayama (1984a). "Burden of Personal Income Tax by Professions." *Contemporary Economics,* No. 84, Autumn, pp. 14–25 (in Japanese).
Horst, T. (1977). "Income Taxation and Competitiveness in the United States, West Germany, France, the United Kingdom, and Japan." Washington, D.C.: National Planning Association.

Ishi, H. (1979). *Economic Effect of Tax Policy.* Toyokeizai-shimpo-sha (in Japanese).

(1981). "Differences in Unreported Taxable Income by Occupations." *Contemporary Economics,* Spring, pp. 72–83 (in Japanese).

Itaba, Y., and T. Tachibanaki (1987). "Measurement of Tax Progressivity When the Forms of Both Income Distribution and Tax Function are Given." *Economic Studies Quarterly,* Vol. 38, June, pp. 97–106.

Jorgenson, D. W., and M. A. Sullivan (1981). "Inflation and Corporate Capital Recovery." In C. R. Hulten (ed.), *Depreciation, Inflation and the Taxation of Income from Capital.* Washington, D.C.: Urban Institute.

Kaizuka, K. (1973). "Tax Base of the Income Tax." In T. Hayashi and K. Kaizuka (eds.), *Fiscal System in Japanese Economy.* University of Tokyo Press (in Japanese).

Kansai Economic Center (1984). *A Study on the Effect of Corporate Tax on Fixed Investment.* Osaka (in Japanese).

Keidanren (1984). *Corporate Tax Systems and Tax Burdens in Industrial Nations* (in Japanese).

King, M. A. (1977). *Public Policy and the Corporation.* London: Chapman & Hall.

King, M. A., and D. Fullerton (1984). *The Taxation of Income from Capital: A Comparative Study of the United States, the United Kingdom, Sweden, and West Germany.* University of Chicago Press.

Komiya, R. (1966). "Post-War Japanese Tax System and Capital Accumulation." *Todai Keizai Ronshu,* Vol. 32 (2), July, pp. 10–35 (in Japanese).

Kuninori, K. (1984). "Estimation of Vintage of Capital Stock." *Kaigin-chosa,* Vol. 5, December, pp. 4–38 (in Japanese).

Kuroda, M., and K. Yoshioka (1984). "Measurement of Services from Capital – Capital Stock by Industries and Assets." *Mita Shogaku Kenkyu,* Vol. 27 (4), October, pp. 12–30 (in Japanese).

Ministry of Finance. *An Outline of Japanese Taxes* (various years).

Zaisei-kinyu Tokei Geppo, Special Issues on Taxation (various years) (in Japanese).

Survey of Corporate Firms (various years) (in Japanese).

Annual Yearbook of Federal Tax (various years) (in Japanese).

Nishina, K. (1982). "Estimation of Profits and Japan–United States Comparison." Report to Keizai Doyukai, Keizai Kenkyu-sho (in Japanese).

Pechman, J. A., and K. Kaizuka (1976). "Taxation." In H. Patrick and H. Rosovsky (eds.), *Asia's New Giant.* Washington, D.C.: Brookings Institution.

Sato, S. (1979). *Japanese Tax Systems.* University of Tokyo Press (in Japanese).

Shoup Commission (1949). *Report on Japanese Taxation.* Vols. 1–4. Tokyo: Shoup Commission.

Tachibanaki, T., and N. Atoda (1984). "Income Redistribution Effect of Tax and Social Security Systems and Horizontal Equity." *Contemporary Economics,* No. 59, Autumn (in Japanese).

Tajika, E., and Y. Yui (1984). "Post-War Corporate Taxation and Fixed Investment in Japan: Estimation of Reduction in Corporate Tax by Industries." *Contemporary Economics,* No. 59, Autumn (in Japanese).

Wada, Y. (1980). *Reconsideration of Tax Policy and Reforms in Tax System in Japan.* Tokyo: Bunshindo (in Japanese).

CHAPTER 4

Corporate tax burden and tax incentives in Japan

Hiromitsu Ishi

1   Introduction

Before the first oil shock in 1973, there was wide agreement in Japanese government and business circles that the tax system should be actively employed to promote economic growth. On the basis of tax-incentive policies, several special measures were formulated to stimulate exports, private savings, and investment. These usually included tax exemptions, tax-free reserves, and accelerated depreciation. Linked with Japanese industrial policies, these tax-incentive policies often received credit when authors tried to explain the rapid economic growth in the 1950s and 1960s.

It is, however, very difficult to ascertain the effectiveness of tax incentives adopted to achieve specific policy purposes. In fact, the evaluation of these policy effects has been controversial, subject to many difficulties. These difficulties are mainly due to the scarcity of quantitative studies examining the effects of tax incentives on economic activity. In some cases, it is almost impossible to quantify the effect of these policies.

Since the late 1970s, the basic strategy of tax policy has been shifted from tax incentives to tax neutrality and equity. The main reason for this is that large fiscal deficits have accumulated since the late 1970s. To curtail future fiscal deficits, the Japanese government decided that a substantial tax increase could not be avoided. As a prerequisite to a tax increase, it is acknowledged that the government should take the initiative in improving the inequitable burden of income taxation. Thus, during the past decade, a number of special measures for tax incentives have gradually been curtailed, especially in the corporate sector.

In recent years, particular attention has been paid to whether or not corporate tax burden is heavy relative to those in other countries. For example, the *Keidanren* (Federation of Business Organizations) presented an estimate to show that Japan has the highest level of corporate tax burden of the major industrial countries. This is mainly because of the recent curtailment of special measures for tax incentives. The *Keidanren* estimate has led to controversy among many economists, including the Ministry of Finance staff.

Although this chapter focuses on tax-incentive policies, a broader purpose is to clarify the debate surrounding measurement of the effective tax burden in the corporate sector. Section 2 gives an overview of tax-incentive policies in postwar Japan. A great deal of attention in this section is paid to the past role played by special tax measures in the corporate sector. Section 3 is devoted to the recent debates on the corporate tax burden and their policy implications. Section 4 estimates additional measures of the corporate tax burden. Finally, in Section 5, some concluding remarks are presented.

2   An overview of tax-incentive policies

2.1   *Special tax measures*

We begin our discussion with a review of the tax-incentive policies that the Japanese government has adopted in the postwar period. Although many studies have discussed this topic (e.g., Komiya, 1966; Pechman and Kaizuka, 1976), it is worth reviewing these developments again to cover the more recent period; see Kaizuka (1984) for a similar discussion.

In the postwar period, numerous tax measures were introduced to stimulate economic growth and achieve other related policy targets that had a high national priority. These measures were included in the "Special Tax Measures Law," which was distinct from the ordinary income tax laws. This special law was formulated to include most, though not all, of the incentive provisions applying to individual and corporate income taxes. However, at the present, a number of significant tax-incentive measures are contained in the ordinary income tax law, rather than in the Special Tax Measures Law. Thus, it is rather ambiguous to distinguish those tax provisions that are considered to be special from those that are not.

In what follows, the concept of "tax incentives" encompasses primarily what the Ministry of Finance (MOF) calls "special tax measures," which might be termed "tax preferences." The items included in the special-tax-measures definition come from both the Special Tax Measures Law and the ordinary income tax law and are chosen depending on a specific definition of policy incentives adopted by the MOF.[1]

Accordingly, as Pechman and Kaizuka pointed out (1976, p. 352), there is no compilation in Japan comparable to the comprehensive list of "tax expenditures" in the U.S. budget document. It does not seem that the scope of "special tax measures" in Japan is narrower than in the United States.

2.2 Significance of the tax incentives

In order to investigate how significant tax-incentive measures have been, we examine a series of annual estimates of revenue losses caused by special tax measures, as compiled by the MOF. Using this series, we are unable to distinguish between revenue losses from corporate income taxes and revenue losses from individual income taxes before 1972, but because this is the only available estimate of the significance of tax incentives, we use it.

Table 4.1 shows the past trend of estimated revenue losses due to the special tax measures. According to these estimates, the revenue loss resulting from the special tax measures varied between 10.6% and 13.2% of total income tax revenue in the late 1950s, fell to 8-9% in 1961-2, rose to 12.0% in 1965, and then declined to 5.1% in the early 1980s. This long-run declining trend is illustrated in Figure 4.1. This trend reflects the fact that many of the special tax measures for specific purposes have been abolished in the past decade to make the tax system more neutral or equitable.

Emphasis should be placed on the recent tendency of curtailing the special tax measures granted to the corporate sector. In Figure 4.2 we have estimates of corporate tax revenue losses due to special tax measures as a percentage of the corporate tax revenue since 1972. In 1972, the special measures relating to the corporate income tax reduced total revenue by 9.0%. This figure declined steadily to as low as 2.2% in 1980. Thereafter, in 1984, it turned upward slightly to 3.2%. Thus, we see that a number of special tax measures have been abolished or diminished in size.

2.3 Development of the tax incentives

The trend in revenue losses resulting from the special tax measures is a good indicator of the past development of tax incentives. In general, special measures are classified into two types: (1) tax exemptions and credits; (2) tax deferrals, including (a) accelerated depreciation and (b) tax-free reserves. Broadly speaking, type (1) was more important in the 1950s, whereas type (2) became more important in the 1960s and 1970s (Ikemoto, Tajika, and Yui, 1984).

The origin of the special tax measures can be traced to the prewar era, when the "Temporal Tax Measures Law" was enacted in 1938 to provide

Table 4.1. *Comparison of estimated revenue losses from special tax measures*

Fiscal year	Total individual and corporate tax revenue (billion yen)	Revenue losses from special tax measures[a]	
		Amount (billion yen)	Percentage of income tax revenue
1958	586.3	77.6	13.2
1959	649.9	82.2	12.6
1960	964.0	99.1	10.6
1961	1,210.1	99.5	8.2
1962	1,359.9	125.8	9.3
1963	1,553.6	157.0	10.1
1964	1,812.8	207.5	11.4
1965	1,897.5	228.2	12.0
1966	2,115.9	248.5	11.7
1967	2,597.6	255.4	9.8
1968	3,205.0	284.4	9.0
1969	4,014.3	357.7	8.9
1970	4,995.4	434.5	8.7
1971	5,445.7	532.7	9.8
1972	6,718.3	580.4	8.6
1973	9,850.2	645.0	6.6
1974	11,166.5	727.0	6.5
1975	9,610.2	796.0	8.3
1976	11,004.5	759.0	6.9
1977	12,144.6	840.0	6.9
1978	15,665.8	933.0	6.0
1979	16,657.9	959.0	5.8
1980	19,722.3	1,026.0	5.2
1981	20,802.9	1,121.0	5.4
1982	21,980.1	1,149.0	5.2
1983	23,467.4	1,193.0	5.1
1984[b]	25,318.0	1,281.0	5.1
1985[c]	28,014.0	1,525.0	5.4

[a]Includes only the items listed as special tax measures by the Tax Bureau excluding revenue gains from the curtailment of corporate special and entertainment expenses.
[b]Figures for revised budget.
[c]Figures for initial budget.
Sources: Tax revenues from Ministry of Finance (1984); revenue losses from special tax measures from data presented to the Budget Committee, National Diet, by the tax Bureau of the MOF.

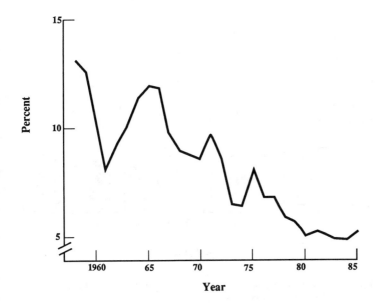

Figure 4.1. Revenue losses from special tax measures: percentage of personal and corporate income tax revenue.

tax incentives for the war effort. After a substantial expansion was experienced during the war and the immediate postwar era, the list of special tax measures was shortened when the Shoup Commission recommended tax reform in 1950.[2]

From 1950 to the late 1970s, the list of special tax measures again expanded. During the earlier period (say in the 1950s), the exemption types of tax-incentive measures were most prevalent. To give two examples, from 1913 to 1966, income raised by producing certain products (mostly petrochemical products) was exempted. To promote export-oriented industries, export income was exempted from 1953 to 1963. Most of the exemption-type measures, however, were abolished in the early 1960s. It is important to notice that these exemptions were not applied to all industries across the board, but only to specific infant or export-oriented industries.

In recent years, the tax-credit device has been used more often than tax exemptions. An important credit is the tax credit for experimental and research expenses, which started in 1966. If a firm's expenses for research and development in any year exceed its outlays in any previous year, 20% of the excess is allowed as a tax credit. The maximum amount of credit is

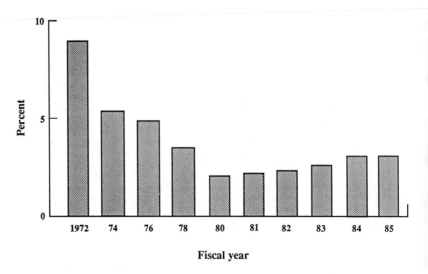

Figure 4.2. Corporate tax revenue losses from special tax measures: percentage of corporate tax revenue.

limited, however, to 10% of the corporate income tax. Since 1981, an investment tax credit for energy-saving equipment has been granted.

Tax-deferral measures include accelerated depreciation and increased initial depreciation. Both are designed to promote business investment. These devices were used often in the 1950s, and some of them have remained in effect since the 1950s. However, many of the accelerated-depreciation and initial-depreciation plans have been altered. For instance, accelerated depreciation for important industrial equipment was made available in the form of a three-year 50%-more-than-normal rate of depreciation from 1951 to 1961. Also, additional initial depreciation for important industries (i.e., an initial-year 50% write-off system) was allowed from 1952 to 1961.

In the 1960s, several depreciation plans expanded to new areas. For instance, accelerated depreciation was granted to small and medium-size enterprises in 1963. The initial depreciation for machinery and equipment used for prevention of environmental pollution was increased in 1967. In the 1970s, the trend of expanding accelerated depreciation for export industries was abolished, and in 1973 increased initial depreciation for important industries was reduced. On the whole, the recent trend has been to reduce the range of accelerated-depreciation provisions.

Another type of tax-deferral measure is tax-free reserves. Although we use the term "tax-free reserves" in English, two types of tax-free reserves usually are distinguished in Japanese. The first represents reserves that are recognized for purposes of business accounting (*Hikiate-kin*), and the second type is designed to stimulate involvement in risky activities (*Junbi-kin*). Because the second type of reserves are not justified by generally accepted accounting principles, the *Junbi-kins* are officially listed as special tax measures.

Both types of tax-free reserves have been allowed since the early 1950s. The tax-free accounting reserves granted reserves for bad debts and special repairs in 1951, reserves for retirement allowance in 1952, and thereafter reserves for bonus payments and losses on returned goods in 1965. The special inducements included reserves for price fluctuations in 1951 and reserves for drought in 1952. Numerous other reserves were added in the 1960s and 1970s.

The size of the tax-free reserves and the amount allowed annually are subject to specific limits, but in all cases the limits are generous in relation to the potential risks the reserves are designed to mitigate. Thus, the tax-free reserves are criticized on the ground that they conceal profits from corporate income taxation.

2.4   Objective of the tax incentives

According to the MOF, the special tax measures of individual and corporate income taxes are classified into six different categories: (1) promotion of savings, (2) promotion of environmental quality and regional development, (3) promotion of natural resources, (4) promotion of technological development and modernization of industrial equipment, (5) strengthening the financial positions of firms, and (6) miscellaneous. These classifications, however, are not useful for economic analysis. Thus, we rearrange them into more meaningful categories.

Table 4.2 summarizes the percentage distribution of revenue losses from the special tax measures, dating back to 1958. The first category, promotion of individual savings and housing, is connected exclusively with the individual income tax. Since 1958, the first category has maintained the highest share. In addition, it has recently been increasing its relative share, because corporate special tax measures have been substantially reduced.

The second largest share is due to promotion of business savings and investment. As was explained earlier, the tax devices used to promote these activities include tax exemptions and credits, accelerated depreciation,

Table 4.2. *Percentage distribution of estimated revenue losses from special tax measures, by type of incentive*

Fiscal Year	Promotion of individual savings and housing (%) (1)	Promotion of business savings and investment (%) (2)	Promotion of export and foreign investment (%) (3)	Promotion of environmental quality (%) (4)	Other (%) (5)
1958	49.5	25.8	18.0	0	6.7
1959	45.6	33.8	13.4	0	7.1
1960	45.6	35.9	12.6	0	5.9
1961	50.3	31.8	12.1	0.3	5.6
1962	49.4	24.2	17.9	0.2	8.2
1963	60.6	15.9	15.6	0.1	7.9
1964	59.3	18.5	13.6	0.2	8.3
1965	59.9	18.7	12.9	0.3	8.2
1966	60.3	20.7	11.3	0.4	7.4
1967	61.0	20.9	10.9	0.8	6.3
1968	59.8	19.3	14.0	0.9	6.1
1969	54.6	18.2	14.8	1.5	10.9
1970	47.0	18.1	19.3	1.6	14.0
1971	44.5	19.9	17.0	5.8	12.8
1972	44.7	27.5	4.7	6.9	16.2
1973	49.6	25.1	3.8	7.3	14.2
1974	49.4	21.4	5.5	8.3	15.4
1975	44.6	22.2	6.5	9.2	17.5
1976	47.0	18.8	5.5	6.7	21.9
1977	48.2	18.9	4.2	4.6	24.0
1978	48.1	18.3	2.8	4.4	26.4
1979	49.7	22.4	2.1	5.5	20.2
1980	53.6	20.6	1.9	3.6	20.4
1981	57.4	20.2	1.7	4.2	16.5
1982	58.0	21.1	2.3	4.3	14.4
1983	57.3	23.4	1.6	4.1	13.7
1984	54.6	26.0	2.4	4.2	12.7
1985	59.0	24.2	2.2	4.1	10.6

Note: The official classification was rearranged into five items as described in the text.
Sources: Same as for Table 4.1.

and tax-free reserves. These devices generally are used in particular industries or activities, and in many cases two or three measures are employed to promote the same objective.

We note that the promotion of export and foreign investment has become a much less important special tax measure. In the 1950s and 1960s, the devices to promote export and foreign investments included both the special deduction of export income from taxation and accelerated depreciation for export-oriented firms. These tax provisions were finally eliminated by the early 1970s. Today, the remaining provisions for exports and overseas investment are minor. Consequently, their relative share in Table 4.2 has continued to fall over the long run.

The fourth category is concerned with the promotion of environmental quality. In the early 1970s, the Japanese economy began to experience the agonies of rapid economy growth, such as rampant inflation, urban congestion, and environmental pollution. Particular attention was paid to the importance of environment policies to prevent air and water pollution. Since then, tax devices relevant to pollution control have sharply increased their share, reaching the highest peak of 9.2% in 1975. Typical measures include special additional depreciation and tax-free reserves for pollution control.

Finally, miscellaneous measures have accounted for 10–20% since the 1970s. Mostly they are composed of elements such as the special deduction of physicians' fees that are not related to the corporate income tax.

3 Earlier studies of the corporate tax burden

3.1 Statutory tax rates

In this section, we construct a simple estimate of the corporate tax burden by using the statutory structure of the corporate income tax. The MOF has traditionally used this formula to estimate the tax burden in the corporate sector.

The present corporate tax has a complicated structure, consisting of several rates (MOF, 1984). At present, the tax rate on retained profits stands at 43.3%, and the tax on dividends is 33.3%. This split rate system has been in effect since 1961 to increase the share of equity capital relative to borrowed capital. In addition to the basic rates, reduced tax rates are applied to small and medium-size corporations with paid-in capital of not more than 100 million yen. For income less than 8 million yen, tax rates are 31% on retained profits and 25% on distributed profits. In addition to these tax burdens at the national level, local corporate taxes are levied on each corporation. When estimating the corporate tax burden, the MOF usually computes what we shall call a statutory rate of tax burden (π hereafter). The formula for this is

$$\pi = \frac{[(70 \times t_r) + (30 \times t_d)](1 + t_e) + (100 \times t_b)}{100 + (100 \times t_b)} \quad (1)$$

where t_r is the tax rate on retained profits, t_d is the tax rate on distributed profits (both t_r and t_d are national taxes), t_e is the tax rate for local corporate income tax, and t_b is the tax rate for local business tax.

Table 4.3. *International comparison of corporate tax rates (%)*

Source	Japan 1984	U.S. 1985	U.K. 1982	West Germany 1984	France 1980
MOF	52.94	51.18	52.00	56.52	50.00
Keidanren	51.57	32.28	18.06	49.84	45.70

Source: Kubouchi (1984).

If we use the actual data of statutory tax rates, π is estimated at 52.94% in 1984 (i.e., $t_r = 0.433$, $t_d = 0.333$, $t_e = 0.173$, $t_b = 0.12$). In this calculation, it is assumed that corporations pay out dividends of 30% of their before-tax earnings. Calculated on the statutory-rate basis, this is the official estimate of the corporate tax burden presented by the MOF.

3.2   *The* Keidanren *proposal*

The MOF estimate considers both national and local taxes on corporate income. However, the effects of tax incentives offered through the special tax measures are not taken into consideration. This omission has been sharply criticized by the *Keidanren* (Kubouchi, 1984).

The *Keidanren* insists that the corporate tax burden should be estimated to take account of the effects caused by tax-incentive policies. Thus, it calculates the effective rate of tax burden in the corporate sector, based on the tax amounts actually paid by corporations. Specifically, the MOF estimate π is changed to the *Keidanren*'s effective rate π_e by applying the following equation:

$$\pi_e = \pi \left(1 - \frac{T_s}{T_s + T_f} \right) \tag{2}$$

where T_s is revenue loss from special tax measures, and T_f is final tax payments.

In Table 4.3, the results from the different estimates are shown for different countries. The most conspicuous result is that the smallest gap between the statutory and effective rates for the corporate tax burden is found in Japan. The statutory-based figure presented by the MOF does not provide a realistic picture of the actual tax burden Japan faces relative to other countries. If more importance is placed on the *Keidanren* estimate, the Japanese tax burden in the corporate sector is higher than that in any other industrialized country.

This reflects the fact that curtailment of the special tax measures has been accelerated especially in the corporate sector. On the other hand, governments in other major countries have taken the initiative in introducing bold measures for tax relief to promote economic revitalization, such as the ACRS (accelerated cost-recovery system) in the United States, or the initial allowance in the United Kingdom. Evidently, the relative levels of effective tax rates between Japan and the other major countries (e.g., the United States) have been reversed in the past seven or eight years (Gravelle, 1983).

3.3   *Effective tax rate by size of corporation*

Although information is limited, the MOF has tried to construct estimates of the actually paid effective tax burden under the special tax measures. These estimates allow us to observe the discrepancy between statutory and actual corporate tax burdens by size of corporation. Table 4.4 summarizes the statutory and actual tax rates at three different levels of paid-in capital for corporations. For the actually paid calculations, corporate incomes are broadened to include the major items eroded by the special tax measures (tax-free reserve, accelerated depreciation, and special deductions). Calculating tax rates on a statutory basis requires making a weighted average of a multiple-rate structure, with split and reduced tax rates.

Figure 4.3 depicts the movements of the two tax rates given in Table 4.4. There are a couple of points worth noting. To begin with, statutory tax rates have consistently shown an upward tendency for corporations of all sizes in the past 10 years. This suggests that the corporate tax burden has been raised by the government on a statutory basis as well as on an actual tax basis. Furthermore, medium-size corporations with 0.1–10 billion yen of paid-in capital have incurred a heavier tax burden than corporations in the other two size categories. Small corporations benefit from reduced rates of taxation and a larger portion of exempted corporate income, whereas large corporations in general can pay out more dividends, which are taxed at a lower level. By contrast, medium-size corporations seem to have relatively fewer opportunities to make use of such preferential tax provisions.

The trends for effective tax rates have shown ups and downs over the long run, reflecting the changing availability of special tax concessions in various periods. It is often pointed out that large corporations are given more advantages to make use of tax-free reserves and accelerated

Table 4.4. *Effective corporate tax rates before and after adjusting for special tax measures, by size of corporation* (billion yen; %)

Fiscal year	Corporate income (1)	Corporate tax revenue (2)	(2)/(1) (3)	Tax-free reserve (4)	Accelerated depreciation (5)	Special deduction for overseas technical service (6)	Tax credit for experimental and research expenses (7)	$\dfrac{(2)-(7)}{(1)+(4)+(5)+(6)}$ (8)
Case 1: less than 0.1 billion yen of paid-in capital								
1973	5,994.2	2,036.9	34.0	162.6	116.2	1.1	1.3	32.4
1974	7,331.1	2,578.7	35.2	58.3	177.9	0.5	1.8	34.1
1975	5,626.5	1,992.2	35.4	−71.1	14.5	1.1	1.6	35.7
1976	5,700.0	2,021.9	35.5	64.6	3.0	0.8	1.6	35.0
1977	5,652.6	2,007.0	35.5	−44.5	15.6	1.7	1.4	35.7
1978	6,395.2	2,274.8	35.6	−7.6	−26.1	1.9	11.0	35.6
1979	8,158.7	2,951.1	36.2	81.6	−11.7	0.8	23.1	35.6
1980	8,960.2	3,254.4	36.3	5.2	42.9	1.3	18.1	35.9
1981	9,098.2	3,406.4	37.4	−154.3	8.0	1.7	13.5	37.9
1982	9,026.2	3,458.8	38.3	4.4	2.0	1.9	6.2	38.2
1983	9,009.5	3,472.0	38.5	−204.8	3.7	3.3	5.9	39.3
Case 2: 0.1–10 billion yen of paid-in capital								
1973	4,072.1	1,445.9	35.3	133.4	60.3	3.5	12.0	33.6
1974	4,483.7	1,675.2	37.4	117.3	91.9	7.6	19.0	35.2
1975	3,055.2	1,182.8	38.7	−55.8	−0.3	6.0	9.0	39.1

1976	3,766.8	1,461.4	38.8	80.5	−26.2	9.5	11.8	37.8
1977	4,480.2	1,742.9	38.9	50.7	27.1	8.8	10.1	37.9
1978	5,092.8	1,984.5	39.0	−46.7	−42.9	10.9	11.6	39.3
1979	6,183.2	2,416.1	39.1	−11.1	−40.1	13.0	15.1	39.1
1980	7,280.7	2,844.8	39.1	39.9	−41.4	17.8	18.1	38.7
1981	7,330.6	2,935.6	40.0	−76.3	−35.3	16.8	21.4	40.3
1982	7,413.5	3,048.2	41.1	−108.8	−32.4	14.6	24.8	41.5
1983	7,583.6	3,115.0	41.1	−107.3	−23.5	17.7	24.0	41.4

Case 3: 10 billion yen or more of paid-in capital

1973	3,074.8	1,078.4	35.1	165.7	106.0	19.0	14.9	31.6
1974	3,108.9	1,151.3	37.0	151.9	103.5	24.6	20.4	33.4
1975	2,650.2	1,014.1	38.3	−6.7	−22.2	12.9	4.7	38.3
1976	3,434.5	1,317.5	38.4	117.3	−41.4	19.9	10.5	37.0
1977	4,296.1	1,647.1	38.3	47.9	39.6	31.1	16.6	36.9
1978	4,359.7	1,683.7	38.6	−61.1	−59.8	25.7	20.6	39.0
1979	5,080.9	1,958.1	38.5	−10.7	−60.7	25.8	30.8	38.3
1980	6,089.1	2,359.0	38.7	32.4	−80.6	30.6	38.3	38.2
1981	6,934.9	2,740.4	39.5	124.2	6.5	30.2	54.9	37.8
1982	7,395.2	3,007.0	40.7	−32.8	−59.0	38.5	63.6	40.1
1983	7,901.8	3,207.3	40.6	−80.9	−72.0	35.8	53.2	40.5

Source: Unpublished data presented to the National Diet by the Tax Bureau of the Ministry of Finance.

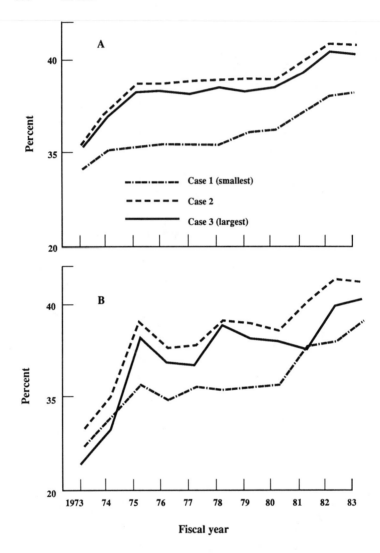

Figure 4.3. Effective corporate tax rates before and after adjusting for special tax measures, by size of corporation. A: Statutory basis. B: Actually paid basis under the special tax measures.

depreciation than smaller corporations. For instance, such tax-free reserves as retirement allowances or bonus payments are used primarily by large corporations. As a result, the regular trends for the three tax rates on a statutory basis are more uneven when we look at the actually paid tax rates. Notice that the largest corporations had the lowest actually paid tax rates in the early 1970s.

4   A new estimate of corporate tax burden

4.1   Basic nature of the Keidanren concept

In this section we present a new method to estimate corporate tax rates. In order to clarify our basic concept, the *Keidanren*'s framework, given in equation (2), is reviewed.

The amount of ordinary income Y is computed as the difference between gross income P and expenses X:

$$Y = P - X \tag{3}$$

These items, Y, P, and X, are all defined in accordance with the ordinary corporate tax law. Taxable income Y_T is derived by subtracting from Y additional deductions X_s that relate to the special tax measures:

$$Y_T = Y - X_s \tag{4}$$

The tax amount T before tax credits is calculated by applying the statutory tax rate π to Y_T:

$$T = \pi Y_T \tag{5}$$

The final tax payment T_f is

$$T_f = T - T_c \tag{6}$$

where T_c are tax credits from the special tax measures.

Thus, revenue loss T_s from the special tax measures is the sum of $\pi X_s + T_c$:

$$T_s = \pi X_s + T_c \tag{7}$$

Using equations (3)–(7), equation (2) is rewritten as

$$\pi_e = \pi \left(1 - \frac{T_s}{T_f + T_s} \right) = \frac{\pi(Y - X_s) - T_c}{P - X} = \frac{T_f}{Y} \tag{8}$$

Thus, the *Keidanren*'s effective rate π_e is the ratio of final tax payment to taxable income prior to the deductions associated with the special tax measures. One problem here is that π_e could change depending on whether the tax-incentive measures are derived from ordinary corporate tax law (included in X) or special tax measures (included in X_s).

It can, however, be concluded that π_e is a more meaningful indicator to explain the real burden of corporate income tax than π, which is calculated on a statutory basis and is used by the MOF.

4.2   A new concept of the tax burden

We now construct a revised concept to estimate the corporate tax burden. Tax-incentive policies provide a number of opportunities to save taxes. Tax exemptions and credits reduce tax burdens in the year they are applied; however, tax-incentive measures like tax-free reserves and accelerated depreciation extend tax savings into the future. This characteristic of tax-incentive policies is observed in the case of tax-free reserves. A corporation is first allowed to accumulate a part of income in a specific reserve account (e.g., bad-debt reserve) for a given period. The reserve then is added back to taxable income and becomes subject to taxation only when the period is over. Accordingly, a corporation can delay payment of taxes levied on a portion of income and as a result benefit from the tax savings due to the tax deferral. The amount of tax savings becomes larger as the period is lengthened. The same holds for accelerated depreciation. In calculating the ultimate tax burden in the corporate sector, this extension of the tax burden over time should be taken into account.

The ultimate rate of corporate taxation is calculated as the ratio of the ultimate tax payments to the economic income that a firm earns in a given business year. We shall call this ultimate tax rate π_u:

$$\pi_u = T_u / Y_E \tag{9}$$

where T_u is ultimately paid taxes, and Y_E is economic income.

In what follows, only the national corporate income tax is created. Economic income Y_E is defined as follows:

$$Y_E = S - C - D_E \tag{10}$$

where S is gross sales, C is costs, excluding depreciation and reserves, and D_E is economic depreciation. Taxable income Y_T is defined as

$$Y_T = S - C - (R_i - R_o) - D_T \tag{11}$$

where R_i and R_o are accumulated (credited) and decumulated (debited) amounts placed in reserve accounts, and D_T is depreciation for tax purposes. In defining Y_T in equation (11), the tax-exemption types of tax-incentive measures are omitted for analytical simplification.

From equations (10) and (11) we obtain

$$Y_E = Y_T + (R_i - R_o) + (D_T - D_E) \tag{12}$$

The difference between Y_E and Y_T emerges from the second and third terms; this occurs when the net accumulation in the reserve account is changed or when economic depreciation and tax-purpose depreciation differ.

The concept of "ultimate" tax burden found in the numerator of equation (9) is used to take into account the tax deferrals derived from tax-free reserves and accelerated depreciation. Let us start by analyzing the effect of tax-free reserves. Generally, the amount (R_i) accumulated in the tax-free reserves is deductible, and the dissolved amount (R_o) from the accumulated reserves is taxable. Therefore, the actual tax payment T_a before tax credits in a single year is computed, given the statutory tax rate π, as

$$T_a = \pi(S - C - R_i + R_o) \qquad (13)$$

This tax amount neglects the tax-deferral effect of R_i in the future.

Now it is assumed that the accumulated amount R_i during this period will be dissolved and added back to taxable income in the $j+1$ period, after it has been kept for j periods in the reserve account. Thus, tax to be paid from R_i is postponed until the $j+1$ period, and tax savings can be realized for the j periods. Given the discount rate r, the ultimate tax burden is expressed in present value as follows:

$$T_u = \pi(S - C) - \pi\left(1 - \frac{1}{(1+r)^j}\right)R_i \qquad (14)$$

The first term in equation (14) indicates the tax payment excluding the tax-free reserves, and the second term of the tax savings is due to the accumulation of R_i. In the case of $j \to \infty$, the second term becomes πR_i, which is equivalent to the exemption type of tax incentive.

From equations (13) and (14),

$$T_u = T_a - \pi R_o + \frac{\pi R_i}{(1+r)^j} \qquad (15)$$

The sum of the second and third terms is called adjusted tax-free reserves.

Next, we deal with the ultimate tax burden in relation to the accelerated-depreciation method. Accelerated depreciation allows a larger depreciation cost during an earlier period of asset life than ordinary depreciation. Accordingly, taxable income can be decreased to obtain tax savings. For simplicity, we ignore the existence of tax-free reserves in order to focus on the effects of accelerated depreciation.

Let us assume that the firm uses ordinary depreciation for investments of I_n, and accelerated depreciation for investments of I_s. We define Z_n to be the present value of ordinary depreciation on a unit of investment. Also, let Z_s be the present value of accelerated depreciation on a unit of investment. In the absence of accelerated depreciation, the present value of depreciation on total investment, $Z_n(I_n + I_s)$, is deducted from taxable income.

On the other hand, when accelerated depreciation is available, the present value of total depreciation increases by $(Z_n - Z_s)I_s$. Thus, the ultimate tax burden T'_u in this case is

$$T'_u = \pi\{(S-C) - [Z_n(I_n + I_x) - (Z_n - Z_s)I_s]\}$$
$$= \pi[(S-C) - (Z_s I_s + Z_n I_n)] \tag{16}$$

From equation (11), when we ignore the term $(R_i - R_o)$, the actual tax payment T'_a is

$$T'_a = \pi Y_T = \pi(S - C - D_T) \tag{17}$$

Therefore, equation (16) reduces to

$$T'_u = T'_a + \pi[D_T - (Z_s I_s + Z_n I_n)] \tag{18}$$

The second right-hand-side term in equation (18) is defined to be the tax payment adjusted for accelerated depreciation.

Finally, we can combine the effects of tax-free reserves and accelerated depreciation to yield the ultimate tax T_u:

$T_u = T_a - T_c +$ (tax amount adjusted for tax-free reserves)

   $+$ (tax amount adjusted for accelerated depreciation)   (19)

The third and fourth terms have been defined in equations (15) and (18), respectively.

4.3   *Ultimate tax burden*

Now we can calculate the ultimate rate of corporate tax burden defined in equation (9) by making use of equations (12) and (19). Basic data are collected from *Actual Performance of Corporate Firms in View of Tax Statistics* from the *Hōjin-Kigyo no Jittai* (National Tax Administrative Agency), and estimates are provided for 1970–82. Statutory average tax rates are estimated to construct a reference level for comparing the ultimate rate of corporate taxation. Statutory average tax rates are defined as the ratio of T_a to Y, which is a weighted average for the multiple-rate structure for national corporate taxes. In Table 4.5, these rates are shown by industry.

Upward trends can be observed in the long-run movements of tax rates, mainly because statutory tax rates have been raised in recent years. For instance, when statutory rates rose by 2% in 1981, the average tax rates in Table 4.5 tended to increase about 1% in each industry. In addition,

Table 4.5. *Statutory average tax rates*

Industry	1970	1971	1972	1973	1974	1975	1976	1977	1978	1979	1980	1981	1982	Average (%)
1	33.5	33.5	33.5	34.4	34.6	35.5	36.3	36.6	37.0	37.4	37.0	38.2	38.4	35.9
2	35.8	35.0	35.5	35.3	38.8	39.4	39.4	39.0	38.9	39.4	39.1	40.0	40.8	39.0
3	33.6	33.6	34.1	34.1	35.2	36.3	36.5	36.3	36.4	36.7	36.5	38.4	39.1	36.2
4	34.0	34.0	34.0	34.8	35.6	35.9	36.8	37.0	37.0	37.4	37.6	39.2	39.3	36.2
5	34.9	34.9	34.3	34.9	37.1	37.7	37.8	38.0	38.3	38.5	38.7	39.5	40.6	37.6
6	33.9	33.9	33.4	34.3	36.5	36.9	36.3	36.1	35.1	37.8	38.1	38.8	40.1	36.7
7	35.1	35.1	35.0	35.1	36.8	37.7	38.4	38.4	38.4	38.6	30.8	39.6	40.8	37.9
8	34.4	34.4	34.1	34.4	35.3	37.0	37.5	38.0	37.9	37.9	37.9	39.8	39.9	37.2
9	34.7	34.7	34.8	34.5	36.5	37.5	37.6	37.4	37.9	38.4	38.4	40.0	40.2	37.7
10	34.1	34.1	34.0	34.6	36.0	36.4	36.9	37.1	36.9	37.6	37.4	39.1	39.7	36.7
11	34.1	34.1	34.3	34.9	36.2	36.4	36.6	36.9	37.1	37.3	37.6	38.6	39.4	36.6
12	32.5	32.5	32.4	32.9	33.9	34.2	35.0	34.9	35.6	35.9	36.0	37.4	38.3	35.0
13	32.4	32.4	32.8	33.4	34.0	34.0	34.3	34.8	35.5	35.8	35.7	37.4	37.9	37.7
14	35.6	35.6	35.6	36.1	37.5	39.0	39.0	39.1	39.2	38.7	38.6	40.1	40.9	38.2
15	33.3	33.3	34.6	34.5	35.5	36.4	35.9	36.2	36.2	36.6	36.5	35.5	38.5	35.7
16	33.7	33.7	32.7	33.5	35.2	36.2	36.5	37.2	37.6	37.2	37.7	38.3	39.6	36.6
17	33.0	33.0	33.6	33.7	34.0	35.5	35.6	35.2	36.1	36.2	36.3	37.5	38.6	37.7
18	34.3	34.3	34.3	34.7	36.2	36.9	37.2	37.4	37.5	37.7	37.9	38.9	39.9	37.0

Note: The statutory average tax rate is computed as the ratio of actual tax payments to taxable income, depending on the statutory tax schedule. The industry numbers correspond to the following industries: 1, agriculture & fishing; 2, mining; 3, construction; 4, textiles; 5, chemicals; 6, iron & steel; 7, machinery; 8, food & beverages; 9, publishing & printing; 10, other manufacturing industries; 11, wholesale; 12, retail; 13, restaurants & hotels; 14, financial institutions; 15, real estate; 16, public transportation & utilities; 17, services; 18, all industries.

there is substantial variation in average tax rates among various industries. Average rates are higher for mining and financial institutions, and
lower for wholesale, retail, and service industries, in which small and
medium-size firms are move involved.

We next investigate the effects that tax-free reserves have on the ultimate rates of corporate taxation ignoring accelerated depreciation. To
do this, we must calculate tax payments adjusted for tax-free reserves as
defined in equation (15). We assume that the outstanding tax-free reserves
are dissolved at the period succeeding the last period (Ikemoto, Tajika,
and Yui, 1984, p. 380). Three types of tax-free reserves (i.e., reserves for
bad debts, for retirement allowance, and for price fluctuations) are considered in the following calculation. In order to show the estimated results more clearly, the deviations from the reference level for statutory
tax rates are computed in terms of a relative ratio:

$$\text{deviation ratio} = \frac{\text{statutory rates} - \text{ultimate rates}}{\text{statutory rates}} \times 100$$

The larger the deviation, the more the actual tax burdens are lowered by
utilizing tax-free reserves. The results are shown in Table 4.6.

First, the deviation ratio tends to fall over the time series, and it has
been reduced substantially in many industries since 1980. Second, the
higher deviation ratios are found in public transportation and utilities,
financial institutions, and textiles, followed by such industries as chemicals, iron and steel, and machinery. The ratios have stayed relatively
higher since 1980 in these industries. It is interesting to note that benefits
from utilizing tax-free reserves have emerged in both growing and declining industries. Third, service industries and wholesale and retail industries are given fewer benefits from tax-free reserves, as evident from the
lower deviation between the two rates.

Because of poor access to data, it is not possible at this time to extract
meaningful results concerning the effects of accelerated depreciation on
ultimate tax rates. Thus, we must look for another approach to evaluate
the effects of accelerated depreciation, apart from the term given in equation (18). We measure the tax savings (expressed in present value) caused
by accelerated depreciation with the term $\pi(Z_n - Z_s)I_s$. The rate of tax
savings is defined as the ratio of $\pi(Z_n - Z_s)I_s$ to T, and it is estimated under the proper assumptions.[3] Table 4.7 presents the rates of tax savings
due to accelerated depreciation for 1970–82.[4] As with the previous findings, we can observe a long-run declining trend in the rates of tax savings among all industries. The highest rate in 1982 was only 2% in public
transportation and utilities. Relatively high rates of tax savings are also
observable in the textile, iron, and steel industries.

Table 4.6. *Deviation between statutory average tax rates and effective rates due to tax-free reserves*

Industry	1970	1971	1972	1973	1974	1975	1976	1977	1978	1979	1980	1981	1982	Average (%)
1	6.38	4.05	2.70	6.50	11.70	6.80	1.86	1.10	4.82	0.33	0.59	1.34	0.36	4.64
2	0.83	3.07	0.27	0.26	1.71	0.95	0.05	0.45	0.35	0.96	0.40	0.22	0.13	1.11
3	1.77	1.41	1.83	2.15	2.26	1.01	1.66	1.36	1.05	1.18	0.61	0.30	0.21	1.51
4	1.81	1.66	0.21	6.05	4.00	2.83	1.63	2.55	0.66	1.46	1.90	1.86	0.85	5.04
5	4.49	3.45	2.03	5.13	6.19	4.72	4.84	3.93	1.95	2.89	2.33	2.24	2.00	4.56
6	4.57	1.14	5.52	4.72	4.54	3.32	4.03	3.94	4.06	2.55	2.70	1.65	2.39	3.52
7	2.67	5.12	4.57	4.91	6.89	3.56	3.64	3.95	3.77	2.60	2.51	3.37	3.09	3.87
8	2.95	2.22	3.58	2.34	4.42	2.37	3.13	1.63	1.72	1.55	0.67	0.72	0.51	2.18
9	0.42	3.33	5.69	0.12	1.89	7.91	0.35	2.47	1.88	3.47	0.82	0.53	0.22	2.44
10	2.69	0.39	3.75	3.59	3.21	1.35	2.59	1.68	1.32	2.53	0.97	1.31	1.44	2.21
11	5.20	4.69	3.45	4.36	3.05	0.92	3.51	0.74	1.88	1.00	0.23	0.14	0.23	2.67
12	1.85	2.79	2.54	2.49	4.88	0.02	1.31	2.02	0.70	0.23	0.47	0.04	0.03	1.83
13	0.28	1.70	0.03	1.68	0.18	0.23	0.88	1.61	0.63	0.51	0.07	0.18	0.36	0.72
14	6.88	10.21	1.07	7.80	2.82	1.56	1.81	0.86	0.85	1.77	0.25	0.19	0.00	5.05
15	0.90	0.38	0.11	0.93	0.91	0.81	1.01	0.27	0.24	0.51	0.19	0.17	0.08	0.56
16	8.95	4.58	4.82	8.33	7.90	2.48	0.87	5.20	3.15	2.26	1.42	0.69	0.60	5.43
17	1.95	0.39	2.16	2.29	1.37	2.32	1.22	1.11	1.57	1.31	0.20	0.63	0.07	1.28
18	4.04	3.80	3.04	4.52	4.18	2.05	3.16	2.38	1.97	1.81	1.21	1.19	1.07	3.22

Note: Deviation is expressed in terms of the following ratio: (statutory rate − effective rate) ÷ statutory rate. The industry numbers are the same as in Table 4.5.

Table 4.7. Rate of tax savings due to accelerated depreciation

Industry	1970	1971	1972	1973	1974	1975	1976	1977	1978	1979	1980	1981	1982	Average (%)
1	1.40	2.25	0.87	1.49	1.76	2.39	1.76	2.07	0.70	0.51	0.20	0.15	0.12	1.13
2	0.56	0.44	0.31	0.59	0.40	0.37	0.40	0.34	0.83	0.41	0.29	0.11	0.52	0.40
3	0.15	0.09	0.13	0.26	0.27	0.22	0.20	0.21	0.18	0.19	0.19	0.14	0.11	0.10
4	2.60	4.00	2.33	1.44	1.42	1.44	1.04	0.90	0.60	0.52	0.62	0.62	0.65	1.31
5	0.99	1.13	0.95	0.73	0.92	0.99	0.77	0.82	0.45	0.24	0.22	0.22	0.22	0.59
6	4.42	2.80	1.90	1.55	1.31	2.18	4.11	1.92	1.43	0.54	0.45	0.46	0.46	1.30
7	1.63	2.03	0.92	0.59	0.72	0.66	0.42	0.41	0.23	0.19	0.19	0.21	0.23	0.49
8	0.57	0.53	0.61	0.74	1.17	0.80	0.65	0.71	0.30	0.35	0.31	0.22	0.30	0.55
9	1.81	1.71	1.44	1.71	1.74	1.13	1.08	1.13	0.68	0.45	0.62	0.42	0.53	0.94
10	1.53	1.42	0.98	0.85	0.94	0.58	0.71	0.69	0.54	0.36	0.37	0.37	0.50	0.67
11	0.11	0.10	0.09	0.06	0.08	0.09	0.07	0.07	0.04	0.04	0.03	0.03	0.03	0.06
12	0.05	0.05	0.05	0.05	0.06	0.05	0.04	0.07	0.05	0.03	0.01	0.02	0.03	0.04
13	0.02	0.05	0.06	0.06	0.05	0.06	0.23	0.09	0.05	0.03	0.03	0.04	0.03	0.06
14	0.05	0.10	0.05	0.06	0.10	0.15	0.09	0.08	0.04	0.02	0.01	0.01	0.00	0.06
15	0.34	0.27	0.19	0.21	0.43	0.53	0.49	0.40	0.27	0.16	0.15	0.12	0.11	0.27
16	3.69	4.95	3.86	2.96	4.73	1.85	1.74	1.31	0.86	0.81	2.47	1.45	1.15	2.01
17	0.15	0.23	0.12	0.17	0.22	0.22	0.17	0.22	0.10	0.09	0.10	0.07	0.06	0.14
18	1.20	1.14	0.58	0.50	0.74	0.56	0.54	0.49	0.31	0.24	0.28	0.29	0.26	0.48

Note: The rate of tax savings is defined as the ratio of tax saved by the use of accelerated depreciation to taxable income. The industry numbers are the same as in Table 4.5.

5   Concluding remarks

In conclusion, there are two points we wish to note. First, special tax measures began to be reduced starting in the late 1970s. This phenomenon has mainly been caused by restricting the use of tax-free reserves and accelerated depreciation in the past decade. This point was made in the *Keidanran* proposal and may have implications for the international competitiveness of firms in Japan. Second, although tax incentives have been institutionally allowed in every industry, they often are not utilized evenly among industries. Thus, they cause unequal rates of corporate tax burden among different industries.

In this chapter we have analyzed the corporate tax burden, focusing on tax-incentive policies. No attempt has been made to clarify the effectiveness of tax incentives to promote private investment and savings. The next step is to investigate further the relationship between tax incentives and their policy targets, including the promotion of corporate investment.

ACKNOWLEDGMENT

I appreciate the computational assistance of E. Tajika and Y. Yui and editorial help from Robert Deckle.

NOTES

1. The definition of special tax measures was officially made clear when the Tax Advisory Commission presented the tax report in 1976. In both the Special Tax Measures Law and the ordinary income tax law, a great deal of effort was made to draw the distinction between incentive measures relating to specific policy purposes and the ordinary tax structure in the relevant area. The tax staff at the MOF asserts that the distinction between the two is clear-cut, given their professional knowledge and understanding of the income tax law. See the Tax Advisory Commission's *Tax Report* for 1976 (pp. 3–4).
2. The Shoup Commission recommendation was proposed by a group of tax specialists, headed by Professor Carl Shoup of Columbia University. The purpose of the Shoup Commission was to recommend a tax system that would contribute to economic stability and would require no changes for several years. The commission's detailed report (65,000 words), which covers the Japanese tax system, both central and local, has been made public.
3. Data on useful lives of assets, the rate of depreciation, etc., are required to calculate Z_n, Z_s, and I_s in the tax savings. Useful lives of assets are collected from *Survey of National Wealth* (1970), and the rates of depreciation for ordinary assets are computed assuming the declining-balance method. In regard to the rate of accelerated depreciation, it is assumed that the law of accelerated depreciation allows one-quarter of asset value to be written off in the first year. Using both this rate and the accelerated-depreciation allowance, the time series for I_s is estimated each year.

4. It is easy to add the rate of tax savings relating to tax-free reserves to that in Table 4.7.

REFERENCES

Economic Planning Agency (1970). *Survey of National Wealth* (Nihon no Kokufu Chosa). Tokyo: EPA.

Gomi, Y. (1984). *Guide to Japanese Taxes.* Tokyo: Zaikei Shohosha.

Gravelle, J. (1983). *Comparative Corporate Tax Burdens in the United States and Japan and Implications for Relative Economic Growth.* Congressional Research Service, report 83-177E. Washington, D.C.: Library of Congress.

Hollerman, L. (1984). "Tax Incentives for Saving, Investment, and Innovation in Postwar Japan." Testimony presented at hearing of the Joint Economic Committee, September 24. Washington, D.C.: U.S. Congress.

Ikemoto, Y., E. Tajika, and Y. Yui (1984). "On the Fiscal Incentives for Investment: The Case of Postwar Japan." *Developing Economics,* Vol. 22, No. 4, December, pp. 372–95.

Kaizuka, K. (1984). "Recent Development in the Japanese Tax System." In W. Block and M. Walker (eds.), *Taxation,* Proceedings of an international conference of the Fraser Institute.

Komiya, R. (1966). "The Levels of Capital Formation and Public Finance in Postwar Japan." *Foreign Tax Policies and Economic Growth* (pp. 39–90). New York: NBER and Brookings Institution.

Kubouchi, Y. (1984). "Tax Burden on Corporate Income: An International Comparison." *Keidanren Review,* No. 87, June, pp. 9–12.

Ministry of Finance (1984). *An Outline of Japanese Taxes.*

Pechman, J. A., and K. Kaizuka (1976). "Taxation." In H. T. Patrick and H. Rosovsky (eds.), *Asia's New Giant* (pp. 317–82). Washington, D.C.: Brookings Institution.

CHAPTER 5

A closer look at saving rates in the United States and Japan

Michael J. Boskin and John M. Roberts

1   Introduction

The saving behavior of a society reveals much about the nature of its economy and demography. It reflects values, institutions, and incentives, as well as the rate of economic growth and the age structure of the population. The saving rate is a fundamental reflection of the relative values placed on the future and the present by its citizens and political institutions.

Saving is important for two related, but conceptually different, reasons. First, saving provides funds to finance investment, which in turn increases productivity and the future standard of living. Second, saving provides the vehicle by which households shift their income over their lifetimes, for example, from peak earning years to years of retirement, and, perhaps to a lesser extent, between generations by bequests.

It is not surprising that much attention has been paid to the apparent tremendous difference in saving rates in the United States and Japan. The United States for many decades has had the lowest traditionally measured saving rate of any advanced economy in the world, and that saving rate has plummeted in recent years. Japan, on the other hand, has had the highest saving rate among the advanced economies, although it, too, probably has fallen somewhat. In 1983, the net national saving rate as a percentage of gross domestic product (GDP) was 2.2% in the United States compared with 15.7% for Japan. Most of the other advanced Western economies had net national saving rates ranging from 7% to 10%. By 1985, the U.S. rate was only a little over 3%.

Numerous commentators, particularly the financial press, tend to correlate saving rates and economic growth rates. Japan has grown much more rapidly than average for the OECD economies, whereas the United States, until quite recently, had been growing less rapidly than average.

121

Thus, many commentators look to the low saving rate in the United States as a cause of its poor economic performance. This may be correct, but it is also likely that the saving rate will be higher in a rapidly growing economy, because this implies that a larger fraction of total national resources will be in the hands of younger, richer workers who are saving, with a smaller fraction in the hands of poorer, dissaving retirees. Further, the comparisons most frequently made in the popular press are between Japanese and U.S. household saving rates, neglecting the saving done in the business sector and by government. We shall see later that the relative saving rates may look quite different when these sectors are examined as well.

Finally, the United States and Japan use different accounting conventions in measuring gross national saving. The United States does not keep a separate capital account for its government, whereas Japan does. Were government investment unimportant, this would not be a problem. But when comparing the Japanese rate as reported by the Japanese national income accounts with the United States rate as reported by the United States national income accounts, the fact that the Japanese government is an enormous net saver is neglected.

The traditional view, simply put, is that the United States has a very low saving rate, and Japan a very high saving rate. Although this is correct, the argument seems to be that the saving rate in Japan is *many times* that in the United States. We believe such pronouncements to be quite misleading, and we believe that it is important to examine the sectoral composition of saving between the public and private sectors, as well as to address a variety of other measurement and conceptual issues.

Recently, a revisionist view has emerged. This view argues that several important components of saving are treated as consumption expenditures in the national accounts – consumer durables and education are two primary concerns – and that once expenditures on these items are included as saving, the U.S. saving rate is not nearly so out of line. An important example is provided by the work of Blades and Sturm. In two important studies, Blades and Sturm (1982) and Blades (1983) discuss alternative measures of saving, the OECD and United Nations standardized national accounts, and a variety of adjustments to them. We review their work more extensively later, but it is interesting to note here that their conclusion is that the gross saving rate in Japan is only approximately one-third larger than that in the United States once one accounts for the treatment of consumer durables and a variety of other issues. There are so many other differences in institutions, growth rates, and demography that such a difference may not appear so startling as that reflected in the traditional view that the saving rate in Japan is a substantial multiple of that in the United States.

The purpose of this chapter is to reexamine this issue in order to shed some light on a variety of conceptually and pragmatically important issues. Is Japan adding to its wealth more rapidly than the United States? What form does this greater saving take? Should we be surprised at the differences in saving rates, whether national or sectoral? What data, measurement, and conceptual issues must be overcome if we are to examine carefully any differences in saving behavior in the United States and Japan? After we examine various adjustments and differences in the two countries' saving rates, what implications are there for policy with respect to saving in each country? Does the current set of policies alter the saving rates? Finally, with these adjustments made, are we closer to the traditional view of the relative saving rates in Japan and the United States or to the revisionist view? Japan and the United States are the two largest economies in the world, and Japan is currently the largest supplier of capital to the world capital market, while the United States has become a large capital importer. What do current and prospective trends in saving rates in the United States and Japan imply for international capital flows and the ability to finance productive investment in the United States, Japan, and the rest of the world?

This chapter is organized as follows: In the next section we discuss some methodological issues. Is net or gross saving the appropriate measure? Or do we need to keep both figures in mind for various purposes? How good are the measures of depreciation in the two economies? Should we be concerned about reallocation of saving between the public and private sectors, and within the private sector, between the household and business sectors? Given that government is a large investor, especially in Japan, and that government capital stocks are large and depreciate, what difference does it make if we attempt to measure government net investment and include the rental flow of government services in national income? Correspondingly, what difference does it make if we treat consumer durables purchases as saving and the imputed rental flow from consumer durables as income? We also discuss a variety of other issues in adjusting saving estimates, such as the importance of education, that we believe to have been greatly overstated by casual observation.

In Section 3, we present a cursory review of some previous studies, including the work of Blades and Sturm (1982), Auerbach (1982), Shoven (1984), and Boskin (1986a). We also discuss the implementation of various saving adjustments.

Section 4 presents our results. We compare gross saving rates under different definitions: that used by the national income accounts in Japan and that in the United States. We also make an adjustment for consumer durables. We then argue that the net saving rate, for many, but not all, purposes, provides a more appropriate comparison. We discuss measurement of net saving in the United States and Japan, including issues of government investment (both military and nonmilitary) and consumer durables purchases. These issues are important because the United States spends a much higher fraction of its income on consumer durables and on military investment, whereas Japan spends a much higher fraction of its national income on government investment, despite its substantial budget deficits. In short, the government sector in Japan is a large net saver, whereas the U.S. government is a large net borrower.

Thus, if we examine *net national saving*, Japan still appears to have a saving rate several times that of the United States. However, if we confine ourselves to private saving, a somewhat different picture emerges: The net saving rate in Japan is still substantially larger, but not nearly so great a multiple as in the net *national* saving figures. In short, a substantial fraction of the difference between the net saving rates in the United States and Japan is accounted for by the substantial net saving done by the Japanese government and the substantial borrowing by the government sector in the United States. This may be due to a variety of factors, including a natural historical evolution: It appears that Japan is undergoing a massive public infrastructure investment that is unlikely to continue indefinitely. The closest analogy in the United States would be the building of the interstate highway system in the early 1960s.

Finally, we conclude in the final section with an agenda for future research. Estimation of the determinants of saving behavior in each economy is an important step toward predicting the future course of that behavior, as influenced by demographic and other trends, and an important step toward understanding the likely effects of various policies on saving behavior in each economy.

2   Methodology in the measurement of saving

Recent studies of aggregate saving behavior have measured saving in a variety of ways. Among the measurement issues are the following questions: whether to use stock changes or flows in measuring saving, the former using financial data, and the latter, NIPA data; whether net or gross saving is the relevant concept, and, if the answer is net, how to measure depreciation; what to include as saving, such as whether or not consumer durables or education ought to be included; whether or not individual savers are affected by whether a corporation, or the government, is saving on their behalf. In this section, we attempt to locate our approach within the spectrum on each point.

"Annual saving" measures the addition made each year to the capital stock.[1] There are two ways that one can measure this change. One is to measure the capital stock each year and calculate the changes. The other is to measure the flow into, and out of, the stock each year, with the difference being saving. In the second method, the capital stock is never measured directly, but rather is inferred from the flows, using the perpetual-inventory method.

The latter method, based on flows, is the most common. This is largely because it can be calculated directly from national income and product account data. One drawback of this approach is that saving is a residual, so that small percentage errors in the measurement of other, larger components can lead to large percentage errors in the measurement of saving.

The first method, based on direct capital stock measurement, has the advantage that it can incorporate market reassessment of the value of assets. It has been implemented for the United States by several authors, including Shoven (1984), Auerbach (1982), and Boskin (1986a). In the United States, the Federal Reserve Board (the "Fed") makes annual estimates of financial wealth. These authors used changes in these estimates, adjusted for inflation, as their estimate of saving.

Unfortunately, in practice, this measure has a number of problems. First among these problems, the Fed reports the value of bonds "at par." Thus, the obvious market adjustment in the value of bonds for changing interest rates or inflation rates is ignored.[2] Second, some economists are skeptical that equity market changes affect behavior in the same manner as other forms of saving. Should the recent upswing in the U.S. stock market be considered as saving? Should a stock market crash be considered as dissaving? Also, many private assets are not publicly traded. Should they be added, simply, to other forms of saving? Because of these misgivings, some authors prefer using the corporate capital stock based on the perpetual inventory method in their studies. But once bonds and equities are eliminated, the categories of capital subject to potentially large market revaluations are small. These include such categories as housing and land.

In our analysis, we analyze only the flow-based methods. Besides incorporating the information that governments generate in constructing their national income and product accounts, these measures also have the advantage of being familiar and of being the subjects of earlier studies that can be used for comparison.

Once flow-based measures are chosen, attention must be focused on the appropriate measures of depreciation. Note that in the market-based approach, depreciation is not an issue, because markets presumably take the wear and tear and obsolescence of the capital of a firm into account.[3] The best way to measure depreciation directly is by examining time series records of the prices of assets as they age. An important recent attempt to do this in the United States was the study of Hulten and Wykoff (1981). They found that the pattern of depreciation for the categories of buildings and equipment for which data were available had a roughly exponential, declining balance pattern. They used a relationship between the traditional "service lives" and their exponential depreciation rates to infer depreciation rates for items for which there was inadequate price data. Their methods have been implemented for the U.S. federal government sector by the current authors (Boskin, Robinson, and Roberts, 1985), and these new estimates of depreciation, and companion measures for the state and local sector, have been incorporated in the estimates we report here. The depreciation rates that are implicit for the appropriate aggregates have been used in calculating depreciation for Japanese government capital. For private sector depreciation, however, we use the estimates reported in the respective national income and product accounts, with one important exception.[4] The Japanese depreciation data are on a historic cost basis and hence may be mismeasuring depreciation in periods of rapid inflation. We convert the historic cost depreciation data to their replacement cost equivalents using the shorthand method proposed by Hayashi (1986).

The U.S. Bureau of Economic Analysis (BEA) calculates depreciation by combining a straight-line depreciation pattern based on service lives with an empirical discard pattern. This method has the advantage of being straightforward and can approximate economic depreciation. However, such approximation is fortuitous. Hulten and Wykoff (1981) found that the BEA method approximated their empirical estimates of depreciation patterns well for equipment categories, but poorly for structures, with the BEA method depreciating structures much too quickly. Although we believe that the empirical approach of Hulten and Wykoff is an improvement, the alternative depreciation method is not crucial to our results.[5]

Although it is true that for measuring additions to the wealth of a society saving net of depreciation is the relevant concept, gross saving rates can also be important. If technical change is embodied in new capital, or if there are substantial learning-by-doing effects related to the introduction of new capital goods, then the higher the rate of replacement of capital, the higher will be the rate of growth. A higher gross saving rate will therefore lead to more rapid growth. But because our main focus here is not on how technical change occurs, but rather on the choice of when to consume, we shall concentrate on the net saving rate.

If individuals are indifferent to which institution is saving on their behalf, the national saving rate will directly reflect the decisions of individuals. It is possible, though, that governments and corporations take actions that the household cannot undo, and thus if we want to analyze the underlying decisions of individuals, we need to disaggregate national saving.

In this chapter, we take the position that the distinction between household and corporate saving does not matter, but that the distinction between public and private saving is important. The issue of the "corporate veil" centers on whether or not people realize that corporate retained earnings constitute savings. The fact that share prices generally reflect previous retained earnings suggests that people do realize that retained earnings constitute savings.[6]

The debate over whether or not people see through the "government veil" is a venerable one in economics, with authors such as Barro (1974) arguing that the veil ought to be transparent, while others, such as Tobin and Buiter (1980) argue that owing to capital market imperfections, all people may not be able to offset every government action. Boskin and Kotlikoff (1985) presented empirical evidence that rejects the Barro conjecture. The recent correlation among high U.S. government budget deficits, high real interest rates, and large trade deficits further suggests that the government veil may indeed be opaque. In what follows, we examine public and private saving separately, as well as national saving. Recall also that for most private capital projects, a market test must be passed; there is no corresponding capital market to value public investment decisions. Indeed, the "value" is estimated by input cost, which only under very strong assumptions concerning the quality of public benefit–cost decisions would approximate the value to citizens.

We consider the question of what to include as savings in more detail in the next section, when we look at Blades and Sturm's thorough treatment of the subject, but it is useful here to review some of the algebra of saving rates. The saving rate (SR) is defined as

$$SR = \frac{Y - C - G}{Y} \tag{1}$$

where Y may be net national product (NNP) or gross national product (GNP), C is consumption by households, and G is consumption by government. If we conclude that some expenditure X has inappropriately been categorized as consumption, when it is in fact investment, then the gross saving rate (GSR) ought to be adjusted as

$$GSR = \frac{GNP - C - G + X}{GNP + RX} \tag{2}$$

where RX is the rental flow from the stock of X, K_X. The rental flow is the sum of the depreciation of K_X, D_X, and the opportunity cost of holding K_X, RK_X, where R is the real rate of interest, assumed in this study to be 2% per year.[7] Because the rent is consumed, it cancels in the numerator.

The net saving rate (NSR) is adjusted as

$$NSR = \frac{NNP - C - G + X - D_X}{NNP + Rent - D_X} = \frac{NNP - C - G + X - D_X}{NNP + RK_X} \tag{3}$$

The denominator is thus adjusted to include only the opportunity cost component of the rental flow.

3   Previous studies

Previous research examining the measurement of saving has included studies implementing the change-in-net-worth method for U.S. data (Auerbach, 1982; Shoven, 1984; Boskin, 1986a) and studies exploring the effect of expanding the definition of savings (Blades and Sturm, 1982; Boskin, 1986a). The Blades and Sturm study is of particular interest because it makes international comparisons and includes estimates of household and gross national saving as well as net national saving. In addition, Blades and Sturm include an interesting discussion of various notions of what constitutes saving.

For their international comparisons, Blades and Sturm examine saving rates for the period from 1970 to 1980 for as many as 24 countries, using OECD data. From their largest sample, they find that the United States has the lowest net national saving rate, and Japan the second highest net national saving rate, among the 24 OECD countries.[8] Further, most countries appear to have saving rates closer to that of Japan than to that of the United States.

The first set of adjustments Blades and Sturm make are to the household saving rate. Some of these corrections are also made in the national saving rate. These include treating expenditures on consumer durables and education as saving. Several adjustments they consider, though, net between the household and corporate sectors, such as corrections for the size of the unincorporated business sector, for the relative importance of private pensions and public social security, and for inflation gains and losses. As we argued earlier, it is likely that individuals see through the corporate veil, and to the extent that business saving varies across countries, examining only household saving may be misleading.

Blades and Sturm then turn to adjusting national saving rates. They expand the basis of the saving concept to include expenditures on consumer durables, education, and research and development (R&D). Although each of these constitutes a way in which societies provide for future consumption, the latter two introduce considerable problems in the measurement of depreciation. Educational investment is certainly fully depreciated when a person dies, but whether the intervening pattern is "one hoss shay" or declining in some way is not a question to which we have a ready answer. We agree with Boskin (1986a) and Auerbach (1982) that net education investment is likely to be quite small as a share of income, and unlikely to alter our basic results. R&D also depreciates, probably rapidly, and there may be a problem in distinguishing between R&D and investment.[9]

Finding these depreciation issues difficult, Blades and Sturm choose to look only at gross saving rates when making their consumer durables, education, and R&D adjustments. But as we mentioned in the previous section, for the purpose of measuring additions to potential future consumption, net saving is a better measure.

Although they do not measure net saving, Blades and Sturm do claim to make the appropriate adjustment to income for the rental flows; see equation (2). However, because Blades and Sturm choose not to consider depreciation, they make an extreme assumption in measuring the rental flow. They assume that depreciation in each year is equal to purchases (which implies bizarre depreciation patterns as purchases fluctuate) and that the opportunity cost of holding these durables is zero. Although this simplifies the calculations, this treatment is equivalent to treating durables as current expenditures and thus is circular, because the purpose was to treat them as savings. In our calculations, we assume an opportunity cost of 2% per year, use our estimates of U.S. government depreciation for that sector, and standard declining-balance techniques for the others.

We do not examine education and R&D adjustments. As we have just argued, depreciation of these intangibles is difficult to measure, and neglecting them is likely to lead to only small errors. We focus on adjustments to include consumer durables expenditures and military investment as saving items, for which depreciation is more readily measured and which are likely to be important in comparing net national saving in the two countries.

4   Results

Table 5.1 reports gross saving for Japan and the United States measured in three ways: first, as the U.S. NIPA reports saving which excludes government investment; second, as the OECD reports saving which includes government nonmilitary investment; third, including both government investment and expenditures on consumer durables as saving. The adjustments for nonmilitary investment and consumer durables leave the U.S. *gross* saving rate only 30% below the gross saving rate for Japan in

Table 5.1. *Japanese and U.S. gross savings rates*
(gross national savings/GNP)

Year	Excluding government nonmilitary investment (U.S. basis)	Including government nonmilitary investment (OECD basis)	Including government nonmilitary investment and consumer durables
Japan			
1970	32.1	40.2	42.1
1971	29.5	38.4	40.3
1972	28.3	37.9	39.9
1973	28.5	38.1	40.2
1974	27.5	36.5	38.5
1975	23.7	32.7	34.9
1976	23.9	32.7	34.8
1977	23.6	32.7	34.8
1978	23.2	33.1	35.1
1979	22.1	32.1	34.3
1980	22.0	31.7	33.7
1981	22.6	32.2	34.1
1982	22.1	31.2	33.1
1983	21.9	30.5	32.4
1984	23.7	31.6	33.5
1970–9	26.2	35.5	37.5
United States			
1970	15.2	18.4	24.8
1971	15.8	18.9	25.6
1972	16.5	19.4	26.3
1973	18.4	21.2	27.9
1974	16.9	19.8	26.1
1975	15.0	17.9	24.4
1976	15.8	18.4	25.2
1977	16.7	19.1	25.9
1978	17.8	20.3	27.0
1979	18.1	20.4	26.8
1980	16.2	18.5	24.7
1981	17.3	19.3	25.2
1982	14.1	16.0	22.2
1983	14.0	15.9	22.4
1984	15.7	17.5	24.1
1970–9	16.6	19.4	26.0

the 1970s, a decade average of 26% versus 37.5%. In contrast, the unadjusted gross saving rate in Japan is 83% higher than that in the United States, at 35.5% versus 19.4%.

Table 5.2 presents the usual net saving rates and various adjustments to them. The chief adjustments are to include consumer durables and both military and nonmilitary investment, net of depreciation, as saving.

The *net* saving rates for Japan and the United States, based on each country's respective national income accounts for the 1970s, were 25.5% for Japan and 7.7% for the United States. In the early 1980s, the U.S. figure dropped below 3%, and the Japanese figure stayed near 20%. Thus, the Japanese saved three times as much as Americans in the 1970s and more than six times as much in the early 1980s. With Blades and Sturm's numbers showing only a 30% shortfall in the 1970s, one would take a much more sanguine view of U.S. saving. But such relief may be misplaced for a number of reasons, chief of which are that the gross saving rates may be inappropriate, as mentioned earlier, and the usual comparisons of net saving rates include different goods as saving in the two countries.

In the following, we attempt to correct for such definitional differences. As an example, the U.S. net saving rate rises by 1.5 percentage points, about 20% for the decade of the 1970s, when put on a corresponding basis to include government nonmilitary investment; compare columns (1) and (2) in Table 5.2. Our remaining adjustments are in this same spirit.

Thus, in column (3) of Table 5.2, an adjustment similar to that in Table 5.1 is made. Net expenditures on consumer durables are included as saving. The definition of saving here is

$$SR = \frac{NNP - C - G + IC - DC + INM - DNM}{NNP + Rent - DC} \tag{4}$$

where SR is the saving rate, NNP is net national product, C is consumption by households, G is government consumption, IC is expenditures on consumer durables, DC is depreciation for consumer-durables purchases, and xNM is the relevant item for nonmilitary government. Because a larger share of saving in the United States than in Japan takes the form of consumer durables, this adjustment shrinks the gap between the U.S. and Japanese savings rates.

Column (4) of Table 5.2 adds government net expenditures on military capital as investment, with the appropriate rent included as income. This adjustment makes little difference for either country in the 1970s, but adds 0.4 to 0.7 percentage point to the U.S. saving rate in the early 1980s. The final column makes the additional adjustment of adding the

Table 5.2. *Japanese and U.S. net national savings rates, alternative definitions*

Year	(1) xNMI	(2) (1)+NMI	(3) (2)+CI +rent	(4) (3)+MI +MI rent	(5) (4)+ govt. rent
Japan					
1970	22.7	30.9	31.5	31.6	31.4
1971	19.6	28.6	29.4	29.5	29.2
1972	18.1	27.7	29.0	29.0	28.8
1973	18.9	28.2	29.8	29.8	29.5
1974	18.4	26.6	27.4	27.5	27.1
1975	14.7	22.6	23.4	23.4	23.0
1976	15.3	22.7	23.6	23.6	23.2
1977	14.9	22.6	23.5	23.5	23.1
1978	14.5	23.1	23.9	23.9	23.5
1979	13.2	21.8	22.8	22.9	22.4
1980	13.2	21.1	21.7	21.8	21.4
1981	13.7	21.4	21.8	21.9	21.5
1982	12.8	19.8	20.4	20.5	20.1
1983	12.4	18.6	19.3	19.5	19.0
1984	14.4	19.8	20.5	20.6	20.2
1970–9	17.0	25.5	26.2	26.5	26.1
United States					
1970	6.9	8.9	10.1	10.1	10.0
1971	7.6	9.5	11.3	11.3	11.1
1972	8.3	9.9	12.3	12.5	12.3
1973	10.5	12.2	14.6	14.6	14.4
1974	8.2	10.0	10.9	10.9	10.7
1975	5.3	6.9	7.9	8.0	7.9
1976	6.3	7.6	9.4	9.5	9.4
1977	7.3	8.4	10.5	10.5	10.3
1978	8.4	9.6	11.7	11.9	11.7
1979	8.4	9.5	11.1	11.3	11.2
1980	5.7	6.7	7.5	7.5	7.7
1981	6.9	7.6	8.5	8.7	8.6
1982	2.8	3.3	4.3	4.9	4.8
1983	3.0	3.5	5.0	5.8	5.7
1984	5.2	5.9	8.0	8.5	8.4
1970–9	7.7	9.2	11.0	11.0	10.9

Note: Column (1): U.S. National Accounts Basis (excludes government investment). Column (2): OECD National Accounts Basis (includes nonmilitary government investment). Column (3): Includes nonmilitary government investment and consumer durables as saving. Income includes imputed rent from consumer durables. Column (4): Adds military investment, and the appropriate rental flow, to the items included in column (3). Column (5): In addition to the items in column (4), includes the rental flow from government investment income.

rental flow from the nonmilitary government capital stock to national product. This last column is our "fully adjusted" case and will provide the basis for our subsequent comparisons. It includes both consumer durables and all government investment as saving and consistently includes the rental flow from the respective capital stocks as income.

As compared with the OECD definition of net saving in column (2), we note that including consumer durables and net military investment as saving raises the U.S. saving rate by 1.7 percentage points during the 1970s, almost a 20% increase. The Japanese saving rate in this period is raised by 0.6 percentage point, only a 3% increase. Japan's saving rate is still 2.5 times that of the United States, however. These adjustments to measures of saving rates still cannot account for a major share of the difference in the national saving rates.

In recent years, the U.S. saving rate has plummeted, mostly as a result of large federal government deficits. Our adjustments make a bigger difference in this period, mostly because of the military buildup. For 1984, the 14-point gap in column (2) is closed by the adjustments to the 12-point gap in column (5). Instead of saving 3.4 times as much as Americans, the Japanese saved "only" 2.4 times as much after the adjustments.

With government net saving seemingly accounting for so much of the U.S. saving shortfall in recent years, it is instructive to look at saving broken into its public and private components. Table 5.3 shows our "fully adjusted" net national saving, as well as private and government saving under the same concept. Government saving is broken into its components, government investment and the deficit, both divided by the fully adjusted concept of NNP. Note that the deficit is for all levels of government.[10] The deficit also does not include accrued government-employee pension liabilities, but rather only current collections and disbursements.

Social security financing adds considerable complexity to an accurate measure of government saving or dissaving. There is an implicit or potential debt due to the unfunded net liabilities in social security (Boskin, 1986b). In each country, this debt may be as large as or larger than the regular national debt. Changes in the net unfunded liabilities conceptually might be thought of as saving or dissaving. Although we are sympathetic to these budgetary implications, we do not deal here with changes in the rate at which unfunded social security liabilities accrue. But even focusing on current revenues and outlays can be a source of confusion. The United States is running a small social security surplus (about 0.5% of GNP, but growing), whereas Japan is running a relatively larger surplus (almost 3% of GNP). In the United States, the social security surplus is reported as part of the federal government figures (i.e., it reduces the federal deficit). The government deficit in Japan excludes the social security surplus, where it shows up either in private saving or as government financial investment.

Table 5.3. *Japanese and U.S. public and private net saving rates*[a]

Year	National saving	Private saving	Government saving	Government investment	Deficit
Japan					
1970	31.4	22.8	8.5	8.2	−0.4
1971	29.2	21.5	7.8	9.0	1.2
1972	28.8	21.9	6.9	9.6	2.7
1973	29.5	21.8	7.8	9.3	1.6
1974	27.1	19.9	7.1	8.2	1.0
1975	23.0	19.5	3.6	7.8	4.3
1976	23.2	21.0	2.2	7.4	5.1
1977	23.1	20.6	2.5	7.6	5.1
1978	23.5	22.0	1.6	8.5	6.9
1979	22.4	19.7	2.7	8.5	5.8
1980	21.4	18.5	2.9	7.8	4.9
1981	21.5	18.1	3.4	7.7	4.3
1982	20.1	16.9	3.2	6.9	3.7
1983	19.0	16.3	2.7	6.2	3.5
1984	20.2	17.6	2.5	5.4	2.9
1970–9	26.1	21.1	5.1	8.4	3.3
United States					
1970	10.0	9.2	0.8	1.9	1.2
1971	11.1	11.3	−0.1	1.8	1.9
1972	12.3	10.8	1.5	1.8	0.3
1973	14.4	12.1	2.3	1.6	−0.6
1974	10.7	9.4	1.3	1.7	0.4
1975	7.9	10.7	−2.8	1.7	4.5
1976	9.4	10.3	−0.9	1.1	1.0
1977	10.3	10.2	0.1	1.1	1.0
1978	11.7	10.3	1.4	1.4	−0.0
1979	11.2	9.2	2.0	1.3	−0.7
1980	7.6	7.6	−0.0	1.3	1.3
1981	8.6	8.7	−0.1	0.9	1.0
1982	4.8	7.8	−3.0	1.2	4.2
1983	5.7	9.0	−3.3	1.2	4.5
1984	8.4	10.9	−2.6	1.1	3.7
1970–9	10.9	10.4	0.6	1.6	1.0

[a] Based on the net national saving concept, adjusted for consumer durables, government investment, and appropriate rents [column (5) of Table 5.2].

The most striking feature of Table 5.3 is the high rate of Japanese government saving. Despite deficits in the later 1970s that represented 5% or 6% of adjusted NNP, government saving always remained positive in Japan because of the high rate of government net investment. Government investment was 8.4% of adjusted NNP in Japan in the 1970s, compared with 1.6% in the United States. This may be related to Japan's rapid growth in the 1960s, which left its infrastructure lagging, so that this component of saving can be expected to continue its recent gradual decline.

With government saving comprising about 20% of total saving in Japan in the 1970s, but only about 5% in the United States in the same period, Japanese private saving was only double U.S. private saving in the 1970s. In 1984, Japan's net private saving rate was 17.6%, whereas the U.S. rate had rebounded to 10.9%. The U.S. private savings rate was only 37% lower than the Japanese rate.

Table 5.4 shows various consumption and investment components as fractions of adjusted NNP. From 1970 to 1979, private consumption as a fraction of NNP was only 4 percentage points higher in the United States than in Japan. Net purchases of consumer durables were 0.9 percentage point higher in the United States. The main differences depressing saving in the United States come in the government sector. Government consumption in the 1970s was 9 percentage points higher in the United States, at 23% of NNP, than in Japan. By the early 1980s, though, Japanese government consumption had risen to 17% of expanded NNP, to within 6 percentage points of U.S. government consumption. As noted earlier, government investment was 7 percentage points higher in Japan than in the United States in the 1970s, at about 8.5% of NNP. Note that this was equal to more than 75% of U.S. net saving in the period, and to about a quarter of Japanese saving.[11]

5   Conclusion

We have examined two extreme views with respect to relative saving rates in the United States and Japan that we have labeled the traditional view and the revisionist view. The former view stresses comparisons of either gross household saving rates out of disposable income or each country's net national saving rate as defined by its own national income accounts. In either case, the saving rate in Japan is several times that in the United States. Much public attention has focused on this apparent enormous difference. The latter view stresses differences in the form of saving among countries and argues, sometimes casually, that inclusion of items such as consumer durables and education would eliminate a large part of the gap in the saving rates between the two countries.

In this chapter we attempt to provide alternative measures of gross and, especially, net national saving rates in the two countries for the period 1970 to 1984. We pay particular attention to adjustment of the data

Table 5.4. *Various components of NNP as fractions of adjusted NNP*

Year	C/NNP	G/NNP	CI/NNP	GI/NNP	MI/NNP	NMI/NNP
Japan						
1970	59.4	10.3	0.7	8.2	0.10	8.1
1971	60.8	11.3	0.8	9.0	0.11	8.9
1972	60.9	11.9	1.3	9.6	0.11	9.5
1973	59.9	12.3	1.6	9.3	0.09	9.2
1974	61.2	13.9	0.8	8.2	0.11	8.1
1975	64.1	15.4	0.8	7.8	0.07	7.8
1976	64.0	15.3	0.9	7.4	0.04	7.3
1977	64.0	15.5	0.9	7.6	0.06	7.6
1978	63.8	15.5	0.9	8.5	0.07	8.4
1979	64.7	15.8	1.0	8.5	0.10	8.4
1980	65.4	16.4	0.6	7.8	0.12	7.7
1981	65.0	16.9	0.5	7.6	0.14	7.5
1982	66.3	17.2	0.7	6.9	0.14	6.8
1983	67.2	17.5	0.7	6.2	0.17	6.1
1984	66.2	17.4	0.8	5.4	0.15	5.2
1970–9	62.3	13.7	1.0	8.4	0.09	8.3
United States						
1970	66.7	23.3	1.3	1.9	0.01	2.0
1971	65.8	23.1	1.9	1.8	0.04	1.9
1972	65.1	22.6	2.4	1.8	0.16	1.6
1973	63.9	21.7	2.5	1.6	0.02	1.6
1974	66.5	22.7	1.1	1.7	− 0.0	1.7
1975	68.3	23.8	1.1	1.7	0.11	1.6
1976	67.6	23.1	1.9	1.4	0.15	1.3
1977	66.9	22.7	2.1	1.1	0.02	1.1
1978	66.5	21.8	2.1	1.4	0.19	1.2
1979	67.3	21.6	1.7	1.3	0.25	1.1
1980	69.7	22.7	0.8	1.3	0.24	1.0
1981	68.6	22.8	0.9	0.9	0.24	0.7
1982	71.4	23.9	0.9	1.2	0.61	0.6
1983	71.1	23.2	1.6	1.2	0.71	0.5
1984	68.8	22.8	2.2	1.1	0.51	0.6
1970–9	66.5	22.6	1.8	1.6	0.08	1.5

Note: C/NNP, consumption; G/NNP, government consumption; CI/NNP, consumer durables; GI/NNP, government investment; MI/NNP, military investment; NMI/NNP, nonmilitary government investment.

for consistent treatment of net saving in the form of consumer durables and in the form of government capital, as well as inclusion of the imputed rental flow from the stock of durables and government capital as income. We pay particular attention to net national saving, but also

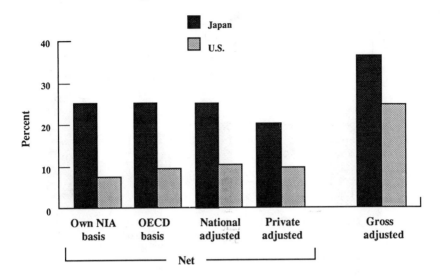

Figure 5.1. Saving rates in Japan and the United States, 1970–9.

distinguish between public and private saving. Figures 5.1 and 5.2 present a graphic summary of our findings. They deal, respectively, with the decade-average saving rate for the 1970s and the saving rate for 1984. In each figure, five sets of comparisons are presented: reading from left to right, four sets of net saving rates and, on the far right, gross saving rates. The far-left and far-right pairs of bar graphs portray pictorially the traditional and revisionist views, respectively. The first pair of bar graphs presents net national saving rates in Japan and in the United States on the basis of each country's own national income accounts (recall that they exclude nonmilitary government investment in the United States, but include it in Japan). Clearly, on this basis, the rate in Japan is several times that in the United States. Moving to the second pair of bar graphs, the two countries' net national saving rates are put on an OECD basis, which includes government nonmilitary investment as saving. This makes no difference to the Japanese saving rate, but increases the U.S. saving rate slightly in the 1970s.

The third pair of bar graphs presents net national saving rates as we have fully adjusted them to include net saving in the form of consumer durables and *all* net government investment as part of saving, and the imputed rental flows from their respective stocks of capital as net income. As can be seen, relative to either of the first two pairs of bar graphs, this raises the ratio of net national saving in the United States to that in Japan.

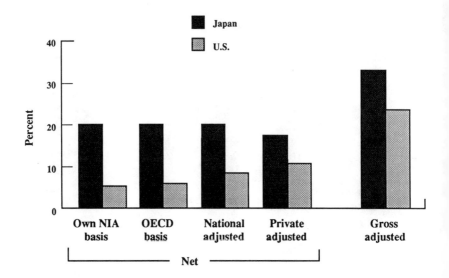

Figure 5.2. Saving rates in Japan and the United States, 1984.

The fourth pair of bar graphs in each figure represents net private saving, including purchases of consumer durables as saving and the imputed rental flow from the stock of durables as part of net national income. The private saving rate, properly measured, is substantially less than the national saving rate in Japan. For the decade average in the 1970s, the U.S. national and private saving rates are roughly the same. However, by 1984, a different result emerges. Whereas the net national saving rate for Japan substantially exceeds the private saving rate because net government saving is still quite substantial (despite large Japanese government deficits), net private saving in the United States exceeds net national saving. Indeed, this diagram is very close to the revisionist view, with the saving rate in Japan exceeding that in the United States by, relative to the previous comparisons, a modest amount. Perhaps the most startling and important finding concerns the comparisons of the third and fourth pairs of bar graphs in Figures 5.1 and 5.2. They document the substantial fraction of total national saving done in Japan through the public sector, in contrast to the substantial amount of dissavings in the aggregate done by the combined governmental units in the United States in 1984.

Finally, we present for comparison the gross national saving rates, adjusted to include purchases of consumer durables as saving, in the far-right pair of bar diagrams, a pictorial representation of what we have called the revisionist view.

What conclusions can we draw from this analysis? Although the difference in saving rates between Japan and the United States narrows considerably when one makes some sensible adjustments to the measures of saving and of income, net national saving in Japan is still more than twice that in the United States. However, net private saving rates in Japan and in the United States are far less disparate. Although the difference is not inconsiderable, the view that the saving rate in Japan is a large multiple of that in the United States, obtained by examining gross household saving rates out of disposable income, is clearly misleading.

Are differences of this magnitude in net national saving and net private saving important and worthy of further study and analysis? We believe the answer is yes. Despite the fact that our analysis suggests that the disparity in saving rates between the United States and Japan, especially for private saving as opposed to national saving, is not nearly so large as is generally supposed, it is still substantial. Differences of this magnitude are likely to be somewhat easier to explain, but still enormously important to the world economy.

First, consider the difference between a net private saving rate of 17% and a rate of 11%, roughly the figures in 1984 for Japan and the United States, respectively. Such a difference could result quite easily from any or all of the following factors:

1. Differences in regard to age structure of the population and rates of economic growth, combined with some amount of life-cycle saving, can lead to a higher saving rate in the economy that is growing more rapidly.

2. Even at similar growth rates, differences in life expectancy and the age of retirement can easily lead to differences in saving rates of this magnitude; the "normal" age of retirement from career jobs in Japan appears to be 55 years, whereas 60, 62, or 65 appears to be historically the age of retirement in the United States (this may drift upward with the elimination of mandatory retirement prior to age 70). Even a five-year difference in the typical age of retirement, given the same rate of time preference, economic growth, and life expectancy, could explain the difference in net private saving rates.[12]

3. Differences in tax structure, particularly with respect to saving. Japan appears to allow a much greater degree of relief from double taxation of saving inherent in an income tax through various tax-free saving devices. Also, these devices appear to provide greater liquidity than our analogues, which usually require funds to be held until age 59.5 years in order to be withdrawn without penalty; our individual retirement accounts (IRAs) have a $2,000-per-year maximum, and approximately half of those who participate contribute the maximum, suggesting that many are at a corner: They would like to contribute more and are doing their

marginal saving at the after-tax rate of return. Of course, in the United States there are various other tax-free vehicles for saving, especially housing, employer-prepaid pensions, and life insurance.

4. Differences in the tax treatment of housing and in financial-market treatment of collateral and financing of housing, as stressed by Makin (1986).

Clearly, we could continue enumerating such factors, but note that we have not had to resort to "cultural differences." In fact, it has been pointed out to us that the saving rate in Japan was much lower in the early part of this century than it is today. Surely, if cultural differences were major causes of higher saving rates in Japan, one might have expected a convergence, rather than a divergence, of saving rates in the more recent period.

Although our estimates of the disparities in net private saving rates between the United States and Japan are much smaller than the traditional view suggests, we do conclude that they are nonetheless important. Japan is the largest supplier of capital to the world capital market. In part, this represents the other side of Japan's trade surplus. The trade surplus and capital exports are determined simultaneously by relative saving and investment rates. The United States has become a large capital importer in recent years, which has prevented its investment rate from falling and interest rates from rising still further, but diverting capital from investment in the rest of the world.

A decade or two ago, an examination of saving rates in Japan by scholars in the United States would have been pursued only by those whose interests focused on Japan. But Japanese saving has become so important to the world economy (especially when we take into consideration the relatively low saving rate in the world's largest economy, the United States, and its new role as a large capital importer) that anyone interested in the current or future course of the world economy must be interested in the saving (and investment) rates in the world's two largest economies: Japan and the United States.

There are reasons to believe that the Japanese private saving rate may fall in the future. A primary reason might be the projected relatively rapid aging of the Japanese population in the coming decades, which should shift resources from younger, richer savers toward older dissavers in Japan.[13] Of course, this may be partly offset by a response of private saving to the maturation of the Japanese public-sector infrastructure. If the Japanese government investment falls substantially, say in a decade or two, is it likely that 20% (roughly, the marginal propensity to save) or more of this decrease will be offset by increased private saving? Or will it merely be soaked up by increased government consumption, as in other countries?

Will the U.S. private saving rate continue to rebound? Will the baby-boom generation begin to save substantially more as it enters its peak earning years? What about the period of its retirement early in the next century? The answers to these questions will have significant effects on the future performance of world capital markets, as well as on the respective economic performances of Japan and the United States. Thus, despite the likelihood that the disparity between the saving rates in the two countries is less than is commonly supposed, explaining the relatively high saving rate in Japan and the relatively low saving rate in the United States, analyzing the effects of current policies on these saving rates, projecting these saving rates into the future, and analyzing the likely influence of possible alternative policies on the future paths of saving in Japan and the United States all are urgent research priorities.

ACKNOWLEDGMENTS

We would like to thank Mariko Fuji and Kazuo Ueda for generous assistance in obtaining data and the American Enterprise Institute (AEI) for financial support for this research. This chapter was originally presented at a conference of the AEI/Ministry of Finance, Japan, April 9–10, 1986, held at the American Enterprise Institute, Washington, D.C. We thank the participants for many valuable suggestions. This research was performed while J. M. Roberts was a John M. Olin Graduate Research Fellow at Stanford University.

NOTES

1. The wealth of citizens could be abroad as well, whether directly or via retained earnings of foreign subsidiaries of domestic parent firms.
2. This is a problem for measuring national saving only to the extent of external holdings of bonds – a growing phenomenon. Obviously, the internal holdings cancel across sectors.
3. This is probably a good approximation for the (actively traded) private sector. For the public sector, obviously, no direct market values are available.
4. We hope in subsequent work to address the issue of measurement of depreciation of private capital.
5. As a comparison, depreciation of private capital was 15.0% of NNP in Japan in 1983, and 13.6% of NNP in the United States, where U.S. NNP excludes nonmilitary government depreciation so as to be comparable with Japan.
6. See David and Scadding (1974). However, to the extent that adverse selection problems lead to a form of credit rationing, one might wish to take separate account of business and household savings, as corporate cash flow will be a determinant of business investment.
7. Boskin (1986a) examines the sensitivity of estimates to alternative estimates of R. We do not believe that plausible alternative values would make much of a difference to U.S. rates; measurement of real rates in Japan is somewhat more complex because of the system of compensating balances.
8. Luxembourg is the highest.

9. These and other issues are discussed in Kendrick (1976).
10. We ignore the capital gains to the government, and capital losses to the private sector, due to inflation eroding the real value of previously issued public debt. In recent years, this adjustment has amounted to as much as 2% of national income.
11. It may seem surprising that net military investment in Japan was so close to U.S. net military investment in the 1970s. This occurs because the much larger stock of U.S. military capital generated much larger depreciation, offsetting higher levels of gross investment. Gross military investment in Japan was 0.3% of NNP in the mid-1970s, but 1.1% of NNP in the United States.
12. We obtain results of this type from sensitivity analysis of simulations of saving rates based on life-cycle models of capital accumulation, such as those in Summers (1981) and Evans (1983).
13. Because of changes in social security laws in Japan, the retirement age in Japan has risen in recent years and can be expected to rise for several more years. We can therefore expect the disparity in saving rates from this source to shrink in coming years.

REFERENCES

Adams, G. F., and S. M. Wachter (eds.) (1986). *Savings and Capital Formation: The Policy Options.* Lexington, Massachusetts: Lexington Books.

Auerbach, A. J. (1982). "Saving in the U.S.: Some Conceptual Issues." In P. Hendershott (ed.), *The Level and Composition of Household Saving.* Cambridge, Massachusetts: Ballinger.

Barro, R. J. (1979). "Are Government Bonds Net Wealth?" *Journal of Political Economy,* Vol. 82, p. 1095.

Blades, D. (1983). "Alternative Measures of Saving." *OECD Occasional Studies,* June.

Blades, D., and P. H. Sturm (1982). "The Concept and Measurement of Savings: The United States and Other Industrialized Countries." In *Saving and Government Policy.* Federal Reserve Bank of Boston Conference Series, No. 25.

Boskin, M. J. (1986a). "Theoretical and Empirical Issues in the Measurement, Evaluation, and Interpretation of Postwar U.S. Saving." In G. F. Adams and S. M. Wachter (eds.), *Savings and Capital Formation: The Policy Options,* Lexington, Massachusetts: Lexington Books.

(1986b). *Too Many Promises: The Uncertain Future of Social Security.* Homewood, Illinois: Irwin.

Boskin, M. J., and L. J. Kotlikoff (1985). "Public Debt and U.S. Saving: A New Test of the Neutrality Hypothesis." In K. Brumner and A. Meltzer (eds.), *The "New Monetary Economics," Fiscal Issues, and Unemployment.* Amsterdam: North Holland.

Boskin, M. J., M. S. Robinson, and J. M. Roberts (1985). "New Estimates of Federal Government Tangible Capital and Net Investment." NBER Working Paper No. 1774.

David, P., and J. Scadding (1974). "Private Saving, Ultrarationality and Denison's Law." *Journal of Political Economy,* Vol. 82, p. 225.

Evans, O. J. (1983). "Tax Policy, the Interest Elasticity of Saving, and Capital Accumulation: Numerical Analysis of Theoretical Models." *American Economic Review,* Vol. 73, p. 398.

Hayashi, F. (1986). "Why is Japan's Saving Rate So Apparently High?" *NBER Macroeconomic Annual.*

Hulten, C. R., and F. C. Wykoff (1981). "The Measurement of Economic Depreciation." In C. R. Hulten (ed.), *Depreciation, Inflation, and the Taxation of Income from Capital.* Washington, D.C.: Urban Institute Press.

Hurd, M. D. (1986). "Savings and Bequests." NBER Working Paper No. 1826.

Kendrick, J. (1976). *The Formation and Stocks of Total Capital.* New York: Columbia University Press.

Makin, J. H. (1986). "Savings Rates in Japan and the United States: The Roles of Tax Policy and Other Factors." In G. F. Adams and S. M. Wachter (eds.), *Savings and Capital Formation: The Policy Options.* Lexington, Massachusetts: Lexington Press.

Shoven, J. B. (1984). "Saving in the U.S. Economy." In M. L. Wachter and S. M. Wachter (eds.), *Removing Obstacles to Economic Growth.* Philadelphia: University of Pennsylvania Press.

Summers, L. J. (1981). "Capital Taxation and Accumulation in a Life Cycle Growth Model." *American Economic Review,* Vol. 71, No. 4.

Tobin, J., and W. Buiter (1980). "Fiscal and Monetary Policies, Capital Formation, and Economic Activity." In G. M. Von Furstenberg (ed.), *The Government and Capital Formation.* Cambridge, Massachusetts: Ballinger.

CHAPTER 6

The Japanese current-account surplus and fiscal policy in Japan and the United States

Kazuo Ueda

1   Introduction

The purpose of this chapter is to analyze the causes of the recent large surplus in the Japanese current account. Among these causes we pay particular attention to the role played by differences in fiscal policy between Japan and the rest of the world, notably the United States.

In 1984, the Japanese current-account surplus reached a historical high of $35 billion. Given that the two economies were close to business-cycle peaks, a significant part of the current-account surplus must have been noncyclical or structural. This noncyclical portion of the surplus is the focus of this chapter. We start with an analysis of savings and investment behavior in Japan and the United States, rather than with the current account itself. This enables us to show how changes in fiscal policy that alter domestic savings and investment lead to changes in the current account.

The analysis of savings and investment behavior is carried out in terms of a simple two-country model in which two endogenous variables, the real interest rate and the real exchange rate, determine savings and invest-ment.[1] The model abstracts from economic growth; therefore, various stock-flow interactions are not explicitly modeled. These include the ef-fect of the capital stock on investment,[2] the effect of a change in wealth on savings, and the effect of a change in net foreign assets on the ex-change rate. Consequently, the analysis of this chapter does not reveal what the levels of savings, investment, and the current account will be in the very long run. On the other hand, the model does tell us whether domestic or foreign, private or public savings or investment has been re-sponsible for the recent current-account surplus.

In the next section, the basic framework of the analysis is explained. In Section 3, the empirical part of the chapter, we apply the framework

145

to the "world" consisting of Japan and the United States. We first estimate the autonomous components of net savings in each country. We then estimate an equation that relates the current account to these components and the cyclical variables. The estimated equation is then used to assess the quantitative importance of cyclical and noncyclical factors. We then look at the noncyclical component of the current account more carefully to determine the contributions of net savings and fiscal policy in the two countries. This analysis reveals clearly the importance of the countries' different fiscal policies in determining the recent movement of the Japanese current account. In the last section we discuss some of the limitations of the analysis.

2   The theoretical framework

In this section we consider a two-country full-employment macroeconomic model in which savings and investment behavior determines the level of the current account. In the model, net domestic savings for each country is a function of the real interest rate. The current account is related to the real exchange rate. In equilibrium, the real exchange rate and the real interest rate are determined by the exogenous parts of savings, investment, and the current account. As stated earlier, we abstract from the dynamics arising from the responses of savings and investment to wealth accumulation. This means that even in the long-run equilibrium of the model, asset stocks may not be at optimal levels. This simplification has been necessary to consider equilibria in which the current account is not equal to zero.

In this model there is a causality running from net savings to the current account. That is, the exogenous parts of the net savings of the two countries affect the current account, but not vice versa. This is a result of the assumption that the real exchange rate does not affect net savings. This assumption may be very restrictive, but it helps to highlight the role of savings and investment in the determination of the current account.

Mathematically, let us consider a world consisting of two economies, a home country and a foreign country, linked by trade in goods and services and in financial assets. We write the goods-market equilibrium conditions of the two countries as follows:

$$PS - f = NX \tag{1}$$

$$PS^* - f^* = -NX \tag{2}$$

where PS, f, and NX are net private savings, government budget deficit, and the current account of the home country, respectively – all at full employment. The variables for the foreign country are shown with an asterisk.[3] Net private savings are assumed to depend on the real interest rate:

$$PS = S_p + s_1 r \qquad (3)$$

$$PS^* = S_p^* + s_1^* r^* \qquad (4)$$

where r is the real interest rate, and S_p summarizes the effects of exogenous variables on net savings.[4] The parameters s_1 and s_1^* are assumed to be positive. Throughout the chapter, we assume that private agents do not fully discount all future tax burdens at the market interest rate, because either liquidity constraints exist or the time horizon of agents is finite. Given this assumption, the level of the government budget deficit affects the equilibrium of the economy.

The current account is assumed to be of the form

$$NX = c_0 + c_1 x \qquad (5)$$

where c_1 is a positive constant, and x is the real exchange rate (foreign price divided by domestic price). In equation (5), we have assumed away interest payments on foreign assets.

Turning to the assets markets, we assume that domestic and foreign assets are perfect substitutes. Given that we do not introduce any dynamics into the model, rational expectations require that the expectation of the change in the real exchange rate be equal to zero. Then, we have

$$r = r^* \qquad (6)$$

Equations (1)–(6) determine the levels of the endogenous variables. The formulas for these are

$$r = r^* = \frac{1}{s_1 + s_1^*} [(f - S_p) + (f^* - S_p^*)] \qquad (7)$$

$$x = \frac{1}{c_1} \left(\frac{s_1^*}{s_1 + s_1^*} (S_p - f) - \frac{s_1}{s_1 + s_1^*} (S_p^* - f^*) - c_0 \right) \qquad (8)$$

$$NX = \frac{s_1^*}{s_1 + s_1^*} (S_p - f) - \frac{s_1}{s_1 + s_1^*} (S_p^* - f^*) \qquad (9)$$

These formulas show the classical nature of the equilibrium in that the interest rate, the real exchange rate, and the current account are mainly determined by the determinants of savings and investment. More specifically, the real interest rate and the current account are determined only by S_p, f, S_p^*, and f^* - autonomous levels of private and government net savings. That is, there is a causality in this model that runs from savings and investment variables to the current account. A shock to the current account – a change in c_0 – will affect only the real exchange rate, not the interest rate or the current account, because of the absence of terms of trade effects on net savings.

Interpretation of the formulas is straightforward. An increase in private or government savings in either country lowers the equilibrium real interest rate. At that real interest rate, one country's total domestic savings may not equal domestic investment. The discrepancy creates an international capital inflow or outflow. The exchange rate is determined at the level where the current account is equal to the negative of the capital account.

Thus, the equilibrium current account tends to improve when net savings in the home country increase relative to those of the foreign country. The magnitude of the impact of autonomous changes in net savings on the current account depends on the interest elasticities of net savings.

3   Empirical analysis

In view of the basic current equation (9), our empirical analysis proceeds in two steps. First, we estimate the major determinants of the equilibrium level of the current account, S_p, f, S_p^*, and f^*. This is accomplished by estimating savings and investment functions for the private sector with full-employment government budget deficits. Second, we regress the current account on these and variables representing cyclical movements in the current account. This estimation allows us to decompose the behavior of the current account into two components, an equilibrium or structural part and a cyclical part consisting of deviations from the equilibrium.

3.1   *Estimation of net savings of private and government sectors*

The series for the full-employment government budget deficit for the United States used in the following is basically the same as that estimated by de Leeuw and Holloway (1983). We also used their estimate of full-employment GNP. For Japan, we constructed a full-employment GNP series using the same method as for the United States. We then estimated tax functions to produce an estimate of the full-employment budget deficit for Japan. The procedure adopted is more carefully explained in Appendix 1.

We now turn to the specification of savings and investment equations. The estimation results and the definitions of the variables are presented in Appendix 2. The equations for fixed investment are of the usual Jorgenson type in which investment depends on the level of production, the initial capital stock, and the user cost of capital, which in turn is composed of the relative price difference between output and investment goods, the real interest rate plus the depreciation rate, and a factor that takes account of the corporate tax system. The levels of investment and capital stock are divided by full employment GNP to adjust for the trends in these variables. Most variables have the right signs and are significant in both the Japanese and U.S. equations.[5]

The equations for housing investment contain as explanatory variables the interest rate (for the U.S. equation, this is adjusted for the tax deductibility of interest payments) and income relative to housing price. Although, theoretically, investment should be affected by a real interest rate, in the case of the United States the use of a nominal interest rate yielded a better estimation result than using a real rate. Therefore, we present two sets of estimation results for housing investment, one with the nominal interest rate and the other with the real rate.

The savings functions are of the usual life-cycle-theory type, but they allow for estimation of the degree to which agents are forward-looking. More specifically, as shown in Appendix 3, the coefficient on the budget-deficit variable measures the extent to which agents discount future income streams at a higher rate than the market rate of interest. The larger the coefficient, the closer the agent's behavior is to the neoclassical or Ricardian case. On the other hand, the complete Keynesian case corresponds to a value of the coefficient equal to 1 minus the propensity to consume out of income.

The estimation results show that the coefficient is close to 0.3 in both countries. This implies that consumers discount future income and taxes at a very high rate. For example, the estimate for the United States indicates that with a propensity to consume of 0.9 and a real interest rate of 5%, people discount future income at a rate of about 350%. In other words, the time horizon for the average consumer is very short.[6] Thus, people do not seem to pay much attention to prospective future tax increases when there is a government budget deficit.

The Japanese equation contains a variable representing the importance of bonus payments in order to capture long-run movements in household savings. This variable has been found to exert a significant impact on the savings rate for Japanese households (Ishikawa and Ueda, 1984).

The estimates can now be used to calculate the autonomous parts of private and government net savings. In order to calculate S_p and S_p^*, we substituted full-employment GNP wherever actual GNP appears. The real interest rate was made equal to a constant of 3.1% – the average of U.S. and Japanese real rates over the last 10 years. The results are shown in Figures 6.1 through 6.6. All series are shown relative to full-employment GNP.

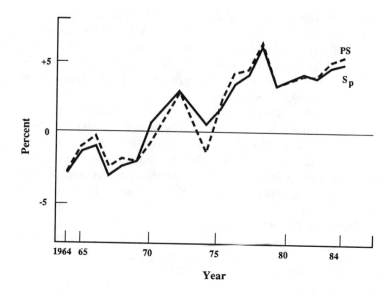

Figure 6.1. Net savings of the Japanese private sector (housing investment 1).

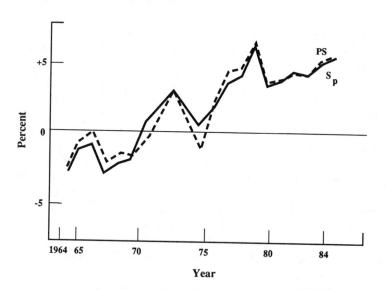

Figure 6.2. Net savings of the Japanese private sector (housing investment 2).

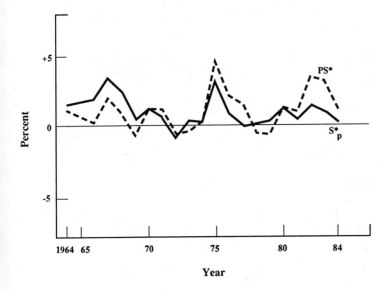

Figure 6.3A. Net savings of the U.S. private sector (housing investment 1).

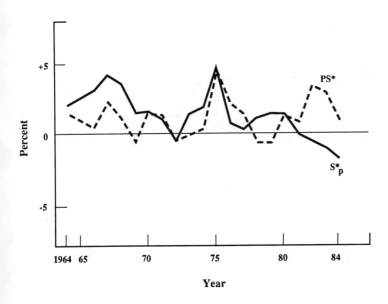

Figure 6.3B. Net savings of the U.S. private sector (housing investment 2).

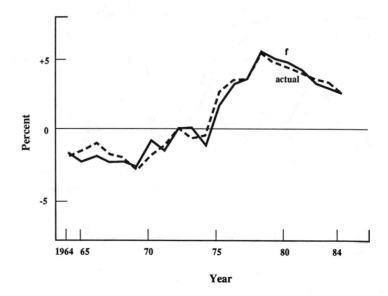

Figure 6.4. Japanese government budget deficit.

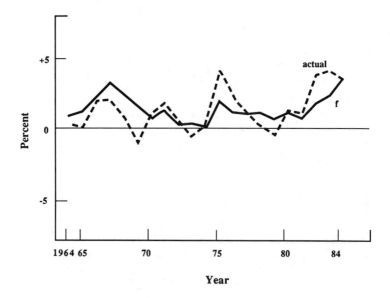

Figure 6.5. U.S. government budget deficit.

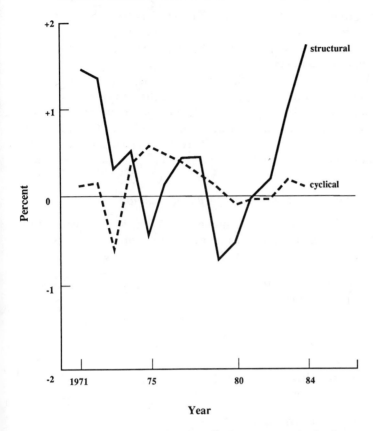

Figure 6.6. Structural and cyclical movements in the Japanese current account: equation (11).

In the United States, S_p^* is much smoother than actual net savings. It seems that a large part of the movement in U.S. net savings is cyclical. In the last few years, the movements in S_p^* have been quite variable, depending on the choice of the housing-investment equation. This, of course, is a result of the difference in the interest elasticities in the two specifications. With the nominal-rate specification, U.S. net private savings decreased sharply in the last few years, whereas this decrease was not as pronounced with the real-rate specification.

There is a positive trend in Japanese net private savings. In the 1960s, S_p was negative, whereas it has been positive since the early 1970s. The increase in S_p in the 1970s was due to stagnant levels of investment. It is important to note that S_p hit its peak in the late 1970s and then decreased sharply in 1979. Although it has increased slightly since then, the behavior of S_p alone does not seem to explain the very large increase in the current-account surplus in the last few years.

It is apparent from Figures 6.4 and 6.5 that there have been very divergent behaviors of the deficits in the two countries in the last few years. The Japanese deficit hit its peak in the late 1970s and has been decreasing steadily since then. The U.S. deficit has increased sharply in the last few years. One would expect that these different movements in f and f^* have had strong impacts on the behavior of the Japanese current account.

3.2   Estimation of the current-account equation

We are now in a position to estimate the current-account equation explained at the beginning of this section. The following two equations have been estimated:

$$\text{NX} = 0.0911 + 0.529(S_p - f) - 0.136(S_p^* - f^*) + 0.234\frac{y^*}{\bar{y^*}} - 0.321\frac{y}{\bar{y}}$$
$$\quad\;\;(1.07)\qquad(5.09)\qquad\quad(-5.28)\qquad\qquad(2.94)\qquad(-2.72)$$

$$R^2 = 0.851, \qquad \text{SE} = 0.631 \times 10^{-2}, \qquad \rho = -0.500 \tag{10}$$
$$\qquad\qquad\qquad\qquad\qquad\qquad\qquad\qquad(-1.77)$$

$$\text{NX} = 0.128 + 0.407(S_p - f) - 0.263(S_p^* - f^*) + 0.0418\frac{y^*}{\bar{y^*}} - 0.169\frac{y}{\bar{y}}$$
$$\quad\;\;(1.24)\qquad(3.02)\qquad\quad(-4.23)\qquad\qquad(0.467)\qquad(-1.25)$$

$$R^2 = 0.788, \qquad \text{SE} = 0.698 \times 10^{-2}, \qquad \rho = -0.328 \tag{11}$$
$$\qquad\qquad\qquad\qquad\qquad\qquad\qquad\qquad(-1.05)$$

The first equation uses the nominal-interest-rate specification for housing investment, whereas the second equation uses the real-rate specification; t-statistics are in parentheses. The variables NX, S_p, f, S_p^*, and f^* are measured relative to *Japanese* full-employment GNP. The period of estimation was chosen to be 1971 to 1984 in view of strong controls on international capital flows that existed in Japan in the 1950s and 1960s.[7]

Both estimation results are consistent with our theoretical framework, although the impact of the cyclical variables is weaker in equation (11).[8] The four net savings variables exert strong effects on the Japanese current account.

The results in equations (10) and (11) can be used to decompose the movements in the current account into structural and cyclical components. The cyclical part is the sum of the constant and the fourth and fifth terms, and the structural part is the sum of the second and third terms.

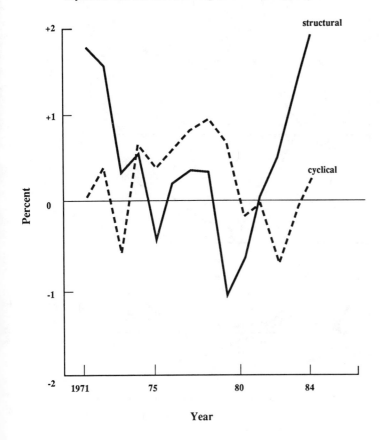

Figure 6.7. Structural and cyclical movements in the Japanese current account: equation (10).

The two components are shown in Figures 6.7 and 6.8. Both figures show that the structural component has increased sharply over the last few years. It is now about 2% of GNP. The remaining surplus of about 1% either is cyclical or is the contribution of the error term. Thus, a major part of the surplus is noncyclical.

Next, we can decompose the structural surplus into its four components. For this purpose we multiply each of S_p, S_p^*, f, and f^* by its coefficient in equations (10) and (11). The results are shown in Figure 6.9.

Among the four determinants of the structural current account, Japanese net private savings and the U.S. government budget deficit have worked to create a surplus, whereas the Japanese government budget

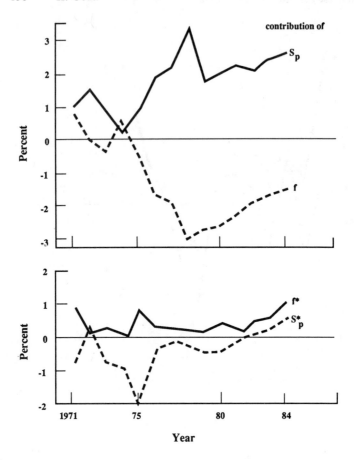

Figure 6.8.

deficit decreases the surplus. U.S. private net savings has not exerted a strong impact on the Japanese current account except during the mid-1970s. Thus, there is an element of truth to the argument that Japan has entered a stage of being a net creditor country as a result of an increase in private savings over investment.

However, the reasons for the recent rise in the structural surplus (by about 2–3% of GNP in the last four or five years) are slightly different. The two figures reveal clearly that the increase in the U.S. budget deficit and the decrease in the Japanese budget deficit are the major reasons for the increase in the surplus. In Figure 6.8, the contribution of the two factors is about 1.6% in terms of the change between 1981 and 1984, whereas

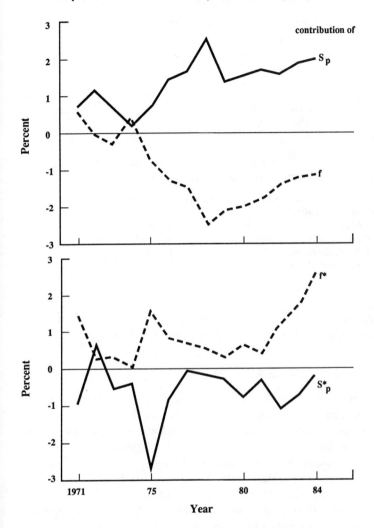

Figure 6.9.

it is 2.8% in Figure 6.9. Whether the U.S. deficit has been more responsible than the Japanese deficit for the increase in the surplus is hard to
determine given the large difference between the two cases. In any case,
*divergence in fiscal policies in the two countries has been the major cause
of the increase in the Japanese current-account surplus.* In addition, both
Japanese and U.S. net private savings have tended to increase the Japanese

Table 6.1. *Effects of policies to reduce the current-account surplus*

Policy[a]	ΔNX		ΔBuD	
	I[b]	II	I	II
A	−1.0	−1.0	−2.67	−1.38
B	−1.0	−1.0	1.77	2.29
C	−0.53	−0.40	0.78	0.78
D	−0.09	−0.07	0.08	0.08

[a]A: Decrease in government expenditures in the United States (ΔBuD is relative to U.S. GNP). B: Increase in government expenditures in Japan. C: Introduction of a 10% investment tax credit in Japan. D: Introduction of a 10% tax credit on purchases of new houses in Japan.
[b]Cases I and II correspond to equations (10) and (11), respectively.

current-account surplus in the last few years. But the contribution of these savings effects is smaller than that of fiscal policy.

3.3   Some policy simulations

In this section we carry out some simulations of policy actions that may lead to a decrease in the structural component of the Japanese current-account surplus. To do this, we can use the coefficient estimates of the individual savings and investment equations and the current-account equations. It may be appropriate to note at this point that one should be very careful about interpreting the results of the simulations. This is because we look at only the effect of, say, a fiscal expansion on the current account in the equilibrium of the model presented in Section 2. This means that we calculate something like a long-run effect, but with variables like full-employment GNP or the capital stock fixed. Also, in the short run, a fiscal expansion might have a stronger impact on the current account through its effect on the cyclical position of the economy rather than through a change in savings–investment balances.[9]

The results of policy simulations are presented in Table 6.1. Given the importance of the divergence in fiscal policies in the United States and Japan, we examine the effects of fiscal policies on the current account. We calculate first the size of a deficit reduction in the United States necessary to bring about a decrease in the Japanese current-account surplus of

1 percentage point relative to GNP. The required reduction in the U.S. budget deficit is fairly large. It is also apparent that complete elimination of the U.S. budget deficit would bring the structural component of the Japanese surplus almost down to zero.

Second, the size of the increase in the Japanese budget deficit required for a decrease in NX of 1 percentage point is calculated. The numbers are again very large. In order to eliminate the structural current-account surplus by only a Japanese action, the deficit must go up to about 6–7% of GNP. The third row shows the impact of a 10% investment tax credit in Japan. The impacts on NX and BuD are not much different from those that would be caused by an increase in government expenditures.

Finally, the last row calculates the impact of introducing a 10% tax credit for housing investment in Japan. The effects are calculated assuming that the policy is equivalent to a reduction in housing price by a factor that depends on the individual income tax rate. The policy is efficient in the sense that it can decrease the current-account surplus and yield only a relatively small increase in the budget deficit. However, we should not place too much importance on this result, given the poor performance of the housing-investment equation.

3.4   Implications for exchange-rate behavior

The analysis of current-account behavior in previous sections has important implications for the exchange rate. This is apparent from the theoretical framework in Section 2. We have focused on the current-account equation, equation (9), thus far. But the model also determines the value of the real exchange rate through equation (8). This can be easily calculated from the parameters of the current-account equation and the equilibrium level of the current account.

An example of such an analysis for a very recent period is presented in Ueda (1985). The procedure used is to estimate simple export and import functions and then to find a level of the exchange rate that equates the current account with the structural surplus calculated in Section 2.2. In the calculation, all variables that appear in the export and import functions are assumed to be exogenous, with the exception of the exchange rate. The difference between the current account and the trade balance is also assumed exogenous.

Figure 6.10 shows the equilibrium (nominal) exchange rate along with the actual exchange rate. For reference, Figure 6.11 shows the exchange rate that balances the current account and the trade account.

Clearly, the dollar has been overvalued. We assume that a balance in the current account is a condition for equilibrium. However, the extent

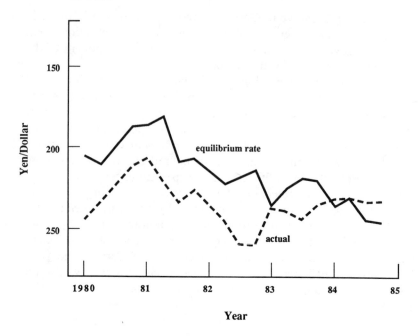

Figure 6.10. Equilibrium exchange rate.

of overvaluation becomes much smaller in Figure 6.10, where equilibrium implies that the value of the current account is equal to its structural component shown in Figure 6.8. The difference between the actual and equilibrium values is almost negligible for 1984.

Therefore, a fairly "high" value of the dollar can be considered an equilibrium rate given the investment–savings patterns in the two countries. This suggests that unless the patterns of savings and investment are changed, any attempt to change the value of the current exchange rate may not be successful except for a short period.

4   Qualification

The theoretical framework presented in Section 2 has been shown to be very useful in explaining the recent behavior of the current account and the exchange rate. More than half of the recent surplus in the Japanese current account is structural and largely a result of the divergent fiscal policies in the United States and Japan. Given the large structural surplus in the current account, the high value of the dollar is not puzzling at all.

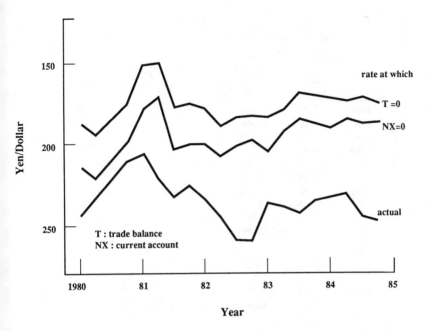

Figure 6.11. Trade balance, current account, and the exchange rate.

However, the analysis has been based on a number of simplifying assumptions. In the following section we discuss the implications of relaxing some of those assumptions.

4.1   Sustainability of the flow equilibrium

One of the most serious shortcomings of the analysis is that it has not paid attention to interactions between flow and stock variables. Among many possible sources of such interaction, let us focus on the large U.S. budget deficit and the imbalance in the current account.

The major problem with these imbalances is that we do not know whether or not the imbalances are sustainable. Given the causality from savings and investment to the current account in the model, the budget deficit is more important than the imbalance in the current account. Therefore, let us first discuss the budget deficit.

It is well known that the ratio of the budget deficit to GNP will increase indefinitely if the interest rate is above the growth rate and if the non-interest-payment component of the deficit stays constant relative to

Table 6.2. *Simulations of U.S. budget deficit and interest rate*

Year	B/Y	BuD/Y	i
Case 1			
1986	0.34	0.040	10.5
1987	0.37	0.044	11.1
1988	0.40	0.049	11.8
1989	0.44	0.056	12.8
1990	0.48	0.064	14.0
1991	0.53	0.074	15.6
1992	0.60	0.089	17.8
1993	0.68	0.111	21.1
1994	0.79	0.147	24.6
1995	0.95	0.196	32.1
Case 2			
1986	0.34	0.040	10.4
1987	0.35	0.038	10.1
1988	0.36	0.034	9.5
1989	0.37	0.032	9.3
1990	0.38	0.033	9.3
1991	0.39	0.033	9.4
1992	0.40	0.034	9.6
1993	0.41	0.036	9.8
1994	0.42	0.037	10.1
1995	0.43	0.039	10.4

GNP. Current statistics ($i = 10\%$, $Y = 5\%$ as of mid-1985 for the United States) show clearly that the U.S. budget deficit is unsustainable according to this criterion. Thus, it is not reasonable to assume that the model in Section 2 describes a long-run equilibrium.

The unsustainability of the budget deficit is not likely to be of great concern for market participants if it takes 20 or 30 years for the deficit–GNP ratio to begin to explode. However, an explosion starting within five years or so might well be of major importance to investors.

Table 6.2 examines this point in a very simple way. It shows the movement of the government-debt-to-GNP ratio (B/Y), the budget-deficit-to-GNP ratio (BuD/Y), and the nominal interest rate (i) for the next 10 years under two different sets of assumptions. Both cases assume that the GNP growth rate for 1985 is 2% in real terms and 5% in nominal terms, the nominal interest rate is 10%, and the stock of government bonds outstanding at the end of 1985 is equal to $1,224.7 billion. We then calculate the time path of the deficit assuming that net private savings will be zero for the next 10 years.

For case 1, we assume that real and nominal growth rates will be the same for the next 10 years, and the noninterest component of the deficit relative to GNP will stay at 1985 levels of 1%. The interest rate is calculated from an estimate of equation (7).[10]

As can be seen from the table, the three variables will start to explode in about four or five years. The mechanism behind this is straightforward. The deficit increases the stock of debt, which leads to higher interest payments. These higher payments, in turn, further raise the deficit and the interest rate.[11] As illustrated by the numbers for 1995, sustainability becomes a critical issue within a very short time in case 1.

In case 2, we assume that the growth rate of real GNP will be 4% from 1986 onward. Also, it is assumed that increases in taxes resulting from the increase in the growth rate will enable the government to cut the noninterest component of the budget deficit by 0.5% of GNP in 1987 and 1988. This noninterest component will be kept at zero thereafter. In sharp contrast to case 1, in case 2 the current equilibrium may be maintained for about 10 years. Consequently, the sustainability of the current situation seems to depend crucially on the medium-term growth rate of the U.S. economy. This might seem an obvious point. But the analysis reveals that a fairly small change in the growth rate will make a large difference in the simulation results. One could say that people who are currently buying U.S. assets and are financing the U.S. current-account deficit are acting on the assumption that case 2 is more realistic.

We can make a similar remark regarding the analysis of Krugman (1985) concerning the sustainability of the high value of the dollar. He calculates the future path of the U.S. current account and external debt given the assumptions built into market prices. His results show that the ratio of U.S. external debt to GNP will increase for the next 23 years and will reach a maximum of about 50%.[12] He concludes that the value of the dollar and the current-account deficit are not sustainable.

However, one can easily change the Krugman result drastically by changing the assumption about the growth rate of the U.S. economy. In Figure 6.12 we reproduce the Krugman result as case I. Cases II and III assume different growth rates for the U.S. economy. The size of the external debt decreases fairly quickly as the growth rate of the U.S. economy increases. Thus, this analysis makes the same point as Table 6.2: The assumption about the U.S. growth rate is a crucial factor in the discussion of the sustainability of the current situation. (The figure also shows the time path of Japanese external assets for comparison.)

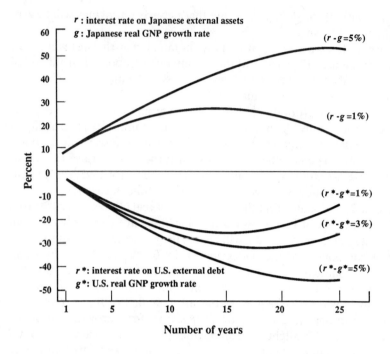

Figure 6.12. Simulating U.S. debt/GNP ratio.

4.2   *An alternative view*

Finally, let us briefly comment on the view that the competitiveness of the Japanese trade-goods sector is the cause of the Japanese current-account surplus.[13] This view is fairly widespread among private economists in Japan.

The competitiveness of the export sector, using the notation in Section 2, will mean either a very high value of x (perhaps an undervalued exchange rate) or a high value of c_0. The former cannot be an explanation of a current-account surplus unless one explains why x is high. The latter cannot be an explanation, either, because it will be offset by a change in x in our model. In this sense, the theoretical basis of the competitiveness view is very weak.

However, we may point out that two restrictive assumptions of our model prevent the competitiveness of the export sector from affecting the equilibrium value of the current account. First, as stated in Section 2, we have assumed that there are no terms-of-trade effects on savings or investment. Relaxing this assumption does make it possible for a change in c_0 to affect the equilibrium value of the current account. However, it still is not clear whether an increase in competitiveness would increase or decrease the current account. The direction of the effect depends on the sign of the assumed terms-of-trade effect.[14]

Second, we have assumed that full-employment GNP or the supply side of the economy is exogenous. However, the level of total income will depend on the way resources are allocated between various sectors of the economy. One might be able to construct a model in which an increase in competitiveness would be associated with an increase in savings, and thus an increase in the current account. Construction of such a model would be an interesting exercise. But it is still uncertain whether or not such a theory would be able to explain the rise in the Japanese current-account surplus in the last few years.

Appendix 1: Estimation of full-employment budget deficits

The United States

De Leeuw and Holloway (1983) presented an estimate of the full-employment deficit of the federal government. In addition, we estimated the full-employment deficits of the state and local governments by running the following equations:

1952–71

$$\frac{\text{BuDL}^*}{p^* \overline{y^*}} = -0.0243 + 0.0214 \frac{y^*}{\overline{y^*}} + 0.000208 \text{Time}$$
$$\quad\quad (-1.83) \quad\quad (1.73) \quad\quad (3.51)$$

$$R^2 = 0.416, \quad SE = 0.00153, \quad D.W. = 1.00$$

1972–84

$$\frac{\text{BuDL}^*}{p^* \overline{y^*}} = -0.0929 + 0.0881 \frac{y^*}{\overline{y^*}} + 0.000611 \text{Time}$$
$$\quad\quad (-3.34) \quad\quad (3.35) \quad\quad (3.48)$$

$$R^2 = 0.575, \quad SE = 0.00227, \quad D.W. = 1.30$$

where BuDL* is the actual deficit of the state and local governments, and time is a linear time trend. The preceding equations were then used to calculate the deficit level for state and local governments at full employment.

The result was added to the de Leeuw and Holloway estimate to obtain the full-employment deficit of the general government.

Japan

First, the series for full-employment GNP was constructed in the same way that the series for the United States was constructed by de Leeuw and Holloway (1983), except that we took a middle expansion path for the annual real GNP series, whereas theirs was based on the quarterly data.

In order to estimate the full-employment government deficit for Japan, we first estimated the following tax functions:

$$\frac{T_c}{py} = \underset{(-2.75)}{-116.8}\frac{1}{py} + \underset{(5.21)}{0.315t_c} - \underset{(-3.12)}{0.232}\frac{t_c p(-1)y(-1)}{py}$$

$$\underset{(-2.84)}{-0.00015d} + \underset{(4.29)}{0.0290t_c D_{78}} - \underset{(-0.280)}{0.00179t_c(-1)D_{78}(-1)}$$

$$\text{D.W.} = 1.68, \qquad \text{SE} = 0.0022$$

where T_c is total corporate tax payments, t_c is the statutory corporate tax rate, d is the number of firms with deficits relative to firms with surpluses, and D_{78} is a dummy taking the value 1 after 1978 to reflect a change in the corporate tax system in 1978. In particular, the d variable was included because the current tax system does not allow a full refunding of taxes when a firm reports a deficit.

Next, the estimation result for the remaining receipts of the government turned out to be

$$\frac{T_{NC}}{py} = \underset{(-1.07)}{-0.0652} + \underset{(1.41)}{1,392.7}\frac{1}{py} + \underset{(0.836)}{0.000690t_p} + \underset{(3.96)}{0.0157t_s}$$

$$\bar{R}^2 = 0.898, \qquad \text{D.W.} = 1.52, \qquad \text{SE} = 0.012$$

where T_{NC} equals receipts of the general government other than corporate taxes, t_p is a variable representing the progressivity of personal taxes (ratio of incomes of those whose marginal tax rate is above 30% to total personal income), and t_s is the average tax rate on social security and public medical insurance systems.

We then substituted full-employment GNP into these equations and assumed that government expenditures were exogenous to arrive at an estimate of the full-employment government budget deficit.

Appendix 2: Estimates for 1953–84 (t statistics in parentheses)

Fixed investment

United States

$$\frac{I_f^*}{p_I^* \overline{y^*}} = \underset{(-0.133)}{-0.291 \times 10^{-3}} + \underset{(7.47)}{0.422 \times 10^{-2} \frac{y^*}{\overline{y^*}}} - \underset{(-2.74)}{0.253 \times 10^{-4} \frac{p_I^*}{p^*}}$$

$$\underset{(-2.03)}{-0.118 \times 10^{-2} C^*} - \underset{(-0.0392)}{0.443 \times 10^{-4} \frac{K^*}{\overline{y^*}}}$$

$R^2 = 0.754, \quad$ SE $= 0.711 \times 10^{-4}, \quad$ mean of $I_f^*/p_I^* \overline{y} = 0.184 \times 10^{-3}$

Japan

$$\frac{I_f}{p_I \overline{y}} = \underset{(-0.0290)}{-0.628} + \underset{(3.67)}{0.660 \times 10^{-2} \frac{y}{\overline{y}}} - \underset{(-6.48)}{0.261 \times 10^{-4} \frac{p_I}{p}}$$

$$\underset{(-2.67)}{-0.120 \times 10^{-2} C} - \underset{(-3.22)}{0.133 \times 10^{-2} \frac{K}{\overline{y}}}$$

$R^2 = 0.637, \quad$ SE $= 0.171 \times 10^{-3}, \quad$ mean of $I_f/p_I \overline{y} = 0.105 \times 10^{-2}$

Housing investment 1

United States

$$\frac{I_H^*}{p_H^*} = \underset{(1.25)}{0.0880} - \underset{(-2.71)}{0.206[i^*(1-S^*) - \pi^*]} + \underset{(5.02)}{0.0358 \frac{p^* y^*}{p_H^*}}$$

$R^2 = 0.363, \quad$ SE $= 0.0556, \quad$ mean of $I_H^*/p_H^* = 0.225$

Japan

$$\frac{I_H}{p_H} = \underset{(-0.101)}{-1.51} - \underset{(-0.542)}{16.15(i - \pi)} + \underset{(6.12)}{0.0598 \frac{py}{p_H}}$$

$R^2 = 0.282, \quad$ SE $= 5.76, \quad$ mean of $I_H/p_H = 7.93$

Housing investment 2

United States

$$\frac{I_H^*}{p_H^*} = -0.0890 - 5.72i^*(1 - S^*) + 0.0888\frac{p^*y^*}{p_H^*}$$
$$\quad\quad (-0.803) \quad\quad (-5.29) \quad\quad\quad\quad (6.76)$$

$$R^2 = 0.575, \quad SE = 0.0416, \quad \text{mean of } I_H^*/p_H^* = 0.0863$$

Japan

$$\frac{I_H}{p_H} = -1.28 - 3.71i + 0.0589\frac{py}{p_H}$$
$$\quad\quad (-.0664)(-.0437) \quad\quad (5.56)$$

$$R^2 = 0.256, \quad SE = 5.78, \quad \text{mean of } I_H/p_H = 7.47$$

Savings

United States

$$\frac{S^*}{P^*} = -9.87 + 0.284\left(y^* - \frac{G^*}{P^*}\right) - 0.0663\left(y^*(-1) - \frac{G^*}{P^*}(-1)\right)$$
$$\quad\quad (-2.63) \quad\quad (7.88) \quad\quad\quad\quad (-1.76)$$

$$+ 0.294\frac{BuD^*}{P^*}$$
$$\quad (4.66)$$

$$R^2 = 0.991, \quad SE = 5.69, \quad \text{mean of } S^*/P^* = 178.5$$

Japan

$$\frac{S}{P} = 27{,}588.3 + 0.581\left(y - \frac{G}{P}\right) - 0.249\left(y(-1) - \frac{G}{P}(-1)\right)$$
$$\quad\quad (1.35) \quad\quad (7.35) \quad\quad\quad\quad (-2.95)$$

$$+ 0.259\frac{BuD}{P} - 0.434\frac{W}{B + W}$$
$$\quad (1.21) \quad\quad\quad (-1.48)$$

$$R^2 = 0.954, \quad SE = 1{,}265.6, \quad \text{mean of } S/P = 9{,}778.8$$

Definitions of variables

P^*	GNP deflator (U.S.), 1972 = 100
P	GNP deflator (Japan), 1975 = 100
y^*	Real GNP (U.S.), 1972 billions of dollars
y	Real GNP (Japan), 1975 billions of yen
$\bar{y}^*$	*Full-employment real GNP (U.S.), billions of dollars*
$\bar{y}$	*Full-employment real GNP (Japan), billions of yen*
I_f^*	Fixed investment of private sector (U.S.), billions of dollars
I_f	Fixed investment of private sector (Japan), billions of yen
I_H^*	Housing investment of private sector (U.S.), billions of dollars
I_H	Housing investment of private sector (Japan), billions of yen
S^*	Gross private savings (U.S.), billions of dollars
S	Gross private savings (Japan), billions of yen
G^*	Expenditures of the total government (U.S.), billions of dollars
G	Expenditures of the total government (Japan), billions of yen
BuD*	Government deficit (U.S.), billions of dollars
BuD	Government deficit (Japan), billions of yen
K^*	Capital stock (U.S.), billions of dollars
K	Capital stock (Japan), billions of yen
p_I^*	Private fixed-investment deflator (U.S.), 1972 = 100
p_I	Private fixed-investment deflator (Japan), 1980 = 100
p_H^*	Private housing investment deflator (U.S.), 1971 = 100
p_H	Private housing investment deflator (Japan), 1975 = 100
i^*	Interest rate on Aaa corporate bonds (U.S.)
i	Interest rate on telephone and telegraphic bonds (Japan)
π^*	Growth rate of GNP deflator (U.S.)
π	Growth rate of GNP deflator (Japan)
S^*	Personal income tax rate calculated as personal tax and nontax payment/personal income (U.S.)
S	Personal income tax rate calculated as personal tax and nontax payment/personal income (Japan)
W	Regular wages
B	Bonuses
C	$[(r+\delta)(1-k-uz)]/(1-u)$
r	Real interest rate calculated as i minus the growth rate of the private fixed-investment deflator
δ	Depreciation rate
k	Rate of investment tax credit
u	Corporate tax rate
z	Present value of depreciation

Appendix 3: Derivation of the savings equation

The savings equations presented in Appendix 2 are based on the following considerations. Let us consider a typical permanent-income-theory consumption function:

$$C = KY^p \tag{A1}$$

where C and Y^p are consumption and permanent disposable income, respectively. Assume that agents discount future income at a higher rate than the market rate of interest (Blanchard, 1985). Then, in a two-period context, Y^p is written as

$$Y^p = y_1 - T_1 + rB_1 + \frac{y_2 - T_2 + rB_2 + B_2}{1 + r + \rho} \tag{A2}$$

where y is before-tax income other than interest on government bonds, T is taxes, B is government bonds at the beginning of the period, r is the rate of interest, and ρ is the factor by which agents discount future income ($\rho > r$). The government budget constant implies

$$T_1 - G_1 - rB_1 + \frac{T_2 - G_2 - (1+r)B_2}{1+r} = 0 \tag{A3}$$

where G is government expenditures. Using (A3), we can rewrite (A2) as

$$Y^p = y_1 - G_1 + \frac{y_2 - G_2}{1 + r + \rho} + \frac{r + \rho}{1 + r + \rho}(G_1 + rB_1 - T_1) \tag{A4}$$

Therefore,

$$S = Y_1 = rB_1 - T_1 - C$$

$$= (1-K)(y_1 - G_1) - K\frac{y_2 - G_2}{1 + r + \rho} + \left(1 - K\frac{(r+\rho)}{1 + r + \rho}\right)(G_1 + rB_1 - T_1) \tag{A5}$$

This is the equation estimated in Appendix 2, except that we replace $y_2 - G_2$, the expectation of future income minus government expenditure, by a weighted average of current and past $y - G$. Note that in the extreme neoclassical case, where $\rho = 0$, the coefficient on the budget deficit becomes largest, equaling $1 - Kr/(1+r)$.

On the other hand, if agents are not forward-looking at all (i.e., $\rho = \infty$), the coefficient equals $1 - K$, and equation (A5) reduces to the usual Keynesian savings function. The specification (A5) allows us to test between the two hypotheses.

ACKNOWLEDGMENTS

The author would like to thank M. Fukao, K. Hamada, R. McKinnon, Y. Shinkai, and L. Summers for useful comments on earlier versions of this chapter, as well as S. Kamesui, T. Sakakibara, and K. Yoshida for able research assistance.

NOTES

1. This model, in its essence, is the same as that employed by Ueda (1985). However, the present analysis is new in its special emphasis on the role of fiscal-policy variables in determining the level of the current account.
2. An example of analysis of the effects of tax policy on investment and in turn on the capital stock and international competitiveness of a country can be found in Summers (1985).
3. It is implicitly assumed that the current account is initially zero. This allows us to use the same NX in the two equations.
4. It would be more appropriate to estimate the equations using a simultaneous-equations method. But, for simplicity, the equations in Appendix 2 are estimated either by ordinary least squares (OLS) or by a first-order autoregressive process (AR 1).
5. The tax factors in the formula for the U.S. cost of capital have been estimated by using the estimates of the effective tax rate by Auerbach (1983).
6. Ishikawa and Ueda (1984) reported a similar result using a different data set and a more elaborate estimation technique.
7. More realistically, controls had been fairly strong until 1980, when a new foreign-exchange law was enacted. However, the period since then has been too short for econometric estimation of an equation.
8. In order to correct the equation for the possible endogeneity of the y variable, we carried out instrumental-variables estimations of the equations using various instruments for y. However, the results were not very different from those reported in equations (10) and (11).
9. See, for example, Ishii, Mckibbin, and Sachs (1985) for an example of policy simulations designed to calculate more short-run impacts of policy changes.
10. For the sample period 1971–84, the estimated interest-rate equation is

$$r^* = 0.125 - 1.44(S_p^* + S_G^*) - 0.563(S_p + S_G)$$
$$\quad\ (1.16) \qquad\ (-3.50) \qquad\qquad (-3.45)$$

$$-1.29\frac{y^*}{\bar{y}^*} + 1.18\frac{y}{\bar{y}}, \qquad \hat{\rho} = -0.459$$
$$\ (-13.6) \qquad (8.40) \qquad\qquad\qquad (-1.51)$$

$$R^2 = 0.975$$

11. Note that given the assumption of zero net private savings, the time path of the budget deficit is also the time path of the current-account deficit.
12. Krugman does not consider the general-equilibrium implication of the movements in the current account. Also, he assumes that the market expects that the real exchange rate will keep changing indefinitely, and hence the real-interest-rate differential between the United States and foreign countries is not zero – an assumption different from that made in Section 2 of this chapter.

13. See, for example, Bank of Japan (1985).
14. See, for example, Deardorff and Stern (1978).

REFERENCES

Auerbach, A. (1983). "Corporate Taxation in the U.S." *Brookings Papers on Economic Activity,* Vol. 2, pp. 451–513.
Bank of Japan (1985). "On External Imbalances." *Monthly Review,* July (in Japanese).
Blanchard, O. J. (1985). "Debt, Deficits and Finite Horizons." *Journal of Political Economy,* Vol. 93(2), pp. 223–47.
Deardorff, A. V., and R. M. Stern (1978). "The Terms of Trade Effect on Expenditure." *Journal of International Economics,* Vol. 8, pp. 409–14.
de Leeuw, F., and T. M. Holloway (1983). "Cyclical Adjustment of the Federal Budget and Federal Debt." *Survey of Current Business,* Vol. 63, pp. 25–40.
Ishii, N., W. Mckibbon, and J. Sachs (1985). "Macroeconomic Interdependence of Japan and the United States: Some Simulation Results." NBER Working Paper No. 1637.
Ishikawa, T., and K. Ueda (1984). "The Bonus Payment System and Japanese Personal Savings." In M. Aoki (ed.), *The Economic Analysis of the Japanese Firm* (pp. 133–92). Amsterdam: North Holland.
Krugman, P. (1985). "Is the Strong Dollar Sustainable?" NBER Working Paper No. 1644.
Summers, L. (1985). "Tax Policy and International Competitiveness." Mimeograph.
Ueda, K. (1985). "Investment–Savings Balance and the Japanese Current Account." Institute of Fiscal and Monetary Policy, Ministry of Finance, Discussion Paper No. 1.

CHAPTER 7

Curing trade imbalance by international tax coordination

Iwao Nakatani

The biggest issue in Japan–United States economic relations over the next few years is likely to be the large and growing current-account imbalance. There are those who deny that this imbalance is a major problem; however, it has aspects that cannot be ignored. There are serious and persistent political issues that arise on the microeconomic level of individual industries, and there is the possibility that investment decisions will be made that will be inefficient from the viewpoint of international resource allocation.

In this chapter I argue that international differences in tax systems can be a major cause of external imbalance. I also make some observations concerning the inefficiency of investment decisions. I intend to demonstrate the importance of international coordination of tax systems as a policy issue for the future.

1 The external impact of surplus savings

The salient feature of the Japanese economy since the first oil crisis in 1973–4 has been the persistence of fiscal deficits and current-account surpluses in the face of a macroeconomic performance so good that it has drawn worldwide attention. To put it another way, the Japanese economy, which is extremely adept at recovering its equilibrium, may be described as macroeconomically well balanced in comparison with the other major industrial economies. At the same time, though, it suffers from persistent imbalances within its private, public, and external sectors. Unfortunately, Japanese economic policy over the past several years has not been based on a solid grasp of this distinctive feature of the country's economy.

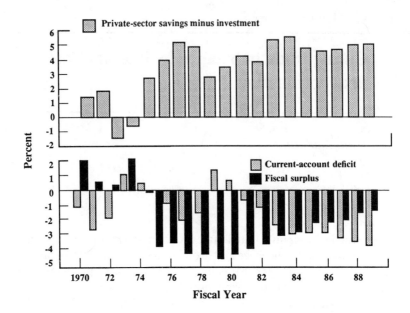

Figure 7.1. Japanese savings–investment balance by sector (ratio to GNP).

Figure 7.1 plots the savings–investment balance in the private sector, in the general government sector (central plus local government), and in the external sector (the current account) as a percentage of gross national product (GNP). The savings surplus (excess of savings over investment) of the private sector grew rapidly after the first oil crisis and has subsequently stayed at a high level. This is because investment in capital goods and in housing has lagged, whereas the savings rate has remained high.

In the national-account calculations, the private-sector savings surplus is identically equal to the sum of the fiscal deficit (the savings–investment gap in the general government sector) and the current-account surplus. Roughly speaking, the demand gap in the private sector is being filled by demand from the government and abroad. This relationship expresses only an ex post identity, not an ex ante relationship between household and corporate demand on the one hand and public-sector and external-sector demand on the other. The equation does not show the causal relationships that may exist among the variables. It does not, therefore, eliminate the possibility that the savings surplus has arisen as a result of the creation of a fiscal deficit and a current-account surplus.

Common sense, however, makes it more plausible to think of the present fiscal deficit and current-account surplus not as deliberate creations but rather as the results of insufficient private-sector demand. Consider, for example, that the current-account surplus has been increasing in spite of the measures implemented to open Japan's markets. This increase has even accelerated recently, and a continued gradual rise is predicted over the present high level. The fiscal deficit and current-account surplus should be seen as the outcome of the savings surplus in the private sector.

The predictions for future years given in Figure 7.1 are based on a projection published by the Japan Economic Research Center in March 1985. An interesting feature of these predicted values is the way the current-account surpluses increase gradually as a percentage of GNP, exactly offsetting the predicted decline in the share of the fiscal deficit. This suggests that although the government's program of fiscal rehabilitation may be able to control the budget deficit to some degree, the implementation of market-opening policies will not reduce the current-account surplus. The natural conclusion, therefore, is that the central issue in future economic policy should not be the fiscal deficit; rather, policy should focus on the external surplus.

The 1985 annual report of the U.S. Council of Economic Advisors states that market-opening measures, such as the removal of trade barriers, cannot alone rectify a current-account imbalance. A possible reason why the effects of market-opening policies are limited is discussed in detail in the next section.

The report correctly points out that a country's current-account balance is determined by domestic savings and investment behavior (including that of the public sector) relative to savings and investment behavior abroad. An imbalance can be redressed only through a change in savings or investment behavior abroad.

Seen in this light, the market-opening policies adopted in recent years have consistently attacked a symptom of the disequilibrium, namely, the current-account surplus, rather than its cause, the savings surplus. Some disorders, to be sure, improve during the course of symptomatic treatment. Needless to say, however, an attack on the root of the malady is preferable. If we follow this line of reasoning, we can see the need to investigate the causes of the persistent savings surplus and to formulate policies that will work directly to restore a savings–investment equilibrium.

2   Why are the effects of market-opening policies limited?

The view that the trade deficit is due to trade restrictions in Japan has received a great deal of attention in both the United States and Japan. Historically, Japan has liberalized its trade since the 1960s, and its tariff barriers are lower today, on average, than those in most other GATT

(General Agreement on Trade and Tariffs) nations, including the United States. However, problems remain, especially in areas such as agriculture, forestry, oil and petroleum products, and capital markets. Their removal not only would increase our trade but also would improve the standard of living for the Japanese, as well as for the consumers of other nations.

Many experts also agree that nontariff barriers in Japan, such as standards and certification procedures, are serious obstacles to the free flow of trade among countries. Prime Minister Nakasone's "action program" announced on July 31, 1985, was a significant step forward, but the general perception has been pessimistic about its actual effect in reducing the trade imbalance between Japan and the United States.

I do recognize that such action is essential, but the nature of the problem is not that simple. What must be understood clearly is the fact that actions that can be taken officially by the government are rather limited compared with all the actions that are needed. The reason is that the government can deal only with explicit and written rules, such as tariffs, quotas, standards and certification procedures, and other regulations.

But, in reality, there are numerous implicit and unwritten rules that dominate people's thinking and behavior in economic and business transactions. Explicit and written rules may be altered in response to changes in the economic environment, domestic or international. They will be changed through an explicit legislative process, as far as such action obtains sufficient support of the electorate.

Implicit and unwritten rules, on the other hand, are generally more difficult to change, and sometimes it is not even desirable to change them. They are constrained by the cultural and social values of each society. They are recognized, often unconsciously, as fair and just inside its cultural border. Some of them may have their roots so deep that their removal or alteration might lead to the loss of cultural identity of the people.

Obviously, these implicit and unwritten rules cannot be changed by governmental or legislative action. At best, what is possible will be "moral persuasion," but habits and customs are difficult to change by moral persuasion alone. At any rate, we have to admit that even if they can be changed, it will take time – perhaps too much time in the case of those who are expecting changes.

As is well known, Japan is among the most homogeneous societies on earth. The United States is a nation of immigrants and perhaps the most heterogeneous society in the world. This difference alone makes communication between the two countries rather complex. In Japan, everyone inherently knows the rules (not ony explicit and written rules but also implicit and unwritten rules) and is comfortable with them. The American system is constantly being tested and redefined in a sometimes adversarial way. This means that the system has to be transparent. But transparency is not always a virtue in Japanese society, where people know the implications of the rules of the system before they are completely exposed.

Some Americans talk about Japanese corporate groups called *keiretsu* as obstacles to free entry to Japanese markets. That may be true, but also there is a solid economic rationality behind them. I have carried out extensive research on the economic role of these financial corporate groups in Japan and have come to the conclusion that such groups substantially stabilize corporate performance over time.[1] We often see in Japan that the member firms in such a group help one another in times of serious business hardship. When a financial difficulty arises, for example, the member banks usually render assistance to the firm in trouble, financial or managerial, sometimes at far greater cost and risk than normal business reciprocity requires. Likewise, in a buyer–seller relationship, the buyer often will accept a somewhat higher price if the seller is in the same group and is facing business difficulties. Of course, in the reverse case, when the buyer is in difficulty, the seller may be willing to sell at a lower price or take other measures such as extending usance on the buyer's bills.

This sort of profit-sharing practice (or, to say the same thing in a different way, risk-sharing) among groups members can be interpreted as an implicit mutual insurance scheme in which member firms are insurers and insured at the same time. As a result of these implicit mutual-assistance programs, the firm in difficulty is able to recover relatively quickly from even the worst situation. To the extent that this sort of mutual-assistance mechanism is effective among group members, there will be fewer bankruptcies and layoffs during times of crisis due to external shocks. This may be one of the reasons why the unemployment rate has not risen significantly in Japan despite the two recent oil crises.

Prices, quality, and delivery are important, but they do not, at least in the short run, entirely transcend this particular relationship among corporations. Foreigners obviously have enormous difficulties to overcome in entering Japanese markets. But this uniquely Japanese system has its own rationality and merit, and if there were no trade frictions, there would be nothing to be condemned.

The attitude of these Japanese companies may be incompatible with short-run profit maximization; they are inherently long-run-oriented. They are simply seeking long-term stability and continued prosperity for their own companies at the sacrifice of short-term profits. Although American corporations are also worried about long-term profits, their approach is clearly different. They rely more on markets, and less on long-term contracts.

These differences in business approaches need not carry a suggestion of right and wrong. But they do raise the question whether or not we can avoid serious trade conflicts when these companies are playing by different sets of rules.

Is there a solution to this problem? This is a difficult question, but, for Japan, it should be made clear that "internationalization" of a country has an immediate implication that it accept "heterogeneity." It is impossible to internationalize any society without accommodating foreigners and tolerating their customs and rules. As far as we take "internationalization" as an objective that is good and worth pursuing, we must be ready to change some, if not all, of our rules of the game (explicit and implicit). Among others, the necessity for making the implicit rules of the Japanese system transparent seems to be rapidly emerging at this time.

3   The U.S. savings–investment balance

Figure 7.2 shows the changes in the savings–investment balance in the United States from 1970 to 1984. It can be observed that the U.S. private-sector savings–investment balance has fluctuated more than that of Japan and that the average level is quite low. The large savings surpluses of 1975–6 and 1982–3 coincide closely with periods of domestic recession. The U.S. economy is less stable than Japan's economy. Wages are set in three-year contracts, industry by industry; this institutional feature is one of several factors that make the United States less able than Japan to adjust to external shocks. Accordingly, there is a strong tendency for the savings–investment balance to show a surplus during troughs in the economic cycle. This large savings surplus, however, is attributable entirely to cyclical factors and – unlike that of Japan – does not persist beyond the short term. The two countries contrast sharply in this respect.

The reason that the U.S. current-account deficit has grown so rapidly in recent years, even though the domestic savings–investment balance is structurally close to equilibrium, is to be found in the huge federal deficit that has arisen from the major tax cuts and spending programs implemented during President Reagan's administration.

Another factor that cannot be ignored is the rapid increase in investment that has resulted from corporate tax cuts. Net capital investment by U.S. private-sector businesses in 1983, for example, was $108.0 billion, a dramatic rise over the previous year's figure of $82.1 billion; it swelled further to $177.6 billion in 1984. The major factor behind this growth, according to the Council of Economic Advisors, is the passage of the

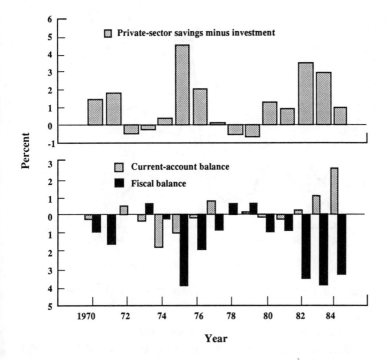

Figure 7.2. U.S. savings–investment balance by sector (ratio to GNP).

Economic Recovery Tax Act of 1981 and, in particular, its provision of an accelerated cost-recovery system and an investment tax credit.

Figure 7.3 compares the changes in corporate tax rates in Japan and the United States. The figures are derived by dividing corporate tax payments by corporate income as it appears in national income accounts. Though they cannot show the effects of specific tax measures or the distortions caused by inflation, they do provide a rough view of trends.

4   Reversal in corporate tax rates in Japan and the United States

From Figure 7.3 we can observe that the Japanese corporate tax rate was almost uniformly lower than the American rate throughout Japan's postwar rapid-growth era (the only exceptions being 1951, 1964, and 1965). We also see that the difference was significant, generally on the order of 10 percentage points; in 1970, in particular, the gap widened to 18 points, with the U.S. rate at 47.9% and Japan's rate at 29.5%.

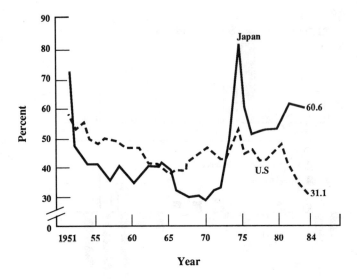

Figure 7.3. Corporate tax rates in Japan and the United States.

When the oil crunch hit in 1973, however, the relationship between the two countries' tax rates was reversed. Since the start of the Reagan administration in 1981, U.S. corporate tax rates have shown a pronounced drop. In Japan, where a campaign to pare the budget deficit is under way, corporate taxation has been made more stringent, and rates have risen significantly. As a result of these opposite trends, the U.S. rate (estimated at 31.3% in 1984) is now only about half of Japan's rate (60.6% in 1983).

Table 7.1 presents a comparison of tax service lives (depreciation periods) by industry in Japan and those in the United States before and after the shortening of depreciation schedules under the accelerated cost-recovery system (ACRS). As I have stated, the tax rate data in Figure 7.3 represent simply the ratio of tax payments to corporate income; they do not show the benefits accruing from the implementation of ACRS. But because ACRS is one of the key elements of the Economic Recovery Tax Act of 1981, any Japan–United States comparison of tax rates must also consider the effects of this system.

It is clear from a glance at this table that in practically all categories the Japanese depreciation period is longer than the corresponding American period under ACRS. For steel, the U.S. depreciation period is 5 years, and for Japan, 14 years. For the American automobile industry, which has recently shown a strong recovery, the period is 5 years for general equipment and 3 years for special tools, whereas in Japan it is 10 years.

Table 7.1. *Tax service lives in Japan and the United States*

United States			Japan	
	Years			
Industry	Former	Current	Type of equipment	Years
Mining	10	5	Oil and natural gas drilling	12
Oil refining	16	5	Oil refining	8
Spinning	11	5	Spinning	10
Forestry	6	5	Manufacture of board and plywood	9
			Manufacture of wood chips	8
Paper	13	5	Manufacture of processed paper and pulp	12
Chemicals	9.5	5	Manufacture of ethylene, acetylene, etc.	9
			Manufacture of polyethylene, etc.	8
Steel	18 (6.5)	5	Manufacture of steel and pipe	14
Nonferrous metals	14 (6.5)	5	Aluminum smelting	12
			Copper, lead, and zinc smelting	9
Industrial machinery	10	5	Manufacture of engines, turbines, etc.	11
			Manufacture of metal-processing machines	10
Electronic machinery	12 (5)	5 (3)	Manufacture of semiconductor elements	5
			Manufacture of printed circuit boards	6
Electric machinery	8	5	Manufacture of industrial and civilian electric appliances	11
Autos	12 (3)	5 (3)	Automaking	10
Ships	12	5	Shipbuilding and repair	12
General				
Computers	6	5	Computers	6
Data-processing equipment	6	5	Teletypewriters, facsimiles	5
Office equipment	10	5	Metal desks, cabinets	15
			Reception-area furniture, display cases	8

Notes: Figures in parentheses are for special manufacturing tools. Former U.S. figures refer to those under the asset-depreciation-range system, which was implemented in 1971; current U.S. figures are those in effect since 1981 under the accelerated-cost-recovery system.
Source: Chōsa geppō (Research Report), Sumitomo Bank, November–December 1983.

Table 7.2 shows the results of hypothetical calculations of corporate taxes that would be paid both in Japan and in the United States by some large Japanese corporations if those corporations were relocated to the United States.[2] These calculations are based on the assumption that those Japanese corporations had moved to the United States in 1976, but received the same business results as they did in Japan, and paid corporate taxes according to U.S. tax systems. The common result of these calculations is that their tax payments would have been drastically decreased (5.2–100%).

However, the investment decision typically is not so heavily affected by average corporate tax rates as by marginal corporate tax rates (which

Table 7.2. *Comparison of corporate taxes (unit: million yen)*

| | Taxable income | | Tax payment in Japan | Tax payment in U.S. | | Rate of increase or decrease |
| | | | | Calculated value | Actual value | |
Year	Japan	U.S.				
Nippon Steel Corp.						
1981	172,614	72,515	89,000	25,075	25,075	−71.8
1982	213,344	121,818	110,000	47,318	47,318	−57.0
1983	131,885	57,721	68,000	5,695	5,695	−91.6
1984	16,486	−56,230	8,500	−47,824	0	−100.0
NEC Corp.						
1981	22,304	6,047	11,500	−1,360	0	−100.0
1982	30,062	11,069	15,500	214	214	−98.6
1983	43,638	30,381	22,500	8,503	8,503	−62.2
1984	49,263	40,629	25,400	13,890	13,890	−45.3
Matsushita Electric Industrial Co., Ltd.						
1981	126,843	114,652	65,400	45,365	54,365	−16.9
1982	180,372	160,675	93,000	79,076	79,076	−15.0
1983	152,250	137,954	78,500	67,393	67,393	−14.2
1984	178,433	179,060	92,000	87,261	87,261	−5.2
Toyota Motor Corp.[a]						
1981	281,420	211,205	145,100	87,938	87,938	−39.4
1982	191,040	109,987	98,500	38,427	38,427	−61.0
1983	304,306	262,231	156,900	133,998	133,998	−14.6
1984	390,807	360,344	201,500	170,610	170,610	−15.3
Daiei Inc.						
1981	17,572	12,139	9,060	5,500	5,500	−39.3
1982	19,414	14,490	10,010	7,035	7,035	−29.7
1983	22,576	18,359	11,640	8,972	8,972	−22.9
1984	14,294	10,690	7,370	5,197	5,197	−29.5

[a]Before 1982, Toyota Automotive Industries.

will henceforth be referred to as *effective tax rates*) and the cost of capital. Table 7.3 compares the effective tax rates for investment in Japan and in the United States based on an investment-decision model by Hall and Jorgenson.[3] According to this table, rates for machinery and equipment, as well as structures, were higher in Japan throughout the period 1975–83. The difference in machinery and equipment rates was especially remarkable. This apparently was caused by the major tax reform in the United States in 1981. This difference was created, as is often pointed out, by the different depreciation systems and the investment tax credit. The

Table 7.3. *Effective tax rates for investment in Japan and the United States*

Year	Machinery and equipment		Structure	
	Japan	U.S.	Japan	U.S.
1975	96.3	30.6	92.6	42.7
1976	81.2	31.9	70.5	43.7
1977	54.9	32.8	48.5	44.6
1978	54.9	42.7	48.5	50.2
1979	97.8	42.0	95.5	49.3
1980	57.6	36.1	50.3	44.4
1981	50.8	−9.6	46.7	38.1
1982	48.4	−16.0	45.2	36.6
1983	49.6	−33.5	45.9	35.8

Table 7.4. *Cost of capital*

Year	Machinery and equipment		Structure	
	Japan	U.S.	Japan	U.S.
1975	21.1	25.7	7.1	12.6
1976	22.0	24.7	8.2	11.3
1977	24.5	23.6	11.4	10.0
1978	24.0	21.3	11.0	7.0
1979	20.7	21.3	6.9	7.0
1980	24.6	24.9	11.5	11.1
1981	26.6	24.8	13.7	15.0
1982	27.0	24.5	14.2	14.9
1983	26.9	23.0	14.0	13.3

effective tax rate for machinery and equipment in the United States has been negative since 1981, because cash flow accruing from the ACRS and investment tax credit has exceeded the return from the investments made.

On the other hand, the difference in cost of capital in Table 7.4 is not as large as that for the effective tax rate. The cost of capital in Japan is sometimes less than that in the United States.[4] The reason that the difference in cost of capital is small relative to that indicated by the effective tax rate is that the tax factors are partly offset by financial factors, such as interest rates and debt–equity ratios.[5] The Japanese interest rate has been much lower than the American rate over the period under investigation, and the debt–equity ratio for Japanese corporations is generally higher than that for their American counterparts. Because of these differences, the average cost of funds has been relatively lower in Japan. Japanese corporations are rather disadvantaged by the effective tax rate, but as far as the average cost of funds is concerned, they are in a better position. Because of these reasons, the difference in cost of capital has become small.

However, since 1981, the cost of capital for machinery and equipment has been far lower in the United States. For example, the difference between the two nations has been as large as 3.9%, comparing Japan's 26.9% and the United States' 23.0%.

5   Differences in tax systems' treatment of savings

As has been shown, the United States has adopted a rather strong pro-investment tax system relative to that in Japan, particularly since 1981. But the difference in tax systems with respect to savings is even more surprising. As is well known, Japan is one of the world's leading countries in regard to preferential tax treatment for savings. The *Maruyū* system provides a tax exemption for interest on deposits up to 14.5 million yen ($70,000) for each wage-earner and 9 million yen ($45,000) for each non-wage-earner (including even infants). *Maruyū* deposits total 250 to 260 trillion yen (about $1.3 trillion), or roughly two-thirds of Japan's total personal financial assets as of 1985. If we assume that they earn 6% annual interest, the interest income under the *Maruyū* system comes to 15 trillion yen ($75 billion), or roughly 5% of Japan's GNP. Thus, huge amounts of interest income are tax-exempt under the *Maruyū* system.

In the United States, by contrast, there is nothing that corresponds to Japan's *Maruyū*, except for the individual retirement account (IRA)[6] – all interest income is taxed together with other income. As a result, marginal tax rates, particularly for those in upper income brackets, are quite high. The U.S. system not only penalizes savings but also encourages borrowing (i.e., dissavings). Under the current system, interest paid by borrowers can be deducted without limit from income. In Japan, there is nothing comparable to this system.

In a lecture at George Washington University in Washington, D.C., on September 23, 1984, Peter G. Peterson, former U.S. secretary of commerce, contrasted the U.S. approach with Japan's pro-savings system, saying that "we have developed some of the world's strongest pro-consumption and pro-borrowing tendencies." A major factor behind these

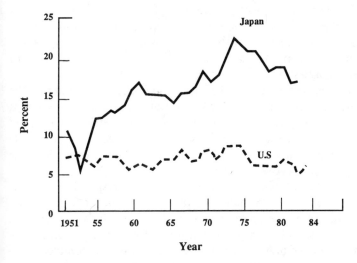

Figure 7.4. Personal savings rates in Japan and the United States (share of disposable income).

tendencies, he suggested, is that the United States, unlike many other countries, was not a battleground during World War II. When the war ended, Peterson said, "our plants and factories were intact; what we needed was strong consumer demand to keep them producing up to capacity. The keys to long term prosperity for Americans seemed to be saving less, borrowing more, and spending heavily on domestically produced consumer goods."

This pro-consumption, pro-borrowing posture produced a fundamental difference in direction between the Japanese and U.S. economies. In 1982, for example, installment plus mortgage debt amounted to only 5.5% of Japan's GNP. In the United States, such debt for consumption and housing was almost 10 times higher as a percentage of GNP (48.2%). In fact, interest paid by American consumers is roughly 5% of U.S. GNP. This huge amount is deducted from taxable income if it was paid by borrowers.

This sharp contrast with respect to the taxation of savings should be stressed. In Japan, 5% of GNP is tax-exempt if people are savers; in the United States, 5% of GNP is tax-exempt if people are borrowers (dissavers). This difference in the two tax systems seems to explain, at least partially, why the personal savings rate is 17–18% in Japan as opposed to a mere 5% in the United States (Figure 7.4).

Of course, the question of what factors determine the savings rate is a perennial issue in economic theory. The return on savings deposits, as measured by the after-tax real rate of return, is, of course, one such factor. It is not the only factor, to be sure, nor do I claim that this factor is one to which savings respond with special sensitivity.

Many observers deny that tax rates affect savings rates. The standard econometric analyses may reveal no significant effect on the savings rate from a change in the tax rate, or they may lead to the conclusion that the degee of responsiveness is extremely slight. But because the tax system is not changed annually, tax rate data for use in econometric analysis tend to be insufficient, and even when the system is changed, not all people react immediately. This is because the decision about savings is made from a lifetime perspective.

Indeed, it is natural that the savings rate does not respond to a changing rate of interest, because changes in interest rates occur typically in a short-term cycle. However, people may change their minds on savings in the case of a large-scale and permanent tax reform. For example, supposing that the tax systems for savings in two nations are completely replaced, we can ask if it is still possible to declare that the saving rates in both nations will not change at all – even after such a large-scale and permanent reform.

6   Taxes and efficient resource allocation

As we have seen, the tax structures in Japan and the United States are diametrically opposed with regard to savings and investment. The Japanese system favors savings and penalizes investment, whereas the U.S. system penalizes savings and rewards investment. This structural difference appears to be among the most important factors behind the long-term evolution of Japan's savings surplus and America's investment surplus.

The reason for the disequilibrium among sectors in the Japanese economy is the occurrence of a fundamental shift since the first oil crisis, a shift that has distorted the relative price structure. To put it another way, we might say that the private sector has ecountered higher prices on the demand side than on the supply side; for the public and external sectors, meanwhile, exactly the opposite situation has prevailed.

Why is the Japanese economy – which is supposed to be good at price adjustment – unable to rectify the imbalances among its sectors? The reason is that the economy is an "open system." In a closed system (or in one which current-account imbalances are instantly corrected by exchange-rate adjustments), as long as interest rates are flexible, savings and investment should balance domestically, regardless of tax-system distortions favoring savings and penalizing investment, or vice versa. This domestic balancing function is effected by movements of the after-tax real rate of return on savings and investment.

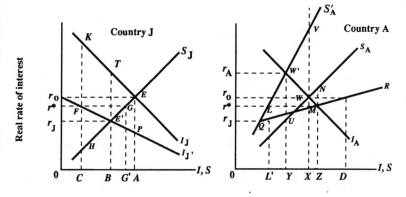

Figure 7.5. Differences in tax structures and international movement of savings.

In an open system, by contrast, people can invest their savings in foreign securities. Because U.S. tax policy is anti-saving and pro-investment, real interest rates tend to be pushed up as a result of serious shortages in savings. Japanese people attracted by these high rates are able to invest their savings in American securities, because the domestic securities tend to be less attractive and promise a lower rate of return, reflecting the savings surplus in Japan. The result is a massive movement of capital away from Japan and into the United States, the strong dollar, and a huge trade imbalance.

Figure 7.5 shows how differences in the tax structure for savings and investments induce movements of capital from one country to another. For this analysis, it is assumed that there are only two countries (J and A) in the world and that, to simplify the following discussion, the sizes of the countries' investment functions (I_J, I_A) and savings functions (S_J, S_A) are identical. They are assumed to differ only in tax structure.

The equilibrium real rate of interest before the introduction of taxes is r_0 for both countries. Savings ($=$ investments) are the same for country J and A $(0A = 0X)$. Suppose now that country J introduces a tax on investments such that, say, a 50% investment tax is levied on the marginal return from investments, but no taxes are imposed on savings. The I_J curve will shift down to I_J', because firms invest up to the point where the after-tax rate of return equals the real rate of interest. The slope of I_J' is half that of I_J, reflecting the marginal tax of 50%. For example, when the before-tax rate of return is AE, the after-tax rate of return is AP, which is half of AE. Therefore, in order for investments of $0A$ to be carried out, the real rate of interest should be as low as AP.

S_J, the savings function, is not affected, because, as before, there is no tax.

Country A, being a pro-investment and anti-savings country, introduces a 50% tax on the return from savings, whereas no tax is imposed on investments. Savers are interested in the after-tax real rate of return. For example, to assure an after-tax return of XW, the rate of interest must be twice as high as XW, that is, XV in Figure 7.5. For savings in country A to be as large as $0X$, the real rate of interest must be as high as XV. Reflecting these factors, the savings function S_A shifts up to S_A', the slope of the latter being twice as steep as that of the original S_A.

As a result of these shifts in the investment curve in country J and the savings curve in country A, the savings–investment equilibria in the two countries move from E to E' (country J) and W to W' (country A), and savings (= investment) for both countries decrease by as much as BA and YX, respectively.

The deadweight welfare losses are TEE' and $W'WU$, respectively, and in a closed system where there is no movement of savings internationally, we cannot judge a priori which method of taxation is preferable. An important difference between taxation of investment and taxation of savings is that the rate of interest is higher for country A, where taxes are on savings, than for country J, where taxes are on investments. Figure 7.5 shows that the rate of interest is r_J for country J and r_A for country A, and we have $r_A > r_0 > r_J$.

Suppose now that the capital market is liberalized, and savings can move freely across borders. Assuming away the effects of changes in exchange rates on the movement of savings, we can say that savings flow out of the country where the real rate of interest is lower into the country where it is higher. Supposing that taxes are imposed based on the "nationality" of those who save, the savings behavior of country J can still be represented by the S_J curve. For simplicity, assume also that there is no direct foreign investment and that all the movement of savings is directed toward purchase of securities.

Under these assumptions, we can show in Figure 7.5 the amount of savings flowing out of country J to country A. The line QR is the total supply of savings for country A, where QS_A' represents domestic supply, and the horizontal distance between QR and QS_A' stands for savings supplied by country J. For example, at the real rate of interest r^*, the amount of savings moving from country J to country A is LM, which is incidentally equal to FG. Because points M and F are located just on the investment schedule of both countries, r^* is the "equilibrium world rate of interest." If the world rate of interest happens to be r_0 ($> r^*$), then gross savings in country A ($= 0D$) exceed total investments ($= 0X$). In this case, r_0 is apparently not the equilibrium rate. On the other hand, if the world rate of interest is less than r^*, then a shortage of savings emerges, and the interest rate will be pushed up to r^*.[7]

From the foregoing simplified analysis it can be said that, first, the outflow of savings from country J ($=FG$) equals the current-account surplus in country J.[8] Second, the social surplus for country J is decreased by the triangular area KEH, country A's social surplus decreased by WNM. From Figure 7.5, area KEH is larger than area WNM, but that does not mean that country A is better off than country J, because the latter receives interest income from the former. This interest income is as much as the rectangular area $LMZL'$, which is exactly equal to $FGG'C$.

Most important is the fact that as a result of the outflow of savings from country J to country A ($FG = LM$), real investment in country J is decreased from $0B$ to $0C$, and it is increased from $0Y$ to $0Z$ for country A. But recall that we have initially assumed that the investment schedules (before tax) are the same and that the marginal efficiency of investment is the same in both nations. That is, there is no efficiency requirement that investments differ between the two countries when the rates of interest are identical. The difference in levels of investment was simply created by the differences in tax structures of the two countries, and it is "inefficient" in the sense of "too little investment in country J" and "too much investment in country A." In other words, in country J, only those investment projects whose rates of return are higher than KC are carried out. On the other hand, in country A, all the investment projects whose rates of return are higher than r^* (the equilibrium world interest rate, which is clearly lower than KC) are carried out. This misallocation of investment will end up with a shortage of real capital in country J and surplus of real capital in country A. What should be clearly understood is that the movement of capital in the foregoing heuristic analysis has been induced not from the efficiency requirement but by the differences in tax systems in the two countries.

In the real world, there is a tendency for Japanese and U.S. interest-rate levels to converge, and with the liberalization of capital movements in recent years, real interest rates have indeed tended to move toward the same level worldwide.

If this process of cross-border interest-rate adjustments works perfectly, differences in tax treatments of savings and investment will lead inevitably to external imbalances. But are external imbalances really a problem? It is true, as the 1984 economic white paper and white paper on international trade insist, that Japan is playing the important role of supplier of capital to a world faced with a savings shortage. From this perspective, no problem arises.

The point to note is that the differences in tax systems are limiting investment in Japan and promoting investment in the United States. If the flow of investment funds from Japan to the United States reflects higher pretax rates of return in the latter country, there is no problem from the standpoint of efficient international allocation of funds. However, because what actually determines the outflow of savings is the after-tax real rate of return, we must consider whether or not the movement of savings that is now occurring is truly a response to higher marginal productivity of capital in the United States.

If the flow of capital from Japan to the United States is indeed artificially induced by tax systems, as in Figure 7.5, then it represents a loss of efficiency in resource allocation. This is the real problem in the Japan–United States current-account imbalance.

7   Beggar thy neighbor?

The following points are clear from the foregoing presentation.

First, current-account imbalances may occur as a result of differences in countries' tax structures.

Second, when this happens, savings will flow from a pro-savings, anti-investment country (like Japan) to an anti-savings, pro-investment country (like the United States). The former country may therefore experience an investment gap, and the latter, excess investment.

Third, this flow of savings will have a serious impact on the efficiency of resource allocation in both countries. The pro-savings, anti-investment country in particular may find its economic growth potential and vitality sapped by insufficient investment, whereas the anti-savings, pro-investment country may be the victim of inefficient investment decisions.

Fourth, like the "export of unemployment," which is seen as saving jobs at home through exports that deprive workers of jobs abroad, this phenomenon will also produce a "beggar-thy-neighbor" effect. In this case, however, the current-account-deficit (capital-importing) country will enjoy increased growth, whereas its current-account-surplus (capital-exporting) neighbor will be "beggared" into lower growth. In short, the capital importer will benefit at the expense of the capital exporter.

If we recognize the clear-cut differences between the Japanese and U.S. tax structures and acknowledge the way they affect the movement of savings, what is an appropriate policy response? If the U.S. stance favoring investment is seen as a beggar-thy-neighbor policy, one approach would be for Japan and the countries of Europe to counter with their own tax breaks for investment. This would amount to avoiding being "beggared" by responding to the United States in kind.

This approach, however, calls to mind the competitive currency devaluations of the 1930s and is clearly undesirable from a global perspective. Simultaneous adoption of an anti-savings, pro-investment stance by every country would aggravate the worldwide savings shortage and probably drive interest rates up sharply. Such a global rise in interest rates would have a serious adverse impact on the world economy, including a worsening of the problem of third-world debt.

It does not follow, however, that we must accept the status quo. Japan may believe that it is doing a good deed by supplying its savings to a world that needs them. But if the return on investment (before taxes) is found not to be lower in Japan than in the United States, then Japan's action does not actually contribute to efficient allocation of capital resources among countries. Some would have it that Japan is now a capital exporter as a result of a natural historical process, but this is an overly deterministic view. Even if we accept the existence of historical factors, we must also acknowledge that capital exports are being promoted artificially by the institutional factor of the tax system. And an institutional factor ought to be amenable to change through policy measures.

8   Proposing a tax summit

Under these circumstances, what policies can we adopt? We must recognize two aspects of the present situation. First, there is a worldwide shortage of savings. The high international levels of interest rates have resulted from the Reagan administration's policies favoring investment. Savings are not high enough to meet the total demand.

Second, in order to avoid the inefficiencies arising from a beggar-thy-neighbor approach, we must avoid unilateral measures taken by each country to protect its own interests and work instead for international coordination of policies. If we all pursue only our own narrow nationalistic interests, we are likely to fall into the trap represented by the "prisoner's dilemma."

Tax policy has traditionally been a domestic concern. But as a result of the rapid internationalization of transactions, both of goods and of money, national borders are losing their meaning. In other words, whereas taxes are set by each country in the light of its own domestic circumstances, economic transactions are carried on freely across borders in a single international market, and this is producing external imbalances. It is therefore necessary for individual countries to reexamine their tax systems from an international perspective and agree to coordinate their policies.

My conclusion is that Japan should call for an international summit conference to discuss the possibility of international coordination of tax policies. Our country, the world's largest supplier of savings, is currently receiving criticism from other countries for its huge current-account surpluses. With regard to the supply of savings, the Japanese government has maintained that they are performing a useful service to the world, whereas on the current-account imbalance it has taken a passive posture. But because the supply of savings and the current-account imbalance are two sides of the same coin, Japan's position is irrational. Japan should instead make the world aware that one of the basic causes of the external imbalance lies in the differences in tax systems and work for a solution that will attack the root of the problem.

The agenda for a tax summit should include achievement of a common understanding that one of the basic problems facing the world economy is the misallocation of capital that has resulted from the tax policies adopted by individual countries. The summit should study the loss of economic efficiency that may be caused by major current-account imbalances (and the capital movements that accompany them). And because excessive pursuit of nationalistic concerns in tax-system reform may confront us with a "prisoner's dilemma," it should seek agreement on an international organ devoted to the coordination and adjustment of tax policy from a global perspective, an "International Tax Policy Coordination Committee," if you will.

In particular, all other industrial countries of the world should join in demanding that the United States overhaul its anti-savings, pro-investment tax system in order to raise its savings rate. Indeed, if the U.S. citizens and government can save a few percentage points more relative to its GNP, the problem of the existing external imbalances may well disappear from the list of worldwide economic diseases.

ACKNOWLEDGMENTS

I would like to extend my gratitude to Professors Chikashi Moriguchi, Yasushi Kosai, Robert Gordon, Lawrence Summers, Kazumasa Iwata, Yukio Noguchi, Hiromitsu Ishi, Yasusuke Murakami, Yoshio Suzuki, Shoichi Royama, Keimei Kaizuka, Yujiro Hayami, Masaaki Homma, Alan Auerbach, and John Shoven for their comments and criticisms on the substance of this chapter on various occasions. Of course, it was impossible to accommodate all the suggestions made by them in revising the chapter, and I am solely responsible for all the possible ambiguities and errors remaining. This study was supported by a Grant-in-Aid for Scientific Research No. 58410013 from the Ministry of Education, Science and Culture.

NOTES

1. See Nakatani (1982, 1984).
2. This table was calculated by Mr. Tohru Inoue, Osaka University. See Nakatani et al. (1986) for details.

3. Hall and Jorgenson (1969); these figures are long-run equilibrium values, because the Hall–Jorgenson model does not incorporate adjustment costs needed to bring the firm to the position of "desired" capital stock.
4. The following relationship holds between the cost of capital, F_K, and the effective tax rate, τ, and financial factors such as nominal interest rate, r, ratio of borrowing, b, and rate of (expected) inflation, π:

$$(1-\tau)(F_K-\delta) = b[r(1-u)-\pi] + (1-b)\rho$$

Here, δ, u, and ρ are the rate of depreciation, the basic rate of corporate income tax, and the cost of issuing new stock, respectively. The left-hand side of this equation shows the after-tax marginal rate of return to capital net of depreciation, which is equal, in equilibrium, to the cost of raising funds, which appears on the right-hand side. The term $r(1-u)-\pi$ represents the fact that interest payments are deductible from the corporate income tax, and inflation lowers the real cost of borrowing. The cost of capital expressed by F_K thus depends not only on the effective tax rate but also on other factors, such as interest rate, inflation, debt–equity ratio, and cost of new stock issue. See Nakatani et al. (1986) for further details.
5. There have been some studies that have made Japan–United States comparisons regarding the cost of capital; for example, see the chapters by Ando and Auerbach and Shoven and Tachibanaki in this volume. Ando and Auerbach reported that the cost of capital is lower in Japan; however, they did not really estimate the cost of capital, but rather the ex post rate of return to capital (earnings–capital ratio). Shoven and Tachibanaki, on the other hand, attempted to estimate the effective tax rate after integrating the corporate sector and individual sector. According to their study, the effective tax rate on the individual investor was much lower in Japan than in the United States, but their definition of the "individual investor" included not only stockholders but also lenders (depositors and bondholders). In addition, they assumed the rate of return to capital net of depreciation to be 10% a priori for both countries. They did not estimate the cost of capital itself.
6. An IRA allows wage-earners to deduct up to $2,000 per year from their taxable incomes on the condition that these funds not be withdrawn until retirement. The total amount of IRAs outstanding has been increasing rapidly since the inauguration of the system in 1981, but the IRA total still remains much smaller than the outstanding *Maruyū* account in Japan. The estimated figure for 1985 is less than $200 billion, which is only one-sixth of the outstanding *Maruyū* deposit (see *Business Week,* December 23, 1985, p. 11).
7. In Figure 7.5, r^* happens to be lower than the equilibrium rate of interest before the introduction of tax, r_0. Obviously, however, by changing the shape of investment and/or savings functions, r^* can be made equal to or higher than r_0.
8. By stating this, we are assuming that investments and savings here include those of the government sector. Also, in the foregoing analysis, it is assumed implicitly that the independent change in current-account balance does not affect savings and investments. That is, we are assuming a one-way causal relationship from savings–investment balance to current-account balance. Kazuo Ueda (1985) analyzes the fluctuations of the current-account balance of the Japanese economy based on this assumption. Although this assumption is not correct, it seems to have some relevance for analyzing the long-term movement of current-account imbalances.

REFERENCES

Hall, R. E., and D. W. Jorgenson (1969). "Tax Policy and Investment Behavior." *American Economic Review,* Vol. 59, pp. 388–401.

Nakatani, I. (1982). "The Role of Intermarket Keiretsu Business Groups in Japan." Pacific Economic Papers, No. 97, Australia–Japan Research Centre, Australian National University.

——— (1984). "The Economic Role of Financial Corporate Grouping." In M. Aoki (ed.), *The Economic Analysis of the Japanese Firm* (pp. 227–58). Amsterdam: North-Holland, 1984.

Nakatani, I., T. Inoue, Y. Iwamoto, and M. Fukushige (1986). *Wagakuni Kigyō Zeisei no Hyōka to Kadai* (Evaluation and Problem of Japan's Corporate Tax System). Kigyō Katsuryoku Kenkyusho (Business Policy Forum).

Ueda, K. (1985). "Sengo Nippon no Keijo Shūshi, Koeki Joken – Chochiku Toshi Baransu Karano Apurochi" (The Current-Account Balance and Terms of Trade in Post-War Japan – An Approach from a Saving–Investment Balance). Paper presented at Zushi Conference.

CHAPTER 8

Picking losers: public policy toward declining industries in Japan

Merton J. Peck, Richard C. Levin, and Akira Goto

1 Introduction

It is well known that the development of a strong indigenous technological capability has established Japan as a leading exporter in several strategically important industries. It is less widely recognized that changes in technology elsewhere, as well as changes in international factor prices, have rendered some Japanese industries noncompetitive in world markets and even caused some to struggle for survival in the domestic market against the pressure of import competition. Like all modern economies, Japan has its share of "lower" industries, but these have received far less attention in the United States than Japan's conspicuous "winners." In this chapter we describe and evaluate Japan's recent experience with public policy measures directed specifically at its declining industries. These policies differ markedly from those commonly employed in both Western Europe and the United States.

National industries that are suddenly thrust into a position of comparative disadvantage tend to be eliminated or scaled down by the working of the free market. Because adjustment to a decline is costly and may involve externalities, market forces do not necessarily guide the adjustment process efficiently. Recent studies by Neary and Mussa show that intervention in the adjustment processes of competitive industries can be justified on efficiency grounds under a variety of circumstances.[1] For example, intervention may be warranted when capital is not perfectly mobile, when factor prices are sticky, when income from capital is subject to taxation, or when private and social discount rates are unequal. When the declining industry is an oligopoly, it can be shown by a straightforward extension of the results of Ghemawat and Nalebuff,[2] that in the absence of intervention, firms may exit in an inefficient sequence. Moreover, the costs of adjustment may be distributed inequitably. In any event, a free-market solution to the problems of declining industries is seldom politically feasible in modern economies.

Recognizing that the unfettered market can be a cruel instrument for solving the problems of industrial decline, the OECD has articulated certain principles to guide policy efforts aimed at "positive adjustment."[3] Noting that some government intervention in support of declining industries is inevitable and perhaps even desirable, the OECD holds that assistance should be (1) temporary, (2) transparent (i.e., observable by trading partners), (3) linked to the phasing out of obsolete capacity, and (4) free of protectionist measures against imports. The Japanese government claims that its measures for declining industries conform to these OECD prescriptions. One objective of this chapter is to assess the validity of this claim.

A second objective is to gain further insight concerning the interaction of market forces and public policy in Japan. We know something about this from the numerous studies of Japanese policy toward its "winners." Much less is known about the "losers," for whom the forms of intervention differ from those used for the widely discussed "winners," such as semiconductors, consumer electronics, and automated machine tools.

Our third objective is to assess whether or not Japanese policy has been successful. The English-language literature contains several descriptions of Japan's structural-adjustment policies,[4] but very little has been reported about the performance of the industries officially designated as "structurally depressed" since the major policy measures were introduced in 1978. Although the data for such an assessment are limited, and the sample of relevant industries is small, we are able to reach some tentative conclusions about the efficacy of the structural-adjustment policies.

Many accounts of Japanese adjustment policies have focused on financial assistance in the form of government loans to companies and public payments to workers. We believe that the emphasis should be placed on a much more distinctive feature of the Japanese approach: the role of firms in the administration of structural-adjustment policies. As in all industrialized countries, the ultimate burden of adjustment is shared by the declining industry's workers, shareholders, creditors, and customers, as well as the taxpayers. But in Japan, the firms in a designated declining industry bear an unusually large share of the burden of adjustment. The firms, rather than public agencies, play a leading role in relocating redundant workers, in phasing out excess capacity, and in assuring the solvency of lending institutions by repaying debt.

Of course, most firms in declining industries, in Japan as elsewhere, operate at a loss. To enable firms to assume the burden of administering and partially financing structural adjustment, Japanese public policy aims to increase the resources available by directly coordinating industry-wide capacity reduction or by permitting cartelization for this purpose. Even where explicit agreement on prices or production levels is prohibited, a planning process or legal capacity-reduction cartels may be expected to restrain the tendencies to engage in the drastic price-cutting that might otherwise accompany extensive excess capacity. Thus, prices may tend to be higher than they would be in the absence of such policies, and this helps firms in the declining industries to undertake certain adjustment activities that are elsewhere undertaken by creditors or government agencies.

A second distinctive feature of our treatment of the subject is that we examine whether or not industry structure influences the effectiveness of Japanese adjustment policies. Though the limitations of the data do not permit a decisive inference, we find that the Japanese approach has tended to work best in concentrated industries; in unconcentrated industries, public policy does not appear to have had much impact.

Japan's first comprehensive attempt to deal with the generic problem of industrial decline was embodied in the 1978 law entitled "Temporary Measures for Stabilization of Specific Depressed Industries." Prior to 1978, Japan had a succession of public measures aimed at facilitating adjustment to declining demand in specific industries, notably textiles and shipbuilding. These policies have been described elsewhere, and although they contained some elements that are prominent in the 1978 legislation, they lacked its comprehensiveness and coherence.

Between 1978 and 1983, the provisions of the new law were applied to 14 designated industries. This is a long enough history and a large enough sample to at least begin the task of policy evaluation. We should caution the reader, however, that the data we have obtained, though very useful for making some preliminary inferences about the efficacy of the 1978 law and the philosophy it embodies, are too sparse to warrant strong conclusions about many important aspects of the law's impact.

In the next section we describe the provisions of the 1978 law, the process by which industries are designated as "structurally depressed," and some characteristics of the designated industries. In Section 3 we describe related legislation providing assistance to firms in the designated industries for the support of workers rendered redundant by industrial decline.

In Section 4 we proceed to evaluate, to the extent that the data permit, the economic impact of the 1978 law and related adjustment policies. Specifically, we indicate the magnitude of planned capacity reduction and the extent to which the designated industries achieved their capacity-reduction goals. We also examine the impact of the law on the efficiency of resource allocation within the designated industries, on the reallocation of resources to other uses, and on the rate of decline in relative prices.

Although our principal focus is on the role played by planned capacity reduction in facilitating structural adjustment, the 1978 law and related legislation provided some financial assistance to troubled industries. In Section 5 we describe the extent of such assistance, and we note some rather special features of the treatment of four designated industries: shipbuilding, aluminum, and cotton and wool textiles.

In Section 6 we examine whether or not the Japanese structural-adjustment policies are consistent with the OECD guidelines on positive adjustment. The Japanese government claims that they are, but the U.S. government disagrees. The issue is of some consequence, because the 14 designated industries represent an $80 billion Japanese market to which U.S. producers believe they have inadequate access. Economists are naturally skeptical about any policy that is alleged to simultaneously stabilize prices and maintain free trade, because import competition would be expected to frustrate stabilization efforts. There are, however, at least some plausible reasons why imports might not expand rapidly even in the absence of formal barriers to trade. We have no conclusive evidence to offer concerning "invisible" trade barriers, but we make some attempt to interpret the evidence on import penetration in the designated industries.

Another natural concern from the perspective of the economist is that "temporary" cartels, once legally sanctioned, may become permanent. In Section 7 we briefly describe legislation enacted in 1983 that extended and modified the 1978 law. Several features of the newer legislation appear somewhat troublesome, although it is too early to evaluate their impact.

In the final section of this chapter we offer some concluding remarks concerning the appropriateness of Japanese structural-adjustment policies in the peculiar context of Japanese industrial organization, and we summarize the achievements and the problems associated with this distinctive set of public policy measures.

2   The 1978 law

The 1978 law, Temporary Measures for Stabilization of Specific Depressed Industries, established the criteria and procedures for designation of an industry as "structurally depressed," and it empowered the Ministry of International Trade and Industry (MITI), or another relevant agency,[5] to coordinate an industry-wide process of planning the reduction of capacity for industries so designated.

The legislation specifically identified seven industries as candidates for designation, and it permitted MITI to identify additional industries if they satisfied four criteria:

1. Most firms in the industry must be confronted with "extremely unstable economic conditions" that are expected to prevail for a long time.
2. The industry's difficulties must have been caused by a drastic change in domestic or international economic conditions.
3. There must be considerable excess capacity in the industry.
4. A reduction in capacity must be both necessary and likely to take a long time without designation.

MITI has issued guidelines to make these legislative criteria more specific. The guidelines explain, for instance, that "a long time" is to be interpreted as three to five years.

Once an industry has been identified, by statute or by MITI, as a candidate for designation as "structurally depressed," consultation takes place between MITI officials and the firms in the industry to determine whether or not the firms favor designation. If two-thirds of the firms in the industry (measured both by number of firms and by the share of sales) agree, they apply formally for designation. MITI then makes a decision concerning designation.

After an industry is designated, the ministry – in consultation with the industry's trade association, its individual firms, its major customers, and independent experts – develops an estimate of the amount of excess capacity to be scrapped. The estimate takes account of expected future demand and anticipated developments in world markets, as well as the current level of capacity utilization. In the course of its consultations, MITI attempts to forge an industry-wide consensus on a capacity-reduction goal and a schedule for its attainment. Once consensus is reached, it is formalized as the industry's "basic stabilization plan" and officially approved by the ministry.

In practice, there is considerable overlap in the sequence of steps just outlined. Discussions with firms and trade associations usually begin before MITI identifies an industry as a candidate for designation. Indeed, MITI will be unlikely to initiate the process unless it is more or less assured in advance that two-thirds of the firms favor designation. Similarly, formal designation of an industry does not strictly precede the development of a capacity-reduction plan. Preliminary attempts to forge a consensus are made in the early rounds of negotiation concerning designation.

Once a Basic Stabilization Plan is approved, the government can do little but exhort the firms in the industry to carry out their intentions to reduce capacity. There are no legal requirements that compel firms to adhere to the plan, and neither the building of new plants nor the expansion of existing ones can be prevented. The 1978 law does provide for modest financial incentives in the form of loans and loan guarantees, but these appear to be relatively unimportant. Somewhat more significant are the subsidies provided under separate legislation, discussed in the following section, to assist firms in relocating, retraining, or retiring workers made redundant by capacity reductions. Yet the government's most important role would appear to be that of coordinator and facilitator of action in the collective interest of firms in the designated depressed industries.

If MITI judges that an industry's capacity-reduction goal, as established by the Basic Stabilization Plan, is inconsistent with the reductions planned by individual firms, it recommends ("indicates") to the industry the formation of a cartel for the purpose of reducing capacity. These "indicative" cartels must be approved by the Fair Trade Commission, and with approval comes exemption from the antimonopoly laws. This permits members of the cartel to meet together to discuss capacity reductions and to agree on the allocation of such reductions across firms.

Japanese antimonopoly laws have long provided for authorization of "recession cartels" for industries suffering from temporary hardship and "rationalization cartels" for industries with secular problems. These cartels, like indicative cartels, must be approved by the Fair Trade Commission. In addition, specific statutes exempt cartels in some industries from the antimonopoly laws, mostly for small and medium-size businesses.

Cartel agreements are, in principle, enforceable as private contracts under Japanese law, but in fact cartels must largely rely on voluntary cooperation to achieve collectively determined objectives. Firms are not obligated to join indicative cartels when MITI recommends that one be formed; indeed, there have been many instances of firms that have stayed outside of these cartels. Some cartel agreements provide for fines to be paid by member firms that do not meet their obligations, and agreements sometimes provide for inspectors, usually trade-association employees, to monitor compliance. Yet firms do not in fact use the courts to compel their competitors to meet their obligations under cartel agreements.

Table 8.1 lists the 14 industries designated as structurally depressed under the 1978 law and the dates at which each was identified, designated, and granted approval for its Basic Stabilization Plan. The table also indicates the time by which capacity reductions were to have been completed; in 12 of the 14 cases, that was the termination date of the statute.

Consistent with the statutory criteria, all 14 industries had substantial excess capacity and subnormal earnings at the time they were designated. The 14 industries consist of three mineral-processing industries (electric-

Table 8.1. *Designation of depressed industries*

Industry	Identification as prospective designated industry	Designation as depressed industry	Approval of Basic Stabilization Plan	Duration of plan	Indicative cartel
1. Industry manufacturing rolled ingots of ordinary steel or semifinished steel products by use of either open-hearth furnace or electric furnace	Prescribed by statute	7/4/78	8/28/78	3/79–6/83	No
2. Aluminum-smelting industry	Prescribed by statute	7/4/78	1/27/79	3/80–6/83	No
3. Nylon-glass-fiber-manufacturing industry	Prescribed by statute	7/4/78	10/23/78	1/79–6/83	Initially yes, later no
4. Polyacrylonitrile-glass-wool-manufacturing industry	Prescribed by statute	7/4/78	10/23/78	1/79–6/83	Initially yes, later no
5. Polyester-glass-fiber-manufacturing industry	Prescribed by statute	7/4/78	10/23/78	1/79–6/83	Initially yes, later no
6. Polyester-glass-wool manufacturing industry	Prescribed by by statute	7/4/78	10/23/78	1/79–6/83	Initially yes, later no
7. Industry building ships by use of a dock or a shipway capable of building ship of 5,000 gross tons or more	Prescribed by statute	8/29/78	11/4/78	3/80–6/83	No
8. Ammonium-manufacturing industry	7/4/78	1/23/79	1/31/79	6/79–6/83	Yes
9. Urea-manufacturing industry	7/4/78	1/23/79	1/31/79	6/79–6/83	Yes

Table 8.1 (cont.)

Industry	Identification as prospective designated industry	Designation as depressed industry	Approval of Basic Stabilization Plan	Duration of plan	Indicative cartel
10. Industry manufacturing phosphoric acid by wet process	7/4/78	1/23/79	1/31/79	6/79–6/83	No
11. Cotton textiles	7/4/78	12/18/78	4/25/79	10/79–6/83	No
12. Spinning industry, including the manufacture of combed wool	7/4/78	12/18/78	2/28/79	8/79–6/83	Yes
13. Ferrosilicon-manufacturing industry	8/29/78	11/10/78	12/26/78	6/79–3/83	No
14. Linerboard- and corrugating-medium-manufacturing industry	3/2/79	4/14/79	6/15/79	9/79–3/83	Yes

Source: Keizai Chōsa Kenkyūkai, Teiseichō keizai ka no sangyō chōsei to kyōsō seisaku (Tokyo: Fair Trade Commission, 1983).

furnace steel, aluminum, and ferrosilicon), four synthetic-fiber industries (nylon filament, polyacrylonitrile, polyester filament, and polyester staple), three chemical-fertilizer industries (ammonia, phosphoric acid, and urea), two textile industries (cotton and wool), linerboard, and shipbuilding.

Most of the designated industries were affected adversely by the sharp rise in energy prices, either because electricity is a major input (as in linerboard and the three mineral-processing industries) or because petroleum products are used as raw materials (as in the four synthetic-fiber and three fertilizer industries). Japan generates much of its electricity from oil, and 99% of its oil is imported. As a consequence, Japan was the industrialized country hit most severely by the 1973 and 1979 oil price shocks.[6]

Three industries designated under the 1978 law were not particularly energy-intensive. Cotton and wool had been problem industries in Japan since the 1960s; their difficulties in the 1970s were more directly attributable to intensified competition from low-wage, newly industrialized countries. Shipbuilding, the last of the 14 designated industries, did not have an energy-intensive technology, but its depressed condition was in part created by the oil price shocks that reduced the demand for tankers, although competition from shipyards in newly industrialized countries, as well as the general economic slowdown, also contributed to the industry's decline.

As Table 8.1 indicates, indicative cartels were formed in 8 of the 14 designated industries: the four synthetic-fiber industries, two fertilizer industries, cotton, and linerboard. The first six of these were among the seven most concentrated of the designated industries.[7] In addition, seven designated industries were authorized to form recession cartels during the period covered by the 1978 law: the four synthetic groups had cartels to limit output from April 1978 to March 1979. Producers of cotton and wool were authorized to restrict output in 1977 and 1978, and again from May to September 1981. In shipbuilding, a first recession-cartel agreement ran from August 1979 until March 1981, and a successor agreement ran from April 1981 through March 1982.

3 Related structural-adjustment legislation

The 1978 law, Temporary Measures for Stabilization of Specific Depressed Industries, is only one element of Japanese public policy toward its declining industries. There are also laws protecting workers and small business enterprises. Here we give a brief account to make more clear the institutional and policy context in which the 1978 law governing capacity reduction emerged and operated.

A related statute enacted in 1978, Temporary Measures for the Unemployed in the Designated Depressed Industries, provides subsidies to assist firms in shouldering the burden of adjusting the labor force to altered patterns of demand.[8] One provision is that the Ministry of Labor reimburse firms for relocating and retraining permanent employees of designated depressed industries. The subsidy can amount to as much as full salary for six months if the government determines that a worker's new employment can be regarded as training. A second category of subsidy covers special allowances related to early retirement. Large Japanese firms typically retire employees between 55 and 60 years of age, and often retirees are paid lump-sum bonuses of three or four times their annual wages, rather than a continuing pension. Permanent discharges tend to be concentrated among older employees, and they receive both a regular retirement bonus and an extra bonus for early discharge. The Ministry of Labor finances a fraction of the cost of the early retirement bonus, although not the regular retirement bonus.

The burden of structural adjustment is also eased by a subsidy for temporary layoffs, provided by the Employment Insurance Act of 1975. Under the system of permanent employment, large firms typically pay a significant fraction of a worker's salary during layoffs, sometimes as much as 85%. The 1975 law enabled the Ministry of Labor to cover half of these payments for large firms, and two-thirds for small and medium-size firms.

A distinctive feature of these laws is that payments are made to firms, not directly to workers. This procedure reflects the fact that large firms in Japan bear the responsibility for providing permanent employment until retirement age. The traditional labor arrangements make exit costs large, because they convert what would be variable costs under arrangements prevailing elsewhere into fixed costs. Subsidies by the Ministry of Labor reduce these exit costs, though the burden on the firms remains substantial.

Employment adjustment is also facilitated by a purely private practice of placing discharged permanent employees in jobs with other enterprises in the same business group. In aluminum smelting, for example, all six primary producers are members of the largest business groups. Although only a relatively small number of workers have been involved (aluminum smelting employed 15,000 workers in 1975 and about 4,000 in 1983),[9] about half the workers who have left the industry have been reemployed by affiliated companies. This mechanism of relocation has been less important in other industries in which group membership is less prevalent and where the numbers of workers discharged have been higher.

Despite the subsidies provided by the Ministry of Labor, layoffs, relocation, and early retirement all require substantial payments by large firms in the declining industries. Indeed, one significant rationale for cartelization is to provide revenue to make these payments. By contrast, in Western Europe and the United States, governments tend to take exclusive responsibility for unemployment-compensation programs and training and relocation schemes. In Japan, government programs are augmented by those of large firms, supported in part by government subsidies.

The Japanese system may have some efficiency advantages. Consider the initial layoff of a worker in response to declining demand. Even after government subsidy, the firm still pays a large fraction of the worker's salary. If there is little chance that the worker will be needed in the future, the firm has a strong incentive to retrain and/or relocate the worker. The manager of a public employment system would be likely to have less information than the firm about a specific worker's prospects for reemployment, and the public manager has no direct financial incentive to reduce the numbers of people on unemployment compensation.

The large Japanese firm also has some incentive to find good jobs for redundant employees. The union monitors these placements, and a poor record is likely to result in demands for higher discharge payments in the next round of labor negotiations. The manager in a public system again has no direct financial incentive to maximize the job satisfaction of those removed from the unemployment rolls.

Finally, the large Japanese firm has the contacts and influence to place its discharged workers with other large firms, especially with directly affiliated firms or with members of the same business group. The Japanese labor market is sharply divided between large and small firms. Large firms provide higher wages, greater employment security, and more extensive fringe benefits than small firms. Competition for jobs in the large-firm sector is keen. Most hiring is limited to young workers who are paid entry-level wages. The manager of a public employment agency would have great difficulty placing older workers in a large firm. A fellow group member can do better, as the record of aluminum smelting demonstrates.

Large Japanese firms have experience in placing workers, because they are accustomed to helping those retiring at age 55 or 60 to find employment. Japanese workers typically reenter the labor market on retirement and remain in the labor force until they are eligible for social security at age 65, or even longer. Traditionally, workers retiring from large firms take employment in small or medium-size subsidiaries. Such firms have a lower wage scale and an older retirement age (or no mandatory retirement age). In the designated declining industries, placing workers in subsidiaries has been difficult, because the subsidiaries tend to be suppliers to the parent, and they have been beset with the same economic problems that have affected their parents.

Finding employment for workers in large firms affiliated with a business group, however, has been a more promising approach in the designated industries populated by large firms. Because group members have wage scales similar to those for the large firms in designated industries, workers have viewed employment with a group member as a good solution. By finding jobs for discharged workers at comparable wages, some of Japan's declining industries have been spared the social tensions felt in the United States among the unemployed of the automotive and steel industries, who cannot find jobs with wages and benefits comparable to those they lost. The unemployment generated in these two U.S. industries, however, was at least an order of magnitude greater than in any Japanese industry.

The arrangements just described are characteristic of large firms. The 1978 law, Temporary Measures for the Unemployed in the Designated Depressed Industries, provides broader protection to workers with at least one year of employment in a depressed industry. Such workers are eligible for 12 months of unemployment compensation, paid directly to them by the Ministry of Labor. This public assistance has been most important to workers in small firms. Such firms typically are not unionized; they lack an established system of permanent employment and the advantages of group membership.

Two other pieces of legislation, less directly connected with the 1978 law, are part of Japan's overall policy toward sectors in trouble. The Depressed District Act extends special assistance to unemployed workers in districts of high unemployment; its provisions are similar to those for workers in the designated industries.[10]

The Smaller Enterprise Business Switchover Act aids troubled industries composed primarily of small and medium-size enterprises, in contrast to the more capital-intensive industries designated under the 1978 law.[11] The switchover act covered the period 1976 to 1986. Table 8.2 lists the industries designated under the act; they produce a wide variety of labor-intensive products subject to import competition from lower-wage Asian countries. This switchover act, quite different from the 1978 law, assists small firms in switching to a different activity. Rather than planning industry-wide capacity reductions, the switchover act permits smaller firms to move to a different industry and to provide continued employment for their workers. The smaller enterprises in designated industries may file plans for a switchover to a new line of activity with the local prefectural government. If the plans are approved by the prefectural governor, the enterprise becomes entitled to (1) low-interest loans from the central government's Small and Medium Enterprise Agency and from the local government, (2) special tax credits on new investment, (3) consulting services from the Small and Medium Enterprise Agency and the

Table 8.2. *Industries designated under the Small Enterprise Business Switchover Act*

Manufacturing and repairing vessels, their engines and parts
Manufacturing of canned or bottled fruits, vegetables, and marine products
Manufacturing of saccharin
Manufacturing of synthetic leather
Manufacturing of rubber footwear and accessories
Manufacturing of plastic footwear and accessories
Manufacturing of leather gloves
Manufacturing of fireworks
Manufacturing of Christmas goods
Manufacturing of metal dinnerware
Manufacturing of porcelain ornaments for alcoves
Manufacturing of porcelain tiles
Manufacturing of rattan blinds
Manufacturing of plastic-film sheet
Silk-yarn spinning
Silk-yarn weaving
Linen weaving
Manufacturing of circular knitted fabrics and goods
Manufacturing of socks and stockings
Manufacturing of embroidery lace
Agalomite mining

Source: Yoshie Yonezawa, "The System of Industrial Adjustment for Trade in Japan" (discussion paper, Japan Economic Research Center, Tokyo, 1979), pp. 44–5.

local government, (4) tax credits for a merger with a firm in another line of activity, and (5) grants for retraining workers and payments to workers to facilitate moves to other jobs.

We have not investigated the operation of this law. We list its provisions simply to indicate that smaller enterprises in economic difficulty are not ignored and that the approach to adjustment in industries made up of small firms is quite different from the capacity-reduction approach of the 1978 law.

4   The economic impact of structural-adjustment policy

In this section we attempt to evaluate the economic consequences of the structural-adjustment policies embodied in the 1978 law and related legislation. Specifically, we examine the behavior of the designated depressed industries in setting capacity-reduction targets and their performance in achieving those targets. We also examine the efficiency with which capacity-reduction goals were attained, by considering the allocation of reductions across firms within each industry to the extent that the data permit. In addition, we look at the extent to which labor was released from the declining industries and the extent to which these released resources were reabsorbed in other sectors of the economy. Finally, we ask whether or not the process of coordinated reductions in capacity had the effect of cushioning the tendency toward price decline that excess capacity might otherwise encourage, thus permitting firms to bear more easily the burdens of partially financing and administering the adjustment process.

Ideally, to draw inferences about the efficacy of Japanese structural-adjustment policies, we would want first to make predictions about what would have happened in the designated depressed industries in the absence of any policy intervention and then compare the predicted effects with what actually occurred. In principle, there would be at least three ways to do this. First, we could have obtained detailed time-series data on each of the designated industries, estimated the production and demand structures with some precision, and generated predictions about the extent of capacity reduction and the decline in prices that would have occurred without intervention. Second, we could have examined the behavior of the 14 designated industries in other countries where factor prices and capital vintages were similar to those in Japan. Third, we could have used data on Japanese industries similar to the designated industries in all respects except designation. These approaches, desirable in principle, were not feasible. It is not clear that satisfactory "control groups" exist for the second and third approaches. Data simply were not available to permit the first approach.

We are left instead with limited data on the 14 designated industries, much of which covers only the period in which the 1978 law was in force or the period just preceding its passage. The conclusions that we can draw are therefore quite tentative.

4.1   Setting capacity-reduction targets

Our interviews with Japanese officials and our examination of the data on industry capacity and utilization suggest that concentrated and unconcentrated industries differed substantially in the magnitude of their capacity-reduction targets and the process as by which targets were established.

Table 8.3 ranks the 14 designated industries by the 1977 value of the Herfindahl index for domestic shipments. In four of the six concentrated industries, plans were established to remove between 84% and 100% of unutilized capacity. In aluminum smelting, the capacity-reduction target actually exceeded the level of excess capacity in 1977, in anticipation that the industry's international competitiveness would continue to decline.

Table 8.3. *Concentration and capacity reduction in industries designated under the 1978 law*

Industry	1977 Herfindahl index	1977 no. of firms	Target as % of initial capacity	Unutilized capacity, 1977 (%)	Target as % of unutilized capacity
Concentrated industries					
Aluminum smelting	2,161	7	57	27	210
Nylon filament	2,079	6	20	21	96
Polyester staple	2,051	8	20	23	84
Polyacrylonitrile staple	1,728	6	20	20	100
Urea	1,566	12	45	50	90
Polyester filament	1,386	8	13	23	55
Unconcentrated industries					
Ammonia	848[a]	18	26	38	68
Ferrosilicon	771	16	20	45	45
Shipbuilding	660	61	35	24	146
Linerboard	622	88	15	37	41
Phosphoric acid	467	21	28	42	67
Wool	377	142	11	36	32
Cotton spinning	304	288	6	29	21
Electric-furnace steel	161	69	14	37	36

[a] 1979 data.
Source: Keizai Chōsa Kenkyūkai, *Teiseichō keizai ka no sangyō chōsei to kyōsō seisaku* (Tokyo: Fair Trade Commission, 1983).

In contrast, only one of the eight less concentrated industries, ship-building, set a target in excess of 70% of unutilized capacity in 1977. Indeed, only three of the eight sought to eliminate as much as one-half of initial excess capacity.

The target-setting process began with a demand forecast made by MITI and each industry's trade association. These forecasts of expected demand less expected imports provided an initial basis for estimating the amount of capacity to be scrapped. In concentrated industries, MITI officials discussed the volume to be scrapped with individual firms, who typically volunteer increasingly large capacity reductions in response to rivals raising their commitments. MITI officials conducted successive rounds of discussions, and the targets were modified to reflect the willingness of firms to reduce capacity.

In unconcentrated industries, MITI officials dealt largely with trade-association executives, who in turn carried on discussions with individual firms. MITI influence with individual firms was relatively small, and the targets for capacity reductions were very conservative.

The low targets, even if achieved, left the unconcentrated industries with the problem that reasonable levels of capacity utilization could not be reached without increases in demand. In most of the industries, demand growth of 30% to 50% would have been required to reach a 90% rate of capacity utilization. This was an unrealistic expectation for industries that had lost their international competitiveness. But a low target has the bureaucratic advantage that it is easier to achieve.

4.2   Achieving capacity-reduction targets

Table 8.4 displays the records for the designated industries in achieving capacity-reduction targets. According to official government reports on the 1978 law, 12 of the 14 industries disposed of at least 90% of the capacity targeted for disposal, as shown in column (3). The two exceptions were polyester filament and cotton spinning.

The official reports are puzzling, however, because they are at variance with other government data. The last column of Table 8.4 shows the net decrease in capacity as calculated from published figures on industry capacity in 1977 and 1983. By these standards, four industries (three of them producing synthetic fibers) failed to reach 90% of their targets. These apparent failures, however, can be explained by an unexpected increase in demand that brought capacity utilization back to 89% in polyester staple in 1979, and it remained high through 1983. The only significant anomaly is the electric-furnace steel industry, which we discuss later, in which industry capacity actually increased by 15%.

Table 8.4. *Actual and planned capacity reductions*

Industry	Equipment	(1) Capacity before disposal (1,000 tons)	(2) Goal as % of initial capacity	(3) Reported disposal as % of goal	(4) Net reduction as % of goal	(5) Net reduction as % of initial capacity
Concentrated industries						
Aluminum smelting	Electric melting furnace	1,642	57	97	97	54
Nylon filament	Spinning machine	367	20	98	83	17
Polyester staple	Spinning machine	398	20	90	76	15
Polyacrylonitrile staple	Spinning machine	431	20	113	92	18
Urea	Synthesizing, separation, granulation facilities	3,985	45	93	93	42
Polyester filament	Spinning machine	350	13	82	35	5
Unconcentrated industries						
Ammonia	Gasification, refining, or synthesizing facilities	4,559	26	100	100	26
Ferrosilicon	Electric furnace	487	20	100	164	34
Shipbuilding	Building berth or dock	9,770	35	105	105	37
Linerboard	Paper machine	7,549	15	94	93	14
Phosphoric acid	Reaction filtration facilities	934	20	92	91	19
Wool	Spinning frame	182	12	96	236	23
Cotton spinning	Spinning frame	1,204	6	78	136	8
Electric-furnace steel	Open hearth or electric	20,790	14	95	—	—

Source: Keizai Chōsa Kenkyūkai, *Teiseichō keizai ka no sangyō chōsei to kyōsō seisaku* (Tokyo: Fair Trade Commission, 1983).

On the whole, however, the capacity-reduction process worked well. Reductions in excess of 14% of initial capacity were achieved in all but three industries: polyester filament, cotton, and electric-furnace steel. In the four industries with the most ambitious targets – urea, ammonia, shipbuilding, and aluminum smelting – more than 25% of initial capacity was removed.

The general success of designated industries in meeting their targets should not be too surprising. As noted, the goals were based essentially on what firms were willing to do, rather than on a prespecified idea of what would be necessary to reach a particular level of prices or profitability. There were no apparent instances of strategic behavior by firms in announcing their commitments; that is, firms did not deceitfully agree to large goals to encourage rivals to increase their commitments.

We have remarked that concentrated industries tended to set more ambitious targets than unconcentrated industries. To be precise, the simple average of targeted reductions as a percentage of initial capacity was 29% in the concentrated industries and 16% in the unconcentrated industries. Yet there was little difference in the experiences of concentrated and unconcentrated industries in reaching their targets, at least not in the data officially reported to MITI. The simple average of reported capacity disposal as a percentage of target was 96% for the concentrated industries and 95% for the unconcentrated industries. If the actual net change in capacity is considered instead of the official figures on disposals, the concentrated industries averaged 79% of their goals, and the unconcentrated averaged 102%. This does not really imply greater adherence to plans in the unconcentrated industries; rather, the opposite is the case: The standard deviations of the attainment percentages just cited are 23 percentage points in the concentrated industries and 97 percentage points in the unconcentrated industries.

In the end, the capacity reductions actually achieved by the concentrated industries were only slightly larger on average than those in the unconcentrated industries. Net reductions averaged 25% of initial capacity in the concentrated industries and 18% of initial capacity in the unconcentrated industries, despite their more conservative goals. If electric-furnace steel, for which capacity actually increased, is excluded, the unconcentrated industries shed 23% of their initial capacity on average.

Achievement of capacity targets does not seem to be strongly linked to the presence or absence of indicative cartels. The eight industries in which indicative cartels were formed achieved net reductions that were on average 101% of their goals. The uncartelized industries achieved 81% on average, but 118% if electric-furnace steel is excluded. Reductions as percentages of initial capacity, however, tended to be somewhat higher in the industries without indicative cartels: 19% in the cartelized industries and 23% in the others, even including the electric-furnace steel industry. This is not surprising; indicative cartels were formed when it was anticipated that capacity reductions would be difficult to achieve.

The electric-furnace steel industry is anomalous because capacity actually increased. Although adherence to the Basic Stabilization Plan was purely voluntary, the plan did expressly prohibit firms from adding capacity. Yet the plan permitted investment to upgrade the production process, even though such investment might lead to an expansion of capacity. As a result, it was difficult to prevent capacity expansion.

The failure of the electric-furnace steel industry to adhere to its plan resulted primarily from the behavior of one deviant firm – Tokyo Steel – which had about a 10% market share. Tokyo Steel disagreed with the consensus view of its competitors and MITI officials that higher electricity prices would diminish the role of electric furnaces in steel production relative to large blast furnaces. Tokyo Steel's managing director, Hideo Ozeki, was quite outspoken in his opposition:

> Why should we go along with them [MITI and the trade association]? I don't see the industry as structurally depressed. We haven't lost our international competitiveness yet. . . . What's surprising is that so many companies go along despite MITI's weakened powers. It must have something to do with the feudal legacy of bowing to authority.[12]

Tokyo Steel undertook an aggressive modernization program that was imitated by some other firms in the industry. But the electric-furnace steel industry was the exception among the designated industries in increasing its capacity. Maverick firms, however, were found in other industries, notably Settsu Paper in the linerboard industry. Settsu expanded its capacity in ways similar to those used by Tokyo Steel.

4.3   Allocation of capacity reductions

We lack specific data on the capacity reductions undertaken by each firm in the designated industries, but data on industry concentration and on the number of firms in each industry, displayed in Table 8.5, suggest very strongly that concentrated and unconcentrated industries differed substantially in the way capacity reduction was achieved.

The table reveals that in the four synthetic-fiber industries, there was essentially no change in the number of firms, and virtually no change in market shares of domestic shipments. Unfortunately, we do not have available a Herfindahl index of capacity, but the extraordinary stability of market shares strongly suggests that capacity reductions were distributed

Table 8.5. *Changes in concentration and numbers of firms for industries under the 1978 law*

Industry	Herfindahl index		% change 1977–82	Number of firms		Number of firms with under 300 employees	
	1977	1982		1977	1983	1977	1981
Concentrated industries							
Aluminum smelting	2,161	2,387	10.5	7	5	0	0
Nylon filament	2,079	2,002	-3.7	6	6	0	0
Polyester staple	2,051	2,029	-1.1	8	8	0	0
Polyacrylonitrile staple	1,728	1,779	3.0	6	6	0	0
Urea	1,566	1,741	11.2	12	8	0	0
Polyester filament	1,386	1,380	-0.4	8	9	0	0
Unconcentrated industries							
Ammonia	848[a]	1,009	19.0	18	14	0	0
Ferrosilicon	771	1,293	67.7	16	10	n.a.	n.a.
Shipbuilding	660	436	-33.9	61	44[b]	32	19
Linerboard	622	577	-7.2	88	79	66	56
Phosphoric acid	467	534	14.3	21	13	n.a.	n.a.
Wool	377	367	-2.7	142	109[b]	122	93
Cotton spinning	304	358	17.8	258[c]	193[b]	215[c]	150
Electric-furnace steel	161	257	59.6	69	57	40	32

[a] 1979 data. [b] 1981 data. [c] 1978 data.

Source: Keizai Chōsa Kenkyūkai, *Teiseichō keizai ka no sangyō chōsei to kyōsō seisaku* (Tokyo: Fair Trade Commission, 1983).

fairly evenly across firms in each industry. By contrast, in the unconcentrated industries it appears that exit played a very important role in achieving industry-wide capacity reductions. More than 20% of all firms exited from the ammonia, ferrosilicon, shipbuilding, phosphoric acid, wool, and cotton industries, with exit concentrated among the smallest firms.

These data are consistent with our general view that "planning" involved serious negotiation between MITI and individual firms in the concentrated industries, whereas in the unconcentrated industries such individual-firm commitments were less common. The data also help explain why several unconcentrated industries drastically overshot their capacity-reduction targets. Presumably, many firms did not "plan" their exit from the market, although there actually were side payments to exiting firms in three industries: urea, ammonia, and linerboard.

The data also suggest that capacity reductions may have been more efficiently allocated in the unconcentrated industries than in the concentrated ones, because exit probably was concentrated among firms with the highest costs. A problem with the planning process in the concentrated industries was that multilateral bargaining, especially among mutually distrustful competitors, may not have resulted in exit of the highest-cost capacity, even though that was a MITI objective. Indeed, the stability of market shares gives at least a hint that the concentrated industries may have reached agreement on prorated capacity reduction, which is not efficient if firms have different mixes of high- and low-cost facilities.

4.4   Unemployment and reallocation of labor

The elimination of excess physical capacity in the designated depressed industries naturally brought with it some displacement of labor, and, as we have noted, the Temporary Measures for the Unemployed in the Designated Depressed Industries were intended to aid firms in relocating, retraining, or retiring displaced workers. We could not obtain detailed data on these programs, but data on employment and on unemployment compensation permit at least a partial evaluation of the success of these policies.

Table 8.6 presents data on employment levels in 10 of the designated industries for 1977 and 1983. In three industries, employment declined by over 50%, and in the aggregate nearly 48,000 jobs were lost, over 15% of total employment in 1977. Notably, shipbuilding is excluded from Table 8.6, because we could not obtain data for 1983. But shipbuilding, the most labor-intensive of the depressed industries, had by far the largest changes in employment: 27,000 jobs were lost in 1978, and another 17,000 were eliminated in 1979. Thus, in just two years, nearly as many shipyard

Table 8.6. *Changes in numbers of workers*

Industry	Number of workers		Absolute change	% change
	1977	1983		
Concentrated industries				
Aluminum smelting	8,557	3,715	−4,842	−56.6
Nylon filament	71,021	61,055	−9,996	−14.0
Polyester staple	66,217	54,801	−11,416	−17.2
Polyacrylonitrile staple	45,270	42,383	−2,887	−6.4
Urea	417	200	−217	−52.0
Polyester filament	81,330	71,144	−10,186	−12.5
Unconcentrated industries				
Ammonia	1,057	746	−311	−29.4
Ferrosilicon	1,474	714	−760	−51.6
Phosphoric acid	467	382	−85	−18.2
Electric-furnace steel	36,400	29,300	−7,100	−19.5
Total	312,210	264,440	−47,770	−15.3

Source: Sankōhō no kaisetsu (Commentary on the Law of Temporary Measures for the Structural Adjustment in Specific Industries) (Tokyo: Sangyō Seisaku Kyoku, MITI, 1983).

jobs were lost as were lost over a six-year period in 10 of the designated industries.

We can draw some inferences about the number of displaced workers who failed to be reemployed by their firms or by their own efforts and who thus applied for unemployment compensation. According to the Fair Trade Commission, 39,000 jobs were lost in the designated industries, apart from shipbuilding, in 1978. A study by the U.S. General Accounting Office reports that on the unemployment-compensation rolls in 1978 there were about 21,000 workers who had been continually employed in a designated industry (other than shipbuilding) for at least a year prior to being laid off.[13] This is 53% of this decline in the number of jobs, which suggests that about half the workers found other employment without showing up on the unemployment-compensation rolls.

The experience of the shipbuilding industry, however, was far worse. There were over 25,000 former shipyard workers on the unemployment rolls in 1978. This indicates that most did not move directly into new jobs. The reemployment of shipyard employees was an especially difficult problem because of the large numbers involved and the geographic distance of some shipbuilding locations from major metropolitan areas. In addition, shipbuilding was a large local employer in several areas. Thus, unemployment in shipbuilding led to additional unemployment in local supply and service industries, aggravating the problems of shipyard workers in finding other employment.

On balance, however, the magnitude of the unemployment problem associated with the designated depressed industries was minor. Unemployment peaked in 1978, with 47,000 workers from depressed industries on the unemployment-compensation rolls. Yet these workers represented less than 5% of the 1 million workers who drew unemployment compensation during that year. By 1979, only 19,000 workers from designated industries drew unemployment compensation.

The relative moderation of unemployment problems cannot be entirely attributed to the 1978 legislation. Two other factors kept measured unemployment of workers from the depressed industries low. First, in two industries (wool and cotton spinning), 71% of the workers were women, who often withdrew from the labor force when discharged. Second, the low economy-wide rate of unemployment made reemployment more likely and the duration of unemployment shorter than would be expected in an economy like that of the United States.

4.5   *Evaluating the impact of structural-adjustment policy*

As we noted earlier, the data available do not really permit a definitive test whether or not Japanese policy toward declining industries achieved substantially better results than a free market would have. But we can draw several conclusions.

First, the process of setting capacity-reduction targets seems to have resembled forecasting more than planning in many of the unconcentrated industries. In the concentrated industries, the targets were more ambitious on average, and they were more closely aligned with the initial extent of unutilized capacity.

Second, most of the industries designated under the 1978 law met the targets for capacity reduction specified in their Basic Stabilization Plans. Indeed, several unconcentrated industries shed substantially more capacity than planned. The synthetic-fiber industries actually scrapped somewhat less than planned, because of an unexpected strengthening of worldwide demand that made possible satisfactory capacity utilization without full attainment of the reduction goals.

Third, capacity reduction appears to have been accomplished largely by means of the exit of small firms in the unconcentrated industries, whereas planned allocation of capacity reductions appears to have been more important in the concentrated industries.

Table 8.7. *Balances of bank loans payable in designated industries: 1977 and 1982 (billion yen)*

Industry	1977 balances (current yen)	1982 balances (current yen)	1981 balances (1977 yen)	% change in real balances
Urea	1,676	202	187	−88
Ammonia	1,532	1,764	1,629	6
Linerboard	709	709[a]	643[a]	−8
Phosphoric acid	181	199	183	1
Electric-furnace steel	285	102[a]	93	−67
Total	4,383	2,996	2,735	−38

[a] 1982 data.
Source: Computed by the authors from data in *Sankōhō no kaisetsu* (Commentary on the Law of Temporary Measures for the Structural Adjustment of Specific Industries) (Tokyo: Sangyō Seisaku Kyoku, MITI, 1983) and Bank of Japan, *Price Indexes Annual,* various issues.

Fourth, with the exception of shipyard workers, the workers displaced by structural adjustment in declining industries appear to have been rapidly absorbed elsewhere in the economy or to have withdrawn from the labor force. Persistent unemployment seems to have been a problem only in the shipbuilding industry and the local economies in which the shipyards are situated.

As we have indicated, the most distinctive feature of the Japanese adjustment policy was that firms in the declining industries, rather than the government, carried most of the burdens of financing and administering the adjustment process. In the concentrated (and the other cartelized) industries, the firms played an active role in planning capacity reductions. Assisted in part by subsidies, firms found new jobs for displaced workers or provided inducements for early retirement. The firms also paid down their bank debt, at least in real terms. Table 8.7 shows, for the five industries for which we could obtain data, that nominal bank debt either declined or increased modestly, whereas real loan balances declined in each case.

In theory, there would seem to be a clear linkage between reducing excess capacity and assuming the burdens of administering adjustment. By reducing excess capacity, the threat of ruinous price competition is minimized, the financial positions of firms are made more secure, and the firms can thus assume the burdens of relocating labor and repaying debt. One might therefore expect to find evidence that designated industries,

Table 8.8. *Annual rates of change in real relative domestic prices: 1975–8 and 1978–83*

Industry	Annual % change 1975–8	Annual % change 1978–83	Improvement in % change
Concentrated industries			
Aluminum smelting	+2.7	+2.8	+0.1
Nylon filament	−1.2	+0.2	+1.4
Polyester staple	−3.4	−4.3	−0.9
Polyacrylonitrile staple	−2.5	−1.7	+0.8
Urea	+3.1	+2.1	−1.0
Polyester filament	−5.4	−4.9	+0.5
Unconcentrated industries			
Ammonia	−2.1	+4.5	+6.6
Ferrosilicon	−1.8	−0.7	+1.1
Linerboard	+0.9	+2.1	+1.2
Wool	+2.2	−1.8	−4.0
Cotton spinning	+4.5	−4.8	−9.3
Electric-furnace steel	+2.2	−5.2	−7.4

Source: Calculated by the authors from data in Bank of Japan, *Price Indexes Annual* (Tokyo, various issues).

especially the concentrated industries, experienced some strengthening of prices after 1978, or at least a reduction in the rate of price decline. The price data, however, provide only mixed support for this hypothesis.

Table 8.8 shows that real relative dometic prices fell in four of the six concentrated industries in the three years prior to 1978. In three of these four industries (all synthetic-fiber industries), prices did indeed fall less rapidly over the next five years. Aluminum prices, however, rose both before and after 1978 at about the same rate, and urea prices also increased in both periods, though more slowly after 1978 than before. In the ammonia industry (the most concentrated of the remaining industries and one that was cartelized), prices did strengthen significantly, but in four of the five other industries for which we have data, relative prices fell after 1978, and the rate of decline accelerated in three of the four cases.

To the extent that planned capacity reduction did strengthen prices or arrest their decline in the concentrated industries, the Japanese consumer thus made it possible for firms in these industries to bear more easily the costs of adjustment. One might reasonably ask if there are any particular advantages to a system in which firms, supported in part by higher prices paid by their customers, bear the costs of relocating workers and repaying creditors, rather than having these input suppliers themselves, or the government, shoulder the burden.

A pure market system would require workers and suppliers of capital to bear the costs of adjustment to decline. But no real-life market economy is so ruthless. In Western Europe and the United States, workers are aided by publicly financed and administered schemes of extended unemployment compensation and retraining programs. Suppliers of capital are protected, in Western Europe especially, by substantial subsidies to prolong the lives of firms in declining industries. Even in the United States, rescue operations often are mounted for very large firms when bankruptcy threatens. If banks get into difficulties because their loan customers cannot make repayment, the government frequently helps bail out the banks.

In Japan, large firms do much of what governments do in Europe and the United States. Of course, workers and creditors do share some of the burdens of decline. Discharged workers often are reemployed in lower-paying jobs in smaller firms, and banks permit large firms in trouble to stretch out repayment schedules or grant them interest-rate concessions. But large Japanese firms in declining industries bear a substantial portion of the adjustment costs, by administering schemes for the relocation or retirement of workers and by repaying creditors as the firms themselves shrink to adapt to adverse market conditions.

There are certain features of concentrated industries in Japan that make reliance on the firms themselves, rather than on market forces or on the government, particularly appropriate. Large Japanese firms have an unusually heavy burden of unavoidable costs. Union agreements and established practices have created a system of permanent employment. Substantial portions of labor costs are not variable; they cannot be avoided by discharging or laying off workers. Large firms are also heavily financed by bank debt, and creditors often have liens against specific facilities. Scrapping such facilities requires repaying these secured loans to preserve the goodwill of regular lenders. To the extent that Japanese firms treat certain costs as fixed that are elsewhere treated as variable, they can endure low prices longer without pressure to exit. The unavoidable costs serve as exit barriers, slowing the reduction of capacity in response to market forces. The structural-adjustment policies embedded in the 1978 law can be viewed as responses that facilitate capacity reduction while preserving the distinctive features of Japanese labor and credit-market institutions. By managing the relocation of their own workers and repaying the debt secured by excess capacity, large Japanese firms are able to adjust to a decline in a manner that is far less disruptive of traditional

Table 8.9. *Loans and loan guarantees under the 1978 law (million dollars)*

Item	1978	1979	1980	1981	1982	1983	Total
Loans	–	3	2	0	8	43	55
Guarantees	20	61	12	0	0	0	93[a]

[a]Guarantees by industry: polyacrylonitrile staple, 12; shipbuilding, 57; ammonia, 11; cotton spinning, 5; linerboard, 8; total, 93.
Source: Data supplied to the authors by the staff of the Japan Development Bank.

arrangements than is direct government intervention to assist workers or to bail out banks.

5 Financial assistance under the 1978 law and special measures for certain industries

Apart from the payments in support of dislocated workers, authorized by separate legislation described in Section 3, the 1978 law itself provided very modest financial aid to the designated industries. In general, the Japanese government has not engaged in the massive subsidization of declining industries that is commonplace in Western Europe. In this section, we sketch the financial-assistance provisions of the 1978 law, and we proceed to discuss additional public intervention in four of the designated depressed industries.

The 1978 law provided for (1) low-interest loans for equipment to facilitate the transfer of a firm to a new line of business, (2) low-interest loans to finance retirement allowances to individuals made redundant by capacity reductions, and (3) guarantees for new loans from private banks to pay off existing loans on plants and equipment.[14] (These new loans replaced loans secured by plant and equipment, thus permitting the capacity to be scrapped.) The loans were made by the Japan Development Bank, and the loan guarantees came from an affiliate of the Japan Development Bank. Both are quasi-government corporations.

Table 8.9 shows that loans and loan guarantees under the 1978 law totaled only $148 million. Also shown in the table is the distribution of loan guarantees by industry. Only five industries received loan guarantees, and except for shipbuilding, the amounts involved were quite small. This modest use of the loan guarantees is a puzzle, because the guarantees used were less than the amount available from the Specific Depressed

Industries Credit Fund. It is possible that the regulations governing the guarantees rendered them unattractive.

Although financial aid under the 1978 law was generally modest, four designated industries were subject to special treatment: shipbuilding, aluminum smelting, and cotton and wool textiles. Shipbuilding was distinguished by the involvement of the Ministry of Transport, rather than MITI, in its planning process. The aluminum industry received a rather unusual form of subsidy in lieu of trade protection, and the two textile industries received financial aid under separate legislation.

Shipbuilding is under the jurisdiction of the Ministry of Transport, which has a tradition of strong "administrative guidance," or informal advice from officials to firms concerning output, pricing, and investment.[15] Apart from this administrative distinction, shipbuilding differs from the other 13 designated industries in that it is almost entirely an export industry. Thus, domestic consumers do not bear the full cost of measures to support prices. These circumstances gave the Ministry of Transport considerable scope to design a comprehensive plan for restructuring the industry.

One major feature of the plan was substantial capacity reduction. According to a report by the U.S. General Accounting Office: "Various sources indicate that industry and government had difficulty reaching an agreement as to how the plan should be carried out. Large and small firms disagreed as to which should bear the burden of capacity reduction. The smaller firms claimed the larger firms could afford to bear a greater proportion of the burden while the larger firms felt all should suffer equally."[16] As Table 8.10 indicates, the larger shipyards made the greatest capacity reductions.

Capacity reduction was facilitated by the statutory creation of a Designated Shipbuilding Enterprise Stabilization Association, which was given a specific exemption from the antimonopoly law. The Stabilization Association purchased nine shipyards owned by smaller firms, with a total capacity of 490,000 tons. This represented about 12% of the capacity that was scrapped. The funds for these purchases came from a 1-billion-yen loan from the Japan Development Bank and a 1-billion-yen loan from private banks. The yards were totally scrapped, and the proceeds from sale of the land were used to repay part of the loans. In addition, each shipbuilder was required to pay 1.3% of the price of its new vessels to the Stabilization Association until the loans were repaid. It should be noted that even here government aid took the form of loans, not grants, and the repayment provision in effect imposed a tax on shipbuilding firms and their customers, not the general public – a procedure consistent with placing the direct burden of adjustment on the depressed industry. The

Table 8.10. *Shipbuilding capacity reductions*

Category of firm	No. of firms	Capacity before disposal (1,000 tons)	Planned disposal	Planned disposal as % of initial capacity	Actual disposal	% of goal achieved
Major	7	5,690	2,280	40	2,240	98
Quasi major	17	2,890	870	30	1,040	120
Medium	16	790	210	27	250	119
Small	21	400	60	15	50	83

Source: 1980 White Paper on Transport (Tokyo: Ministry of Transport, 1980).

Ministry of Transport also took several measures to increase the demand for new ships: low-interest loans for ships purchased by Japanese shipping firms, subsidies for the retirement of Japanese-flag vessels, and increased government purchases of military and patrol ships.

Finally, the Ministry of Transport organized a recession cartel. The cartel, approved on August 1, 1979, limited each shipbuilder to 39% of its previous peak output until March 1981. A second cartel, from April 1, 1981, until March 31, 1982, limited output to 51% of the previous peak.

The Japanese shipbuilding industry had poor financial results in the late 1970s, and its share of world output declined from 50.1% in 1975 to 36.6% in 1979. Beginning in 1980, its share recovered, and its financial results improved. By 1985, its share of world output was about 45%.[17] In the fall of 1984, an OECD committee concluded that to help reduce the continuing worldwide excess capacity in shipbuilding, the Japanese government should limit output and capacity to 40% of world demand.[18] The recommendation was not well received by either the Ministry of Transport or the Japanese shipbuilding industry.

Aluminum smelting suffered severely from the 1973 and 1979 energy shocks. Aluminum smelting requires vast amounts of electricity, and as noted earlier, most electricity in Japan is generated in oil-fired plants. Unlike producers in other countries, Japanese primary producers of aluminum ingot had no long-term contracts for electric power to moderate the impact of rising electricity prices. The Basic Stabilization Plan for aluminum smelting targeted 56.7% of the 1977 capacity for removal, more than in any other designated industry. To reach this ambitious goal, a tariff-quota system was applied in 1978 and 1979.[19] Japanese primary producers and fabricators were allowed to import aluminum ingot at reduced tariff rates on a first-come, first-served basis until the total amount of these imports equaled the amount of the demand in excess of the capacity that was to be retained under the Basic Stabilization Plan. Once this limit or quota was reached, importers were again subject to the normal tariff. The importers, in turn, paid their tariff savings (less a handling fee) to the Association for the Promotion of the Structural Improvement of the Aluminum Industry. The association then made payments to primary producers of 6.6% of the book value of the capacity that the firm had scrapped or mothballed. The subsidy served to cover the interest cost associated with capacity that was no longer in operation.

In 1982, the tariff-quota system was replaced by a tariff-exemption system. This system allowed primary producers to import aluminum up to the amount of the capacity they had closed under the Basic Stabilization Plan without paying tariffs. In effect, producers could pocket the tariff, which was then about 9.3% of the import price.

The amount of the subsidy under both systems is estimated to have totaled 28 billion yen ($112 million) through 1984. In addition, the government financed the Light Metal Stockpiling Association, which bought 61.6 billion yen ($246 million) of ingot from 1976 to 1983. There were also some low-interest loans to primary producers from the Japan Development Bank, as well as low-interest loans to convert electricity-generating plants from oil to coal. These loans were part of an energy-conservation program, not a specific measure for the aluminum industry, but generating plants owned by aluminum producers were eligible. Finally, the Research Association on the New Smelting Process for Aluminum received government subsidies to carry out basic research on new smelting processes.

The aid to the aluminum industry under these various measures was significantly greater than that for the typical industry designated under the 1978 law. Still, public assistance was less than the losses borne by aluminum companies, which amounted to 186 billion yen ($436 million) from 1976 to 1983.

The cotton and wool textile industries received assistance under a variety of government programs during the 1978–83 period. Among the laws covering the textile industries were the Exceptional Textile Act, the New Textile Act, the Act for the Promotion of Rationalization by Enterprises, the Act for Joint Activity by Small and Medium Enterprises, the Act for Modernization by Small and Medium Enterprises, the Act for Small and Medium Enterprises Affected by the Generalized System of Preferences, the Smaller Enterprise Business Switchover Act, and the Higher Yen Act.[20] The extent of duplicate coverage is difficult to determine; all of these laws had different definitions of the cotton and wool industries, and some were limited to small and medium enterprises.[21]

Two interventions appear to have had significant impact on the cotton and wool industries as defined under the 1978 law. First, recession cartels to restrict output operated intermittently during 1977 and 1978 (for about 15 months in all) and again for four months from May to September in 1981. The life of the second cartel was cut short by the Fair Trade Commission's refusal to extend it.

The second measure was 16-year interest-free loans to trade associations under the Textile Industry Joint Scrapping Plan. The loans were intended to encourage trade associations to buy small firms and scrap their capacity. The industry categories used in the 1978 law and in the Joint Scrapping Plan do not match exactly, which makes it difficult to determine the role of subsidized scrapping in the Basic Stabilization Plan for cotton and wool. We do note, however, that the number of small firms covered by the Basic Stabilization Plan in cotton declined from 215 in

1978 to 150 in 1981, and in wool, from 122 in 1977 to 93.[22] It is probable that some of this decline was the result of purchases subsidized by the Joint Scrapping Plan. According to a Japanese official, the loans for wool under the plan amounted to 10.3 billion yen ($42 million); we have not been able to determine the total assistance granted to the cotton-spinning industry.

It is unclear how the loans under the Joint Scrapping Plan are to be repaid by the trade associations at the end of 16 years. Unlike the situation for shipbuilding, there is no provision for a levy on industry sales to repay the loans. The trade associations have realized significant amounts from sale of the land and buildings of the firms they purchased, and these revenues have been invested. One trade association has placed 40% of its interest-free loans into interest-bearing accounts to finance eventual repayment.

6   Structural adjustment and protection

We have noted that one objective of the 1978 law was to provide, through a planning process to reduce excess capacity, a greater degree of price stability than unrestrained competition in the presence of substantial excess capacity might have encouraged. By indirectly supporting prices, or at least slowing their rate of decline, the law made it easier for the firms in designated industries to bear the burdens of financing and administering the relocation of labor and the repayment of debt. But it is paradoxical that prices should be supported in industries that have lost their international competitiveness. Absent barriers to trade, one would expect efforts to support domestic prices to be thwarted by increased import penetration. This observation has led many observers, especially in the United States, to suggest that Japanese structural-adjustment policies have been accompanied by overt or disguised protectionist measures.

It is quite clear that overt protection is not an issue in the designated depressed industries. Government officials insist that Japan is committed to free trade and to the OECD principle that depressed industries shall not be protected. The 1978 law made no provision for protection from import competition, and published tariff schedules confirm the claim that there has been no move toward protection. Table 8.11 shows tariff rates in 10 of the 14 designated industries. In four cases, tariffs have actually declined, and in none has there been an increase. Nor has Japan introduced such trade-limiting devices as pressuring others to adopt voluntary export restraints, a technique that has been employed by the United States and by several European countries.

Table 8.11. *Tariff rates for products of selected industries under the 1978 law (percentage of product value)*

Industry	1978	1984
Ferrosilicon	4.0	3.7
Aluminum	9.3	9.3
Polyacrylonitrile	8.0	8.0
Polyester staple	10.0	10.0
Nylon filament	10.0	10.0
Polyester filament	10.0	10.0
Ammonia	4.0	3.7
Urea	Free	Free
Phosphoric acid	6.0	5.2
Linerboard	12.0	9.3

Source: Custom Tariff Schedule of Japan (Tokyo: Japan Tariff Association, 1984).

Still, there remains an inherent inconsistency in seeking to stabilize prices and maintain free trade. The U.S. government claims that there has been substantial protection in the form of "invisible" trade barriers. We can narrow the scope of this claim by investigating, first, whether or not the trade data reveal any suggestion of invisible trade barriers in any of the designated industries. We can then proceed to a more detailed description of trade practices in those industries in which invisible barriers appear to be present.

Table 8.12 contains data on imports as a share of Japanese consumption in 11 of the 14 industries designated under the 1978 law for which data are available. Invisible barriers cannot be very important in at least two industries: ferrosilicon and aluminum, in which import penetration increased dramatically between 1978 and 1983. Invisible barriers also are not at issue in the phosphoric acid industry, in which high transportation costs make the barriers to import penetration "natural" rather than artificial. Finally, trade barriers are not a major source of protection for the electric-furnace segment of the steel industry, because its principal competition comes from domestic steel produced by conventional blast furnaces.

Seven industries remain in which protection might be suspected: the four synthetic-fiber industries, two chemical-fertilizer industries, and linerboard. In these seven cases, imports remained a small share of Japanese

Table 8.12. *Percentage import penetration in Japan's designated depressed industries (total imports as share of Japanese consumption)*

Industry	1978	1979	1980	1981	1982	1983
Electric-furnace steel	*	*	*	*	*	*
Ferrosilicon	31.0	27.0	32.0	48.0	57.0	65.0
Aluminum	44.0	37.0	57.0	66.0	81.0	83.0
Polyacrylonitrile staple	7.6	12.8	4.8	4.0	3.3	2.4
Polyester staple	7.1	5.0	3.4	1.4	2.0	4.3
Nylon filament	1.6	2.3	3.0	3.8	2.9	2.9
Polyester filament	5.7	3.1	5.5	6.1	4.8	4.2
Ammonia	*	*	*	*	*	*
Urea	0.3	0.3	0.5	1.2	3.4	6.4
Wet-process phosphoric acid	7.9	9.4	9.4	7.2	6.6	n.a.
Linerboard	2.5	2.6	4.8	5.9	4.8	5.0

*Insignificant import penetration.
Source: *Report of the U.S.–Japan Study Group on Trade Frictions* (privately printed, Tokyo, 1985), p. 65.

consumption throughout the entire period covered by the 1978 law. Yet we cannot conclude that invisible barriers to trade are present in all seven cases. The four synthetic-fiber industries, for example, actually remained competitive in international markets. Table 8.13 shows that exports continued to account for a substantial share of Japanese production throughout the period, and Japanese domestic prices actually fell slightly, relative to world prices, in all four of these industries between 1978 and 1983.[23] In these industries, at least, there appears to be no contradiction between the objectives of supporting domestic prices and maintaining free trade, because the phasing out of capacity did not cause domestic prices to increase relative to world prices.

Linerboard remained an essentially self-sufficient industry throughout the period; imports rose modestly, but not enough to eliminate possible concerns about hidden forms of protection. The price data, however, are quite inconclusive. Real prices for the two principal products of this industry (linerboard and corrugating material) moved in opposite directions. The former rose sharply after 1979; the latter was lower in 1983 than it had been in 1978.

The real issue about hidden protection, on close examination, appears to be confined to the chemical-fertilizer industries: ammonia and urea. The former has experienced no import penetration, despite a substantial increase in domestic prices since the mid-1970s. The latter, as seen

Table 8.13. *Exports as percentages of domestic production for selected depressed industries: 1977–83*

Industry	1977	1978	1979	1980	1981	1982	1983
Nylon filament	39	30	25	24	30	25	28
Polyester filament	46	46	43	46	46	46	46
Polyester staple	56	48	39	44	47	39	43
Polyacrylonitrile staple	53	50	45	47	51	46	50
Linerboard	3	3	3	4	2	3	4
Ammonia	3	2	2	1	1	1	0
Urea	60	56	47	51	47	28	12

Source: Keizai Chōsa Kenkyūkai, *Teiseichō keizai ka no sangyō chōsei to kyōsō seisaku* (Tokyo: Fair Trade Commission, 1983).

in Table 8.13, is no longer an export-oriented industry, as it was before 1982, but import penetration remains very small considering the large discrepancy between domestic and world prices. To illustrate, Rapp notes that the average domestic price of urea at the factory was $228 per metric ton in 1983.[24] To support what remained of their diminished Japanese export activities, Japanese export prices averaged $195 per metric ton during the same year. At the same time, U.S. producers were quoting prices for bulk urea landed in Japan at $145 per metric ton, but were unable to gain a substantial share of the Japanese market. It is not surprising that urea has been a focus of U.S. criticism of Japanese trade policy.

Invisible protection does appear to be a prominent feature in the chemical-fertilizer industries, but its presence does not seem to be directly attributable to the structural-adjustment policies embedded in the 1978 law. High domestic prices are sustained by the Fertilizer Price Stabilization Law, passed in 1964, which covers urea, ammonia, and other agricultural chemicals. The dual intent of this law was to assure a stable supply of fertilizer (presumably by keeping prices from fluctuating widely) and to protect Japanese farmers from exploitation by the oligopolistic chemical industry.

Under the Fertilizer Price Stabilization Law, fertilizer can be sold to farmers only by the National Federation of Agricultural Cooperatives (Zennoh) or comparable organizations. Zennoh, the largest cooperative, in turn purchases about 70% of the total urea sold in Japan for agricultural use. Each year, Zennoh negotiates prices for chemicals with the chemical producers. The prices must be approved by MITI and the Ministry of Agriculture.

Given these arrangements, Zennoh and other cooperatives are legally free to buy chemicals abroad and resell them to farmers at the official price. The cooperatives could then pass the savings from purchasing cheaper imports along to their owner-customers. Zennoh does operate some urea capacity of its own, and this may constrain such behavior in part, but Zennoh could in principle substitute imports for what it purchases from higher-priced domestic producers.

Zennoh has in fact been willing to buy some types of chemical fertilizers abroad, most notably ammonium phosphate. Indeed, one reason for the declining fortunes of the Japanese phosphoric acid industry is that phosphoric acid is an input in ammonium phosphate production.

Urea and ammonia, however, are much more significant to Japanese agricultural-chemical firms than is phosphoric acid. Each has a sales volume that is roughly three times that of phosphoric acid. This may account for the press reports suggesting that the Ministry of Agriculture and MITI have pressured Zennoh to restrict its purchases of imported urea and ammonia.

It would be misleading to attribute the creation of invisible trade barriers in the fertilizer industries to the 1978 law. The 1978 law neither authorizes nor condones import restrictions. Given the institutional structure established by the Fertilizer Price Stabilization Law some 14 years earlier, and given the long tradition of government involvement in capital-intensive industries with large firms, invisible trade barriers might well have emerged in the fertilizer industries even without passage of the 1978 law. It is true, nonetheless, that in the process of coordinating capacity reduction, especially in the concentrated industries in which "planning" is more in evidence, both industry and MITI officials may incline to the view that sharp increases in imports would be disruptive. Where the buyer side of the market is also heavily concentrated, as is the case with fertilizers, it may be easier to reach tacit or explicit agreements to discourage imports. At most, however, the institutions and processes established by 1978 law might be said to have indirectly reinforced tendencies favoring the imposition of invisible trade barriers.

7   The 1983 law

The 1978 law, Temporary Measures for Stabilization of Specific Depressed Industries, was intended to expire in 1983. By that time, capacity reductions were to be completed and the depressed industries restructured. In the official view, the sharp rise in energy prices in 1979 upset this timetable. Thus, a second law was passed in 1983 to cover the period 1983 to 1988. In this act, entitled Temporary Measures for the Structural Adjustment

Table 8.14. *Industries designated under the 1983 law and capacity-reduction targets*

Industry	Goal as % of industry capacity
Industries previously designated under the 1978 law	
Electric-furnace steel	14
Aluminum smelting[a]	57[a]
Nylon filament	0
Polyacrylonitrile staple	0
Polyester filament	0
Polyester staple	0
Ammonia	20
Urea	36
Phosphoric acid (wet process)	17
Ferrosilicon	14
Linerboard and corrugating material	20
Industries designated for the first time under the 1983 law	
Fused magnesium phosphate fertilizer	32
Compound fertilizer	13
Ethylene	36
Polyolefin	22
Polyvinyl chloride	24
Ethylene oxide	27
Unplasticized polyvinyl chloride pipes	18
Paper (excepting Japanese paper)	11
Viscose rayon staple	15
Sugar refining	26
Cement	23

[a]The goal includes capacity already closed under the 1978 law.
Source: Tsūshō Sangyō Chōsakai, *Sankōhō no kaisetsu* (Commentary on the Law for the Structural Adjustment of Specific Industries) (Tokyo: Sangyō Seisaku Kyoku, MITI, 1983).

of Specific Industries, the criteria and procedures for designation of industries are the same as in the 1978 law. Table 8.14 lists the industries designated under the 1983 law.

It is striking that 11 of the 14 industries designated under the 1978 law remain covered by the 1983 law. There are only three "graduates" – shipbuilding, cotton, and wool. The last two are still covered under separate textile laws, and shipbuilding operates under the administrative guidance of the Ministry of Transport. It is thus unclear whether or not any industry has completed its restructuring. Of course, the planning for the 1978 law did not anticipate the 1979 energy price increase, but keeping industries under special legislation is inconsistent with the OECD precept that adjustment assistance should be temporary.

The 1983 law adds 11 new industries. Two of the new industries produce fertilizers, one produces a synthetic fiber, and one produces paper products. These industries have input and demand characteristics similar to those of the previously designated industries. Five new entries are in petrochemicals, a sector that is energy-intensive like most of the others. Cement is also energy-intensive, though it is not currently subject to import competition.

The 1983 law differs from its predecessor in two important respects. First, as Table 8.15 indicates, the 1983 law provides for a broader range of financial-support measures. It is not clear how substantial the subsidies and tax benefits are. Some provisions are actually not new; for example, incentives for investment in energy-conserving equipment had been authorized by separate legislation prior to the 1983 law.

The second major change is the provision for "business tie-ups" – contractual arrangements among firms in the same industry. These may cover production, transportation, or marketing agreements, or, in the extreme, mergers. As Table 8.16 indicates, 10 of the 22 designated industries now have approved business tie-ups. In two industries, mergers were permitted, a phenomenon far less common in Japan than in the United States. In five industries, there are production or transportation tie-ups aimed at cost reduction. In the remaining three industries, there are joint-sales arrangements.

Production tie-ups are intended to facilitate the exit of underutilized, high-cost capacity by allowing one company to produce for a competitor, who then sells the product to its own customers. Transportation tie-ups are intended to reduce cross-hauling by allowing the company nearest the customer to make delivery for sales made by other companies. In each case, the company working as an agent receives payment from the principal at a price stated in the tie-up plan.

Under the antimonopoly law, transportation and production agreements are of dubious legality. The 1983 law requires advance approval of all tie-ups by the Fair Trade Commission, thus removing legal uncertainty. The procedure is analogous to the business-review process of the Antitrust Division in the U.S. Department of Justice, in which the division indicates in advance whether or not it will bring action under the Sherman Act against a particular business proposal.

Another type of tie-up involves the formation of a common selling agent for several companies. The Fair Trade Commission will approve

Table 8.15. *Comparison of financial provisions in the 1978 and 1983 laws*

Provisions	1978	1983
Government loans and guarantees	1. Japan Development Bank low-interest loans for equipment funds needed for a shift in business	1. Japan Development Bank low-interest loans for equipment investment and for modernization and improvement
	2. Low-interest loans to pay for retirement allowances necessitated by equipment disposal	2. Low-interest loans to pay for retirement allowances arising out of equipment disposal
	3. Establishment of a Specific Depressed Industries Credit Fund to guarantee liabilities with respect to the borrowing of security-release funds as well as funds for retirement allowances	3. Expansion of activities of the former Specific Depressed Industries Credit Fund (renamed the Specific Industries Credit Fund) to widen the scope of guarantees and to ease the conditions of guarantees (including a lowering of the present re-guarantee rate by two-thirds)
Government subsidies	No provisions	1. Grants for construction of coal-fired thermal power plants to replace oil-fired plants
		2. Grants for R&D to develop energy-conservation technologies
		3. Grants for R&D to develop new products and lower production costs
Taxation provisions	No provisions	1. Special depreciation system for modernization and capacity-reduction investment
		2. Extension of period for carryforward deductions from 5 to 10 years
		3. Reduction of fees for registration of mergers, investment in kind, and transfer of business, as well as for license tax and real estate acquisition tax

Source: "Expectations Placed on the New Law Concerning Measures for Basic Materials Industries," *Quarterly Survey of Japanese Finance and Industry,* July–September, 1985, p. 3.

Table 8.16. *Business tie-ups under the 1983 law*

Industry	Nature of business tie-up	Number of cases
Compound fertilizer	Merger	1
Paper (except Japanese paper)	Merger	1
Phosphoric acid (wet process)	Concentration of production	1
Fused magnesium phosphate fertilizer	Concentration of production	2
Ethylene	Concentration of production	1
Ethylene oxide	Rationalization of transportation	1
Unplasticized polyvinyl chloride pipes	Rationalization of production and transportation	4
Polyolefin	Joint-sales companies	4
Polyvinyl chloride	Joint-sales companies	4
Cement	Joint-sales companies	5

Source: Tsūshō Sangyō Chōsakai, *Sankōhō no kaisetsu* (Commentary on the Law of Temporary Measures for the Structural Adjustment in Specific Industries) (Tokyo: Sangyō Seisaku Kyoku, MITI, 1983).

such an arrangement only if the participants have a combined market share of 25% or less. In two designated industries there are exactly four joint-sales companies (polyolefin and polyvinyl chloride), and in another industry there are five (cement). The joint-sales companies convert industries with 12 or more sellers into industries with four or five sellers, thus making them significantly more concentrated. The objective is to raise or at least stabilize prices by facilitating oligopolistic coordination. Higher prices, in turn, yield the revenue to finance the costs of adjustment.

Capacity reduction under both the 1978 and 1983 laws relied in concentrated industries on encouraging joint action through indicative cartels. The depression cartels found in the synthetic-fiber and shipbuilding industries extended the scope of joint action beyond capacity reduction to current production and prices, but such arrangements were approved for only short time periods. The business tie-ups also extend the scope of joint action, but they are more permanent arrangements. The tie-ups increase the tendency to cooperation among rivals, and in that way they may facilitate realization of capacity-reduction goals. Of course, they may also increase costs to the Japanese consumers in the long run by permanently reducing competition.

8 Concluding comments

In Japan's less concentrated declining industries, many firms lack the distinctive features of large-scale Japanese enterprise, such as permanent employment. In these industries, the 1978 law appears to have done little that would not have been accomplished directly by market forces. The Basic Stabilization Plans were essentially forecasts, not plans, and capacity reduction was achieved primarily by the exit of small firms unburdened with the large exit costs characteristic of oligopolists in Japan.

The role of policy in concentrated industries is more interesting. Moving resources out of these industries is difficult. First, in the context of the permanent-employment system, substantial job reductions are highly disruptive. Under existing union contracts, as well as established norms, large firms have a continuing obligation to support or compensate laid-off or discharged workers. Second, large firms are heavily debt-financed, and reducing capacity requires repaying loans secured by the capacity to preserve the goodwill of customary lenders. The combined effect of the labor and loan obligations is to impose high exit costs on large Japanese firms. These can be avoided only by bankruptcy, which in turn has major ramifications for both financial and labor markets. Even in the absence of these distinctive Japanese labor and credit arrangements, public policy in the United States and Western Europe goes to considerable lengths to avoid bankruptcy of large firms. It is not surprising that Japanese public policy is the same, particularly because in the Japanese context bankruptcy may involve even higher social costs than in the United States and Western Europe. Indeed, in Japan, large firms' status as quasi-permanent social institutions means that they are not dissolved lightly. Even mergers are viewed as social upheavals in Japan, in sharp contrast with the United States.

The Japanese approach to industrial decline is particularly appropriate to this institutional environment. By coordinating capacity reduction, sometimes through cartels, public policy seeks to maintain prices at levels sufficient to permit large firms to shoulder a substantial share of the burden of labor relocation and debt repayment, thus preserving these unique institutional features. Higher prices mean that the consumers of the products of declining industries bear a burden, but the approach may be justified as a particular form of second best, given the institutional constraints.

Compared with a policy of subsidization, as is common in Western Europe, managing decline through coordination and cartelization has some distinct advantages. Ideally, subsidies would be provided for costs of adjustment and reallocation; in practice, subsidies tend to support firms in a declining industry and retard the exit of resources. Although cartelization may delay the exit of resources relative to what might result from unrestrained market forces, cartelization at least has the virtue that its adverse effects are self-limiting. There is only so much that consumers can be made to pay to support the continued existence of a declining industry. Taxpayers, however, have deeper pockets. Resources would undoubtedly have left the British coal industry or the Swedish shipbuilding industry much more quickly under a policy of cartelization than under the massive subsidies that have been provided.

In principle, the Japanese approach to declining industries appears to be consistent with the guidelines suggested by the OECD. The 1978 law was intended as a temporary measure; the statute had a duration limited to five years. The measures appear to be transparent; because we have been able to charaterize them, we assume that trading partners can do so. Support measures are linked to capacity reduction; indeed, capacity reduction is the principal goal of the policy. The approach, on paper at least, does not rely on protectionist measures; no tariffs have been increased in the designated depressed industries.

In practice, however, the policies have not been unambiguously consistent with the OECD guidelines, nor have the policies been unambiguously successful on their own terms.

First, none of the industries designated under the 1978 law completed its restructuring in five years. Many "temporary" stabilization plans have entered a second five-year period, and the 1983 law nearly doubled the number of designated industries. Particularly troublesome is the creation of business tie-ups, especially the joint-sales agencies, that threaten to become permanent arrangements. Democratic governments everywhere have found that temporary measures that confer rents tend to become permanent measures.

Second, although capacity reduction has proceeded more or less as planned, the plans, based largely on what firms were willing to do, may not have been sufficiently ambitious. In no industry was capacity entirely eliminated in response to lost international competitiveness. Comparative advantage might dictate, for example, complete abandonment of the urea industry. Only aluminum smelting has approached this outcome; the current stabilization plan calls for a reduction in capacity to 25% of the 1975 level.

Third, although the evidence is murky, it appears that the structural-adjustment policies have in fact been contaminated with protectionist measures. The precise extent of informal trade barriers in the chemical-fertilizer industries is unknown, and probably unknowable, but the price discrepancies in urea, for example, are too large to support any conclusion other than that imports have been restricted.

Despite these imperfections, the Japanese approach to declining industries seems on balance to be uniquely suited to the peculiar institutional environment of large-scale, concentrated Japanese industry. It may be unrealistic to insist that all structural adjustment be completed in five years, that loser industries completely scrap all capacity, and that protectionist measures be avoided entirely. It would certainly be difficult to argue that other countries have had greater success in phasing out their loser industries. Given the marked international differences in labor and credit arrangements, Japan's approach to picking losers probably would be inappropriate in an institutional environment like that of the United States, but in its context it has achieved reasonably satisfactory results.

ACKNOWLEDGMENTS

The authors would like to thank those who assisted in gathering the data and information used in this chapter: officials of the Ministry of International Trade and Industry, the Fair Trade Commission, and the Economic Planning Agency, Professor Sueo Sekiguchi of Seikei University, and Kazuyuki Suzuki of the Japan Development Bank. Christopher Erickson provided valuable research assistance, Virginia Casey typed the manuscript, and Junichi Goto assisted in translating certain Japanese-language material. Helpful comments on a previous draft were provided by Junichi Goto, Roger Noll, Hugh Patrick, and Andrea Shepard.

NOTES

1. See J. Peter Neary, "Intersectoral Capital Mobility, Wage Stickiness, and the Case for Adjustment Assistance," in J. N. Bhagwati (ed.), *Import Competition and Response* (University of Chicago Press, 1982), pp. 39–67, and Micheal Mussa, "Government Policy and the Adjustment Process," in Bhagwati (ed.), *Import Competition and Response,* pp. 73–120.
2. Pankaj Ghemawat and Barry Nalebuff, "Exit," *The Rand Journal of Economics,* Summer 1985, pp. 184–94.
3. These principles are summarized in a 1984 work printed privately by the Japanese–American Trade Study Group, entitled "Structurally Depressed Industries."
4. See, for example, Yoshie Yonezawa, "The System of Industrial Adjustment Policies for Trade in Japan," a 1979 discussion paper for the Japan Economic Research Center; Garry Saxonhouse, "Industrial Restructuring in Japan," Journal of Japanese Studies, Vol. 5, No. 2, pp. 237–42; Jimmy W. Wheeler, Merit E. Janow, and Thomas Pepper, *Japanese Industrial Development Policies in the 1980s: Implications for U.S. Trade and Investment* (Croton-on-Hudson: Hudson Institute, 1982), pp. 161–90; and Masu Uekusa, "Industrial Organization: The 1970s to the Present," in Kozo Yamamura and Yasukichi Yasuba (eds.), *The Political Economy of Japan, Vol. 1: The Domestic Transformation*

(Stanford University Press, 1987). A notable recent contribution by Michael
K. Young emphasizes the role of firms in the depressed industries in shaping
the policies that govern them: "Structurally Depressed and Declining Industries in Japan: A Case Study in Minimally Intrusive Industrial Policy," in
Joint Economic Committee, *Japan's Economy and Trade with the United
States* (Washington, D.C.: U.S. Government Printing Office, 1986), pp. 133–
50. Policies for depressed industries should be distinguished from those for
specific large firms that are in financial difficulty. Mazda is the most frequently
cited example. See Thomas Rohlen and Richard Pascale, "The Mazda Turnaround," *Journal of Japanese Studies,* Vol. 9, No. 2, pp. 213–63.

5. In the case of the shipbuilding industry, the Ministry of Transport is responsible for administering the provisions of the 1978 law.

6. According to a study by Shinohara, oil accounted for 73% of Japan's primary energy supply in 1977, in contrast to 59% in France, 53% in West Germany, 48% in the United States, and 44% in the United Kingdom. Miyohei
Shinohara, *Industrial Growth, Trade, and Dynamic Patterns in the Japanese
Economy* (University of Tokyo Press, 1982), p. 17. According to a study by
Dunkerley, real energy prices paid by industrial consumers rose 55% in Japan
from 1973 to 1976; prices over the same period rose 13% in France, 23% in
the United Kingdom, 25% in West Germany, and 45% in the United States.
Joy Dunkerley, *Trends in Energy Use in Industrial Societies: An Overview*
(Washington, D.C.: Resources for the Future, 1980).

7. See Table 8.3.

8. For a discussion of this law, see the report of the U.S. General Accounting Office, *Industrial Policy: Japan's Flexible Approach* (Washington, D.C.: GAO,
1982), pp. 69ff.

9. Data on employment in the aluminum-smelting industry were obtained from
the Fair Trade Commission.

10. Information about the Depressed District Act was obtained from interviews
with Japanese officials.

11. For a discussion of the Smaller Enterprise Business Switchover Act, see Yonezawa, "The System of Industrial Adjustment Policies," op. cit. (pp. 41–3).

12. As quoted in Edward Boyer, "How Japan Manages Declining Industries,"
Fortune, 10 June 1983, p. 63.

13. Calculated by the authors from data in U.S. General Accounting Office, *Industrial Policy: Case Studies in the Japanese Experience: Report to the Chairman, Joint Economic Committee, U.S. Congress* (Washington, D.C.: GAO,
1982), pp. 66–7.

14. Information on public assistance was obtained from the *Quarterly Survey of
Japanese Finance and Industry,* July–September 1983, p. 3.

15. Except where otherwise noted, our principal source of information on the shipbuilding industry was a report of the U.S. General Accounting Office, *Industrial Policy: Case Studies in the Japanese Experience,* Appendix V, op. cit.

16. Ibid., p. 62.

17. Information on the shipbuilding industry's share of world output in 1985 was
obtained in interviews with Japanese officials.

18. Information on the OECD committee's recommendations was obtained in
interviews with Japanese officials.

19. Information about subsidies to the aluminum industry is drawn from Akira
Goto, "The Aluminum Industry in Japan," in M. J. Peck (ed.), *The World*

Aluminum Industry in an Era of Changing Energy Prices (Washington, D.C.: Resources for the Future, in press).

20. For a discussion of these laws, see the report of the U.S. General Accounting Office, *Industrial Policy: Case Studies in the Japanese Experience,* op. cit.

21. Although the definition has changed over time, "small and medium enterprises" currently are those with fewer than 300 employees or less than 100 million yen in share capital.

22. See Table 8.5.

23. The price data discussed here and elsewhere in this section are taken from a Bank of Japan, Research and Statistics Department, publication: *Price Indexes Annual,* 1980 and 1983.

24. William V. Rapp, "Japan's Invisible Barriers to Trade" (unpublished paper, Tokyo, 1985).

CHAPTER 9

Corporate capital structure in the United States and Japan: financial intermediation and implications of financial deregulation

James E. Hodder

1 Introduction

Over the last decade, capital-structure differences between U.S. and Japanese firms have been the source of considerable comment.[1] Much of the discussion has focused on overall debt-to-equity ratios, with several authors attempting to provide an economic rationale for the apparently greater borrowing propensity of Japanese firms. Other authors have suggested that the generally higher debt-to-equity ratios of Japanese firms result in lower overall capital costs and a consequent competitive advantage relative to their U.S. counterparts. Still other authors have argued that the apparently higher debt-to-equity ratios are largely accounting artifacts.

Despite the acknowledged problems with accounting measures, there do appear to be substantial differences in borrowing practices between the two countries. Not only are average debt-to-equity ratios somewhat higher for Japanese corporations, but they are extraordinarily high (by U.S. standards) for some firms. Furthermore, the maturity composition of this debt, as well as the role played by financial intermediaries, has been quite different for Japanese borrowers.

One purpose of this chapter is to explore such differences and see what they can tell us about the plausibility of different capital-structure theories. Another purpose is to examine the use of financial intermediation and delegated monitoring (monitoring by the primary creditor) in dealing with bankruptcy risks. Particularly with regard to Japanese lending practices, this chapter will emphasize the role of financial-market regulation. Indeed, the past nature of that regulation fostered development of the "main-bank" lending system in Japan. This system is unique and appears to be a critical feature in allowing heavy borrowing by some Japanese

241

firms. However, the viability of that system may be seriously threatened by certain aspects of financial deregulation.[2] This leads to some interesting questions regarding future trends for capital structure and borrowing practices in Japan.

The next section provides a brief overview of capital-structure theories. Section 3 discusses the usefulness of these theories in explaining differing capital-structure patterns in the United States and Japan. Section 4 examines the role of financial intermediation with delegated monitoring in Japan. Finally, Section 5 provides some summary observations as well as conjectures about future trends for capital structure and borrowing practices of Japanese firms.

2   Capital-structure theories

There has been considerable theoretical controversy regarding the economic rationale underlying firm capital-structure decisions, as well as whether or not an optimal structure even exists. Currently, there are two major themes regarding corporate motivations for borrowing. One theme rests on potential advantages from the tax deductibility of corporate interest payments. The other suggests that information or managerial-control asymmetries may provide an incentive for borrowing. It is generally acknowledged that some form of market imperfection (taxes, asymmetric information, etc.) is necessary to provide a positive motivation for borrowing. Otherwise, Modigliani and Miller's (1958) "leverage-irrelevance proposition" holds, and a firm's value is unaffected by its capital structure.

Assuming that some market imperfection exists to motivate borrowing, we need a countervailing effect to obtain an optimal capital structure that is not essentially all debt. Various such effects have been suggested. Generally, they relate to the risk that a firm will encounter financial distress. Even if the firm does not enter bankruptcy, it may lose tax shields and incur losses on distressed sales of physical assets. Also, attempts by employees, suppliers, and potential customers to protect themselves against a possible corporate liquidation can seriously impair firm value. There may also be "agency costs" that are an increasing function of leverage and the probability of the firm being unable to fulfill its debt obligations. Such costs result from lenders' actions to protect themselves against management moves (such as investing in high-risk projects) to benefit shareholders at the expense of debtholders.[3] In what follows, the aggregate of the foregoing effects will be referred to for labeling purposes as the "cost of financial distress." We also follow the usual practice of assuming that this cost is an increasing convex function of the firm's debt-to-equity ratio.

The typical textbook approach suggests that an optimal capital structure represents a trade-off between a linearly increasing value of interest tax shields from borrowing and the cost of financial distress. The motivation for borrowing in this approach is based on Modigliani and Miller (1963, 1969), who argued that the tax deductibility of corporate interest payments means that leverage increases a firm's value. This result appears in the well-known formula

$$V_L = V_U + \tau D \tag{1}$$

where V_L denotes the firm's levered value, V_U is its unlevered value, D is the firm's debt level, and τ is the corporate tax rate.

In his presidential address to the American Finance Association, Miller (1977) raised serious questions about the general validity of equation (1), as well as whether or not there is an optimal capital structure for an individual firm. There are two key ingredients to Miller's analysis. First, he considers the effects of both personal and corporate taxes. Second, he argues that in equilibrium, an individual should be indifferent between an after-tax dollar of interest income and an after-tax dollar of equity income.

Using the same basic approach as Modigliani and Miller (1969), it is easy to show that with both personal and corporate taxes,

$$V_L = V_U + \left[1 - \frac{(1-\tau)(1-\tau_{PE})}{(1-\tau_P)} \right] D \tag{2}$$

where τ_P is the personal tax rate on interest income, and τ_{PE} is the personal tax rate on equity income (including both dividends and capital gains). For comparison purposes, equation (2) can be written as

$$V_L = V_U + \delta D \tag{3}$$

where

$$\delta = 1 - \frac{(1-\tau)(1-\tau_{PE})}{(1-\tau_P)}$$

The second part of Miller's argument implies that in equilibrium, $(1-\tau)(1-\tau_{PE}) = (1-\tau_P)$ should hold. In that case, $\delta = 0$ and $V_L = V_U$. In other words, the firm cannot increase its value by debt financing, and there is no optimal capital structure at the firm level.

In Miller's analysis, the personal tax rates (τ_P and τ_{PE}) are for marginal individual lenders and equity-holders. Consequently, there may be value to the tax deductibility of interest payments, but that value is captured by lenders in low tax brackets rather than by borrowing firms. As a result, there may be an economy-wide optimal capital structure without an optimum at the firm level. Note that under these circumstances, corporate borrowing does not result in a lower overall cost of capital for the firm. Consequently, the notion of a competitive advantage for high-debt-to-equity firms is inconsistent with Miller's equilibrium.

Miller's ideas have been extended and modified by several authors, including DeAngelo and Masulis (1980) and Barnea, Haugen, and Senbet (1981a). The basic thrust of those studies was to consider agency costs and the probability of losing noninterest tax shields (e.g., depreciation) as a function of firm debt levels. These considerations represent additional costs to borrowing not considered by Miller and result in an equilibrium in which $(1 - \tau_P) > (1 - \tau)(1 - \tau_{PE})$. In these extended versions of Miller's model, there is an economy-wide ratio for $(1 - \tau)(1 - \tau_{PE})/(1 - \tau_P)$ that depends on the equilibrium marginal agency cost, and so forth, for corporate borrowing. Because the agency-cost function and the extent of noninterest tax shields are firm-specific, there is an optimal capital structure at the firm level in these models. Consequently, there is a cost-of-capital advantage to borrowing. However, that advantage may be relatively small, because it depends on the net effect of corporate versus personal taxes.

Considering the other main theme regarding borrowing motivations, the most interesting developments for our purposes are contained in recent studies by Myers (1984) and Myers and Majluf (1984).[4] These studies develop what Myers calls the "pecking-order theory" of corporate capital structure. According to this theory, firms prefer to finance new asset acquisitions from internal sources (retained earnings and depreciation). If external funds are necessary, additional debt is preferred to new equity issues as long as the firm's debt remains approximately default-free.

The preference for debt over equity issues comes from a problem with asymmetric information similar to Akerlof's (1970) "lemons model." Managers are assumed to have superior information regarding potential investment projects as well as future values of the firm's existing assets. They are also assumed to make decisions based on the welfare of current shareholders. Under these circumstances, potential new shareholders believe that management may try to exploit them by issuing shares when it has unfavorable information. Consequently, there is a tendency to undervalue shares issued to finance what are actually favorable projects. The cost implied from such an undervaluation results in a preference for borrowing when a potential new project requires external funding. If the firm's debt is sufficiently risky, management may opt for an equity issue, but only if the project is valuable enough to offset the cost of issuing undervalued equity. Otherwise, potentially desirable projects may be deferred or rejected entirely.

The motivation for borrowing in this pecking-order approach is simply to avoid issuing undervalued equity. A firm's capital structure is largely a cumulative function of its ability to generate internal funds more or less rapidly than it invests in new projects. There is no optimal target for its debt-to-equity ratio or any presumption that the tax deductibility of interest imparts an added benefit to debt financing, although this latter notion is not precluded by the theory.

Thus, we currently have two rather different notions of why corporations borrow. However, with both the modified Miller model and the pecking-order approach the amount of borrowing is limited by what we call the costs of financial distress. In order to see how well these theories perform, we now turn to some evidence on capital structures in the United States and Japan.

3 Corporate capital structures in the United States and Japan

First of all, let us consider some data on aggregate capital structures. Table 9.1 displays aggregate balance sheets for manufacturing corporations in the United States and Japan.

As mentioned earlier, Japanese firms appear to have much higher debt-to-equity ratios than their U.S. counterparts. In Table 9.1 this is illustrated, with net worth (equity) being a relatively low percentage of total assets for Japanese firms. Furthermore, this equity-to-asset percentage has increased substantially since 1976, when it reached a low of 17.2% after declining from roughly 33% during the mid-1950s. In contrast, reported net-worth-to-asset ratios for U.S. manufacturers have declined rather steadily since the mid-1950s, when net worth equaled approximately two-thirds of total assets. In other words, the gap between equity-to-asset (or debt-to-equity) ratios for U.S. and Japanese manufacturers has been closing since the mid-1970s; however, it had widened significantly from the mid-1950s to the mid-1970s. Currently, the gap still appears quite substantial.

In making capital-structure comparisons such as the preceding, we need to be aware that accounting differences as well as enormous appreciations in market values of book assets (particularly land and securities) have raised questions about reported equity-to-asset ratios for Japanese firms. For example, Aoki (1984a) attempts to adjust for a variety of possible distortions using aggregate numbers for all nonfinancial corporations listed on the Tokyo Stock Exchange. His results indicate that adjusted equity values for 1981 represent about 40% of total assets for a typical firm, roughly twice the reported figure.[5] On the other hand, U.S. manufacturers presumably also have book-asset values below market

Table 9.1. *Aggregate balance sheet for manufacturing corporations in the United States and Japan (1983)*

Balance-sheet entries	U.S. firms		Japanese firms	
	Billions of dollars	Percentage of total	Trillion yen	Percentage of total
Assets				
Cash and marketable securities	107	6	27	14
Accounts and notes receivable	263	15	49	25
Inventories	291	17	35	18
Fixed assets	662	39	71	36
Other assets	381	22	16	8
Total assets	1,704	100	198	100
Liabilities				
Accounts and notes payable (trade payables)	156	9	47	24
Short-term debt	74	4	36	18
Long-term debt	314	18	30	15
Other liabilities	325	19	36	18
Total liabilities	869	51	149	75
Net worth	835	49	49	25
Total liabilities and net worth	1,704	100	198	100

Sources: U.S. Federal Trade Commission, *Quarterly Financial Report for Manufacturing, Mining and Trade Corporations;* Bank of Japan, *Economic Statistics Annual.*

because of inflation, as well as unrealized gains on low-interest, long-term debt. Consequently, the U.S. equity-to-asset ratio probably is also understated, but to a lesser extent than for Japanese manufacturers.

It is also important to recognize that aggregate figures tend to conceal extremes in both directions. There are Japanese companies that have very little debt and massive financial resources in the form of cash and marketable securities. There are also major Japanese manufacturers with reported equity-to-asset ratios of 10% or less. Even doubling the reported equity figures for some of these firms would still indicate firms operating on 80–90% debt financing. Clearly, it has been possible to operate a major firm in Japan on a much more highly levered basis than would generally be acceptable to U.S. lenders; however, not all firms have chosen that path.

There are several other points worth noting from Table 9.1. Japanese firms tend to maintain large cash and receivables positions. The former typically results from compensating balance requirements on bank loans. The latter is part of a pattern in which generous trade credit is used by large firms to help finance their smaller affiliates.

On the liability side, the Japanese firms have a heavy concentration of payables (part of the trade-credit-financing mechanism) and short-term debt. Together, these represent 42% of total financing and over 2.5 times their long-term debt positions. Note that short-term debt actually exceeds long-term debt for Japanese manufacturers. This results from the practice in Japanese city banks of lending for a short term and then "rolling over" the loans to effectively provide long-term financing.[6]

One point that is not apparent from Table 9.1 is the small fraction of bonds in the long-term debt of Japanese industrial firms. For example, in 1984, bonds composed only 4% of the capital structure for all nonfinancial companies listed on the Tokyo Stock Exchange. That group includes utility companies, which, at least in recent years, have accounted for roughly three-quarters of nonconvertible corporate bond issues. Consequently, straight bonds all but disappear from the balance sheets of Japanese manufacturers. In contrast, convertibles have become relatively popular in what appears to be primarily an equity-issue mechanism. We shall return to this point.

A similar perspective on the relative importance of corporate bond issues appears in Table 9.2. That table also indicates that the sale of new equity has been a rather minor source of funds and that the vast majority of external funding by Japanese firms has been obtained by borrowing from private financial institutions (primarily banks and insurance companies). Since the mid-1970s, approximately 50% of net industrial funds have been generated internally. Of the remaining half, roughly 75% was borrowed from private financial intermediaries.

Table 9.3 presents comparable data for U.S. nonfinancial corporations. Again, there are interesting contrasts. U.S. firms financed a considerably larger portion of their expansion with internally generated funds (70% vs. 52%). Also, corporate bonds represent a much larger fraction (roughly one-third) of external funding. If we include the use of tax-exempt industrial-revenue bonds, bonds account for 41% of average external funds. This is an order of magnitude greater than the relative use of corporate bonds in Japan. Altogether, the use of market debt instruments (bonds, commercial paper, and acceptances) slightly exceeds borrowing from financial institutions. Again, this is a very different picture from that for Japan.

One feature that appears in both Tables 9.2 and 9.3 is the minimal use of new equity issues as a funding source. Also, in both countries, large fractions of corporate funding needs are met from internal sources. Both

Table 9.2. *Net sources of industrial funds in Japan (%)*

Year	Equity issues	Corporate bonds	Loans from private financial institutions	Borrowing from government institutions	Internal funds (depreciation & retained earnings)
1950	3.7	5.1	43.6	7.6	40.0
1955	6.3	1.7	30.8	5.8	55.3
1960	9.2	3.0	40.6	4.3	42.9
1965	2.7	2.2	41.1	4.5	49.5
1970	3.9	1.4	40.4	4.0	50.3
1974	3.4	1.9	46.9	6.7	41.0
1975	4.0	4.1	45.4	7.2	39.3
1976	2.6	2.0	43.6	6.2	45.6
1977	3.3	2.1	34.5	6.0	54.2
1978	3.1	2.0	28.2	5.3	61.3
1979	3.5	2.3	28.5	6.8	58.9
1980	3.3	1.3	34.8	5.7	54.8
1981	4.4	2.2	35.4	6.6	51.4
1982	4.2	1.3	36.5	4.8	53.3
1983	2.7	0.6	36.3	3.0	57.4
Avg. for 1974–83	3.5	2.0	37.0	5.8	51.7

Source: Bank of Japan, *Economic Statistics Annual.*

these facts are clearly consistent with the pecking-order theory. That theory is also consistent with substantially different capital structures across firms within a given industry – a characteristic that occurs in both countries. There are several other features of Japanese finance that also support the pecking-order model.

From the early 1950s until the mid-1970s, Japanese firms were generally growing at rapid rates. For example, Kurosawa (1981) provides estimates that total assets for such firms grew at an average rate of 15.6% from 1955 to 1974. During that same period, these firms had annual operating profits before interest or taxes that averaged 9.4% of assets. If these firms had been totally equity-financed and had paid no dividends, their after-tax earnings would have financed roughly a 4.7% growth rate, less than one-third of the growth that actually occurred. Instead, these firms were highly levered and were paying substantial dividends.[7] Consequently, they had enormous external-funding requirements. Those requirements were largely met through borrowing, with the result that equity-to-asset

Table 9.3. *Net sources of funds for U.S. nonfinancial corporations (%)*[a]

Year	Equity issues	Corporate bonds	Industrial-revenue bonds	Commercial paper & acceptances	Loans from private financial institutions	Internal funds (depreciation & retained earnings)
1974	2.6	12.6	1.0	3.5	24.3	54.9
1975	6.6	18.1	1.7	−1.8	−4.3	79.5
1976	5.6	12.1	1.3	1.4	8.5	71.0
1977	1.2	10.0	2.9	1.0	16.5	68.5
1978	~0	8.2	3.0	1.5	18.0	68.6
1979	−2.8	6.2	3.6	3.6	20.8	68.2
1980	4.6	9.4	3.9	1.7	12.9	67.0
1981	−3.6	6.8	4.2	5.2	15.6	71.5
1982	3.6	5.9	4.8	−1.7	13.3	73.8
1983	7.8	4.4	2.6	−0.3	8.4	77.2
Avg.	2.6	9.4	2.9	1.4	13.4	70.0

[a]Rows do not add to 100% because we excluded loans from the U.S. government. Such loans averaged 0.3% of the annual totals during this period.
Source: Board of Governors, Federal Reserve System, *Flow of Funds Accounts.*

ratios declined steadily over the period. This result is quite consistent with a pecking-order model, indeed, more so than with an optimal-capital-structure approach.

The manner in which Japanese firms have raised new equity funds is also significant. Prior to approximately 1970, virtually all new issues were rights offerings at par to existing shareholders. Although rights offerings still account for approximately 20% of new equity funds, they are much less important than previously. The interesting feature of rights issues is that they can avoid the problem of potential exploitation of new shareholders.

Also, about 1970, Japanese firms began issuing substantial amounts of convertible bonds. In fact, the annual market value of convertible-bond issues has generally exceeded that for public offerings of new equity since the late 1970s. From 1978 to 1983, convertible issues totaled 9 trillion yen, with 60% being issued in overseas markets (primarily Europe). During the same period, public equity offerings amounted to 6 trillion yen, including slightly over 600 billion yen equivalent in foreign markets.

When issuing these bonds, the conversion price is set quite close to the market price for the firm's shares – the guideline is a 5% premium (*Japan Securities Research Institute, Securities Markets in Japan 1984*). As a consequence, the vast majority of these bonds are converted. In some cases, this occurs very rapidly (e.g., 85% conversion within six months of issue). Indeed, the issue of convertibles by Japanese firms is widely viewed as largely an equity-raising mechanism. For our purposes, the interesting thing about convertibles is that they represent a combination of common stock plus a "put option." If the value of the stock falls (or fails to rise), purchasers of convertibles can, in effect, put the underlying stock back to the firm by holding the bond to maturity without exercising the conversion privilege. Thus, the firm is issuing securities that partially protect the purchaser against the asymmetric information problems described by Myers and Majluf.

Let us now turn to the tax-incentive models of borrowing. These models obviously have difficulty in explaining significant capital-structure differences across similar firms, which is a characteristic of industries in both countries. Because corporate tax rates are similar in the two countries, the simple Modigliani–Miller model in equation (1) does not indicate a substantial differential incentive for borrowing by Japanese firms.[8] However, that model is a special case of the more general approach that includes personal as well as corporate taxes. Consequently, we need to consider how the value of δ in equation (3) differs between the two countries.

There are several reasons to believe that personal taxes on investment income (interest as well as dividends and capital gains) are generally lower in Japan than in the United States. With some exceptions, capital gains are not taxable for individuals in Japan. Also, interest income and dividend income are generally taxed at lower rates than regular personal income. Most important, very large percentages of personal financial assets in Japan are held in tax-exempt or tax-deferred forms. According to the Bank of Japan's *Economic Statistics Annual*, as of March 1984, 58% of personal savings were in tax-exempt accounts. A further 18% were held in (tax-deferred) insurance policies, for a total of 76% in essentially untaxed holdings. This number has been growing rather steadily over the last decade, rising from approximately 60% in 1974.

In a recent study, Flath (1984) estimated a model similar to that of Miller for Japan as well as for the United States using 1971 data. His estimates indicated δ values of 0.406 and 0.354 for Japan and the United States, respectively.[9] These represent average rather than equilibrium δ values, because Flath estimated marginal tax rates for an average of investors in each country, rather than the "marginal investor" hypothesized in Miller's model. Consequently, we cannot tell if there was a differential tax incentive at the margin for corporate borrowing across the two countries. However, those estimates indicate larger average tax benefits (accruing to lenders) in Japan on the existing stock of debt. His analysis ignored the very substantial fraction of Japanese personal savings in tax-exempt accounts. Consequently, the average tax benefits for Japanese lenders presumably were greater than indicated by Flath's estimates. Thus, there appear to have been tax benefits on an economy-wide basis in 1971 that were consistent with greater aggregate leverage for Japanese firms, without necessarily implying a greater incentive for borrowing at the firm level.

There are a couple features of the recent past that are somewhat inconsistent with a Miller equilibrium in Japan. First of all, equity-to-asset ratios have been growing rapidly since the mid-1970s at the same time that average tax benefits should have been growing because of the increasing fraction of tax-exempt personal savings. A possible explanation for this apparent contradiction is an increase in the risk of financial distress following the "first oil shock" and subsequent recession in 1973–4.

Kurosawa (1981) and Kurosawa and Wakasugi (1984) document a substantial increase in earnings volatility and a somewhat lower return on assets for Japanese firms since 1974. This shift in the business environment is consistent with an increased probability of financial distress and a lower desired debt level for firms in a modified Miller model. This, of course, implies an optimal capital structure at the firm level that shifted across a wide number of firms more or less simultaneously. What the modified Miller model does not explain is the gradual shift in Japanese capital structures observed over the last decade. If the optimal debt-to-equity ratio changed in the mid-1970s, why was there not a rapid recapitalization by exchanging equity for debt to return to an optimal position?

A recapitalization of the type mentioned earlier is generally thought to benefit lenders at the expense of shareholders; however, in Japan there is a substantial overlap between the two groups. Table 9.4 provides information on the distribution of share ownership in Japan. The shares listed under financial institutions are held almost entirely by banks and insurance companies. Also, substantial portions of the holdings by business corporations involve either parent-subsidiary or cross-holding relationships. From an aggregate perspective, with those interfirm holdings netted out, financial institutions control roughly half the remaining (externally held) shares. Furthermore, as we shall discuss shortly, the major banks in Japan have enormous power to influence corporate policies.

If the advantages to a recapitalization had been large enough, presumably it could have been accomplished fairly rapidly, perhaps with financial institutions compensating other shareholders out of the net gains. The adjustment is taking place, but it is occurring slowly. Also, it is basically being carried out via greater internal funding and less borrowing (see Table 9.2). This gradual adjustment, plus the fact that new share

Table 9.4. *Share ownership of Japanese firms by type of investor: 1984 (all listed companies)*

Investors	Percentage of listed shares	Percentage of market value
National and local governments	0.2	0.3
Financial institutions	38.0	35.9
Investment trusts	1.0	1.5
Securities companies	1.9	1.7
Business corporations	25.9	27.6
Individuals & others	26.8	24.2
Foreigners	6.3	8.8

Source: Tokyo Stock Exchange, *Tokyo Stock Exchange Fact Book 1985.*

issues are not playing much of a role, indicates rather substantial costs associated with equity issues. This is exactly the point behind the Myers–Majluf model.

It is also true that the aggregate growth of Japanese firms has slowed since 1974. In contrast with the rapid growth from 1955 to 1974 (15.6% annually), Kurosawa (1981) found an average growth rate of only 6.5% for the 1975–9 period. Kurosawa and Wakasugi (1984) used a somewhat different sample, with 377 large manufacturing firms. They found that although sales continued to grow (at a slower rate) after 1974, capital investment actually declined in real terms at a 1.8% annual rate from 1974 to 1980. It is unclear whether a less profitable business environment led to slower growth or whether the slowdown was at least partially caused by the need to adjust corporate capital structures. However, the latter would certainly be consistent with the pecking-order model.

Aoki (1984b) suggested a rather different rationale for the relatively high debt positions by Japanese firms. His argument basically had two parts. First, financial institutions (particularly banks) were able to extract substantial rents via spreads between deposit interest rates for investors and effective lending rates to firms (adjusted for compensating balances). Second, banks were able to use their positions as both lender and shareholder to induce greater corporate borrowing than would have been preferred by individual shareholders.

The first part of this analysis suggests that the major Japanese banks were able to siphon off some of the tax benefits associated with corporate borrowing. In turn, the Japanese government apparently recaptured some of those benefits by requiring banks to effectively underwrite government bond issues at below-market rates. Although the mechanism differs from that in Miller-type models, the tax incentive for borrowing is again greatly reduced from the firm perspective. Thus, some motivation other than tax incentives is needed to explain heavy corporate borrowing.

The second part of Aoki's argument addresses this motivation issue; however, his analysis presumably applies best to firms with modest amounts of leverage. His model excludes the possibility of bankruptcy; consequently, the results do not reflect the relatively large option component in share values of highly levered firms. With the possibility of bankruptcy, there should be a reversal in a bank's attitude toward further firm borrowing at debt levels at which this option effect starts to outweigh the bank's rent-extraction capabilities. However, such debt levels may be relatively high in Japan because of the monitoring and control abilities of main banks, as discussed in the next section. To the extent that Aoki's analysis holds at lower debt levels, it could be viewed as an additional motivation for borrowing beyond the asymmetric-information arguments of Myers and Majluf.

4 Financial intermediation, delegated monitoring, and the risk of financial distress

It is clear from our discussion that the risk of financial distress plays an important role in capital-structure decisions. A particularly interesting aspect of Japanese finance is the way the expected cost of financial distress has been controlled by the financial intermediation process.[10] This is crucial to an explanation of the high debt-to-equity ratios of some major firms.

First, it is important to recognize that the costs involved if a major firm actually fails are potentially much higher in Japan than in the United States. There tends to be a strong dependency for sales as well as trade finance between smaller Japanese firms and their major (sometimes only) customers. Consequently, failure of a larger customer could drag down a number of affiliated suppliers. There also appears to be more reliance on sole-sourcing of components in Japan, and so failure of a key supplier could create costly problems for a customer firm. Perhaps most important of all, labor mobility in Japan is limited, and pension benefits have been largely unfunded firm liabilities. Thus, employees of a failed firm may lose their accrued retirement benefits and have considerable difficulty in obtaining comparable jobs at other firms. This latter point is particularly true for management personnel.

The key to lowering the expected value of the costs that will be incurred if a firm fails is to reduce the probability of failure. This would appear to be a difficult problem for firms operating with heavy leverage, but at least in theory, it is relatively simple. There are two basic requirements. One is the ability of lenders to monitor and control management's risk-taking behavior. This not only reduces the bankruptcy risk but also dramatically decreases agency costs associated with possible management actions to benefit shareholders at the expense of lenders. The other requirement is the ability to smoothly and quickly reorganize a firm in financial difficulty while maintaining the confidence and support of customers, suppliers, and employees.

For small firms, reorganization often is handled by a large customer, who typically has been supplying much of the smaller firm's funding via trade credit and perhaps a significant equity position. Assuming that the small firm is inherently viable, the larger firm protects both a source of supply and its financial stake in the smaller firm. For small firms, the process appears rather straightforward. For a major firm in financial difficulty, there are similarities, but the rescue process is complicated by a larger number of major interested parties and the magnitude of funds involved.

Usually a major firm's main bank takes the lead in organizing (or not) such a rescue effort.[11] The bank's decision regarding whether or not a particular firm can be resuscitated is the critical first step; however, it is also very important that the bank be able to execute the rescue smoothly while causing minimum damage to the firm's ongoing business operations. This requires credibility and a clear commitment that lenders and/or equity-holders are willing to supply sufficient additional funding to make the reorganization successful.

The case of Toyo Kogyo (Mazda) provides a dramatic illustration of this rescue process. In late 1974, Sumitomo Bank sent several of its own executives to top positions at Toyo Kogyo and called a meeting of the firm's lenders. It announced that it would stand behind the automaker – in effect, guaranteeing the other lenders' loans. It also announced that Sumitomo Trust (Toyo Kogyo's second largest lender and a member of the Sumitomo Group) would provide any necessary new loans. According to Pascale and Rohlen (1983), not one of the other 71 lenders called a loan or refused to roll over existing credits. Also, there were no layoffs, although a large number of production workers "voluntarily" became salespeople for an extended period of time.

Clearly, Sumitomo Bank's actions were credible to other lenders as well as Toyo Kogyo's customers and suppliers. The firm's employees, management, and shareholders also cooperated, although presumably they had little choice, because the bank could essentially dictate whether or not the firm would survive. Pascale and Rohlen drew a strong contrast between the smoothness of the Toyo Kogyo rescue and the incredible difficulty of organizing a similar rescue effort for Chrysler. Eventually it required the U.S. government's loan guarantee as well as considerable "arm-twisting" to obtain the necessary cooperation to save Chrysler. What is it about the position of a bank like Sumitomo that allows it to exercise such power and command such credibility? To begin answering that question, we need to take a closer look at the capital structure of Japanese firms.

Previously we focused on overall leverage; however, recall that roughly 75% of external funding is in the form of loans from private financial institutions. Those same institutions are providing over a third of the equity funding and, except for electric-power companies, purchasing almost 70% of domestic corporate bond issues. If we exclude government loans, financial institutions have typically provided between 90% and 95% of private external funds for major industrial firms.

Not only is virtually all nongovernmental funding of large firms coming from financial intermediaries, but almost all of those funds are coming from a highly concentrated group of lenders. Until recently, the ability of Japanese firms to borrow from foreign lenders had been very limited. Prior to the amended Foreign Exchange and Foreign Trade Control Law of 1980, overseas borrowing by Japanese residents required prior approval by the Ministry of Finance. A few large corporations received approval for foreign bond issues starting in the late 1960s; however, as we have already seen, bond issues are not a major funding source. Similarly, access of foreign banks to the Japanese markets has been strictly controlled, and their relative position is very small. At the end of 1984, they accounted for only about 3% of the lending done by Japanese banks. Thus, until recently, borrowing from foreign sources had been an almost negligible factor.

The number of major domestic lenders to large businesses is also limited. Excluding government agencies, there are the 13 city banks, 3 long-term credit banks, and 7 trust banks, as well as the large life-insurance companies. Among the 21 domestic life-insurance companies at the end of 1980, the top three (Nippon, Dai-Ichi, and Sumitomo) controlled 50% of total assets, and the top eight controlled 82%. The non-life-insurance companies also lend to large businesses, but are not a significant fraction of the total. Although the 64 regional banks lend to large firms, they generally focus on loans to smaller firms and individuals. Regional banks represented 31% of total bank loans outstanding at the end of 1984; however, given the focus of their lending, their fraction of total private lending to large corporations is perhaps 10% or less. In summary, 25 to 30 financial institutions are providing roughly 85% of private external funding for large Japanese industrial firms, with almost 90% of these funds in the form of loans.

In practice, the number of key lending institutions has been even smaller than the 25 to 30 indicated earlier. Realistically, the top 6 to 8 city banks plus the Industrial Bank of Japan (a long-term credit bank), and to some extent the Long-Term Credit Bank of Japan, have largely controlled lending to major Japanese corporations.[12] This group of 10 or so institutions is rather tightly knit. Their senior executives know each other; many went to school together, and several are former Ministry of Finance officials. In some cases, several institutions belong to the same industrial group – for example, Sumitomo Bank, Sumitomo Trust and Banking, and Sumitomo Mutual Life are all members of the Sumitomo Keiretsu. Although competition among lenders can sometimes be intense, the small number of key lending institutions, plus common interests and knowledge of each other, has facilitated a coordination of lending policies that has greatly reduced lending risks.

A major industrial borrower typically has one of the foregoing set of 8 to 10 banks acting as its main bank. The relationship between a firm and its main bank tends to be both long-term and very close, with the bank being privy to extensive and confidential information on the firm's operations, as well as its medium- and long-range plans. Consequently, the main bank's loan evaluation typically is accepted with little question by other lenders.

The intensity of the main-bank relationship appears to be largely a function of the indebtedness and consequent need for bank support by the client firm. At one extreme, the main banks of cash-rich companies primarily benefit from corporate deposits, as well as foreign-exchange and fee-generating transactions. There is apparently relatively little flow of confidential information.

For heavy borrowers, there are extensive formal and informal contacts between the firm and its main bank at a variety of levels. In addition to providing a substantial fraction of the firm's borrowed funds, the main bank acts as a financial advisor, as well as an agent on other loans. The bank has considerable influence and in some cases veto power over capital-spending plans. In the extreme, a firm in financial difficulties may suddenly find several of its top executives replaced by bank personnel.

The main bank's power comes from several sources. As we discussed in Section 3, over half the loans to Japanese manufacturers are short-term. The continuing requirement for bank approval to roll over those loans is a source of considerable power. Assuming that other lenders would follow the main bank's lead, they could force most firms into bankruptcy at any time they chose. Also, Japanese banks have rights to take assets, seize collateral, or offset holdings to counter possible losses in the event of a threatened insolvency even though there is no literal default.[13] Furthermore, the main bank typically is trustee on corporate bond issues, almost all of which are mortgage bonds. Indeed, the criteria for issuing unsecured debt in Japan are still quite stringent (despite substantial relaxation) and only large and highly creditworthy companies can qualify. Thus, for a variety of reasons, the main bank is in a very strong position with respect to heavy borrowers.

The other side of the main bank's role is an implicit guarantee to other lenders. The main bank is providing a monitoring function for itself and for those other lenders. It has much better information, and the other lenders rely on its evaluation. They also expect the main bank to absorb a disproportionate share of loan losses in the event of a client bankruptcy.[14]

In order for the main-bank system to work well, there must be a small number of major lenders with considerable confidence in each other. Minor lenders (including bondholders) can be repaid if necessary to eliminate disagreements. However, as the number of major lenders or the fraction of nonintermediary borrowing becomes large, the system becomes unwieldy and starts to break down. Thus, the restriction of foreign borrowing and the concentration of Japanese lenders were crucial in the development of a main-bank lending system.

A critical feature of this system is confidence that the main bank will carry out its responsibilities and not abuse its position, either with respect to other lenders or with respect to the client firm. The reason for such confidence appears to be a powerful enforcement mechanism based on reputation. Reputation is so important to a major Japanese bank's long-run profitability and even existence (not to mention the status of its executives) that abuse of its position becomes virtually unthinkable, even when meeting its obligations can be very expensive. For example, when Ataka (a large trading company) went bankrupt in 1977, its two main banks took almost all the losses. Sumitomo Bank wrote off 106 billion yen, and Kyowa Bank lost 46 billion yen. According to Prindl (1981), foreign creditors of Ataka lost nothing, although their loans were basically unsecured.[15]

Overall, the main-bank lending system seems to have been an effective mechanism for reducing lending risks for large, highly levered firms. It also appears to be a relatively efficient system, because one bank does the monitoring, which tends to minimize associated costs. In turn, further delegating the monitoring and financing responsibilities for small firms to their large customers simplifies the task of major financial institutions. The level of main-bank monitoring for larger firms also seems to be an increasing function of the firm's debt level – a trade-off of monitoring cost versus risk reduction. In addition to being efficient regarding monitoring costs, this system appears to be capable of dramatically reducing deadweight losses in financial-distress situations. The main bank can make a liquidation or rescue decision and take control rather smoothly without resorting to time-consuming bankruptcy procedures and litigation of asset claims. Aside from possible legal costs, it is clear that the ability to reorganize with minimum disruption to customer, supplier, and employee relations is quite valuable. The Toyo Kogyo case is an excellent example.

5   Capital structure and financial-market deregulation in Japan

Recent Japanese experience indicates that the risk of financial distress is an important determinant of capital structure even under a main-bank lending system. A shift in that risk seems to have been a significant factor behind the capital-structure adjustments taking place over the last decade. The gradual nature of those adjustments also strongly implies substantial costs to rapid recapitalization. Such costs are clearly missing from even the extended versions of Miller's model, seriously limiting the ability of such tax-incentive models to explain observed capital structures. In contrast, a tax incentive for firm borrowing (considering both personal and corporate taxes) is not fundamentally inconsistent with a pecking-order approach.

With either pecking-order or tax-incentive models, an interesting issue is the implication of financial deregulation for capital-structure trends in Japan. The previous section emphasized the importance of the main-bank lending system in dealing with the costs of financial distress. That system has clearly been fostered by a variety of financial-market restrictions, which raises questions about the system's viability when those restrictions are relaxed. Of particular significance is the increased openness of Japanese financial markets.

With a dramatically increased number of potential lenders, it is much more difficult for the main bank to control actions of client firms. This is particularly true when foreign lenders are involved, for whom reputational threats regarding the Japanese market may be of only marginal significance. Indeed, recent bankruptcies such as those of Riccar and J. Osawa seem to indicate a weakening of main-bank control over heavy borrowers.[16] Also, in both those situations there apparently was no main-bank guarantee to other lenders, because lending took place without main-bank concurrence.

Opening up Japanese financial markets does not necessarily mean the disappearance of the main-bank system. Some foreign lenders are becoming cautious about loans to highly levered firms and are recognizing that lending without main-bank concurrence can eliminate any guarantees. If this becomes a general trend, the system's continued viability will be greatly enhanced.[17] Nevertheless, it appears that the position of the main bank has been fundamentally weakened.

In the context of the pecking-order model, a main-bank relationship can allow more rapid growth by reducing the need for expensive equity issues. This and the potential for main-bank assistance in the event of financial difficulty are presumably more valuable to some firms than to others. Thus, some firms may find it desirable to limit their borrowing from "nontraditional" sources in order to maintain a strong main-bank relationship. Slower-growing or more profitable firms (with less need for bank funds) presumably will attach less importance to a main-bank relationship and will behave much more independently. To some extent, such a two-tier structure already exists; but it probably will become more accentuated as financial deregulation progresses.

Overall, the role of financial deregulation in weakening main-bank control suggests that the aggregate equity-to-asset ratio for Japanese firms will continue to increase. There is also apt to be more reliance on long-term loans and bond issues by the relatively independent firms, which suggests that aggregate maturity patterns and sources of funds may increasingly look more like those for U.S. firms. Nevertheless, the relatively rare ability of the main-bank system to reduce lending risks suggests that highly levered capital structures may remain a characteristic of some Japanese firms and that those firms will adhere to fairly traditional funding patterns.

ACKNOWLEDGMENTS

Portions of this chapter, particularly Section 4, draw on Hodder and Tschoegl (1985). Valuable comments from Masahiko Aoki and Thomas Roehl are gratefully acknowledged.

NOTES

1. See, for example, Aoki (1984a, 1984b), Baldwin (1986), Elston (1981), Flath (1984), Hodder and Tschoegl (1985), IBI (1983), Kurosawa (1981), Kurosawa and Wakasugi (1984), Rappa (1985), Sarathy and Chatterjee (1984), Suzuki and Wright (1985), and Wallich and Wallich (1976). Toy et al. (1974) and Stonehilll et al. (1975) provide multilateral comparisons.
2. Regarding the ongoing deregulation of Japanese financial markets, see Hayden (1980), Pigott (1983), and Sakakibara and Kondoh (1984).
3. See Barnea, Haugen, and Senbet (1981b) for a useful review of the literature on agency theory and capital structure.
4. Although they do not develop the idea, Barnea et al. (1981b) also mention the informational-asymmetry issue that is central to the Myers and Majluf (1984) model.

5. These results are also consistent with those from confidential studies by the Japanese government and various securities firms, as summarized in Bronte (1982).

6. Although the maturity structure has been lengthening, as of March 1984 only 34% of the outstanding loans from the city, regional, and trust banks had maturities greater than one year.

7. Dividend rates in Japan are generally tied to the par value of stock and represent a low yield in terms of market price. However, the dividend payout rate as a percentage of profit is quite substantial. For example, in 1984 the average dividend yield for firms listed on Japanese stock exchanges was slightly over 1%; however, this represented a payout rate of 37%. See Hodder and Tschoegl (1985) for a discussion of corporate dividend policies in Japan.

8. Considering local as well as national taxes and assuming a 30% dividend payout rate (with partial tax reduction), the marginal tax rate for a typical large Japanese corporation has been estimated to be 51.6%. See, for example, Japan Securities Research Institute (1984), *Securities Markets in Japan 1984*. If we assume that U.S. firms face 6–10% (deductible) state and local taxes, with a 46% federal tax rate, the implied overall tax rate is between 49.2% and 51.4%.

9. Using our notation, Flath estimates $(1-\tau_P)-(1-\tau)(1-\tau_{PE})$ for each country. He denotes this value as G and estimates that it is 0.378 for Japan and 0.244 for the United States. To transform his estimates into δ values, we need to divide by $(1-\tau_P)$ for each country. He estimates τ_P as 0.07 for Japan and 0.311 for the United States, which implies δ values of 0.406 and 0.354, respectively. Note that these estimates implicitly assume that the Japanese and U.S. financial markets are segmented from each other and from the rest of the world. Otherwise, the relevant personal tax rates are not necessarily those of local individuals (as hypothesized in Flath's study). This segmentation assumption appears reasonable for Japan in 1971, but it is more open to question for the United States in 1971 and for both countries today.

10. Imai and Itami (1984) describe this process as an example of the effective interpenetration of organizational and market mechanisms in the Japanese economy.

11. Suzuki and Wright (1985) provide empirical evidence that a strong main-bank relationship is more important than financial measures, such as equity-to-asset ratios, in determining whether or not firms in financial difficulty will be rescued.

12. Such lending was also subject to the views of the Ministry of Finance and the Bank of Japan, who exerted considerable and sometimes detailed influence over major lenders.

13. Prindl (1981, p. 60). Apparently these rights are part of a set of General Business Conditions that are the same for all Japanese banks and must be accepted by client firms in order to establish a borrowing relationship. These General Business Conditions effectively replace the variety of loan convenants prevalent in the United States, while giving Japanese banks more flexibility and power.

14. Wallich and Wallich (1976) describe the situation as follows: "It is taken for granted that the main bank assumes a special responsibility with respect to the borrower. In an emergency other creditors therefore can expect their claims to effectively though not legally outrank those of the main bank" (p. 273).

15. Prindl was general manager of Morgan Guaranty's Tokyo office at the time.
16. Apparently, in both cases, the availability of funds from foreign lenders at least partially undermined main-bank influence. See IBI (1984) for an interesting account of the Osawa failure.
17. Extensive borrowing in bond markets may not represent a serious problem. Highly levered firms are apt to have difficulty floating bonds because of continuing market regulations regarding quality, as well as low ratings on their debt by foreign bond-rating agencies. Parenthetically, it has been suggested that rating agencies such as Moody or Standard and Poor should apply different criteria to rating bonds of Japanese firms. That suggestion appears fundamentally incorrect, because direct borrowing in financial markets (bonds or commercial paper) reduces the influence of the main bank and increases the risk to all lenders. Consequently, it would seem that market debt of a highly levered firm should indeed receive a relatively unfavorable rating.

REFERENCES

Akerlof, G. A. (1970). "The Market for 'Lemons': Quality and the Market Mechanism." *Quarterly Journal of Economics,* Vol. 84 (3), August, pp. 488–500.

Aoki, M. (1984a). "Aspects of the Japanese Firm." In M. Aoki (ed.), *The Economic Analysis of the Japanese Firm* (pp. 3–43). Amsterdam: North Holland.

(1984b). "Shareholders' Non-Unanimity on Investment Financing: Banks vs. Individual Investors." In M. Aoki (ed.), *The Economic Analysis of the Japanese Firm* (pp. 193–224). Amsterdam: North Holland.

Baldwin, C. Y. (1986). "The Capital Factor: Competing for Capital in a Global Environment." In M. E. Porter (ed.), *Competition in Global Industries* (pp. 183–223). Boston: Harvard Business School Press.

Bank of Japan. *Economic Statistics Annual.*

Barnea, A., R. A. Haugen, and L. W. Senbet (1981a). "An Equilibrium Analysis of Debt Financing Under Costly Tax Arbitrage and Agency Problems." *Journal of Finance,* Vol. 36 (3), June, pp. 569–81.

(1981b). "Market Imperfections, Agency Problems, and Capital Structure: A Review." *Financial Management,* Vol. 10 (3), Summer, pp. 7–22.

Board of Governors, Federal Reserve System. *Flow of Funds Accounts.*

Bronte, S. (1982). *Japanese Finance: Markets and Institutions.* London: Euromoney Publications.

Bureau of Statistics, Office of the Prime Minister. *Japan Statistical Yearbook.*

DeAngelo, H., and R. W. Masulis (1980). "Optimal Capital Structure Under Corporate and Personal Taxation." *Journal of Financial Economics,* Vol. 8 (1), March, pp. 3–29.

Elston, C. D. (1981). "The Financing of Japanese Industry." *Bank of England Quarterly Bulletin,* Vol. 21 (4), December, pp. 510–18.

Federation of Bankers Associations of Japan (1982). *Banking System in Japan 1982.*

Flath, D. (1984). "Debt and Taxes: Japan Compared with the U.S." *International Journal of Industrial Organization,* Vol. 2 (4), December, pp. 311–26.

Hayden, E. W. (1980). "Internationalizing Japan's Financial System." Occasional paper of the Northeast Asia–United States Forum on International Policy, Stanford University.

Hodder, J. E., and A. E. Tschoegl (1985). "Some Aspects of Japanese Corporate Finance." *Journal of Financial and Quantitative Analysis,* Vol. 20 (2), June, pp. 173–91.

IBI (1983). "Recent Trends in Japanese Corporate Finance." Report prepared by International Business Information, Inc., Tokyo.

(1984). "J. Osawa & Co., Ltd.: An Assessment of What Went Wrong." Report prepared by International Business Information, Inc., Tokyo.

Imai, K., and H. Itami (1984). "Interpenetration of Organization and Market: Japan's Firm and Market in Comparison with the U.S." *International Journal of Industrial Organization,* Vol. 2 (4), December, pp. 285–310.

Japan Company Handbook: First Section Firms. Tokyo: Toyo Keizai Shinposha.

Japan Securities Research Institute (1984). *Securities Markets in Japan 1984.*

Kurosawa, Y. (1981). "Corporate Financing in Capital Markets." Mimeograph, Research Institute of Capital Formation, Japan Development Bank.

Kurosawa, Y., and T. Wakasugi (1984). "Business Risk, Dividend Policy and Policy for Capital Structure: An Empirical Study of Japanese Enterprises." J.D.B. staff paper, Research Institute of Capital Formation, Japan Development Bank.

Miller, M. M. (1977). "Debt and Taxes." *Journal of Finance,* Vol. 32 (2), May, pp. 261–75.

Ministry of Finance. *Financial Statistics of Japan.*

Modligliani, F., and M. M. Miller (1958). "The Cost of Capital, Corporation Finance and the Theory of Investment." *American Economic Review,* Vol. 48 (3), June, pp. 261–97.

(1963). "Corporate Income Taxes and the Cost of Capital: A Correction." *American Economic Review,* Vol. 53 (3), June, pp. 433–43.

(1969). "Reply to Heins and Sprenkle." *American Economic Review,* Vol. 59 (4), September, pp. 592–5.

Myers, S. C. (1984). "The Capital Structure Puzzle." *Journal of Finance,* Vol. 39 (5), July, pp. 575–92.

Myers, S. C., and N. S. Majluf (1984). "Corporate Financing and Investment Decisions When Firms Have Information That Investors Do Not Have." *Journal of Financial Economics,* Vol. 13 (2), June, pp. 187–221.

Pascale, R. T., and T. P. Rohlen (1983). "The Mazda Turnaround." *Journal of Japanese Studies,* Vol. 9 (2), pp. 219–63.

Pigott, C. (1983). "Financial Reform in Japan." *Federal Reserve Bank of San Francisco Economic Review,* Winter, pp. 25–45.

Prindl, A. R. (1981). *Japanese Finance: A Guide to Banking in Japan.* New York: Wiley.

Rappa, M. A. (1985). "Capital Financing Strategies of the Japanese Semiconductor Industry." *California Management Review,* Vol. 27 (2), Winter, pp. 85–99.

Sakakibara, E., and A. Kondoh (1984). "Study on the Internationalization of Tokyo's Money Markets." JCIF Policy Study Series, No. 1, Japan Center for International Finance.

Sarathy, R., and S. Chatterjee (1984). "The Divergence of Japanese and U.S. Corporate Financial Structure." *Journal of International Business Studies,* Vol. 15 (3), Winter, pp. 75–89.

Stonehill, A. I., T. Beekhuisen, R. W. Wright, L. Remmers, N. Toy, A. Pares, A. C. Shapiro, D. Egan, and T. Bates (1975). "Financial Goals and Debt Ratio Determinants: A Survey of Practice in Five Countries." *Financial Management,* Vol. 4 (3), Autumn, pp. 27–41.

Suzuki, S., and R. W. Wright (1985). "Financial Structure and Bankruptcy Risk in Japanese Companies." *Journal of International Business Studies,* Vol. 16 (1), Spring, pp. 97–110.

Tokyo Stock Exchange. *Annual Statistics Report.*

Tokyo Stock Exchange (1985). *Tokyo Stock Exchange Fact Book 1985.*

Toy, N., A. I. Stonehill, L. Remmers, R. W. Wright, and T. Beekhuisen (1974). "A Comparative International Study of Growth, Profitability, and Risk as Determinants of Corporate Debt Ratios in the Manufacturing Sector." *Journal of Financial and Quantitative Analysis,* Vol. 19 (4), November, pp. 875–86.

Wallich, H. C., and M. I. Wallich (1976). "Banking and Finance." In H. Patrick and H. Rosovsky (eds.), *Asia's New Giant* (pp. 249–315). Washington, D.C.: Brookings Institution.

CHAPTER 10

The Japanese bureaucracy in economic administration: a rational regulator or pluralist agent?

Masahiko Aoki

1 Introduction: three views of the bureaucracy

Diverse views have been advanced regarding the role of the bureaucracy in the Japanese economy. These views can be roughly grouped into three streams of thought: the "rationality" view, the "adversary" view, and the "interest-representation" view. In the first view, the bureaucracy is regarded as contributing to the efficiency of the Japanese economy by being an independent rational actor in the political-economic process. In contrast, the second view regards bureaucratic intervention in the market mechanism as ineffective and redundant at best. Bureaucratic intervention is even considered to be harmful to economic efficiency and other social values (e.g., Friedmanian citizen-cum-consumer's sovereignty, anti-elite democratic ideals, etc.). The third view holds that the bureaucracy represents specific or pluralist interests in the economy. In this view, the bureaucracy is regarded as maintaining a kind of principal–agency relationship with constituent interests. This chapter attempts to synthesize these views, focusing on the dual role of the bureaucracy as a rationalist-cum-pluralist agency.

Even among those holding the rationalist view there is a wide variety of viewpoints. They range from the view holding that the Japanese economy is a bureaucracy-led coherent system to the view that sees the bureaucrat's role as only complementary to the function of the market mechanism. The former view is bruited mostly by journalists, as represented by the "Japan, Inc." theory, but even some non-Japanese political scientists, albeit much more subtle and sophisticated, lean toward this view.[1] The latter view is generally found in the writings of economists. Examples of this complementary role are many. Some argue that economic planning administered by the government complements the failure of future markets to arise and thus helps form consensual expectations in the private sector. This then provides a foundation for individual firms to make macro-consistent investment plans.[2] Another claim that is often heard is that industrial policy fosters the growth of infant industries to become internationally competitive.[3] A recent version of this view holds that government-sponsored research-and-development cooperatives in the computer industry are functionally equivalent to the risk-taking venture-capital market lacking in Japan.[4]

The rationality view has been challenged by the adversary view. Some leading neoclassical economists in the period of high economic growth, such as R. Komiya, T. Uchida, and T. Watanabe, among others, were ardent advocates of removal of government intervention from the competitive process – based on an earnest belief in the supremacy of the market mechanism. A subtle, eclectic view was offered by T. Yakushiji, who submitted empirical evidence of what he calls the "dilemma of policy intervention": Once the policy of fostering a stable structure in a particular industry becomes successful, the industry inevitably starts to drift away from intervention. At that stage, the bureaucracy tends to become coercive, and unless a new relation is created, the intervention is no longer lasting or effective.[5] In this view, the two faces of government alternate: rationalistic and adversary.

An early version of the interest-representation view may be found in the traditional theory of the "triad." This theory holds that the exclusive coalition of the bureaucracy, the ruling Liberal Democratic Party (LDP), and big business rules the Japanese polity. This has long been the dominant view among leading Japanese scholars in political science.[6] Recently, some authors have noted that the bureaucracy, in coalition with the LDP, has come to mediate the interests of a greater variety of social groups: first big businesses, then farmers, small businesses, relatively poor localities, and pensioners, and even wage-earners and salary-earners to a certain extent. The bureaucracy-LDP coalition strikes balances between these demands by distributing the social surplus made possible by economic growth.

I once characterized the bureaucratic budgetary and planning processes as a "quasi-social bargaining game" played by various bureaucratic entities that act in the dual roles of agents of respective constituent social groups cum referee of the game.[7] Similar thoughts have been coined as "bureaucratic-led, mass-inclusionary pluralism" by T. Inoguchi, "channeled pluralism" by S. Sato and T. Matsuzaki, and "patterned pluralism" by M. Muramatsu and E. S. Krauss.[8]

Muramatsu and Krauss have maintained that although diverse interest groups have access to the policy-making process at various points, rendering boundaries between the state and society somewhat blurred, the bureaucracy is still strong enough to structure policy patterns. A somewhat different interpretation was offered by Y. Kosai, who suggested that the role of the ruling party in interest mediation has been steadily gaining in importance, whereas the power of the bureaucracy has been waning.[9]

Mediation among various interests through social bargaining is universally observed in developed countries, either in the context of corporatist states or in T. J. Lowi's pressure-group pluralism.[10] However, the interest-mediation process in Japan is distinctive because of the unique and prominent role played by the bureaucracy. In the interest-mediation role, bureaucrats may be thought of as acting as agents for their constituent interests. But their role is different from that of agents in ordinary principal–agency relations, as envisioned for Western congress–bureaucracy relations, because of the unique incentive and tenure structures in which bureaucrats are embedded. Also, in order to mobilize and accumulate the political resources necessary for effective interest representation, Japanese bureaucrats also need to legitimize their behavior by asserting that their actions are beneficial to national interests that lie beyond specific interests. This need, together with the institutional structure in which they are embedded, places the bureaucracy in two inseparable roles: that of a *semiautonomous rational regulator (policymaker)* and that of a *quasi agent of specific interests* in the economy. This chapter presents a model that accounts for the dynamics of the Japanese political economy, focusing on the dual role of the bureaucracy in its interactions with the private sector.

One reason that I consider the following model important and relevant to an understanding of the Japanese political economy is that there seems to be an important *isomorphism* between, on the one hand, the bureaucratic process viewed from this perspective and, on the other, some aspects of the micro-micro-coordination mechanism within the Japanese firm. The existence of such isomorphism suggests, in my opinion, a deep-seated characteristic of the Japanese social system, and comprehension of this characteristic is essential to understanding the way the Japanese social system functions.[11]

This isomorphism will be formally introduced later, but its essence may be intuitively grasped from consideration of the following notion: Once a general policy/strategic orientation is framed, both the bureaucracy and the firm adapt to emergent demands and needs arising from constituent units in a "diffused" way. The bureaucracy and management of the firm do not control constituent units vertically according to a clear demarcation of control and task performance. Also, they resolve conflicts, or coordinate tasks, between constituent units as much as possible through horizontal bargaining. They do not dictate a centralized solution according to a well-defined, centralized objective. As I clarify later, these properties provide the political process with an aspect of pluralism administered by the bureaucracy. These properties also provide the micro-micro-economic adjustment process with an aspect of semiautonomous problem-solving cum semihorizontal (rather than hierarchical) coordination. These characterizations may appear to be at odds with the stereotypical view that the Japanese social system is more hierarchical and authoritarian than the Western system, but they are consistent with the impression often held by foreigners who have had first-hand contact with Japanese bureaucrats or businessmen: It is not clear who does have the real decision-making power in Japanese organizations.

The organization of this chapter is as follows: Section 2 describes the two faces of the bureaucrat as a rational regulator cum agent of particular interests of society motivated by unique incentive and tenure structures. Section 3 describes the bureaucratic process as quasi-social bargaining among pluralist interests, refereed by a coordinating agency. I call this *administered pluralism*. Section 4 provides a conceptual framework for comparison of the micro-micro-coordinating process of the firm with the bureaucratic process and suggests an important structural isomorphism between the two. Section 5 suggests an implication of this isomorphic structure for the dynamics of the firm and the bureaucracy. Section 6 sketches significant current phenomena that may lead to modification of administered pluralism and the changing roles of the bureaucrat and the politician. Section 7 concludes the chapter by speculating on the future transformation of administered pluralism in Japan.

2   The two faces of the bureaucracy

The Japanese bureaucracy is neither a monolithic, rational social engineer nor a self-sustaining club of power elites. It is a multitude of entities (ministries and agencies and their bureaus, divisions, etc.), each of which has its own jurisdictional sphere,[12] acquires its political resources through interactions with other bureaucratic and private entities, and is staffed by bureaucrats whose motivations are conditioned by unique structures of rewards and tenure. Each bureaucratic entity seems to reveal two faces in its operations: one face that of a rational/adversarial public regulator over private activities in its jurisdictional sphere, and the other face that of an agent representing the interests of its jurisdictional constituents[13] vis-à-vis other interests in the bureaucratic coordinating processes: budgetary, administrative, and planning.

The first face of the bureaucrat as a public regulator is the focal point of the rationality/adversary paradigmatic perspective. But, as we shall see presently, this face is intrinsically inseparable from and intertwined with the second or representative face. Through this representative role, each bureaucratic entity provides its jurisdictional constituents with an important port of access to policy-making. In contrast to the situation for high-level political appointees in the American executive branch, however, the tenure of the Japanese career bureaucrat is insulated from changes in the cabinet and electoral results. Why, and how, are they then receptive to the needs of constituent interests? What is the mechanism of incentive that drives them to act as quasi agents of their constituents?

Most elite bureaucrats start their careers by passing the "upper-class A (*ko-shu*)" civil service examination while enrolled in one of the prestigious universities. They are then recruited to particular ministries on graduation. There is a tacit pecking order among ministries regarding which ministry will get the best and brightest. The Ministry of Finance (MOF) normally gets first pick, followed by the Ministry of Home Affairs and the Ministry of International Trade and Industry (MITI). Those elite bureaucrats referred to as "qualified" persons on the "career *gumi* (team)" – who number a little more than 10,000 – normally remain in one ministry until retirement from the bureaucracy, except for occasional temporary transfers (*shukko*) to related ministries in midcareer. However, they are regularly rotated among various sections and bureaus within a ministry throughout their careers.

Bureaucrats progress through the administrative hierarchy rather rapidly during the first years of their careers. Many become heads of sections (*kakaricho*) at the average age of 29.1 years. Progression beyond that rank becomes increasingly competitive. The average age for a director of a division (*kacho*) is 42.1 years, and that for a director-in-general of a bureau (*kyokucho*) is 50.2 years.[14] The pinnacle of bureaucratic prominence is the permanent vice-ministership (*jimujikan*) in a ministry, which is attained at the average age of 55 years. By the time a member of the bureaucracy attains that position, all members of the same entering class except the most successful will have retired ("descended") from the "heaven" of the elite bureaucracy and become available as important human resources in the areas of national and local politics, business management in private and public corporations, and other consulting activities. This practice is called *amakudari* ("descent from heaven").[15] The term of a permanent vice-minister is not long; it normally lasts one to two years, and then he also practices *amakudari*.

The demand for *amakudari* bureaucrats is diverse. The LDP in relatively underdeveloped localities recruits potential candidates for governors and Diet members from among retired members of the Ministries of Home Affairs, Finance, Construction, and so forth, to promote local interests. Industrial associations and private companies recruit spokesmen and managers from the Ministries of International Trade and Industry, Finance, Health and Welfare, and so forth.[16] Some of the most successful retired bureaucrats take executive positions in public corporations that are engaged in financing private jurisdictional concerns with public funds. Still others hold memberships on various councils that report to their respective ministers and continue to mediate the various private interests represented there. Even the research institute sponsored by the Japan Federation of Labor (*Nihon Sodomei*) has recruited a reputable former Economic Planning Agency bureaucrat who also frequently sits on councils and government panels, representing a labor point of view in the process of economic planning.

By putting to use the expertise and the personal communications networks (*jinmyaku*, or human context) that were cultivated during their tenure as bureaucrats, the *amakudari* bureaucrats can gain access to important policy information that may very well be relevant to the interests of the constituencies to which they have been recruited. Sometimes they may even be able to promote the interests of those constituencies effectively. However, the relationship between the *amakudari* bureaucrat and the incumbent bureaucrat is indirect and subtle. It is not normally the case that *amakudari* bureaucrats can exercise direct influence or bring pressure to bear in regard to concrete intraministerial policy decisions. Because incumbent career bureaucrats are regularly rotated among various sections and bureaus, they are insulated to a great extent from interests that are too specific. Individual bureaucrats are too proud and too ambitious, particularly when young, to be susceptible to specific jurisdictional interests. Thus, although *amakudari* bureaucrats often provide an effective interface between their former ministries and their jurisdictional constituents, the incumbent screens jurisdictional interests with relative autonomy.

Notwithstanding the relative autonomy of the incumbent bureaucrats, however, because *amakudari* opportunities offer considerable rewards to successful bureaucrats in pecuniary and/or nonpecuniary terms, they are motivated to develop their ministerial and individual reputations throughout their careers to enhance their postbureaucratic opportunities by being duly receptive to constituent interests. On the other hand, *amakudari* bureaucrats who are exceptionally successful have achieved and are maintaining their positions linking the private sector and the public sector by the careful cultivation of an influential communications network within and beyond the ministries for which they worked. Therefore, although *amakudari* bureaucrats are not in a position to exercise direct influence over incumbents' decision making, opinions circulating in this elitist network may provide nonnegligible input to the building of "general reputations" of incumbent bureaucrats, which in turn may affect their bureaucratic careers and postretirement opportunities.[17] Thus, the *amakudari* practice seems to provide a subtle but important mechanism for absorbing constituent interests into the bureaucratic process.

Another important port for "grass-roots" access to the policy-making process concerns the increasingly active and influential *zoku* (political "tribes") of the LDP. The *zoku* of a ministry is an informal group of influential LDP Diet members clustered around the ministerial jurisdiction. A Diet member becomes recognized as a *zoku* member corresponding to a particular ministry by acquiring knowledge, influence, and power related to the affairs of that ministry. One gains such influence by having served as parliamentary vice-minister (*Gyosei Jikan*), as chairman of a subsection of the Policy Research Council (*Seichokai*) of the LDP corresponding to the appropriate ministerial jurisdiction, and in other important roles, successively. Because of their experience, *zoku* members have gained considerable expertise and access to information regarding the activities and affairs of the relevant ministries. They sometimes exercise tacit or overt influence over appointments of retiring bureaucrats to important positions in public corporations and other institutions.

Until the late 1960s, bureaucrats were considered to have a substantial informational advantage and superior expertise as compared with LDP politicians. But whereas bureaucrats are rotated among various sections and bureaus in order to be safeguarded from developing ties too close to specific interests, *zoku* politicians are continuously involved in certain strategic issues in related ministries. Given such steady involvement, *zoku* politicians have come close to, and in some cases have even surpassed, the bureaucrats in terms of capabilities.[18] The commitment of the *zoku* is, needless to say, indispensable for the ministry in ensuring the passage of desired legislation in the Diet. Thus, the bureaucrat must treat the *zoku* carefully and cordially. The extent of *zoku* politicians' influence may be illustrated by the fact that the long-standing attempt of MOF to overhaul the tax-exempt status of interest income from small savings accounts has been frustrated by the opposition of the *Yusei* (Ministry of Posts and Telecommunications, MPT) *zoku*.

Thus, the *zoku*, together with *amakudari* bureaucrats, have become important vehicles in recognizing and channeling emerging constitutent demands to the relevant ministries. Notwithstanding the growing receptiveness of bureaucratic entities to constituent interests, the relationship between the bureaucracy and its constituents is not a simple principal-agency relation as bureaucratic–congressional relations are viewed in the United States.[19] Precisely speaking, in principal–agency relations, an agent must normally follow the principal's instruction, and the authority of an agent normally can be terminated by the principal at any time. But Japanese ministries are authorized to draft and propose laws on their own initiative, as they deem necessary, to the Diet through the prime minister, according to Article 11 of the Administration Organization Law. Furthermore, Japanese ministries are perpetual bodies established by statutes and staffed with career bureaucrats whose terms of employment do not normally terminate with either a change in the cabinet or an electoral result. Thus, Japanese ministries have relatively more autonomy than a typical agent in the ordinary principal–agency relation. What, then, is the objective of a ministry? How is it related to constituent interests and to the motives of its career bureaucrats? The following simple conceptual framework may be helpful in considering these questions.

Although career-long competition among individual bureaucrats within a ministry is keen, a common and primary concern for them all is the maintenance and growth of the political influence of their ministry. Fulfillment of their ambitions, idealistic and personal, is not possible without the political viability of the ministry. A strong ministry will enhance their lifetime economic and political opportunities. The more politically powerful the ministry and the more instrumental the roles these bureaucrats have played in it, the better their chances in postretirement positions in the private sector and in the influential network of communications connecting the bureaucracy and the private sector.

However, the political viability of a ministry cannot be maintained without sustained reproduction of the political resources available for policy implementation. Thus, in language familiar to economists, the lifetime career opportunities, during as well as after bureaucratic service, for bureaucrats may be said to be related to maximization of the political stock of the ministry in which they work.[20] This is analogous to the following situation in the typical Japanese firm: Although the career-long competition among permanent employees within the Japanese firm is keen, their individual lifetime opportunities are related to the growth and survival of the employing firm made possible through efficient accumulation of firm-specific resources, including financial and human factors.[21]

The resources that the ministry can mobilize to implement its policy include the following:

1. Fiscal funds allocated to the ministry and available for public expenditure in the interest of jurisdictional constituents; financial funds financed mainly through postal savings and allocated, according to the legislated annual Public Investment and Financing Plan, to public financial corporations under ministerial control and made available as loans to or investment in jurisdictional interests[22]

2. Incumbent officials recruited through the highly competitive civil service examination and trained on the job; the network of its *amakudari* bureaucrats through which ministerial policy may be effectively propagated to the private sector and through which jurisdictional interests may be effectively absorbed

3. Authority to propose laws to the Diet through the prime minister, and good working relations with *zoku* politicians that can be relied on to strengthen the possibility that proposed laws will become enacted in the Diet

4. The capability of exercising regulatory power, either according to statutes or by moral suasion, often referred to as administrative guidance (*gyosei shido*).

The reproducibility of these resources may be considered to depend mainly on two factors: the "utility" of ministerial policy to its jurisdictional constituents and the reputation of the ministry among the general public (or the legitimation of its policy in a broader perspective beyond specific interests). In other words, these two factors are important determinants of the political stock of a ministry. The utility of a ministry to its jurisdictional constituents is basically determined by the effectiveness of its representation of those constituents' interests in the bureaucratic process. But straightforward interest representation is not sufficient. Without a good reputation among the general public, it is difficult for a ministry to sustain command of political resources, and its longterm viability may become weakened. For instance, the Ministry of Agriculture, Forestry and Fisheries cannot possibly legitimize sustained protection for farmers through the costly rice price-support program without appealing to the general public's concern with the national-security implications of excessive dependence on foreign food supplies.

By supplying "utility" to jurisdictional constituents and building its reputation among the public, a ministry can enhance the political prestige and career opportunities, bureaucratic and postbureaucratic, for its officials. It can also mobilize the effective political support of the *zoku* in favor of budgetary demands and desired legislation. It can recruit more able entrants to bureaucratic careers, and it can legitimize continued use of discretionary regulatory power.

However, as can be easily imagined, the utility of a ministry to its constituents and its reputation among the general public may not necessarily be harmonious. Even among the constituents of a ministry, there may be partly harmonious, partly conflicting interests. For instance, the exercise of certain regulatory powers may be of protective value to the interests of incumbents in a particular jurisdictional market, but may deter new entry of outsiders and hinder efficient, competitive operation of the market.

Also, depending on the life-cycle stage of the targeted industry, the same regulatory power may increase or decrease the political stock of a ministry, as illustrated by Yakushiji's previously mentioned theory of the "dilemma of policy intervention." If a ministry (or a bureau or a section) attends to the specific interests of one group of constituents to the neglect of others, or if it continues to coercively intervene in a jurisdictional constituency even after the constituency's maturity makes such intervention obsolete, the legitimacy of the budgetary demand to sustain that policy may become questioned. If the general reputation of a ministry is severely damaged, its ability to recruit competent and promising college graduates in competition with other ministries may also be compromised. Under the career-long employment system, a ministry cannot recruit an effective troubleshooter to help it recuperate from a damaged reputation.

Therefore, each ministry must strike a proper balance between constituent interests and the general welfare (national interest) in its policy-making and implementation so as to maximize its political stock. Dual representation of both general and specific interests gives the bureaucracy the appearance of relative autonomy and neutrality from specific interests, in spite of its quasi-agent role. The rationality view and the adversary view referred to at the beginning of this chapter focus their analyses on one face of the bureaucracy, that of a public regulator, and assess the welfare implications of the regulatory role from either a positive or negative perspective. I submit that such analysis, albeit instructive, is one-sided, as it disregards the subtle, inseparable dual character of the bureaucracy. This dual character may best be clarified in the context of interministerial coordination and competition.

3   The bureaucratic process as quasi-social bargaining

I suggested in the preceding section that pluralist interests have come to have some access to the policy-making process in Japan. One distinct feature of this process is that conflicts between diverse interests are arbitrated through intrabureaucratic coordination, rather than being resolved by open and direct bargaining among interest groups themselves, as is the case in L. Johansen's "bargain society."[23] One may say, as will be elaborated later, that direct social bargaining is substituted by quasi-social bargaining by various bureaucratic entities, each acting as the quasi agent of constituent interests. I call this political process *administered pluralism*.

In the preceding section, I spoke as if each bureaucratic entity (ministries, bureaus, divisions, and sections) controls and represents its own jurisdictional constituency. Precisely speaking, however, there are two types of bureaucratic entities, and only one type has a clearly delineated jurisdictional sphere. Bureaus (and sections), which often are referred to as *genkyoku* (the "original bureaus"), are of this type. The Banking Bureau of the MOF, the Automobile Industry Division in the Machinery and Information Industry Bureau of the MITI, the Pharmaceutical Affairs Bureau of the Ministry of Welfare and Health, the Postal Savings Bureau of the MPT, and the Local Bond Division of the Ministry of Home Affairs are obvious examples. These original bureaus maintain close contact with various organizations representing their jurisdictional constituents through which they absorb constituent interests and implement regulation over their jurisdictional spheres (e.g., the National Federation of Banking Associations, the Automobile Industrial Association, the Japan Drug Manufacturing Industrial Association, the Japan Drug Manufacturing Industrial Association, the Specific Postmasters Association, and local governments). The other type encompasses the bureaus whose primary functions are coordination, budgeting, planning, and monitoring. Let us call them coordinating offices. The Budget Bureau of the MOF, the Coordination Bureau of the Economic Planning Agency (EPA), the Administrative Inspection Bureau of the Management and Coordination Agency, and the minister's office of each ministry are examples.

One of the most important bureaucratic processes, which directly deals with the distribution of political resources, the budgetary process, may be styled as follows: Each *genkyoku* is responsible for drafting annual budgetary demands (*gaisan yokyu*) related to its jurisdictional interests. In this process, "requests" (*chinjyo*) for the allocation of budgetary funds and preferential tax treatments are made by constituent members to working officials concerned. These requests often are backed up by informal lobbying of politicians and *amakudari* bureaucrats. The first draft of budgetary demands at the bureau level is coordinated and adjusted at the minister's office of each ministry. At this point, the political influence of *zoku* politicians and the minister is exercised. By representing the interests of constituents successfully, politicians obviously can increase their own political stock (i.e., vote-getting power). On the other hand, the bureaucrats of each ministry cannot ignore the pressures of *zoku* politicians at this stage, because the exercise of their political influence on behalf of the ministry is valuable in the later stage of the interministerial budgetary process. This reciprocal dependence of the ministry and its *zoku* politicians has recently been strengthened.

Primary budgetary demands at the ministerial level are then submitted to and scrutinized by the Budget Bureau of the MOF, and at this stage, hard bargaining between MOF bureaucrats and other bureaucrats takes place. Normally toward the end of each calendar year, the Budget Bureau acts as a referee in the budgetary distributive game and, in consultation with and approval from LDP leaders, drafts a final budgetary plan. This plan is still subject to the "second budget revival demand" by each ministry, but at this stage, even powerful *zoku* politicians are able to exercise only marginal influence. The final plan must still be discussed and approved by the Diet. At this stage, the budget for minor additional expenditures may be appropriated by negotiation between the ruling LDP and opposition parties representing the interests of small shopkeepers, government employees, and so forth.

This short, stylized description of the budgetary process reveals one fundamental feature of the administrative process – *quasi-social bargaining*. Each *genkyoku* and ministry represents constituent interests and is engaged in quasi-social bargaining. This bargaining is not directly multilateral, however, and it is subject to the multilayered arbitration of coordinating offices (first by the minister's office of each ministry and then the Budget Bureau). The arbitration of coordinating offices is directed less by a well-defined policy objective than by ad hoc rules of thumb such as "incrementalism" (Y. Noguchi) "$-X\%$ ceiling." This will be discussed later, but the essential idea may be simply stated as follows: The budget allocations to (or the budget demands by) ministries increase (or decrease) equiproportionally every year.[24] Therefore, once a budget-allocation pattern is set, the discretionary power of the coordinating office is rather limited.

The limited power of the coordinating office is more apparent in the case of economic planning. Economic planning is officially discussed and formulated by the Economic Council on the request of the prime minister and then reported to the cabinet for its official sanction.[25] The Economic Council is dominated by representatives of business leaders, but also includes academics, representatives of the communications media, consumers, labor unions, and *amakudari* bureaucrats in various capacities. The prime minister sets the general orientation of the plan at the outset in his official letter of request for planning. Economic planning then becomes a sort of interest-arbitration process within that framework. The Planning Bureau of the EPA functions as the secretariat for the Economic Council. It prepares the agenda and statistics and draws a draft of the plan, which is then subject to minor revisions at the final meeting of the council. During the deliberation on the plan at the Economic Council, bureaucrats from other ministries are dispatched to this bureau or sit as observers at council meetings to make sure that the plan will not be drafted counter to their ministries' interests. Economic planning does not "plan," but rather creates a consensus on, or an atmosphere for, very general economic targets by giving pluralistic interests proper shares and a place in the future perspectives.

Aside from consensus formation, however, the economic plan does not have binding power over any party. However, it may legitimize, in a very broad sense, the budgetary demands of the ministries consistent with the plan in the first few years of its "implementation." The MOF carefully intervenes in the plan-making process, behind the scene at Economic Council meetings and through its *amakudari* bureaucrats in the council, so that any commitment to limit its discretionary power in the budgetary process will not be made. Thus, the coordinating role of the Planning Bureau in the actual allocation of fiscal resources is at best modest. However, its role of mediating a consensus in setting national economic targets and promoting macroeconomic stabilization through formation of common expectations should not be overlooked.[26]

Also to be noted in regard to the bureaucratic process as a quasi-social bargaining process is that, parallel to this official coordination among ministries, "shadow bargaining" among corresponding *zoku* takes place. *Zoku* politicians normally are influential members of the LDP, and important conflicts between ministries often are settled among them. Such political settlements often are quick and decisive, whereas interministerial disputes, if completely left to bureaucrats, sometimes are difficult to settle and often end in stalemate.

Characterization of the bureaucratic process as a quasi-social bargaining process gives rise to the following theoretical question: Is the conventional rule of incrementalism (or its negative version, manifested by the uniform $-X\%$ ceiling on budgetary demands by ministries) consistent with efficient and stable resolution of conflicts among political-stock-maximizing ministries? In a somewhat different context of bargaining within the firm viewed as a coalition of the body of stockholders and the body of employees, I have proved a theorem that may suggest a clue to the answer.[27] According to this theorem, under certain regularity conditions, efficient and stable resolution (in the sense of a Nash solution) of the partly conflicting, partly harmonizing interests of utility-maximizing participants in the firm dictates that rents accrued to the firm be distributed to each constituent body according to a respective-share parameter and that other managerial decisions regarding layoffs, investments, and so forth, be made by averaging policies optimal to the constituent bodies, again with the corresponding share parameters as weights: The share parameters represent relative bargaining powers of the constituent bodies. Under this rule, which may be called the *dual parametric rule,* management acts as a sort of arbiter among constituent bodies of the firm.

I conjecture that a similar analysis of the bureaucratic budget allocation process would reveal that under similar regularity conditions, parametric distribution of fiscal resources under the rule of incrementalism and accompanying policy implementation remains the efficient and stable resolution (in the sense of Nash) for the partly conflicting, partly harmonizing interests of political-stock-maximizing ministries, provided that distributive parameters are chosen properly at the outset. The Budget Bureau as the custodian of fiscal resources acts as the efficient arbiter between ministries by following the apparently passive rule of incrementalism. It seems obvious, however, that parametric distribution can be neither efficient nor stable if the jurisdictional demarcation between ministries becomes obsolete and dispute-ridden. In such cases, the coordinating office must become more active in interministerial conflict resolution to be efficient and stable.

4   The isomorphic structure of the bureaucracy and the firm

Section 3 described an aspect of quasi-social bargaining in the bureaucratic process. Pluralistic interests are absorbed through the *zoku* and *amakudari* intermediaries into the corresponding bureaus and ministries and are arbitrated through the administrative processes, such as budgetary, planning, and dispute settlement. I also hinted at an element of structural isomorphism between the firm and the bureaucracy: The role of management in the firm and that of the coordinating office in the bureaucracy are essentially identical in regard to management of intraorganizational conflict resolution (i.e., arbitrative). In this section I submit that the isomorphism extends to the internal informational and structural aspects of Japanese firms and the Japanese bureaucracy. This isomorphism may suggest an intrinsic property of the Japanese social system, and therefore its recognition may be a key to understanding the relative stability of the Japanese polity and the competitive efficiency of Japanese industry.

First, let us consider the Japanese firm to be composed of multiple operative units, shops/divisions. Assume that strategic decisions regarding investment, diversification, and research and development are made and implemented by management according to the parametric distributional rule, as described in the preceding section.[28] Given the general framework of production by such strategic decisions, the problem of coordinating operations among component units responding to emergent events remains; these events might include unpredictable changes in consumer demand for various types of outputs, malfunction of machinery, supply shocks, and so forth.

The conventional neoclassical model of hierarchy envisions the solution of this problem as follows: Each component unit is specialized in a particular task, and the coordination of activities between component units responding to emergent events may also be ascribed as a specialized function of the coordinating office (i.e., management).[29] Management monitors emergent events affecting the productivity of component units and, on the basis of centralized information, decides on an appropriate set of operational instructions for the component units. Although the capacity of management to gather relevant information, to compute a proper solution, and to monitor its implementation at the operative level may be bounded, the guiding principle of this model is purposeful problem-solving based on centralization of information, coupled with efficiency achieved through the specialized separation of control and operation.

As I have described and modeled formally elsewhere,[30] the coordinating mechanism operating in the Japanese firm has somewhat different features. First of all, instead of formal job specialization, the merit of flexible job demarcation is emphasized. In some successful firms, this flexibility has developed into intentional training of multifunctional workers and the practice of job rotation on the shop floor. The objective is to make workers familiar with various aspects of the work process so as to foster their capabilities for semiautonomous, on-the-spot problem-solving. This aids quality control and keeps the cost of products down. Needless to say, the long-term incentive scheme, characterized by seniority wages and lifetime employment, is intended to motivate such collective learning on the shop floor.[31]

What, then, is the similarity between bureaucratic organization and the organization of the firm at the component-unit level? The similarity may be subtle, but it can be described as follows: The bureaucrat is also rotated among various bureaus within a ministry (and even dispatched to other ministries) in much the same way as the quasi-permanent employee of the Japanese firm is rotated among various jobs and divisions within the firm. As already discussed, through this practice the bureaucrat is nurtured to be an effective agent to absorb the interests of diverse constituents in a broad perspective. This is analogous to the industrial situation in which the employee of the firm is nurtured to develop a wider range of skills and related knowledge useful for coping with emergent events semiautonomously at the shop-floor level. In both cases, the emphasis is on semiautonomous, diffused problem-solving.

Next, let us back up a little from the shop-floor level and look at the intershop coordination mechanism. Here, too, the structure is not as centralized as the conventional model of hierarchy envisions. A good example is provided by the *kanban* system at the Toyota factories.[32] After a general framework for the production plan is set out centrally on a weekly or biweekly basis, the fine tuning of the production plan (there can be more than 10,000 variations for one model produced on a line, depending on combinations of parts, color, etc.) is made in response to daily fluctuations in demand. Coordination of operations between different shops is achieved through the horizontal flow of *kanban* (a card put in a vinyl envelope). This enables each shop to order from shops immediately upstream (or subcontractors) particular amounts of materials, tools, parts, or processed goods at a particular time.

This system, which bypasses centralization of information and decision making, contributes to the efficiency of a firm in many ways: It allows faster adaptation of final assembly lines to changing market conditions, reduces inventory and waste, uncovers bottlenecks, quickly responds to defective parts and malfunctioning of machines, and reduces managerial personnel. This semihorizontal coordination has also proved to be effective in other industries in which the product portfolio is diverse and the assembly of a great number of components is involved.[33]

The similarity between interministerial coordination and intershop coordination has to do with the absence of purposeful hierarchical control of component units by the coordinating office. Both in the bureaucratic structure and in the firm organization, the main role of the coordinating office (either the Budget Bureau or management) is to facilitate arbitration or horizontal coordination between component units by providing a general framework, as in the yearly budgetary ceiling or weekly output target.[34]

For semihorizontal coordination across component units within the firm to be workable and to contribute to organizational efficiency, sharing of knowledge and outcomes among the bearers of the intrafirm mechanism seems indispensable.[35] Without the sharing of knowledge, there might be shirking and strategic haggling between units in regard to relative expenditures of effort by the various units, and this would prevent efficient coordination. Without a sharing of outcomes in the long term, however, there may not be incentive among the bearers to share knowledge and to cooperate.

At this point, a difference arises between the firm and the bureaucracy. Because the component units of the bureaucratic coordination process are political-stock-maximizing ministries, there would seem to be no sharing of tangible outcomes; hence, there would seem to be no direct incentive for sharing knowledge. In fact, ministries sometimes are observed to distort and misrepresent information to their own advantage in interactions with others.[36] In ongoing bargaining situations, such as budgetary negotiations, however, bureaucratic entities may come to mutually accumulate, albeit to a limited degree, knowledge relevant to quasi-social bargaining. Knowledge sharing is also fostered by the practice of mutual dispatch (*shukko*) of personnel to relevant ministries,[37] as well as through school and other ties among officials across ministerial boundaries. This limited sharing of knowledge makes the bargaining situation more or less transparent to bargaining parties, which is a prerequisite for an efficient and stable settlement of the problem.

Table 10.1. *Isomorphic relations*

Level	The bureaucracy (administered pluralism)	The firm (Japanese management)
At component unit	Diffused reception for emergent demands of constituent interests	Semiautonomous problem-solving responding to emergent events
Between component units	Quasi-social bargaining	Semihorizontal coordination
Role of coordinating office/management	Arbitration	Arbitration
Mutual linkage	Limited sharing of knowledge; mutual concern with general welfare	Sharing of knowledge
Distribution	Incrementalism; reciprocity	Parametric sharing of outcomes

Furthermore, it is to be recalled that accumulation of political stock by each ministry depends partially on its contribution to the general welfare and national interest. The mutual concern with general welfare and national interest may deter ministries from consistently engaging in uncooperative, inefficient strategies vis-à-vis each other that may deplete mutual political stocks. Rather, ministries engaged in repeated bargaining often may yield by turning to bargaining partners in the expectation of reciprocity in the next round of bargaining. The principle of the *kashikari kankei* (the borrowing–lending relation of favoritism), or something similar to the so-called tit-for-tat strategy (R. Axelrod), seems to prevail in the quasi-social bargaining among ministries. This is merely the strategy of starting from cooperation, and thereafter doing what the other player did in the preceding round.[38] However, if uncontrollable factors affect the outcomes of reciprocated actions, and if ministries cannot perfectly infer their bargaining partners' choices based on the observed outcomes, this reciprocity game may result in an inefficient social outcome.[39] But as the uncertainty about the relation between individual choices and their outcomes is reduced, this simple decentralized strategy of reciprocity tends to secure and maintain cooperation. Thus, knowledge sharing among ministries, such as to mutually clarify the objective situations of the bargaining game, seems to be a crucial prerequisite for efficient and stable decentralized coordination based on reciprocity between ministries.

One may then summarize the isomorphic relation between administered pluralism and the Japanese firm as in Table 10.1. In this table, the "component unit" refers to the *genkyoku* bureau or the ministry in the case of bureaucracy, and to the shop or division in the case of the firm.

5   Operational mechanisms and strategic orientations

In the preceding section, we discussed a possible isomorphism between the structure of the bureaucracy and the structure of the firm organization at the operational level when strategic decisions provide the condition of stable internal composition. But how are strategic decisions that may fundamentally alter the internal composition of the system made in this context? Specifically, do the characteristics of the bureaucratic process or industrial coordination, as discussed earlier, react on the mode of strategic decision making? If so, how? In this section, I present one simple hypothesis on this issue.

First, let us make a distinction between two types of decision making in the firm: *entrepreneurial* and *managerial*. The entrepreneurial type involves exploring new business opportunities, being active in research and development, being willing to take risks in new lines of business, and so forth. In contrast, the managerial type is concerned with pursuing efficiency in established lines of business. The orientation of the Japanese firm in the late 1960s and early 1970s was more or less managerial, as increasing penetration into international markets for established domestic businesses was the typical goal. To pursue operative efficiency, however, decision-making power over operational matters was gradually delegated to shop floors, as described earlier. The quasi disintegration of the large firm through the ever-increasing hiving-off of subsidiaries and extensive deployment of subcontracting also intensified during this period.

In the late 1970s, when the mechanism of semiautonomous problem-solving and semihorizontal coordination based on knowledge sharing reached a certain state of development, some Japanese firms became more consciously entrepreneurial to achieve international competitiveness. Does this entrepreneurial orientation within the organizational framework based on knowledge sharing create a different approach to innovation than that in a hierarchical context? This question is yet to be investigated. But it may be pointed out as a starting point of discussion that penetration into different lines of business (the commercialization of innovation) normally requires a restructuring of the internal organization of the firm. One such restructuring might be creating new component units (divisions/shops) that can be linked into the existing coordinating network. Under hierarchical control based on specialization and functionalism, this restructuring is done by "coupling" the new component units to the existing system under the entrepreneurial initiative of management. Alternatively, an entrepreneur may create an entirely new, equally efficient coordinating mechanism from scratch. Probably the relative ease of this type of restructuring under hierarchy cum specialization explains why in the United States the dominant firms have grown more by acquisition and divestiture. It also probably explains why the commercialization of new innovation takes place in the form of start-up companies more often in the United States than in Japan.

If, on the other hand, the intrafirm coordination mechanism is based more on knowledge sharing among incumbent employees and component units, the restructuring of the firm through coupling/decoupling of separate units or start-ups may not be as efficient as through internal bifurcation. This is so because the knowledge sharing necessary for efficient operation of the mechanism of semiautonomous problem-solving and semihorizontal coordination may not be readily available after coupling or in a new start-up. Therefore, firms relying on knowledge sharing may orient themselves toward growth through internal diversification, made possible by in-house development of knowledge, rather than by acquisition of other firms. There also may be fewer incentives to initiate start-ups, because the usefulness of managers, researchers, and engineers will be partly lost when they are dissociated from the organizational context in which they have developed their expertise.

This hypothesis is yet to be tested. However, there is plenty of anecdotal evidence to show that many innovations in Japan have arisen because the knowledge accumulated within the firm through production experiences has been developed and applied to related, albeit often not obvious, fields. For example, many companies active in research and development in biotechnology are traditional food-processing companies that are aiming at taking the traditional brewing or amino acid fermentation techniques acquired from production experience and applying them for screening and breeding of new microorganisms that have been genetically modified by the use of recombinant DNA.[40]

A parallel line of thought may be applied to a nation's political orientation. Let us start with distinguishing between the two types of political orientation that characterize the basic stance of the polity: *promotional (policy innovational)* and *administrative*. The former absorbs and promotes demands of hitherto unrecognized social interests by breaking away from old constituencies of the government or altering the balance of power among interest groups in a fundamental way. Under the administrative type, the polity absorbs and arbitrates among the officially recognized and established constituencies. In general, the promotional policy stance is likely to appear only occasionally, because its permanence would undermine political stability.

Is administered pluralism consistent with the promotional policy orientation? It may be, but only if the promotional policy is able to absorb emerging new demands without decreasing the existing benefits to recognized social groups by generating a larger amount of social surplus. This self-expansion process is somewhat analogous to the situation in which the firm incorporating the mechanism of semiautonomous and semihorizontal coordination expands itself through self-organizing bifurcation, rather than discontinuous development by the method of coupling/decoupling or start-up.

However, if a promotional policy is to hurt some social groups and/or necessitate a substantial alteration in the existing balance of interests among social groups, it will not be implemented smoothly within the framework of administered pluralism. This is so because administered pluralism essentially relies on consensus-making (bargaining) among bureaucratic bodies, each representing officially recognized constituencies, and the arbitrating role of the coordinating office. Thus, there seems to be an inherent difficulty for administrative pluralism in promoting unrecognized interests on its own initiative, particularly when the political resources of the bureaucracy are limited. Implementation of a redistributive promotional policy then may require, at least temporarily, strong political leadership from the cabinet or, more likely, the political initiative of politicians exercised through the party and parliamentary processes outside the sphere of the bureaucracy. Whether a strengthening of the cabinet leadership or the extrabureaucratic initiative to promote new interests will be secured as a result (thus modifying the fundamental nature of administered pluralism) or the political process will settle back to the normal pattern of administered pluralism after the promotional reorientation will depend on the nature and circumstances of the policy innovation. In the next two sections, I argue that currently in Japan there is emerging a situation in which some realignment of ministerial functions may be needed for efficient operation of the bureaucracy, but that a decisively promotional policy toward that direction, in a way to alter the fundamental nature of administered pluralism, would seem difficult to come by in the near future.

6   Administered pluralism at bay

Administered pluralism started taking clear shape in the 1960s. As I have stated elsewhere,[41] this corresponds to the time when the Japanese firm started developing a unique structure: a coalition including the body of employees.[42] The polity, in that decade, successively recognized and responded to the emerging demands of various social groups in addition to big business: To farmers they provided price support for rice, construction of irrigation projects, and preventive measures for snow disaster; to small and medium-size firms they provided financing through public finance corporations, favorable tax treatment, and regulation of the entry of large businesses into traditional commerce arenas;[43] to salaried employees, blue- and white-collar, they provided the benefit of periodic tax reductions, among other things. The LDP functioned as a network for recognizing and adapting to various interests, old and new. Even opposition parties played a certain role in feeding the interests of small businesses and workers into the policy-making and budgetary processes. Fiscal resources were increased annually because of the high growth of national income and were distributed almost equiproportionally among ministries (so-called budgetary incrementalism). Ministries balanced the interests of their own constituent groups within this budgetary framework. The 1960s were the heyday of administered pluralism. Under this administered pluralism, the political stocks of ministries and LDP politicians were enhanced substantially, and an unprecedented stability of LDP rule followed.

Around the turn of the decade from the 1960s to the 1970s, however, the irritation of city-dwellers concerning the spillover effects of industrial growth, such as pollution, congestion, and the lack of decent housing stock, began to increase. This discontent culminated in successive defeats of conservative candidates in gubernatorial and mayoral elections in the major metropolitan areas of Tokyo, Osaka, Yokohama, and Kyoto. Alarmed by this political signal, the LDP and the bureaucracy began to move swiftly to accommodate the welfare-oriented policy of the opposition parties and "progressive local autonomies" (*kakushin jichitai*). Generous social security provisions were introduced in 1973 without precautionary calculations of their impact on the future fiscal burden. The Tanaka cabinet elected in 1972 also tried to solve the deficiencies of the social infrastructure and private housing by the now notorious Plan for Reshaping the Japanese Archipelago, which ignited feverish land speculation, backed up by excess liquidity created in the process of the faltering shift to the flexible exchange system. The first oil shock aggravated the impact of severe inflation.

In the aftermath of the great inflation, the central government began to resort more and more to debt financing. The impact of the earlier reform of the welfare system began to be felt. The ratio of bond issues to the total revenue of the general account of the central government exceeded 30% in 1977, an upper limit that the MOF insisted be kept. A tax reform, including the introduction of a general consumption tax, seemed to be inevitable, and the MOF began to maneuver for its early introduction.

But a tactical mistake was committed by Prime Minister Ohira in making the introduction of a new value-added tax a campaign issue in 1979, and the near defeat of the LDP made tax reform politically unfeasible for some time to come.

Instead of a tax reform, a 0% ceiling on increases in budgetary demands, except for defense expenditures and foreign aid, was introduced in the early 1980s by the MOF as a means of keeping the fiscal deficit at a manageable level. Later, the ceiling was further lowered to −10%. However, the method of controlling budgets below the ceiling was largely left to the discretion of individual ministries. This was the negative "budgetary incrementalism," and the parametric distributional nature of the budgetary process remained intact.

Meanwhile, big businesses considerably reduced the amount of employment per sales in the second half of the 1970s by spinning off operational activities in the form of subsidiaries, more systematic reliance on subcontracting relations, and speedier semihorizontal, semiautonomous intrafirm coordination. These organizational efforts, called genryo keiei (trimming management), led to a substantially more efficient organizational form of the business firm.[44] Regaining the confidence that had been shaken by the anti-corporate public sentiment in the aftermath of high inflation and land speculation in the mid-1970s, business leaders became increasingly frustrated by and critical of the mounting fiscal deficit and the size of the bureaucracy. They started to insist that similar organizational innovation should be undertaken by the government.

Also, the demand for government services started to decrease in the part of the private sector that had gained a substantial competitive edge, particularly when the supply of services involved the exercise of discretionary regulatory power. In addition, in face of mounting trade disputes, it had become increasingly difficult for the bureaucrat to maneuver away from the pressure of foreign governments and businesses to remove protective regulations.

For the purpose of solving the fiscal imbalance in the long-term perspective and realizing a small, efficient government, the government, on the enactment of the Diet in 1981, appointed the second Ad Hoc Council on Administrative Reform (Rincho) headed by a widely respected business leader, Toshio Doko, and authorized it to report on a wide-ranging administrative-reform plan (gyokaku). Prime Minister Suzuki pledged that every recommendation by the Rincho would be implemented. This initial pledge gave unprecedented power to the Rincho, to the point that some have even raised the question of constitutionality. Thus, the Rincho was assigned a quite different role from those of other councils (shingikai), whose primary tasks normally are to deal with either interest arbitration or specialized administrative issues within a given administrative framework.

The scope and range of the *Rincho* recommendations and their implementability are not yet fully known. But the impacts of these activities are already far-reaching, and a modification of administered pluralism as it functioned in its heyday in the 1960s and early 1970s seems to be inevitable. The administrative reform, if implemented fully according to the council's recommendations, is not likely to result in a Pareto-improving move; rather, a stringent budget ceiling is being imposed on every ministry, and some *genkyoku* will be deprived of important regulatory powers, whereas some coordinating offices may be given greater power. Some examples: The profitable and innovative National Telephone and Telegram Public Corporation was smoothly privatized under the leadership of Wataru Shindo, a close business associate of Doko, but the recommended dissolution and privatization of the debt-striken Japan National Railways (JNR) were at first resisted fiercely by the former management and by the union; pension reform will render government employees worse off, and health-insurance reform will curb doctors' interests.

Will the bureaucracy undergo a significant change as a result of the *gyokaku* and other political developments, so that the fundamental character of the polity as administered pluralism will be altered? More specifically, will there be a significant shift in the relationship between *genkyoku* bureaus and coordinating offices, as well as between the *zoku* and the bureaucrat? There currently are two important developments having to do with the bureaucracy that are relevant to these questions.

The first is the continuing scarcity of fiscal resources that the *genkyoku* bureau can command to administer pluralist interests. The MOF still imposed the -10% ceiling on budgetary demands by ministries for the fiscal year 1986. But this state of affairs seems to need careful reading and interpretation, as the actual situation is far from the imminent danger of crowding out. The household sector is supplying savings in excess of investment that amounts to about 10% of national income, on average, in the 1980s, and capital equivalent of around 3% of national income flew out to foreign markets in 1984. Further, the number of new issues of national bonds for financing new fiscal resources has recently tapered off at 10% of the general account of the central government (and an additional 10% for the cost of debts outstanding). The general government as a whole, including local governments and social security funds, still records a surplus in the current account and is incurring a debt only to finance a portion of investment in the social capital stock.

The continuing restraint of fiscal expenditures may thus be regarded now as a political choice, rather than being strictly an economic necessity. The restraint policy certainly limits the capacity of *genkyoku* bureaus to supply bureaucratic services to the private sector, but also it may enable the bureaucrat to fend off excessive demands made by *zoku* politicians. A covert motive behind the stringent policy of the MOF may well have been to rebuff the ever increasing external political pressure and preserve bureaucratic autonomy and power. But an ironic consequence of the MOF's imposition of the minus ceiling on budgetary demands by ministries is that the near-final coordination among competing budgetary demands is done at the ministerial level to meet that constraint. This means that there is less room left for the MOF to exercise discretionary arbitrative power. The MOF seems to have unexpectedly lost relative power vis-à-vis other ministries in the process of fiscal stringency.

The second important problem facing the bureaucracy is the increase in jurisdictional disputes among ministries. Jurisdictional dispute is a phenomenon intrinsic to the bureaucracy, but its potential significance has recently increased, for two reasons: the increase in competition among ministries for scarce political resources, and the increase in the importance of cross-jurisdictional policy issues caused by the growing complexity of and rapid changes in the domestic and international environments. Among such changes are the breakdown of traditional industrial boundaries caused by the development of high-technology industries, the increasing integration of national economies into the world markets, and the resulting necessity of coordinating economic policy as well as overhauling regulatory systems in ways consistent with international norms and demands. The dispute between the MPT and the MOF over the management and taxation of postal savings is one example of ministerial competition for fiscal resources. A recent dispute beween the MPT and the MITI over regulation of the information industry provides a good example of a cross-jurisdictional issue. In the case of the development of biotechnology, the MITI, the Science and Technology Agency, the Ministry of Welfare and Health, the Ministry of Agriculture, Forestry and Fisheries, and the Ministry of Education compete for jurisdictional hegemony.

The continuing scarcity of political resources and the increase in jurisdictional disputes among ministries suggest that the coordinating functions of arbitrating the allocation of resources (fiscal resources as well as regulatory power) as well as settling jurisdictional disputes are assuming an increasingly important role. One important development in this regard is that LDP politicians are assuming an increasingly active role in interministerial coordination, in addition to their traditional role of feeding constituent interests into corresponding ministries. Accordingly, it is becoming more important for ministries to have close working relationships with their *zoku* politicians. Recently, many ministries have been sending greater numbers of their own former bureaucrats to the Diet.

An interesting example of ministry–*zoku* alliance may be found in the case of the MPT. The MPT has the association of masters of specific

(*tokutei*) postal offices under its jurisdiction. These postmasters, number-
ing approximately 17,800, are licensed to open post offices in residential
areas by providing facilities, and they have access to information concerning neighborhood families (family composition, profession, economic
status, etc.) through their postal and postal savings services. This knowledge is of enormous value to politicians for election campaigns. In return
for political support for *zoku*, postmasters are rewarded by commissions
for postal savings services. Through this symbiotic relationship, the MPT
and its *zoku* have built an important alliance, and the *zoku* are very effective in blocking the removal of tax-exemption schemes on postal savings and delivering significant regulatory power to the MPT in the communications arena.

An advantage of political arbitration in the LDP is the ability to make
quick decisions when interministerial disputes become stalemated. But
zoku politicians' perspectives often may be shortsighted and inclined toward the immediate interests of their constituents. Particularly, most politicians have very strong ties to specific domestic interests, and they may
lack international perspective.[45] Also, the reliance on *zoku* is double-edged
for the bureaucrat. Whereas the *zoku* can be mobilized as useful political
resources of the ministry to get favorable settlements of interministerial
disputes that are beyond their control and to get desired legislation passed
by the Diet, there is the danger of overreliance. If the bureaucracy relies
on the *zoku* too much, that may undermine the political stock of the
ministry in the long run by contradicting the raison d'être of administrative autonomy – expertise and relative neutrality from specific interests.

Theoretically, there are two ways for the bureaucracy to preserve its
relative autonomy vis-à-vis immediate and shortsighted political influence
under the condition of increasing scarcity of resources, but both may alter the fundamental nature of administered pluralism as characterized
in Sections 2–4. One is to strengthen the power of coordinating offices
within the administration; the other is to reorient the role of the ministry
in the direction of insulating it from the need to respond to immediate
and specific interests on a case-by-case basis.

There have been some attempts toward centralization of interministerial coordination within the administration. This can be illustrated by the
September 1985 cabinet decision on the reorganization of the prime minister's Secretariat and the increasing role played by the newly created Management and Coordination Agency, both of which were based on the report of the *Rincho.* According to that decision, "in order to strengthen
the Cabinet function of systematic coordination," the prime minister's
Secretariat was to be reorganized to include a Domestic Policy Coordination Office, a Foreign Policy Coordination Office, and a National Security
Office. But these offices are predominantly staffed by officials temporarily

dispatched from relevant ministries, and it appears dubious that these offices can exercise autonomous coordinating functions free from inter-ministerial haggling.

Some of the explicit functions of the Agency for Administrative Affairs are to coordinate and integrate administrative structure and to review the restructuring of administrative organs and fix the number of personnel. When this agency was created, it was generally expected that its impact would be rather limited. As it turns out, it started to play a certain active role in implementing and monitoring administrative reform. One source for the rather unexpected strength of this agency may be found in the creation of the Administrative Inspection Bureau, which was empowered to monitor administrative activities of governmental agencies and public corporations and to make necessary recommendations. There have even been a few instances in which the activities of this bureau have been effective in promoting administrative reform.[46] But the potential extent of the role of this agency is not yet fully known.

The other alternative to check the growing influence of *zoku* and other politicians in the coordinating function is for the bureaucracy to move in the direction of limiting its functioning to general policy-making (rendering it less prone to bend to the specific needs of a segment of the society) and operating according to more explicit, neutral, and codified rules, rather than relying on pragmatic, case-by-case administration. Of course, there have always been rules to be followed by the bureaucrat, but they have always been applied flexibly and, whenever necessary, have been reinterpreted to fit the given situation. During the first oil shock, when speculative accumulation of oil inventory by petroleum-refining companies and the resulting scarcity of kerosene aroused the anger of consumers, the MITI displayed an ingenious rule-manipulating ability by charging petroleum companies with violation of the Fire Prevention Law. The ministry had to do something to calm the public, and it proved it could contrive something with the existing rules. The rule of incremental budget distribution in the heyday of administered pluralism, despite its formality, was also flexible enough to accommodate the emergent interests of diverse interests because the growing economy was capable of generating ever increasing fiscal resources.

Obviously, the favorable conditions that made discretionary and pragmatic adaptation possible are disappearing. Discretionary maneuvering on a case-by-case basis with limited resources may not be neutral toward various interests in its welfare effects. Also, discretionary regulation by the bureaucrat is increasingly perceived to be burdensome rather than paternalistically helpful to the private sector as it gains international competitiveness. Further, international pressures for making regulatory rules more transparent, neutral and consistent with international trade practices are mounting. Finally, the increasing uncertainty of the economic environment may make a pragmatic and adaptive approach potentially more destabilizing. We have seen that this instability in fact occurred in the 1970s: The sudden accumulation of fiscal deficits was followed by the adoption of fiscal stringency.

However, a general shift to policy-oriented, rule-bound administration would require some restructuring of the bureaucracy, which is organized on the traditional concept of jurisdiction. Efficient policy-making in such cross-jurisdictional arenas as the information and biotechnology industries, financial markets, and international economic relations would now seem to require a redefinition of jurisdictional demarcation or at least a more effective functioning of the coordinating office. But attempts at such restructuring would be bound to elicit bureaucratic resistance. For example, within the MOF, regulation over banking, securities, and international finance is compartmentalized in separate *genkyoku* bureaus, and financial deregulation often is hampered by interbureau jurisdictional disputes. However, *Rincho*'s informal inquiry into the possibility of spinning off those *genkyoku* bureaus from the MOF into the consolidated Agency for Monetary Finance, which would thereby make the MOF a purely coordinating office, was said to be flatly rejected by the MOF.[47] Thus, restructuring of jurisdictions in a way consistent with a policy-oriented, rule-bound administration will need to be promoted by strong political leadership.

The concept of a policy-oriented, rule-bound administration is somewhat akin to T. J. Lowi's model of "juridical democracy" in emphasizing the importance of neutral rule.[48] Lowi proposes, however, that the groundwork for making rules should be laid down by legislative enactments. Of course, no legislative enactment is free from a certain degree of ambiguity, so that, in his model, agencies would need to supplement law by frequent administrative rules. But they would do so on the basis of the responsibility delegated to them by Congress in enabling statutes, and Congress would also regularly and routinely revise its laws in light of administrative experience. Thus, the functions of policy-making and rule-bound administration would be clearly separated between the legislative body and the bureaucracy. However, it is not clear to me how congressional enactments would be made free from the shortsighted haggling of interest-group politics.

One important feature of the Japanese polity is that, as already pointed out, the ministry is endowed with the authority to draft and propose laws to the Diet through the prime minister. Until now, the bureaucracy has mostly drafted laws on its own initiative, although in some areas the

Table 10.2. *Three prototype models*

Aspect	LDP-mediated pluralism	Centralized administration	Neo-neoclassical administration
Genkyoku	*Zoku* control	Quasi agent cum regulator	Policy-oriented, rule-bound
Coordination	LDP arbitration	Centralized cabinet control	Specialized function of coordinating office
Principle of integration	LDP rule	Hierarchy	Functionalism (hierarchy)

legislative initiative has begun to shift toward the LDP.[49] Laws drafted by career bureaucrats may be based more on a long-term perspective and perhaps may be more free of logrolling among a combination of interests. On the other hand, the bureaucracy may be too opportunistic to draft laws that call for significant change. Furthermore, unification of the drafting function and the administration function may give too much centralized power to the bureaucracy, especially if the Diet cannot check it effectively. From one point of view, the rising power of the LDP vis-à-vis the bureaucracy may be regarded as a growing countervailing force against the administrative power.

7   Concluding remarks: three vectors of modification

In preceding sections we have seen that there are three important vectors of force operating that potentially can alter the nature of administered pluralism: the strengthening of LDP influence; the strengthening of the coordinating function within the administration; and the incorporation of some elements of a policy-oriented, rule-bound administration. But, thus far, none of these vectors has been strong enough to produce great change, and the polity has tended to gravitate toward maintenance of the essential elements of administered pluralism. In the future, is it likely that one of these vectors or a combination of them may dominate the others, ending the era of administered pluralism?

In order to consider this question, let us first imagine three prototype models in which one of those vectors dominates. Then we can consider whether or not a transition from administered pluralism to any of the prototype models is likely. The three prototype models may be schematized as in Table 10.2.

The first column, LDP-mediated pluralism, corresponds to the prototype model in which the current tendency toward a strengthening of LDP influence vis-à-vis the bureaucracy is pushed to an extreme. In this model, the *genkyoku* becomes an instrument to which the interests of *zoku* politicians are fed. Interest-group coordination becomes a function of intra-LDP politics. The principle of integration is the collective goal of LDP politicians to sustain LDP rule in politics. I have indicated that in administered pluralism, shadow bargaining between different *zoku* occurs, corresponding to primary quasi-social bargaining among ministries. In this LDP-arbitrated pluralism, the relation between the primal and the dual is reversed.

The second column, the centralized-administration model, corresponds to the prototype model in which there is a clear and rational separation between cabinet control and administrative operation of the *genkyoku*. The dual role of *genkyoku* as quasi agent cum regulator over its jurisdiction remains, but the principle of integration is vertical control by the cabinet, rather than hierarchically ordered bargaining among bureaucratic bodies of different levels and different ministries.

The third column, the neo-neoclassical administration, corresponds to the prototype model in which the neoclassical ideal of functionalism is revived within the administrative framework. According to this model, each *genkyoku* performs the task of policy-making and rule-bound administration over its own jurisdiction. Coordination of cross-jurisdictional issues becomes itself a specialized function of the coordinating office, so that there is an element of hierarchical structuring.

Is it likely that any of these prototype models will supersede the current model of administered pluralism? Will the LDP grow into the dominant bearer of pluralistic politics and replace the adjective "administrative" with "LDP-arbitrated" to define the nature of the Japanese polity? Will the current or future government be able to strengthen the function of the cabinet? Or will the bureaucracy transform itself into a neo-neoclassical administration more comprehensible to and consistent with the Western system? I am skeptical that any single alternative will become visibly dominant in the near future, although it seems inevitable for the Japanese polity to incorporate elements of some or all these models, for the reasons stated in the preceding section. I submit that the Japanese polity will maneuver between the three courses, using its well-known flexibility, making the Japanese polity indeed a complex system.

First of all, a decisive shift of power to the LDP politicians is unlikely. Although there has been a recent strengthening of LDP power, there also are factors that check its momentum. The increasing scarcity of fiscal resources is one factor to arrest the LDP's enhanced role of representing specific interests. The bureaucracy will also make efforts to retain its relative autonomy vis-à-vis LDP politicians. It has already been pointed out that the current fiscal stringency is partly chosen by bureaucrats to retain their budgetary control. Because of the career system, the bureaucracy is endowed with unparalleled human resources to administer pluralism. Even increasingly powerful politicians cannot ignore their utility. Every ministry carefully makes sure to expand its influence within the LDP by sending former bureaucrats to the Diet. So the pluralistic aspect of the polity will likely be characterized by balancing administered pluralism and LDP-arbitrated pluralism.

Reorientation to the centralized-administration model or to neo-neoclassical administration will require strong promotional political leadership that will not spontaneously emerge from administered pluralism, for the reason hypothesized at the end of Section 6. Whether or not the *Rincho* will provide such expediency is not yet clear. However, it is noteworthy that although the increasing importance of cross-jurisdictional issues and the scarcity of fiscal resources will require a stronger coordinating function, a complete transition to either of the two models will introduce a principle of integration and coordination diametrically opposed to the current mode, which is hierarchical integration based on functionalism. Whether or not such a complete transition will be viable or valuable remains undetermined.

We have seen that there has been an important development of isomorphism between, on the one hand, the mechanism of semiautonomous problem-solving and semihorizontal coordination in the Japanese firm and, on the other hand, administered pluralism in the polity. The two have the following common features: pragmatic (technical/political) problem-solving by the use of on-the-spot knowledge and consensual coordination among component units, as opposed to rationalist problem-solving by hierarchical control or a priori rule. From the political perspective, the common feature may also be conceptualized as a sort of decentralization in the sense that access to decision/policy-making is diffused. This isomorphism, together with the resulting duality of political stability and industrial efficiency, suggests that elements of administered pluralism are rather deep-seated in the Japanese social system and more in accord with prevailing social values. Neo-neoclassical administration may be, on the other hand, too alien and impersonal for the Japanese. Also, the possibility of centralized administration may rouse the "democratic" media and public. Some politicians who are skillful in dealing with grass-roots sentiments will not fail to ride such a public mood to their own political advantage.

In sum, the inertia of administrative pluralism seems to be still strong. However, as repeated often, the polity needs to incorporate some elements of LDP arbitration, stronger coordinating offices, and a policy-oriented, rule-bound administration in the changing domestic and international environment. Japan's administered pluralism may adapt itself to these needs with its customary flexibility and transform itself gradually. In this process, politicians, on the whole, will try to enhance their influence as promoters of constituent interests. In addition, some leaders will take the initiative to institutionalize a more centralized coordinating mechanism within either the LDP or the administration. The future course does not seem to be clear-cut, and it is not obvious what the eventual model will be. In any event, one thing is certain: The future of the Japanese polity will be different from any image drawn by linear extrapolation from the past.

ACKNOWLEDGMENTS

I am extremely grateful to several colleagues for detailed critical comments and kind suggestions regarding earlier versions of this chapter: Professors Kent Caldor, Takashi Inoguchi, Shunpei Kumon, Michio Muramatsu, Daniel Okimoto, Seizaburo Sato, Gary Saxonhouse, and John Shoven. They are, of course, not responsible for any errors that may remain or for the views expressed herein. I would also like to acknowledge the helpful editorial assistance of Ms. Stacey Tanaka. The research leading to this chapter was partially supported by grants from the Center for Economic Policy Research and the Center for Research in International Studies, both at Stanford University.

NOTES

1. C. Johnson's work on the Ministry of International Trade and Industry may be considered a sophisticated version of this view: C. Johnson, *MITI and the Japanese Miracle: The Growth of Industrial Policy* (Stanford University Press, 1982).
2. See, for instance, M. Aoki, "Aspects of the Japanese Firm," in M. Aoki (ed.), *The Economic Analysis of the Japanese Firm* (pp. 31–6) (Amsterdam: North Holland, 1984).
3. A most notable recent work on this subject is that of R. Komiya, M. Okuno, and K. Suzumura (eds.), *Nihon no Sangyo Seisaku (Industrial Policy in Japan)* (University of Tokyo Press, 1984).
4. See G. Saxonhouse, "Industrial Policy and Factor Markets: Biotechnology in Japan and the United States," in H. Patrick (ed.), *Japan's High Technology Industries: Lessons and Limitations of Industrial Policy* (pp. 97–135) (Seattle: University of Washington Press, 1986).
5. T. Yakushiji, "The Government in a Spiral Dilemma; Dynamic Policy Intervention vis-à-vis Auto Firms, c. 1900–1960," in M. Aoki (ed.), *The Economic Analysis,* op. cit. (pp. 265–310).

6. For a survey of the literature, see M. Muramatsu and E. S. Krauss, "Bureaucrats and Politicians in Policy-making: The Case of Japan," *American Political Science Review*, Vol. 78, 1984, pp. 126–46.

7. See M. Aoki, "Keizai Keikaku no Kino Saiko (Functions of Economic Planning Reconsidered)," in T. Murakami and K. Hamada (eds.), *Keizaigaku no Atarashii Nagare (New Currents in Economics)* (pp. 163–91) (Tokyo: Toyo Keizai Shinpo-sha, 1981).

8. See T. Inoguchi, *Gendai Nihon Seiji Keizai no Kozu: Seifu to Shijyo (Framework of Contemporary Japanese Political Economy: Government and Markets)* (Tokyo: Toyo Keizai Shinpo-sha, 1983); S. Sato and T. Matsuzaki, *Jiminto Seiken (LDP Governmental Power)* (Tokyo: Chuo Koron-sha, 1985); M. Muramatsu and E. S. Krauss, "The Conservative Policy Line and the Development of Patterned Pluralism," in Y. Yasuba and K. Yamamura (eds.), *The Political Economy of Japan Vol. 1: The Domestic Transformation* (pp. 516–54) (Stanford University Press, 1987).

9. Y. Kosai, "The Politics of Economic Management," in Y. Yasuba in K. Yamamura (eds.), op. cit. (pp. 555–92).

10. See T. J. Lowi, *The End of Liberalism* (New York: Norton, 1979).

11. Similar isomorphic structures seem to be found in other social systems, such as in the legal system and educational system. See J. Haley, "Law, Culture and the Political Economy of Postwar Japan" (mimeograph, 1986); T. Rohlen, "Conflict in Institutional Environments: Politics in Education," in E. Krauss et al. (eds.), *Conflict in Japan* (Honolulu: University of Hawaii Press, 1984), pp. 136–73.

12. Precisely speaking, there are bureaucratic entities that do not have any jurisdictional sphere in the private sector and whose functions are intrabureaucratic coordination. I discuss this division of functions within the bureaucracy later.

13. For example, the computer industry is a jurisdictional constituent of the Machinery and Information Industries Bureau of the MITI, and the banking industry is a jurisdictional constituent of the Banking Bureau of the MOF.

14. M. Muramatsu, *Sengo Nihon no Kanryosei (The Bureaucracy in Postwar Japan)* (chap. 2) (Tokyo: Toyo Keizai Shinpo-sha, 1981).

15. The history of the *amakudari* phenomenon is not long. It began in earnest in the 1950s, possibly caused by the need and pressure not to block the opportunities for career advancement for relatively younger bureaucrats. Because the so-called career team in the bureaucracy more than doubled in size between the Manchurian Incident in 1931 and the end of World War II, these pressures became very intense during the 1950s. This coincided with the beginning of the era of rapid growth, and relatively high-paid positions in the private sector and in expanding public corporations were available to retiring bureaucrats. Demand and supply happily matched. See C. Johnson, "The Reemployment of Retired Government Bureaucrats in Japanese Big Business," *Asian Survey*, Vol. 14, November 1974, pp. 953–65.

16. K. Caldor provides evidence that the relatively "disadvantaged" segment of the private sector is more active in the recruitment of *amakudari* bureaucrats. For example, companies located in the Kansai area, as opposed to the metropolitan Tokyo area, and companies that do not belong to major *keiretsu* groups, or are foreign-owned, or have fewer Tokyo University graduates on their boards of directors, have relatively larger numbers of *amakudari*

bureaucrats on their boards. Caldor thus characterizes the practice of *amakudari* as an "equalizing process." See K. Caldor, "Elites in an Equalizing Role: Ex-bureaucrats as Coordinators and Intermediaries in the Japanese Government–Business Relationship (mimeograph, Princeton University, 1986).

17. K. Caldor, who has done interesting work on this subject, observed the following: "Interviews of twenty present and former MITI and Ministry of Finance officials by the author during the summers of 1979–80 revealed that former bureaucrats do not frequently contact working-level officials (generally 30 or more years their junior) with specific requests. But the junior working level officials who handle day-to-day policy almost unanimously feel a need to tread cautiously in relation to their retired *senpai*, or seniors, due to uncertainty as to what the latter may say privately to superiors who are still within the ministry" (Caldor, op. cit.).

18. See Nihon Keizai Shinbun-sha, *Jiminto Seichokai (The Policy Research Council of LDP)*, 1983, for a detailed account of *zoku*.

19. See, for instance, B. R. Weingast, "A Principal–Agent Perspective on Congressional–Bureaucratic Relations" (unpublished); T. M. Moe, "The New Economics of Organization," *American Journal of Political Science,* Vol. 28, pp. 739–77.

20. This conceptual framework is similar to the resource-dependence perspective of J. Pfeffer and G. R. Slancik, *The External Control of Organizations* (New York: Harper & Row, 1978).

21. This analogy is drawn from an unconventional theory of the Japanese firm as a coalition of the body of stockholders and the body of permanent employees, rather than the property of the former. See M. Aoki, *The Cooperative Game Theory of the Firm* (Oxford University Press, 1984); M. Aoki, "The Japanese Firm in Transition," in Y. Yasuba and K. Yamamura (eds.), op. cit.; M. Aoki, *Microtheory of the Japanese Economy: Information, Incentives, and Bargaining* (Cambridge University Press, 1988).

22. For example, funds allocated to the Public Housing Finance Corporation ultimately accrue to the construction industry under the jurisdiction of the Ministry of Construction. A large proportion of funds allocated to public finance corporations now originate in postal savings.

23. See L. Johansen, "The Bargain Society and the Inefficiency of Bargaining," *Kyklos,* 1979, pp. 497–522.

24. See Y. Noguchi, "Decision-making Rule in the Japanese Budgetary Process," *Japanese Economic Studies,* Vol. 7, 1979, pp. 51–75.

25. See K. Komiya, "Planning in Japan," in M. Bornstein (ed.), *Economic Planning: West and East* (pp. 189–227) (Cambridge, Mass.: Ballinger, 1975), for a detailed description of the economic planning process.

26. For the stabilizing effects of economic planning, see M. Aoki, "Aspects of the Japanese Firm," op. cit. Many expected the same modest role for the Management and Coordination Agency when it was created in 1984 by the merger of the Administrative Management Agency and some bureaus of the prime minister's office, with interministerial coordination of administration as its function. It is noteworthy, however, that there is some indication that this agency is gaining a modicum of centralized power. I discuss the implications of this new development in the last two sections.

27. See M. Aoki, *The Cooperative Game Theory,* op. cit. (pp. 74–80).

28. See M. Aoki, *The Cooperative Game Theory, Part II,* op. cit.

298   M. Aoki

29. See the recent formulation of the hierarchy by economists such as J. Cremer, "A Partial Theory of the Optimal Organization of a Bureaucracy," *Bell Journal of Economics*, Vol. 11, 1980, pp. 683–93; J. Geanakopolos and P. Milgrom, "A Theory of Hierarchies Based on Limited Managerial Attention" (mimeograph, Yale University, 1985).

30. See M. Aoki, "Horizontal vs. Vertical Information Structure of the Firm," *American Economic Review*, Vol. 76, 1987, pp. 971–83.

31. See M. Aoki, "Incentive to Share Knowledge: An Aspect of the Japanese Industrial Organization," in S. Hedlund (ed.), *Incentive and Economic Systems* (pp. 57–75) (London: Croom Helm, 1987).

32. For the *kanban* system, see Y. Monden, *Toyota Production System* (Atlanta: Industrial Engineering and Management Press, 1983); J. Abegglen and G. Stalk, Jr., *Kaisha: The Japanese Corporation* (chap. 5) (New York: Basic Books, 1983).

33. In the article referred in note 30, I attempted a rigorous mathematical analysis to examine under what conditions this semihorizontal coordination mechanism may reduce the total expected costs of the production system, as opposed to hierarchical control, whose rationality is bounded.

34. The tendency of the Japanese firm not to integrate as many activities as the Western firm and to rely on a relatively small number of semiautonomous subcontractors for supplies on a long-term basis may be understood in the same manner from the informational systematic point of view. Semiautonomous management of the subcontractor and semihorizontal coordination between subcontractor and prime manufacturer may save on information costs inevitable in excessive integration (e.g., time lag and distortion of information due to excessive hierarchical layering).

35. See M. Aoki, *Microtheory*, op. cit. (chap. 3).

36. One of the latent roles of the neutral rule of incrementalism may be found in the avoidance of inefficient haggling among ministries by freeing budget allocation from case-by-case judgment.

37. The number of dispatched bureaucrats has increased from 2,106 in 1975 to 3,345 in 1993. S. Sano, *Kanryo, Fuyu no Judai (Bureaucrat: Their Winter Season)* (Tokyo: President-sha, 1985, pp. 189–90).

38. See R. Axelrod, *The Evolution of Cooperation* (New York: Basic Books, 1984).

39. J. Bendor, "In Good Times and Bad: Reciprocity in an Uncertain World" (mimeograph, Stanford University, 1985).

40. Incidentally, this consideration casts some doubt on the view prevailing in the United States that the marginal development in Japan of institutional arrangements to facilitate start-ups, such as the frequent interfirm mobility of researchers and the venture-capital market, may be disadvantageous to innovation without government support to complement or substitute them. See G. Saxonhouse, "Industrial Policy and Factor Markets," op. cit.

41. M. Aoki, "Aspects of the Japanese Firm," op. cit. (pp. 3–43).

42. It is generally agreed that during the 1950s, the model of a more exclusive ruling triad applied. See note 1.

43. See H. Patrick and T. Rohlen, "Small-Scale Family Enterprises," in Y. Yasuba and K. Yamamura (eds.), op. cit. (pp. 331–84).

44. In my estimation, the subsidiarization alone contributed to a 3.5–4.5% reduction in the employment/sales ratio (in real terms) in the electric-machinery

and electronics industry over the period 1973–82, controlling the effect of laborsaving technological progress and the scale effect. The autonomous rate of laborsaving per sales due to internal-organization innovation is estimated to be about 10.0% per annum. See M. Aoki, "Innovative Adaptation Through Quasi-Tree Structure: An Emerging Aspect of Japanese Entrepreneurship," *Zeitschrift für Nationalökonomie (Supplementum)*, Vol. 44, 1984, pp. 177–98.

45. A good example of such shortsightedness can be seen in the aforementioned MPT–MITI dispute over regulation of the communications network. Because manufacturing was under the jurisdictional control of the MITI, the MPT targeted the "user" side of the information industry and, by mobilizing the political power of its *zoku*, was assured of exclusive jurisdiction over the communications arena by the enactment of the 1984 Law for Regulating the Electric Communications Businesses. But the 1984 law was so preoccupied with establishing the MPTs domestic jurisdictional authority that some provisions invited international criticism for being closed and "not transparent." Particularly, the provisions that concerned the establishment and management of a public corporation for inspection of communications-terminal equipment and those that concerned the regulatory procedure for setting up value-added networks (VAN) drew the most criticism from abroad, although those provisions were not intended to pose a trade barrier as much as a domestic jurisdictional barrier. Because of this backfire from the international arena, the MPT was later compelled to modify its discretionary power.

46. An example is provided by the replacement of the top management of JNR in 1985. Against an impending recommendation by *Rincho,* the top management of JNR resisted the dissolution and privatization of the debt-stricken JNR with backup from some transportation *zoku* politicians. But when the Administrative Inspection Bureau made public the knowledge that JNR owned a substantial amount of off-balance-sheet assets, the credibility of the case against privatization was seriously impaired, and those in top management were compelled to submit their resignations to the prime minister the following day. This unusually speedy de facto dismissal of top management was greatly facilitated by the effective monitoring activity of the bureau.

47. In contrast to this conservative stance of the MOF, R. Komiya regards the restructuring of the MITI in the 1970s as more progressive from a policy-oriented, rule-bound administrative point of view. In the MITI, the number of bureaus that have direct jurisdiction over particular industries has been reduced to three bureaus and one agency: the Basic Industries Bureau, the Machinery and Information Industries Bureau, the Consumer Goods Industries Bureau, and the Agency of Natural Resources and Energy. Furthermore, the weights in the intraministerial policy-making process are said to have relatively declined. Instead, across-the-board bureaus, such as the International Trade Policy Bureau and the Industrial Policy Bureau, have been gaining in importance. Thus, the MITI seems to be making some attempts to reorient itself toward general industrial policy-making as a part of macroeconomic management, rather than continuing to respond to the interests and needs of particular industries. See K. Komiya, "Introduction," in K. Komiya et al. (eds.), *Industrial Policy,* op. cit. A similar intraministerial restructuring was made more on a functional basis at the Ministry of Transport.

48. T. J. Lowi, *The End of Liberalism,* op. cit. (chap. 11).

49. For example, the specifics of the tax-scheme changes are now very much in the hands of the LDP Tax Commission, whereas the government Tax Commission that reports to the MOF is concerned only with deliberating on a more general policy framework. This shift in actual legislative power is considered responsible for the difficulty in legislating any major tax change that would hurt any beneficiaries of the current tax system.

CHAPTER 11

Japan's energy policy during the 1970s

Chikashi Moriguchi

1 Introduction

Japan's response to higher energy prices was relatively swift. Its performance in saving energy in both the industrial sector and the household sector was the best among the comparable industrial economies. From the beginning of the first OPEC price hike to the end of the second, Japan's energy consumption per unit of real gross national product declined by 28%. Energy consumption per unit of manufacturing output decreased by 29%. In the household sector, total energy consumption grew as total consumption expenditure rose by 30%. However, energy consumption "per unit of real consumer spending" dropped by 10%.

The industrial structure of Japan changed in the 1970s because of the high energy prices and also because of the development of high technology concentrated in microelectronics. When examining Japan's energy policy, we must consider the joint effects of these two factors. Development of microelectronics technology was one of the primary targets of Japan's industrial policy. Energy policy was not viewed as an industrial policy in Japan, although it does affect the petrochemical, oil-refining, and coal-mining industries. Energy policy does have a national focus, however, and this focus has evolved throughout the two oil price shocks.

In 1973–4 the energy price hike coincided with a general excess-demand condition in the market. In response, the government focused on dealing with day-to-day matters, such as controlling the price of petroleum products, securing a heating-oil supply, and drawing up a contingency plan in case the oil embargo was prolonged.

By the time of the second OPEC price shock, the MITI's industrial policy had undergone a remarkable change in style. This change was from government leadership based on a development plan and coercive policy

301

instruments to a market-oriented stance based on a limited subsidy program. After the second price increase for oil, Japan, under the Ohira government, pursued a noninterventionist policy with respect to price formation in the energy industry, and the monetary authority kept tight control on the rate of expansion of the money supply. The cost of energy rose throughout the economy, but there was no acceleration of inflation because of the general deflationary situation produced by a leakage of income abroad (oil bill) and the monetary squeeze. Energy policy was targeted at a more medium-term perspective during this period.

Thus far, I have focused on the relatively successful demand aspect of the energy problem. Government policy on the supply side of the energy industry has resulted in a mixture of failures and successes. The handling of coal policy has been a poor adjustment policy; the recent development of structural depression in the oil-refining industry is another.

Meanwhile, Japan's natural-gas policy has made a significant contribution to Japan's diversification of its energy supply. The use of nuclear power to generate electricity has made steady progress in Japan. The relative share of nuclear energy in total electric-power generation increased from 2% in 1970 to 11% in 1983. Despite the potential for adverse public sentiment toward nuclear power, a few factors have contributed to relatively generous acceptance by the public. One is a social recognition that Japan is a country with poor energy-resource endowments. Another factor is the record of safe performance of nuclear power plants in Japan. There has not been a major incident at any nuclear power-generation plant in Japan.

The purpose of this chapter is twofold: first, a brief sketch is given of the development of Japan's energy policy from 1973 to 1982, with special reference to industrial policy; second, an assessment of the "effects" of energy-demand policy as distinguished from autonomous adjustment through the market mechanism is made. This seems to be an impossible task, but in order to assess the significance of a public policy, we need to obtain some rough measure of the "policy effect." Of course, there are some nonmeasurable aspects of public policy in terms of effects on the real economy. However, calling the public's attention to a certain issue is important, as it helps the public adjust to a new policy environment. In such cases, measurement of the effectiveness of a public policy should consider not only the degree of accomplishment but also the swiftness of public response.

With respect to the supply side of energy policy, assessment of the domestic coal policy and the overseas oil-development policy remains a crucial issue. These issues are mentioned in the first half of this chapter, but most of this problem is left for future study.

2   Development of Japan's energy situation and energy policy
        during the 1970s

Prior to 1970, Japan had completely finished its switch to oil as its major
and almost exclusive source of energy. The domestic coal-mining industry that once had recorded over 50 million tons of annual production sur-
vived in some local areas and produced an annual output of roughly 20
million tons. The swiftness with which the economy shifted from coal to
petroleum was important in supporting rapid industrial growth of Japan
in the 1960s.

Toward the end of the 1960s, the energy problem had two basic aspects. One was an environmental problem; consumption of heavy oil by
the electric-power industry was regulated in order to control sulfoxide
(SO_x) emissions. Expansion of nuclear power plants was slowed because
of rising concern among the public. The second aspect was a "backward"
adjustment problem in the coal-mining regions. When Tanaka came to
power in 1972, he proposed a plan for "remodeling the Japanese archipelago." Thus, a backward-adjustment policy in which public spending
for workers' readjustment and welfare programs was increased was incorporated as a part of regional development plans.

Because of the ready availability of cheap imported oil, serious efforts were not made to raise the degree of energy self-sufficiency. Power
plants shifted their primary energy source from coal to heavy oil and
later to "raw petroleum" as pollution control was tightened. Some electric-
power companies shifted to burning imported liquid natural gas (LNG)
and became pioneers in diversifying their sources of energy supply. At
that time, the MITI tried to promote the shift using a subsidy program
on the grounds that LNG was a cleaner source of energy than heavy
oil.

When the first OPEC price shock hit Japan, inflation was already in
progress; the annual rate of monetary expansion exceeded 20%, and some
industrial sectors were in an excess-demand situation. Oil price hikes and
the possibility of an oil embargo brought about a mild panic. Heating-oil
prices allegedly were raised by agreement among the domestic suppliers'
association, who thought they had a "rare chance" for profit.[1]

The administration stabilized the near-panic situation by means of price
controls and administrative guidance to suppliers. Unfair practices by
retailers of fuel and some petrochemical products were the targets of social complaints. The government quickly responded to this situation and
enacted a series of regulations to deal with the short-term excess demand
that was aggravated by speculation.

3   Long-run policy in the early stage

In addition to the day-to-day administrative activities carried out by the policy authority, there was an attempt to make long-run policy. An interesting example was the pricing policy introduced for the electric-power industry. It was a progressive rate system, and with the support of the MITI, all of the nine electric-power companies (all serving large separate regions) set three ranges of progressive electricity rates for households. With respect to the industrial sector, the rates were coupled with a policy to cut peak-load demand by means of a "special off-peak" contract. However, the effectiveness of the progressive price system in reducing electricity consumption was minimal. Price ranges were set without considering the sizes of households, and the rate of progression was rather modest.

4   Policy toward coal and petroleum

Domestic coal once was viewed as an alternative domestic source of energy. However, the coal-mining industry experienced a severe process of adjustment covering nearly 20 years. Annual output was below 20 million tons in 1973 (down from 50 million tons in 1966), and production costs were far above levels that would have been competitive against imported coal. In 1972, just before the oil-supply situation changed, the government of Japan decided to maintain the domestic coal-mining industry at a level of 20 million tons by granting increased subsidies and other measures to ensure survival of the industry. It was an extended adjustment policy that had much to do with domestic politics.

In 1975, the coal policy was reviewed. Because it was accepted that energy sources needed to be diversified, continued operation of major domestic coal mines was agreed on. Problems still existed, however, because domestic coal prices were higher than the low prices of imported coal. The high value of the yen and rising costs of coal mining because of domestic inflation contributed to a further widening of the price differential. The problem still remains today.

Overseas oil development was started in the 1960s, and the success of Arabia Oil and a few other ventures encouraged the public feeling that Japan ought to develop its own independent sources of oil. However, because of the high sulfur content in the oil found and the disadvantage of being latecomers to oil exploration, overseas oil development did not grow as had been hoped. Besides, Japan's domestic petroleum-product market was dominated by the network of major oil companies, and it proved difficult for independent producers to find a continuous outlet for processing. After substantial amounts of spending for oil exploration and development, Japan now gets only 10% of its total imported crude oil through its independently developed channels. The original target was 30%.

5   Policy toward nuclear energy

The pace of construction of nuclear power-generating plants by the electric-power industry had slowed by the turn of the 1970s. That slowdown was the culmination of a number of environmental concerns among the public. A series of minor "incidents" reported by nuclear power plants lowered the level of operations generally, and the "lead" time required to build new nuclear power plants became substantially longer.

As of 1973, nuclear energy accounted for 2% of the total electricity supply of Japan; only 6 plants were in operation, but 16 plants were under construction. Five years later, 21 plants were operating and supplying over 10% of Japan's electricity. In 1978, only five new plants had been authorized for construction in the preceding five years. Despite the oil crisis and the changed perception of the public, the process of building a nuclear plant (starting with basic survey, public hearings, and authorization by the Atomic Reactor Safety Commission) became lengthened because of rising societal demands and requirements for safety. This has been part of a worldwide tendency. Even so, Japan belongs to a group of fast developers, together with France, West Germany, and the United States.[2]

Given that rapid adjustment was needed in response to the first OPEC price hikes, Japan fortunately had an asset of 16 nuclear-reactor power plants under construction. These power sources were one reason that Japan did not increase its relative share of demand for oil in the world market in the following years.

In the latter half of the 1970s, Japan's nuclear policy shifted toward developing a stockpile of enriched uranium. Japan purchased a large amount of enriched uranium, partly because of the necessity of reducing Japan's mounting trade-balance surplus. This accumulation reflected Japan's desire to enhance its self-sufficiency in enriched uranium and was aimed at achieving a comprehensive "nuclear cycle."

6   Rapid decline in energy input

After a time lag in adjusting to higher energy costs, Japan's industrial sector began to show rapid progress in raising its energy efficiency. One factor was the relative price shock itself; the second was rapid development of microelectronics (ME) technology in the manufacturing industry; the third was rapid change in Japan's industrial and trade structure that was accelerated not only by high energy prices but also by the rising value of the yen.

The MITI had already decided that ME technology would play a strategic role in its projection for Japan's industrial future. Conservation of materials, including energy, was seen as crucial in restoring Japan's balance-of-payments accounts following the first OPEC shock. A "knowledge-intensive" industrial structure was MITI's "key word" for the latter half of the 1970s and for the 1980s. ME technology development was pursued as a new target of industry policy, and "mechatronics," a combination of electronics and machinery industries, was viewed as a powerful instrument for lifting Japan into a new phase of economic development free from energy and environmental problems. In the latter half of the 1970s, there was an industry-wide campaign for a "lighter, shorter, and smaller" standard of output. It could not have been achieved without the developments of the ME revolution.

Meanwhile, Japan's import structure was shifting to processed-material imports; an example was that aluminum imports began to soar. One factor was a consequence of cost disadvantages; products from North America that relied on low-priced hydroelectric energy flowed in. Second, some of Japan's domestic producers went abroad in search of similar cost advantages and then imported their output from their overseas operations. Energy embodied in imported aluminum contributed significantly to the reduction in domestic energy consumption, and increasing steel imports from the Republic of Korea made a similar contribution.

Changes in import structures made it necessary to adjust domestic productive capacity in import-competing industries. Aluminum smelting, some steel-processing sectors, and petrochemical and oil-refining industries have faced this problem since the turn of the decade. These adjustments may not be directly connected with Japan's energy policy. However, the adjustment process may have a significant indirect effect on the course of Japan's energy-policy development.

7   Energy policy in the later stage

By the time there was another sharp rise in oil prices, Japan had already gotten rid of the inflationary pressures of 1973-4. The monetary authority learned from the inflationary experience, and it switched to a more monetarist stance in the management of the money supply.

The experience of policy managers in the chaotic 1973-4 period taught the government bureaucrats the difficulty of regulating and intervening in market forces. Many bureaucrats simply tired of pressures arising from conflicts among consumers, industrialists, and politicians over energy issues. During this period, the government shifted to a so-called soft stance against the energy price hike; that is, they left price adjustments to the market and controlled inflation solely by keeping an eye on monetary aggregates.

Yet there remained some room for interventionist policy with respect to the relative prices of various oil products, domestic coal, and electricity. In comparison with the U.S. situation, where the energy industry was under strong regulation at least until 1979 (MacAvoy, 1983), the degree and range of Japan's regulatory policies were much larger. Except for the case of coal, Japan was free from conflicts caused by international and domestic price differentials of primary energy. Thus, Japan's regulation policy was not as complicated as that of the United States.

From 1977 to 1979, the government tried to incorporate various fragmentary energy policies into a comprehensive systematic policy framework. In 1978 the petroleum tax law was enacted to generate financial resources for energy policy; however, the rest of the tax system that was related to energy had not yet been reorganized.

8   Oil stockpiling

In a 1983 review by the International Energy Agency (IEA) of member countries' energy policies, Japan had a policy "recommendation" that emphasized the building and maintenance of adequate oil reserves "considering the present low level of reserves compared to other IEA member countries."[3]

As of mid-1983, Japan maintained a 90-day oil reserve by the private sector, and 26 days of government reserve.[4] Reserves as expressed by the number of days of consumption had increased owing to the decline in consumption. In 1984, Japan had a hot summer and a severe winter, and consumption and import levels went up; some of the reserves were released by the private sector. This consumption conflicted with the long-term policy objectives of Japan, but in a sense it met the original purpose of stockpiling.

The optimal sizes of oil reserves to be held by oil-importing countries are matters worth considering. The situation in the world oil market has changed; the OPEC share of world oil production has come down to close to 40%, and world interest rates remain higher than in the 1970s. Given that the world economic environment has changed, the solution to this optimization problem could be different from what we considered in the middle of the 1970s.

9   Policy for energy conservation

The Japanese government enacted a policy package for energy conservation in the 1979 Act of Rationalization of Energy Use. It was a response to the agreement made at IEA. Policies were introduced to encourage business investments that would conserve energy and housing investments making use of specified materials designed for energy conservation. The MITI and the Ministry of Education cooperated by adopting new standards for school-building construction and a subsidy program to install solar water heaters.

The "Moonlight Project" continued, with increasing budgets; this project financed basic technological research in magnetohydrodynamic power generation, fuel-cell power generation, high-efficiency gas-turbine engines, and so on. Also, scientific cooperation with the United States and France in these fields was supported by this project.

Starting with the modest financial support of 2 billion yen in 1974, a project called the "Sunshine Project" has been consistently growing into a comprehensive research program covering solar, geothermal, and wind energy sources, as well as tranformation of coal and hydrogen systems. As of 1983, its budget was 5 billion yen, and the Special Energy Account of the General Account was earmarked to cover the whole field of energy policy. The New Energy Development Organization (NEDO) was set up in 1980 to incorporate existing individual agencies; NEDO bears sole responsibility for assessing research projects and allocating financial resources for these projects.

The new energy research programs have reached the stage of reviewing and refocusing. Reexamination of the prospects for research is not being done. For example, support for solar-heating power-generation systems was discontinued, whereas photovoltaic-system research will continue.

10   Present state of energy policy

Today, the Special Energy Account is well established in the government's annual budget. The total budget for fiscal 1984 was 800 billion yen. Although it is still a small sum, and a large part is allocated to some backward-adjustment needs, the total budget keeps increasing because a certain amount of fiscal revenue is earmarked to it from indirect taxes on electricity and petroleum. At a time of worldwide reductions in government spending, this is an unusual situation. It is important that we examine the efficiency of the present scheme.

Table 11.1. *Energy consumption by industry*

Industry	1970	1973	1970-3 (%)	1975	1973-5 (%)	1980	1975-80 (%)
Foodstuffs	4,121	4,871	5.7	4,764	−Δ1.1	4,580	−Δ0.8
Textiles	5,440	6,586	6.6	6,597	−Δ0.1	5,086	−Δ5.1
Paper pulp	5,340	6,534	7.0	5,630	−Δ7.2	5,165	−Δ1.7
Chemicals	35,113	39,129	3.7	32,641	−Δ8.7	31,443	−Δ0.7
Ceramics	11,605	14,111	6.7	11,735	−Δ8.8	13,220	2.4
Steel	44,926	57,187	8.4	54,789	−Δ2.1	48,540	−Δ2.4
Nonferrous	3,862	4,628	6.2	3,775	−Δ9.7	4,121	1.8
Machinery	6,648	7,328	3.3	6,110	−Δ8.7	7,258	3.5
Others	6,801	10,628	16.0	8,510	−Δ10.5	11,469	6.1
Total	123,871	151,000	6.8	134,553	−Δ5.6	130,883	−Δ2.7

Note: Unit = 10^{10} kcal; % = average annual rate of change.
Source: Table of Energy Balance, Institute of Energy Economics, Tokyo.

11   Energy conservation by industry: a quantitative exploration of policy effects

Total energy consumption by Japan's manufacturing industries peaked in 1973, with the iron-and-steel industry accounting for more than a third of total consumption (Table 11.1). From 1973 to 1975, total energy consumption declined at an annual rate of 5.6%. This decline was mostly due to a change in the composition of Japanese output, not to any improvement in energy efficiency. Actually, energy efficiency deteriorated because of the loss of scale economy (see steel and ceramics in Table 11.2).

A remarkable change began to take place after 1975. By 1980, energy input per unit of manufacturing production decreased to 71 from 100 in 1975. This contributed to an annual rate of decline in total energy consumption of 6.4% during those years.

Improvements in energy efficiency can be attributed to two causes, the first of which is a shift in output composition, a shift away from energy-intensive composition. This can be seen even within each industrial sector; for example, the nonferrous-metal industry saw a sharp drop in aluminum production levels.

We estimate energy demand under the assumption that the general activity level is the same as in 1980 and the relative price of energy remains the same as in 1970. Table 11.3 shows an estimate. The difference between the estimate and the actual consumption level amounts to a decrease in

Table 11.2. *Energy input coefficient by industry*

Industry	1970 (%)	1973 (%)	1975 (%)	1980 (%)
Foodstuffs	51.3 (100.0)	55.9 (109.0)	53.8 (104.9)	46.1 (89.9)
Textiles	55.1 (100.0)	60.4 (109.6)	68.8 (124.9)	51.2 (92.9)
Paper pulp	72.1 (100.0)	71.6 (99.3)	72.6 (100.7)	53.3 (73.9)
Chemicals	560.9 (100.0)	497.6 (88.8)	450.8 (80.4)	320.2 (57.1)
Ceramics	150.5 (100.0)	146.4 (97.3)	152.2 (101.1)	134.9 (89.6)
Steel	573.1 (100.0)	595.7 (103.9)	682.3 (119.5)	497.3 (86.8)
Nonferrous	57.8 (100.0)	49.8 (86.2)	50.2 (86.9)	42.4 (73.4)
Machinery	113.7 (100.0)	101.8 (89.5)	100.0 (88.0)	73.7 (64.8)
Manufacturing total	1,837.8 (100.0)	1,766.1 (96.1)	1,825.7 (99.3)	1,312.8 (71.4)

Note: Unit $= 10^{10}$ kcal per unit of production index with base year of 1970 ($= 100$); figures in parentheses are indices of energy input coefficient.
Source: Table of Energy Balance, Institute of Energy Economics, Tokyo.

energy consumption caused by factors other than the income effect. As for the transport, household, and commercial sectors, we see that the energy conservation achieved is not impressive.

According to a study based on input–output analysis, of the 33% energy conservation achieved by the industrial sector, 20% was accounted for by changes in input coefficients, and 13% by changes in output composition (Research Institute of Electric Power Industry, 1984).

We attribute the entire part of energy conserved by a change in output composition to market forces. Only one point is to be made regarding the role of indirect import of energy. By shifting from domestic production to imports of aluminum and other metals, Japan saved approximately $3,280 \times 10^{10}$ kcal of energy in 1980 (Table 11.4). This amounted to 5.1% of total conserved energy for 1980. One might say that this was in part a market force, but there remains a question whether or not import liberalization might have been a result of a policy action initiated by the MITI to shape the industrial adjustment of the metals industries.

Table 11.3. *Estimation of conserved energy, 1970–80*

Industry	1970	1973	1975	1980
Manufacturing				
Actual	123.9[a]	151.0	134.6	130.9
Simulated[b]	123.9	157.3	144.1	195.6
Saved	0	6.3	9.5	64.7
Transport				
Actual	40.0	45.9	48.5	57.6
Simulated	40.0	49.7	50.4	64.6
Saved	0	3.8	1.9	7.0
Household/commercial				
Actual	35.5	47.1	48.2	54.6
Simulated	35.5	45.2	46.8	56.4
Saved	0	−1.9	−1.4	1.8
Total saved	0	8.2	10.0	73.5
Savings ratio		1.1%	2.9%	27.0%

[a] All entries × 10^{13} kcal.
[b] Simulated case is based on energy efficiency of 1970 with the actual growth path.

Table 11.4. *Indirect energy import through metals imports*[a]

Product	1975	1980	1982
Aluminum (1,000 tons)	—	957	1,477
Energy saved[b]	—	2.1	3.0
Steel product (1,000 tons)	608	24,270	39,800
Energy saved[b]	0.03	1.2	1.9

[a] Based on energy input observed in Japan in the respective years.
[b] × 10^{13} kcal.

12   Effects of tax incentives on energy conservation

The remaining part of energy conserved is attributed to changes in input coefficients, which not only include declines in energy input coefficients in various industrial sectors but also include decreases in material input coefficients. Most of these changes were consequences of both energy conservation and the new ME technology. In some cases, the MITI's administrative guidance to some sectors for reducing material content had some influence; a well-known case involved the auto industry, in which thinner steel plates and lighter coatings for car bodies were pursued.

The government introduced a system of tax incentives for energy-saving investments that consisted of investment tax credits, special depreciation allowances, and low-interest loans from the government's fund. A 10% tax credit for energy-saving investments and a 25% special depreciation allowance in the first year were introduced as options for firms.

Here we have to deal with a well-known difficulty in estimating the magnitude of the effects of tax incentives on investment activity. At the first stage of increased energy costs, many corporate firms had opportunities for cost reductions. In many cases, typically in the steel industry, an additional investment for heat recovery and reutilization yielded a high capital return.[5] In this case, tax incentives may have been redundant. However, tax incentives were given rather selectively. The Ministry of Finance specified that only a large investment with visible equipment for energy conservation was to be granted the credit or loan.

According to the investment survey conducted by the Japan Development Bank, 1.5% of total Japanese investment has been made "mainly for the purpose of saving energy" since 1979. From 1976 to 1979 the ratio was a little higher. Additional investment programs were targeting either at improving the efficiency of productive processes or at switching energy sources from oil to other alternatives.

In order to avoid overestimation, we assume that from 1976 to 1980 only 1.5% of total business fixed investment was investment for saving energy and that half of that investment was profitable. We assume that it takes two years for recovering initial costs, and the initial expense of the remaining half is recoverable only after 10 years. Under these assumptions, we can estimate the value and amount of energy saved from the actual price of oil.

Results show that as of 1982 the accumulated investment for energy conservation should have saved energy totaling 18.8×10^{13} kcal, a contribution that amounted to 34% of the total energy saved. Comparing that with the 22×10^{13} kcal that was saved because of changes in input coefficients in the manufacturing sector (Table 11.5), we can say that our estimation is not unreasonable.

The next problem is to determine how much of this saving should be attributed to tax incentives. Given that large price increases create rich investment opportunities, it seems probable that most of these results were consequences of firms' spontaneous responses to changed environments. But this does not reject the whole idea of tax-incentive policy. First, it

Table 11.5. *Estimation of effects of energy-saving investments, 1976–82*

Year	Investment (billion yen)	Energy price (yen/kl oil)	Energy saved (10^{13} kcal)
1976	200	23,502	5.1
1977	195	22,917	7.6
1978	200	18,372	9.9
1979	240	26,120	13.0
1980	270	47,188	15.6
1981	300	51,556	17.2
1982	300	53,980	18.8

Sources: Investment survey by the Japan Development Bank, based on a rough estimate of rate of return on investment as collected from various sources.

might have given an additional push to energy-saving investment by presenting an extra bonus. Also, when implementing a public policy, the speed of implementation is crucial. Second, with fewer high-return investment projects, tax-incentive policy should be effective by giving a marginal edge in assessing competitive projects within a firm.

There is a problem in Japan's tax-incentive scheme that is related to the second point; it is that the specification for qualified investment projects entitled to tax privileges is rather restrictive. Energy-saving investment projects are becoming less easily distinguishable from other projects; they tend to be parts of combined projects for investments other than energy savings. Broader application of incentive schemes is needed for further encouragement of energy conservation.

13 Concluding remarks

Japan's industrial policy changed during the 1970s, moving from "hard stance" based on incentive schemes (subsidy, tax concessions, and low-interest loans) to a new "soft stance" that relies on the capability of the government (typically the MITI) to compile information, draw up an industrial master plan (called "vision"), and mobilize resources for research for the future.[6]

Japan's energy policy can be viewed as being guided by this new "soft stance," but as it was organized into a "comprehensive policy" targeted at securing energy supply, developing alternative energy sources, and conserving energy, it absorbed some of the old-style backward-adjustment policy in relation to coal mining, aluminum smelting, and oil refining. Programs for new energy belong to the new aspect related to high-technology development.

As of 1984, the Special Energy Account had a budget of 970 billion yen (200 for development of electric power, 400 for petroleum development policy, 130 for coal policy, and 53 for research on non-oil energy sources). The two main sources of funds to support this account are an indirect tax on electricity and a tax on oil and oil products.

Of the 400 billion yen for petroleum policy, nearly half goes for oil stockpiling, which includes a subsidy to the private sector. Of the 130 billion yen for coal policy, a considerable part is spent to subsidize the domestic coal industry and finance a social security program for coal-mining areas. Programs for energy conservation account for only a small portion of the total.

It is clear that the "new aspect" of energy policy as a public policy in Japan is rather inconspicuous. In order to make a comprehensive assessment of Japan's energy policy from a cost–benefit viewpoint, we need to evaluate the effectiveness of the following specific policies: (1) oil stockpiling policy in the present situation, (2) coal policy, as one of the most inefficient backward-adjustment policies, and (3) protection for the domestic oil-refining and petrochemical industries.

Appendix: Chronological sketch of Japan's energy policy

1972   Two coal mines closed. Adjustment policy for coal mine area.

1973   Basic Plan for Rationalization of Coal Mining Industry (20 million tons by 1976), August.

Increased purchases of enriched uranium from the United States, September.

OPEC raised oil prices by 70%. This was followed by an embargo plan against those countries that stood with Israel, October.

Emergency Measures Against Oil Supply Situation (a guideline by the government), November.

Administrative guidance to control consumption of petroleum and electric power, November.

Freeze on retail price of kerosene, November.

Ceiling was set on retail price of LPG, December.

Act for Stabilization of Civil Life, Act for Optimizing Oil Product Supply, December.

1974   OPEC lifted oil embargo against the United States, March.

The regulated price of city gas and electricity raised, May.

Japan–Iraq Agreement on Economic and Technology Cooperation, August.

Government lifts the Declaration of Emergency Situation and lifts price controls on oil products, August.

Sunshine Project (Development Plan for New Energy Research) was launched, September.

1975 Projections on Long-Term Demand for Energy.

Government proclaims "Direction of Comprehensive Energy Policy," December.

Act of Oil-Stockpiling proclaimed.

1976 Increase in electricity prices, July–August.

Review of nuclear power-generation plan, December.

1977 Organization for comprehensive energy policy proceeds. Task force was started in the cabinet, February.

New target for oil stockpiling was set, March.

Energy conservation came up as a high-priority policy target. Necessity of nuclear power generation was widely recognized after a several-year "cooling period."

1978 Petroleum Act Tax enacted; purpose was to secure financial resources for comprehensive energy policy, June.

Acceleration of overseas coal and coal mine development, a report of the Policy Committee of the Energy Council, July.

Partial discount of electricity bill was implemented in view of the lowered domestic price of oil (thanks to a strong yen rate), September.

Oil stockpiling by tankers starts, October.

OPEC meets at Abudabi, announces a new raise to $13.34/bbl, December.

Oil embargo by Iran.

1979 Council of International Energy Agency agrees on 5% cut in oil consumption by member countries, March.

Experts meet on energy problems for Tokyo Summit, April.

Act of Rationalization of Energy Use proclaimed, June.

Tokyo Summit. Agreement on 5% cut in energy consumption up to 1980. Review of energy demand by individual countries.

Conference by Energy Ministers of Summit Seven, September.

IEA sets energy demand in import target by individual countries for 1980 and 1985, December.

1980 Price increase by electricity and gas industries, March.

Iran embargoes its oil shipment to Japan, April.

IEA sets a target of oil dependency in total energy demand and a target of energy-demand elasticity with respect to GNP at 0.6 as of 1990, May.

Enactment of a law to develop alternative energy sources to oil and accelerate its import.

OPEC meets in Algiers and sets a ceiling price of $32/bbl, June.
New Energy Development Organization launched, October. Reorganized old institutions to be responsible for New Energy Research and Development.

Development Commission for Coal Mining Area released a new review, November.

OPEC meets in Bali, setting ceiling price at $36/bbl, December.

1981   A New Petroleum Supply Plan for 1981–5 and a new target of oil stockpiling was set, May.

IEA Council agreed on plans for development and import of non-oil energy, June.

New Petroleum Supply Plan was revised downward, August.

Council of Coal Mining Industry decided to extend the term of law dealing with compensation for pollution and disaster; special measure taken for a coal-mine disaster in Hokkaido, December.

1982   Council of Oil Refinery reports on the necessity of reducing overall supply capacity, March.

Energy Council and Electric Power Industry Council revised long-term demand projections downward, April.

Public hearings by electric-power industry for nuclear power plants proceed nationwide.

1983   OPEC meets in London, lowers price from $34 to $28/bbl, March.

Council of Oil Refinery releases a supply plan for 1983–7; adjustment to lowering demand, May.

Review of Long-Term Energy Demand Projection, September. New report was released, November.

1984   Council of Oil Refinery releases a plan for merger by domestic oil refineries, February.

NOTES

1. A lawsuit filed by a consumer group for the losses caused by the unfair pricing policy of oil refineries at that time is still going on. A high court reversed the verdict reached by the local court and ordered defendants to pay out compensation for the losses.
2. West Germany and the United States have slowed down; France remains the one country in the free world going ahead with nuclear-reactor power plants without hesitation.
3. International Energy Agency (1984, p. 268).
4. Of the 90-day reserve of the private sector, half is stocked as real stockpiled reserve. The remaining half is working inventory.
5. At the beginning stage, the investment cost was recovered within two years.
6. See Uekusa, in Komiya et al. (1985, chap. 3).

REFERENCES

International Energy Agency (1984). *Energy Policies and Programs of IEA Countries, 1983 Review* (Paris: OECD).
Komiya, R., M. Okuno, and K. Suzumura (eds.) (1985). *Japan's Industry Policy* (Tokyo University Press) (in Japanese).
MacAvoy, P. W. (1983). *Energy Policy: An Economic Analysis.* New York: Norton.
MITI (1973). *Nippon no Energy Mondai (Japan's Energy Problems).*
MITI (1980). *Long-Term Vision of Japanese Industries.*
MITI (1984). *21 Seiki eno Energy Jukyu Tenbou (Projection of Energy Demand and Supply into the 21st Century).*
Research Institute of Electric Power Industry (1984). "Factor Analysis of Japan's Performance in Energy Conservation" (unpublished, in Japanese).
Shibata, H. (1983). "The Energy Crises and Japanese Response." *Resources and Energy,* Vol. 5, July.

CHAPTER 12

Industry structure and government policies in the U.S. and Japanese integrated-circuit industries

W. Edward Steinmueller

Recent public concern over international trade issues has focused on the integrated circuit (IC) industry, in which the United States has begun to lose its international dominance to Japanese producers. For 25 years, the U.S. IC industry has been one of the most technologically dynamic of all U.S. manufacturing industries. Few industries can match its record of growth in employment and productivity and its price and performance improvements. Technological improvements in ICs have been sources of technological revolutions in computers, telecommunications, and other electronics manufacturing activities. Price reductions and performance improvements in IC products have provided opportunities for new entry and innovation in the production of electronics goods. In short, the U.S. IC industry has been a major source of long-term economic growth and employment in the U.S. economy.[1]

The last decade of economic growth in the IC industry has been accompanied by major changes and stresses. In this respect, the IC industry shares features with other maturing industries. With maturity, the seemingly boundless opportunities confronting a new industry are constrained by problems of meeting competition for existing major markets, coordinating new product innovation with existing products, and making the investments necessary for sustained expansion. Maturation of the IC industry has occurred during a period of increasing convergence of industrial output and technological capabilities within industrialized nations. This convergence in industrialized economies has led to both larger international markets and more direct competition among firms for participation in these markets. For the U.S. semiconductor industry, the emergence of the Japanese semiconductor industry as a technological and economic rival in the struggle for international IC markets is the most significant economic development since the commercialization of the transistor. This

319

chapter examines the roles played by strategic government policies and industrial structure in the convergence of the U.S. and Japanese IC industries. The strategic behaviors to be considered include subsidization of factor markets and protectionist measures in both the United States and Japan.

1   Ascent of the Japanese semiconductor industry

During the past decade, Japanese IC producers have progressed from a position of technological backwardness to parity with their U.S. competitors in many important areas of technology.[2] Japan's IC industry has attained a position of strength in the international market through a sustained catch-up effort. The two most important factors responsible for the success of this effort are the structure of the Japanese electronics industry and the actions of the Japanese government. In Japan, the largest producers of ICs are also the largest producers of electronics equipment. The role of this structural feature in the catch-up effort and in competition is analyzed in the first half of this section. The second half of this section examines Japanese government policies that have contributed to the ascent of Japanese firms. The difficulty of this ascent reflects the importance of dynamic factors such as the accumulation of general technical expertise and more specific technical learning for maintaining a strong domestic IC industry.

Japan's IC industry is highly concentrated, a fact that is apparent when the output of the 10 largest firms is examined (Table 12.1). The output of the five largest firms dominates Japan's domestic production of ICs. In 1984, the five largest firms produced 76% of the Japanese industry's production value.[3] The five companies are, in order of size, NEC, Hitachi, Fujitsu, Toshiba, and Mitsubishi. Table 12.1 shows the value of IC sales, share of Japanese production by firm, and proportion of internal consumption to total production for ICs in 1978 and 1984–5.[4] The concentration of the Japanese industry has been increasing over time. In 1978, the 10 largest firms accounted for 86% of all Japanese IC production, and the five largest firms produced 65% of the value of output. By 1984, the share of domestic production by the top 10 had increased to 96%, and the share of the top five had increased to 76%.[5]

The five largest producers of ICs are also the largest producers of electronics equipment, and their IC production is a small percentage of their total sales.[6] This correlation might suggest that Japanese IC producers are "captive" producers – established solely to supply ICs for the parent company's electronics systems. Table 12.1 reports the value of internal consumption in 1978 and estimates of internal consumption in 1985.[7] Table

Table 12.1. *Japanese IC industry statistics (1978 and 1984-5)*

Company	IC production 1984 ($ million)	Share (%)	IC production 1978 ($ million)	Share (%)	Internal-consumption share (%) 1985 (est.)	1978
NEC	1,655	21	442	19	25	16
Hitachi	1,600	21	322	14	20	25
Fujitsu	1,085	14	269	11	50	41
Toshiba	910	12	139	6	15	30
Mitsubishi	665	9	202	9	10	34
Subtotal	5,915	76	1,373	58	25	
Matsushita	600	8	226	10	55	57
Oki Electric	285	4	139	6	15	44
Tokyo Sanyo	235	3	120	5	75	43
Sharp	165	2	101	4	20	43
Sony	105	1	96	4	65	80
Subtotal	1,390	18	682	29	48	
Totals:						
Top 10	7,305	94	2,054	87	30	
Others	495	6	298	13		
Total	7,800	100	2,352	100		

Notes: (1) The Nomura statistics for 1978 report sales and internal use separately. To compare with 1982 production figures from ICE, add sales and internal-production-value columns. (2) The share figure reported under internal-production columns represents the share of internal-consumption value in sales plus internal-consumption value (this sum is the production value).
Sources: 1978, Nomura Research Institute, *Microchip Revolution in Japan* (Tokyo: NRI, January 7, 1980); 1984-5, William J. McClean (ed.), *Status 86* (Scottsdale, Arizona: Integrated Circuit Engineering, 1986).

12.1 shows that among the largest Japanese IC producers, only Fujitsu, Matsushita, Tokyo Sanyo, and Sony use 50% or more of the value of IC production internally. The others have significant internal consumption, but sell the predominant portion of their output to other companies. As of 1985, none of the top 10 IC producers can be characterizd as "captive producers" of ICs.

The variability of internal consumption revealed in Table 12.1 shows the existence of substantial differences among Japanese companies in their internal needs for IC products. The high internal consumption of Fujitsu reflects the importance of specialized ICs for computer production. For

Matsushita, Tokyo Sanyo, and Sony, specialized ICs (linear bipolar devices) for their consumer products are responsible for high internal consumption. Of the other companies, NEC is the only company that increased its internal consumption from 1978 to 1985. This increase reflects NEC's expanding role in computer production, where it uses specialized ICs.

In Japan, the high proportion of production value that is sold outside the firm directs both R&D and manufacturing capacity toward external markets. This expectation is confirmed when one examines the diversity of product areas these companies have entered. However, it appears that Japanese companies are somewhat more specialized than their U.S. counterparts. The Bank of America observed in 1980 that Motorola was likely to offer 80% of the devices needed by a customer, whereas Hitachi was likely to offer 50%.[8] The continuing importance of memory products is another measure of this external-market orientation. In 1984, metal oxide semiconductor (MOS) memory products accounted for over 40% of the top five firms' production.[9] However, during downturns in the industry, such as the 1985 industry recession, internal consumption provides some buffer from the general market. In 1985, memory sales of the top five producers were around 25% of the value of production.[10]

In order for internal company sales to be something other than a local peculiarity of Japanese IC producers, its specific advantages must be identified. The significance of this industrial structure is that Japanese firms are well positioned to take advantage of the accumulation of knowledge from system production while at the same time building major capacity for open-market sale of IC products. A further potential strategic advantage would be possible if Japanese firms specialized in the production of ICs, either by process or by product type. Despite the major significance of such cartelization of Japanese *output* decisions for arguments about international trade, little evidence for this behavior currently exists.[11]

Companies with large internal production face organizational problems in maintaining a strong external-market position. Internal-production demands reflect specialized requirements of the systems divisions of these companies. Such specialized demands may conflict with external-market products. For example, while cost is an issue for specialized production, the value added of system production often can finance higher R&D and production costs for specialized ICs. When specialized product design and packaging considerations become more important than price and standard designs, it is more difficult to participate in external markets. According to one engineering manager at Toshiba, it is often necessary to set up two divisions, one for internal and one for external products.[12] While such organizational problems exist, internal consumption fell from 1978 to 1985 in 7 of the 10 major Japanese IC producers. Two of the three exceptions, NEC and Fujitsu, produce high-value-added specialized chips for computers. In other respects these companies are very vigorous competitors for external markets. The remaining exception, Tokyo Sanyo, primarily a consumer-goods producer, is the best example of internal demands dominating the growth of external-market sales. In 1984 and 1985, Tokyo Sanyo produced the highest proportion of linear bipolar devices, which are used primarily for consumer products, and the lowest proportion of MOS memory devices, which have the broadest external markets, of any of the top 10 Japanese IC producers.[13]

The conclusions one draws about the role of internal consumption and external-market orientation in the Japanese catch-up effort are important for conclusions about the effects of this market structure and complementary Japanese government "targeting" activities that favor the growth of the Japanese IC industry. In a seminal paper on industrial targeting, Paul Krugman distinguishes three sorts of knowledge involved in IC production: process knowledge, product-design knowledge, and knowledge of how to innovate.[14] He then argues that these knowledge categories vary notably in their implications for externalities. In particular, he argues that the process knowledge underlying cost reduction through learning is completely internalized by firms and hence generates no external economies. Because product knowledge is observable in the output of products, Krugman argues that it can be duplicated or imitated by other firms in any nation with similar technical capabilities. Finally, knowledge of how to innovate in the IC industry may create externalities favoring a domestic industry because they build a country- or region-based knowledge pool. The evidence for this last proposition cited by Krugman is the geographical concentration of IC production near Boston and in California.[15]

Based on the foregoing analytical distinctions, Krugman states that Japanese targeting policies should emphasize the third category of knowledge, where social returns to the Japanese economy, as opposed to firm-appropriable knowledge, would be largest. Krugman cites Japanese firms' early focus on memory products as evidence that targeting has had the principal effect of building firm-appropriable assets rather than country-specific externalities. This conclusion is incorrect on two counts. First, Japanese government targeting policies have in fact focused specifically on improving the sharing of process technology among the larger Japanese firms and stimulating domestic demand for electronics-system products. Both of these policies will be discussed later. Second, Krugman's analytical distinctions need to be independent; that is, there cannot be significant spillover from firm-specific process knowledge to product design and innovative capability. Unfortunately for U.S. producers, the sources of knowledge accumulation and mechanisms of knowledge transfer are not sufficiently independent to carry Krugman's conclusions. Although it is likely true that the process of designing IC memory does not create firm- or country-specific advantages, production of memory creates two types of spillover. First, knowledge generated in the production of state-of-the-art memory ICs is primarily knowledge about large-scale process technology. Commercially successful memory production results in the construction of large-capacity state-of-the-art production facilities and the complementary knowledge of how to run these facilities at high yields, knowledge that can be applied to the production of other IC components. Second, precisely because memory products are standard, they require the least investment in support and distributor networks to generate large exports. Cost-efficient production of memory devices is therefore the most rapid route to building a domestic IC industry that can be used for other products, a fact that Korean producers are now exploiting to build their own domestic capability. Moreover, because memory designs have less firm-specific design content than other products such as microprocessors, Japanese firms producing such devices provide little in the way of externalities to U.S. producers who have better support and distribution networks and might have been able to capture returns from Japanese investments in product designs.

If Japanese firms were unable to proceed to the next step (exploitation of the capacity and knowledge generated by memory chips in the production of other IC products), Krugman's argument would still be forceful. For example, we would expect that Japanese firms' memory production would be displaced by that of Korean firms, who would be displaced by firms in other developing nations such as the Republic of China or Singapore. However, the structure of the Japanese industry is particularly well positioned to transform the gains in process knowledge and economies of scale resulting from memory-chip production into production of other types of ICs. That is exactly the path that Japanese firms have followed in expanding their product lines.

By firmly occupying the positions of high reliability, rapid delivery, and low cost, which are all consequences of investment in capacity and process learning, Japanese IC producers have quickly moved to a position of competitive strength in all products where purchasers highly value these characteristics. In areas where product innovation and user support and interaction are very important, U.S. firms maintain an advantage. But this advantage is eroding for three reasons: (1) These areas also value reliability, rapid delivery, and low cost. (2) Japanese firms are making major investments in building the U.S. networks necessary to succeed in these markets. (3) Experience in their own equipment markets has created knowledge that commonly offers Japanese firms advantages over U.S. firms in specific markets. What is left to U.S. firms is pure product innovation based on their past investments in vertical interaction with users.

In this area, prior U.S. industry structure has focused the most intense vertical interactions within the captive-production facilities of equipment producers and left merchant firms to produce the standard and hence internationally appropriable products. Even with this handicap, we might conclude that U.S. producers still have design advantages. However, while the costs of capacity expansion and hence requirements for improving process capability have been steadily increasing, the costs of design capacity have been steadily falling with the advent of computerized design capabilities. Sophisticated designs can be developed in the United States, manufactured in Japan or elsewhere in Asia, and sold internationally. Existing U.S. IC firms may have no absolute advantage in such a scenario or industrial organization and therefore may shrink indefinitely. Moreover, there is no reason to suppose that product-design capabilities should indefinitely favor new or currently existing U.S. companies with currently greater specific knowledge of vertical markets, advanced knowledge of product-design techniques, or other generalized innovative capabilities. These capabilities are also subject to investment, and gaps that are commercially valuable are likely to be closed by Japanese investment.

To summarize, the Japanese IC industry is highly concentrated and is becoming more concentrated over time. In order to catch up with the established product-design and process sophistication of U.S. IC producers, Japanese firms have focused on their own internal requirements and on standard products introduced by American firms. Standard products can be produced in sufficient volume to create economies of scale and spillovers to the design of ICs for internal requirements. The choice of these products directly compensates for U.S. technological and production leads. The use of internal markets is a difficult management problem, and the focus on standard products makes Japanese firms dependent on swings in external-market demand. Despite these problems, Japanese firms have grown very rapidly; between 1978 and 1984, the average annual rate of growth for the 10 largest firms was 24%.

The historical development of the Japanese IC industry structure has occurred in two major phases. During the first phase, which began with NEC's acquisition of Fairchild's planar-process patents in 1962, Japanese technical progress in the application of transistors to consumer products was extended to include ICs. The rapid development of Japanese IC production was primarily limited to Japanese companies and consumer products. Foreign direct investment in Japan was foreclosed by government control over direct investment. The only exception was Texas Instruments

(TI).[16] By 1973, the rapid growth of computer and industrial products began to overshadow the consumer-goods market, thus marking the end of the first phase of development of Japan's IC industry.

During the second, post-1973 phase of development, IC requirements for consumer products continued to be important in total IC sales, but became less important for sales growth and technical progress. The second phase of the Japanese IC industry's development encompasses developments from 1973 to the present, during which time Japan has emerged as a major world IC and computer producer. However, it was not until the 1970s that the computer markets for ICs began to outstrip consumer applications, and domestic production began to outstrip imports. Between 1974 and 1977, the value of the installed computer base grew by 60%, while the value of computer imports declined.[17]

Between 1973 and the present, Japanese firms have attempted to achieve state-of-the-art technological parity with U.S. firms. This effort was closely linked to the desire of Japan's six major computer producers, who are also important IC producers, to achieve competitive parity with IBM in the Japanese domestic market. By 1978, 21% of the value of Japanese IC production was used by the computer industry.[18] In 1977, Japan became the "only industrialized nation in which U.S. company-made computers have less than 50% of the market" (42% in 1977).[19] Nomura Research Institute further contends that Japanese success in the computer market is linked with increasing Japanese capability in producing high-quality large-scale-integration (LSI) ICs.[20] The growing importance of computer-related ICs in the 1970s has brought the composition of demand in the Japanese domestic market closer to that in the United States.

A major factor in the rapid growth of Japanese computer manufacture has been the support of the Japanese government for this industry. Government policies aimed at inhibiting entry of foreign industry and encouraging growth of domestic computer manufacturers have been used. By encouraging the rapid growth of domestic demand for computer-related ICs, these policies have had important effects on the Japanese IC industry. Government policies toward the computer industry may be roughly classified as follows:

1. Import and direct-investment trade barriers
2. Preferential procurement by government-related organizations
3. Preferential procurement policies of Japan Electronic Computer Co. (JECC)

The objective of import and direct-investment trade barriers was to foster a protected domestic market for development of Japan's infant computer industry. The principal policies used were import restrictions, high tariffs, and restriction of direct investment. Import restrictions were implemented primarily through the preferential policies of government and JECC procurement, as discussed later. Tariffs were set at maximum GATT (General Agreement on Tariffs and Trade) rates, 15% for mainframes and 25% for peripheral equipment. Tariff barriers were not completely effective because of the high proportion of system cost devoted to software investment. However, effective software investment required support that was unavailable from many foreign suppliers because of prohibitions against direct investment during the early development of the domestic industry. IBM, like TI, was allowed direct investment in Japan in exchange for technology licensing. However, the Japanese government closely monitored and regulated its activities, as they had done with TI. Policies of discouraging direct investment severely limited other companies' entry into the nascent Japanese computer market, assuring the market for domestic companies.

The prohibition of direct investment may have been the most effective means of isolating the Japanese market from the competitive influences prevailing in international markets. This prohibition prevented U.S. and European companies from setting up the coordinated manufacturing, distribution, and support systems that have been shown to be important to competitive success in the international computer industry.[21] As Harman states:

> Since computers are capital goods providing services over an extended period, and since they are new, relatively unfamiliar tools for many potential users, local support facilities for servicing and consulting as well as marketing are essential. Thus direct investment not only protects the company's latest developments in technology, it also provides the necessary presence of support facilities close to users.[22]

In addition to tariff and direct-investment barriers, the Japanese government developed policies for preferential procurement of data-processing equipment. In the 1958–64 period these restrictions were largely informal, relying on the import license as a tool for obtaining compliance. Beginning in 1964, the government permitted purchasers using public funds to specify bidders. This meant that foreign firms could effectively be excluded from the market prior to bidding. By the 1970s, Japanese computer firms were well established, and protectionist measures were lifted.[23]

A final government policy aimed at nurturing Japan's computer industry was the formation of JECC, which was created to finance Japanese manufacturers' sales of computers and to assure users of reliable maintenance and support; U.S.-owned Japanese computer companies were not permitted to participate in JECC.[24] On negotiation of a suitable lease between the user and producer, JECC purchases the computer from the producer. The producer is then obligated by JECC to give maintenance and software support, for which it is compensated by JECC. Given the extremely large and risky investment that finance of computer sales represents, the existence of JECC is a major benefit to both suppliers and users of equipment. In addition, JECC's market power over suppliers may be used as a means for implementing government policies and restricting the entry of foreign suppliers.

Industrial growth and government support of Japan's computer industry have had a major impact on the Japanese IC industry. With relatively stable growth in demand except for 1975–6, IC manufacturers have been able to accurately predict future demand and install capacity systematically. At the same time, computer manufacturers have been confident of a market for their products, because competition has been regulated by direct and indirect government policies as well as by effective exclusion of foreign companies. The long-term goal of this building process is expansion into international markets where competition will be more severe and demands on IC manufacturers may require more specialized circuits.

Government policies fostering industry growth are important in the communications industry as well. Japan's telecommunications company is Nippon Telephone and Telegraph (NTT). Unlike its U.S. counterpart, American Telephone and Telegraph (AT&T), NTT does not have a manufacturing subsidiary and is owned by the Japanese government. ("Privatization" of NTT equity ownership has been announced and will occur gradually over the next several years.) Instead, NTT relies on four domestic supplier companies: Oki, NEC, Hitachi, and Fujitsu. These four suppliers produce both components and systems for NTT under a complex set of arrangements that include R&D and investment support as well as price incentives. These companies also produce communications equipment for competition in international markets. Thus, Japanese companies that supply telecommunications equipment are able to pursue both domestic and international markets.

NTT's research laboratory is the Musashino Electrical Communication Laboratory (MECL), which employes 3,000 individuals to perform both basic and applied research. MECL appears to perform functions similar to those of Bell Laboratories, although more directly focused on problems of basic and applied research thought to be directly relevant to telecommunications. The close links between MECL and the research efforts at supplier companies provide a rapid and efficient means for transferring basic research advances and monitoring company research performance on NTT projects. NTT's development of new communications technology, involving a considerable amount of digital technology, requires research complementary to the national effort in computer development.

The connection of NTT to its four supplier companies serves as a technology communications link, a means to assure markets for advanced ICs, and an alternative channel for serving government policy aimed at supporting the development of the computer industry. NTT provides subsidies for the IC industry whenever NTT pays higher prices, subsidizes component and systems research, or provides technology licenses at preferential rates for products that will eventually be competitively marketed. Whether or not NTT will remain an important source for IC industry technological support and demand for leading-edge products when it becomes a privately held company remains to be seen.

A final area where the Japanese government has had a role in the growth of the semiconductor industry is in the organization of cooperative research activities. The first of these programs, the VLSI project, was organized by the Ministry of International Trade and Industry (MITI), and its $200 million cost was financed by long-term loans to be repaid from future semiconductor-industry profits. During the four years it was in existence (1976–9), this project was concentrated on improving the capabilities of participating firms in process technology. The five firms participating in the VLSI project also were the five largest IC producers: Fujitsu, Hitachi, Mitsubishi, NEC, and Toshiba. The VLSI project led to 600 patents and provided a demonstration that research cooperation among competing firms was possible.[25] Several other projects were begun in 1981. These programs were the Fifth Generation Computer Project ($426 million), a project in optoelectronics ($82 million), and a project in new-function elements ($114 million). Of these projects, the new-function-elements project continues the VLSI project's focus on advancing Japanese capabilities in the process area and if successful will be a major source of process innovations in the 1990s.

The Japanese government has supported demand for systems products using ICs and of research for improving domestic IC producers. While industry participants often identify the VLSI program and its successors as the principal sources of government support, the sustained demand-side support in computers and telecommunications is also very significant. U.S. firms have cooperatively funded a research corporation, the Semiconductor Research Corporation, partly in response to Japanese research programs. Management of the demands for electronics-systems products is likely to be much more difficult in the U.S. economy, where coordination between financial and industrial policies is limited to preferential tax treatments, preferences that for the most part have been dismantled by the tax-reform act of 1986.[26] Japanese government actions have been aimed at reinforcing the strength of domestic vertical ties that will improve the accumulation of knowledge in IC firms concerning user requirements or have been aimed at remedying technological gaps in process technology to put Japanese firms on an equal footing with U.S. firms. Japanese government policies aim at closing the gap between Japan and U.S. technological capability and the structures of demand in the two nations' industries.

2   The U.S. IC industry

The history and structure of the U.S. IC industry are markedly different from those for the Japanese IC industry. I have argued that the vertical integration of Japanese IC producers is responsible for their success in efforts to catch up with U.S. producers. This industry structure is an important source of Japanese IC industry competitive strength in external markets. By comparison, the U.S. IC industry is organized very differently. In the U.S. industry, vertical integration between equipment and IC production for external markets has been uncommon. If this same sort of vertical integration is an important source of advantage for Japanese IC producers, why has it been uncommon in the U.S. industry? This section examines the origin and current structure of the U.S. industry and explores several reasons why nonintegrated "merchant" IC firms have been the U.S. norm. In the next section, I examine the role of recent technological developments in determining industry structure and patterns of competition. In the final section, I return to the role of government policy, with a discussion of the limitations of U.S. military markets for improving the health of the U.S. merchant IC industry.

Production of semiconductors by U.S. firms is divided between captive and merchant producers. In 1984, the total value of IC production by North American firms was $16.53 billion, according to Integrated Circuit Engineering, Inc. (ICE).[27] Of this total, $12.25 billion was produced by merchant companies, and $4.28 billion by captive producers. In 1984, the market equivalent value for the largest seven captive IC producers was estimated at $3.97 billion by ICE, or 32% of total IC production by U.S. companies. The seven major U.S. captive firms were IBM, AT&T Technologies, Delco, Hewlett-Packard, Honeywell, Rockwell, and Digital Equipment Corporation, who consume virtually all of their production internally.[28] A large number of smaller captive firms are responsible for $315 million of output.[29] IBM, in turn, completely dominates the production value of the captive producers. Its 1984 IC production was estimated by ICE to be $2.8 billion, or approximately 65% of the value for all captive U.S. firms' production in 1984.[30] In the same year, AT&T Technologies, which is the second largest U.S. captive producer, manufactured ICs with an estimated value of $480 million, making it only one-sixth as large as IBM.[31]

Table 12.2. *Top 10 electronics*
firms, U.S., 1985

Company	Electronics sales ($ million)
1. IBM	37,085
2. AT&T Technologies	8,331
3. General Electric	6,935
4. ITT Corporation	6,602
5. Hewlett-Packard	6,455
6. Motorola	5,500
7. Sperry Corporation	5,413
8. RCA	4,981
9. Hughes Aircraft	4,876
10. Honeywell	4,736

Source: Electronics News, August 19, 1985,
Section II, p. 3.

In 1984, the production value for the 10 largest merchant producers (TI, Motorola, Intel, National, Advanced Micro Devices, Signetics, Fairchild, RCA, Harris, and Analog Devices) was $9.22 billion.[32] Like the Japanese industry, the U.S. industry is quite concentrated; the top five merchant firms produced 58% of the production value for all merchant firms. However, because of IBM's large production, two different pictures of U.S. IC production are possible. Because IBM sells virtually none of its output to other companies, it is reasonable to define a merchant market in which IBM is excluded as a producer. Thus, the top five produce 58%, which is more comparable to the Japanese industry at 76%. When IBM's production is included, the value of U.S. merchant-company semiconductor production falls to 47%. IBM's production in 1984 ($2.8 billion) was 20% larger than that of the largest merchant producer, TI, which produced $2.32 billion worth of ICs in that year. IBM's production is also much larger than that for Japanese IC firms. In 1984, the largest Japanese firm was NEC, with ICE-estimated production of $1.66 billion, about 60% of IBM's production.[33]

The contrast between the vertical structure of the Japanese and U.S. IC industries is dramatic. Recall that the 10 largest Japanese electronics-goods producers are also the 10 largest producers of ICs. Table 12.2 shows the 10 largest electronics-goods producers in the United States. Each of the 10 largest U.S. companies has some semiconductor manufacturing capabilities. Two of the companies are also among the largest 10 merchant IC producers. Motorola ranks second as an IC producer and sixth as a producer of electronics goods. RCA ranks eighth as an IC producer and eighth as an electronics producer. Of the 10 largest U.S. electronics companies, four are among the top six captive producers of ICs: IBM, AT&T Technologies, Hewlett-Packard, and Honeywell. The four firms that remain after accounting for the two merchant producers and four large captive firms are General Electric, ITT, Sperry Corporation, and Hughes Aircraft, all of which are small captive producers.

This ranking is very different from that in the Japanese industry. In the United States, the largest producers of electronics goods are captive producers or less significant merchant producers of ICs. In Japan, the largest IC producers are uniformly the largest electronics-goods producers. The size of the Japanese electronics companies is not responsible for this observation. The electronics-goods production for five of the Japanese firms in 1984 (Matsushita, Hitachi, NEC, Toshiba, and Fujitsu) was large enough to place them among the top 10 U.S. electronics-goods producers.[34] This comparison shows that Mitsubishi is quite unlike its Japanese rivals. Mitsubishi has over 75% of its total sales in ICs. Mitsubishi's electronics sales would not qualify it to be among the top 50 U.S. electronics producers.[35] Thus, except for Mitsubishi, a direct comparison of large electronics producers shows that the Japanese firms are major merchant IC producers, and the U.S. firms are not.

Captive IC production in the largest U.S. communications (AT&T) and computer (IBM) companies provides the same advantages of vertical integration in designing components for specific system products that were noted for Japanese IC producers. In addition, despite being captive producers, the very large sizes of these companies' internal markets for ICs allow investments in design and production facilities similar to those for merchant producers. The resulting control of the entire electronics-systems design process offers these captive producers advantages in the design of electronics systems.

However, in contrast to the Japanese industry, the concentration of U.S. captive semiconductor production in the dominant U.S. computer and communications companies weakens the structure of the U.S. merchant industry. In Japan, computer and IC production is dispersed among the leading electronics companies. For 1983, sales of computers, related equipment, and services for Japan's leading computer companies were $2.85 billion for Fujitsu, $2.24 billion for NEC, and $1.91 billion for Hitachi.[36] Communications-equipment production is also dispersed among the four domestic suppliers to NTT: Oki, NEC, Hitachi, and Fujitsu.

While the less concentrated Japanese computer market may weaken Japanese computer producers, it strengthens their capabilities for IC design and capacity investment.

The strength of captive production in the United States has had a major impact on the demand for merchant ICs. ICE has estimated external-market purchases in 1984 for 10 major U.S. electronics companies.[37] These purchases totaled $4.6 billion, or 50% of merchant IC production. Recall that captive production of the largest seven captives totaled $3.97 billion, with IBM alone accounting for $2.8 billion. Hence, 10 of the major electronics companies purchase roughly 50% of their requirements externally. A significant reduction in this degree of vertical integration would have a major impact on U.S. merchant producers. For example, if IBM were to purchase half of its requirements externally, it would triple its merchant IC purchases, from $700 million to $2.1 billion. If the captive producers as a whole were to purchase half of their requirements from the external market, the U.S. merchant industry would grow by about 20%. Of course, such changes are unlikely to occur and in a prosperous year could not be quickly absorbed by the U.S. merchant industry. Nevertheless, this exercise indicates that U.S. captive production is removing a significant amount of IC demand from merchant producers and that even with the high level of captive production, merchant producers are heavily reliant on the major electronics-systems companies for their sales.

Captive production also redirects research investments. The concentration of research follows that of production, except for AT&T, which, prior to divestiture, funded a disproportionately large R&D effort. AT&T's R&D expenditures on ICs in 1981 have been estimated in excess of $130 million.[38] Estimates of IBM expenditures on IC R&D are unavailable, but are likely to have been in excess of $220 million in 1981. According to Semiconductor Industry Association (SIA) estimates, U.S. merchant firms spent $573 million on R&D in 1981, or 9.8% of sales, an estimate that excludes R&D spending by other captive suppliers.[39] In the same year, the SIA estimates that Japanese firms spent $394 million on R&D.[40] The R&D advantage of U.S. firms is reinforced by the larger national stock of experienced scientists and engineers created by captive-producer efforts.

In summary, captive production provides part of the explanation for current U.S. merchant IC companies' difficulties in international competition with Japanese IC producers. Two questions remain: How has the U.S. merchant industry succeeded in maintaining its independence? Why have U.S. electronics-system companies not played a more active role in the U.S. merchant IC industry?

The most important reason for the independence of the U.S. merchant industry is its success at product and process innovation. This success began with the invention of the IC by merchant semiconductor producers.[41] During the early history of the U.S. IC industry, product and process innovations occurred very rapidly, beginning with digital logic families that could be used for creating computer systems. By 1970, IC memories became an important source of demand for IC products and growth for IC producers. Because merchant IC producers were very successful at reducing the price and increasing the storage capacity of these devices, both existing and new-entrant systems producers purchased ICs from the merchants, rather than establishing their own facilities. With the invention of the microprocessor, again a merchant-industry innovation, opportunities for creating inexpensive but complex electronics systems received a major boost. During this period, electronics-systems producers continued to develop their own production capabilities, but most did not enter the merchant market. Systems producers may not have entered because they were unable to combine product innovation with the process improvements necessary to match the low prevailing prices in the merchant IC market, or systems producers may simply have been uninterested in the low profit margins in merchant IC production compared with systems production. In either case, the merchant industry grew rapidly during the 1970s. By 1980, limitations of product innovation as a source of sustained growth began to be apparent.

The rate at which product innovations can be translated into major contributors to the overall growth of a firm has slowed with the overall size of IC product revenues. In this environment, often characterized as the "maturing" of an industry, industry structure becomes more significant. In particular, greater vertical integration and accompanying financial resources for capacity expansion may begin to dominate the innovative flexibility and intensity of smaller firms. This outcome, while common in the manufacturing industry, is not preordained. The importance of firm size and vertical integration can be directly addressed by closer "strategic links" between suppliers and vendors, joint ventures, and stable procurement contracts. In addition, vertical integration is less likely to lead to the creation of standard products that can address the requirements of a diverse group of users. As observed earlier, the joint management of internal and external markets is a significant problem for Japanese companies. It is also a major reason for the unwillingness of U.S. systems companies to enter the merchant IC business.

In a maturing industry, vertical relationships often are rearranged. Historically, the U.S. merchant IC industry has served existing and new-entrant electronics-systems producers with a common set of product and process innovations. However, many systems producers have also matured and found the same limitations to growth through innovation that IC producers face. One consequence of the maturation of system markets, particularly in the computer industry, is the growth of captive U.S. IC production that allows product differentiation based on specialized ICs. During 1985, when the U.S. merchant-industry output contracted by 24%, the captive industry grew by 9%.[42] Captive producers smaller than the top seven grew even faster, at 16%. While the level of production of the smaller captive producers is still very modest ($365 million in 1985), continued expansion may further contribute to merchant focus on the most standard ICs, where direct competition between U.S. merchant producers and Japanese producers is most intense. For the larger U.S. captive markets, IBM and AT&T, the conclusion of a long period of antitrust dispute has created a markedly different competitive environment, freeing both companies to more vigorously pursue foreign and domestic competitors.

AT&T was prohibited, by a 1956 consent decree arising from a U.S. Justice Department antitrust suit, from entering markets other than the provision of telecommunications equipment and services.[43] This decree was interpreted to exclude AT&T's entry into both component and systems sales to non-Bell companies, with certain minor exceptions. A second provision of the 1956 decree affecting U.S. and international semiconductor industries was the requirement that all patents controlled (as of 1956) by the Bell System be licensed to others on request. Brock states:

> Licenses under all other existing or future patents were required to be issued to any applicant at a "reasonable royalty" with provision for the court to set the royalty if the parties could not agree. AT&T was also required to provide technical information along with patent licenses on payment of reasonable fees.[44]

These two provisions of the 1956 consent decree had the effect of removing Western Electric from competition for the emerging U.S. semiconductor market and guaranteeing access to that technology to any company that wanted it. As a consequence, companies with no previous electronics-industry experience entered the emerging semiconductor market – among them a small geophysical-instrument company, TI, which has since grown to be the largest merchant IC producer. Entry by Fairchild, Intel, and other merchant firms followed. This pattern of entry was instrumental in the creation of a U.S. merchant semiconductor industry.

The important precedent of successful entry by TI and other companies has influenced the development of industry structure and the availability of technology. Entry was facilitated by the accessibility of Western Electric patents and technological knowledge created by the 1956 consent decree. Access to technological improvements was further improved by the cross-licensing of technological improvements among major producers. Cross-licensing was a means for Western Electric to extract some value for the enforced transfer of technology it had developed. Later, it became a mechanism for avoiding lengthy and risky patent disputes among producers. As a result, major innovations have been cross-licensed within the industry, promoting technological exchange and access. The continuing influence of AT&T as a source of basic research and technology must be contrasted with AT&T's historical absence as a producer of equipment or components for the general market.

IBM also has been influenced by a long history of antitrust actions. IBM has actively competed in virtually every data-processing market. However, IBM has never elected to produce semiconductors for external markets for reasons that are less obvious than AT&T's enforced absence from the merchant market. Threats of antitrust action, limitations on the profitability of semiconductors relative to systems production, and advantages to proprietary circuit development have probably all played roles in keeping IBM from entering the components market.

The existence in the United States of these two major IC producer companies outside of the commercial market has had a fundamental influence on U.S. merchant companies. Major antitrust suits against AT&T and IBM filed by the Justice Department have now been resolved. All the repercussions of these actions have not been determined. Legislative action and a variety of private legal actions may yet change the capability or desire of AT&T and IBM to enter IC markets. However, the basic outcome of U.S. Justice Department withdrawal from litigation against IBM and settlement of the case against AT&T was to free both IBM and AT&T to engage in more vigorous competition, including possible merchant IC production. As of 1985, AT&T had launched a merchant IC effort and recorded sales of $25 million, according to ICE.[45] Although this is a modest start for a company of AT&T's size, the company is clearly positioning itself to be a significant merchant producer, with memory, microprocessor, and more specialized merchant telecommunications ICs.[46]

Several brief notes complete the answer to the questions posed earlier in this section: How have U.S. merchant firms maintained their independence, and why have electronics-systems producers not been more active in merchant markets? Vertical merger of IC producers with larger electronics-systems producers has affected 6 of the 10 largest merchant IC producers, a development that indicates that U.S. merchant IC producers are losing their independence. In addition, systems producers have become more active in merchant markets. Captive producers have been increasing their merchant activity, and new vertical ties have been formed between merchants and systems houses. According to ICE, several companies with captive IC production capability have recently entered merchant markets.[47] However, to date, these efforts have been relatively modest. Vertical ties for joint development of standard and proprietary ICs have occurred among all of the merchant producers.

The acquisition of U.S. merchant IC companies has had a troubled history. The vertical-merger trend began to have an impact on the 10 largest merchant producers with the acquisition of Signetics by Philips, one of Europe's largest electronics companies, in 1975. In 1985, Signetics experienced the worst contraction of the top 10 U.S. merchant producers.[48] In 1979, Fairchild was acquired by Schlumberger, a French company specializing in oil-field reserves. Fairchild was experiencing major financial losses at the time of acquisition, losses that have continued to the present. There have been four significant acquisitions of U.S. IC merchant companies by U.S. electronics companies: AMI by Gould, Synertek by Honeywell, Mostek by United Technologies, and Intersil. AMI has grown since the acquisition, while Intersil has remained about the same size. Synertek was in financial distress when purchased and was shut down in December 1984. Mostek, the largest of the four acquisitions, was also the most disastrous; United Technologies liquidated it in 1986, although some value may have been salvaged in technology transfer to other parts of the company. This history is sufficiently bleak to cause hesitation in future acquisitions. An alternative that is currently being explored is equity investment.[49] Siemens, the other of the largest European electronics companies, purchased a 20% equity interest in Advanced Micro Devices in 1977.[50] IBM, over a period of time, acquired approximately a 20% share of Intel.[51] Altogether, these vertical ties involve the middle 6 of the 10 largest U.S. merchant IC producers. The two largest firms, TI and Motorola, and the two smallest, Harris and Analog Devices, have thus far been unaffected.

In summary, the complementary relationship between merchant IC producers and electronics-systems manufacturers has been an important economic foundation for merchant-company growth and for the innovative character of the U.S. electronics industry. It is difficult to imagine what the evolution of the U.S. IC industry would have been without the existence of merchant IC firms. Perhaps the IC would have been independently invented, perhaps at a later time, by an employee of an electronics-systems producer. If electronics-systems producers who developed IC technology were willing to sell IC products and if a similar path of technological innovation had been followed by systems producers, whose incentives would differ from those of merchant IC producers, then perhaps the U.S. and Japanese industries would be more similar today.

In such an imaginary scenario, U.S. electronics-systems producers would be selling ICs to one another to prevent the entry of merchant firms. However, the IC pricing and product innovations of such firms might well be influenced by competitive strategies in electronics-systems markets. An equilibrium that would continue to forestall entry of merchant producers and yet contribute to the competitive strength of systems producers is one in which electronics-systems markets would likely be less competitive. A structure based entirely on captive production, perhaps through patent or copyright protection of IC innovations and greatly restricted cross-licensing, likely would have led to major increases in market power of electronics-systems producers. Neither the Japanese model of vertical integration or a possible U.S. model of solely captive IC industrial organization is likely to have led to the rapid entry and growth of innovative small electronics-systems producers that has characterized the last 20 years in the U.S. electronics industry. Whether these same reductions in competition would follow from the dismantling of the current U.S. merchant industry depends in large measure on the process of adjustment that would accompany such a dismantling. If the outcome of current competitive struggles leads to Japanese dominance of merchant production, greater captive production of U.S. systems companies will quickly follow. Such a scenario raises serious questions of performance for the resulting industry structure. Would Japanese IC producers, who are also systems producers, have the same incentives as U.S. merchant firms to price competitively and introduce product innovations for customers who would ultimately be competing in the same electronics-systems goods markets? Would U.S. firms offer technologically advanced ICs to existing or new-entrant domestic rivals? Some insight into these questions is available by reviewing current technological trends in the IC industry.

3   Effects of technological trends on IC market competition

The division of U.S. IC production between merchant and captive suppliers and the success of merchants have historically relied on the success of "standard" IC product designs. The simplest definition of a "standard" IC product is that the product is sold to a number of customers. This definition differentiates standard products from "custom" or "proprietary" products, which are designed for a specific purchaser. "Standard" has also been used to connote the market success of a particular design. Hence, a "standard" product is likely to yield more significant revenues than proprietary IC designs, which are tailored to a specific application common to a small number of firms.[52]

From an economic viewpoint, the term "standard" and the market success of particular IC products is closely linked. This section examines the impact of technological change on the market for standard merchant ICs. For producers, the primary reason for standard products is that large production runs reduce costs and permit amortization of design costs. For purchasers, the primary reasons for adopting standard products in their designs are cost, time to delivery, and reliability. Lower costs are consequences of the higher levels of production of such products and the competition between IC producers. Standard products are available immediately. Systems designs based on standard products can therefore be completed more rapidly than systems designs based on custom products, which require longer design and testing processes. Standard products are more reliable, because many users have the opportunity to test a product early in the product's life and complain about the idiosyncratic features of the product.[53] In custom designs, less experience in the use of the product is achieved, and more hidden idiosyncratic features or "bugs" are likely.

The principal advantage of custom products is that they are tailored to the specific needs of an individual systems producer. A custom product is therefore likely to offer higher systems performance and greater differentiation of the systems product from systems produced by rivals. Higher performance is not guaranteed. Because producers of standard products compete in product performance as well as price, the rate of technical improvement in standard products is rapid. Moreover, custom products often are created with slightly older processes that have become more predictable.

The tension inherent in the decision of systems producers to make (or contract for the custom manufacture of) an IC or to purchase an existing standard IC is an important determinant of the demand for merchant IC products. Certain electronics-systems functions are almost always performed better and less expensively by standard products. Examples include basic logic functions, memory, and simple digital processing. As the systems functions performed by standard products become more complex, the user requires greater amounts of technical support and more technically related products. For example, user application of microprocessor ICs requires detailed technical documentation, example applications, and, perhaps most important, a diverse set of "support" ICs that allow the configuration of subsystems to serve different users' application needs.

Technical progress in the IC industry has permitted very high levels of complexity for individual IC products. As a consequence, the number of products that require technical support has increased. At the same time, demand for the most standard products, those requiring little additional support beyond accurate technical-specification documentation, has also grown. Hence, the tension in the make-or-buy decisions facing systems producers is reproduced in the IC industry in the choice between very complex standard products that require technical support and related ICs and products that require little technical support.

Three closely related merchant IC markets that serve the application needs of systems producers can be identified. The first of these markets is for mass-produced "standard" ICs such as those used for memory and basic circuit functions.[54] The second includes markets for more complex "standard" products such as microprocessors, telecommunications ICs such as "modem" chips, and signal-processing chips such as digital signal processors. The third merchant IC market is the combined market for custom and "customizable" chips, referred to as the application-specific integrated-circuit (ASIC) market. Customizable chips are ICs that at some stage of manufacture can be customized to various end-user requirements. Competition for these markets will likely shape the future of the U.S. and Japanese merchant IC industries, because the first market is likely to be a Japanese stronghold, and the second will likely favor U.S. firms.

Japanese firms have been very successful in the production of IC memory devices. Memory devices store binary information and are complements in demand to microprocessors and other digital-signal-processing ICs. Beginning with the 16K RAM, Japanese firms have become major competitors in international markets for memory ICs.[55] Fujitsu was the first company to introduce the 64K RAM in 1978. By 1983, Japanese firms had gained a 70% share of the market for this state-of-the-art device.[56] Memory devices have been the focus of trade frictions because of their very important contribution to the revenue mix of IC companies. In 1983, *Electronics Week* estimated that the largest category of memory devices, and the one in which Japanese firms were most active, dynamic random-access memory (RAM), accounted for $1.98 billion, or 15% of the $13.5 billion worldwide market for ICs.[57] This one segment of the memory market was approximately equal to the entire market for microprocessor ICs and was the single most important IC product in revenue terms.[58] By 1984, the dynamic RAM market was $3.0 billion, or about 14% of the world IC market.[59]

Japanese firms have used the technical capabilities created in the production of memory ICs to attain technological parity in the production of more complex ICs such as the microprocessor and its associated "support" chips. However, Japanese firms have had problems in gaining U.S. market acceptance of more complex products, such as microprocessors, for several reasons. Engineering of applications requires complementary investments within the systems firm to accumulate experience in the application of complex standard products. The cost of these investments is reduced by close relationships between the IC producer and the systems producer. Although these relationships exist within Japanese firms, they have proved difficult for Japanese firms to reproduce in U.S. markets. As a consequence, prior acceptance of U.S. microprocessor designs in products like the personal computer constitutes a market barrier to Japanese firms' designs. Intel has licensed production of the 8088, the microprocessor in the commercially successful IBM PC personal computer, to several Japanese firms, and most Japanese personal-computer makers have incorporated this chip or its more advanced companion, the 8086, into their designs, rather than using Japanese-designed microprocessors.[60] Japanese firms have been successful with microprocessor designs in a number of markets where purchasers have the design resources to take advantage of price advantages and no prior commitment to a particular U.S. design. Japanese firms plan to introduce their own designs in the developing 32-bit microprocessor market.[61] Whether or not these designs will provide the basis for major growth in exports of Japanese microprocessor products remains to be seen.

A potentially contentious area is the licensing of U.S. IC designs for successful advanced-logic devices. Recently, Intel sued NEC for copyright infringement in the design of a new NEC chip that is meant to be compatible with Intel's popular 8088 and 8086 microprocessors.[62] Intel's suit appears to be based on alleged copyright violations under the 1909 and 1976 copyright laws. More recent legislation has extended copyright protection to IC designs. Whether or not the copyright law will serve as a means for extending U.S. companies' control of advanced-logic IC designs and a further barrier to Japanese expansion in these markets remains to be seen.

The third important market for competition between U.S. merchant IC producers and Japan is the market for applications-specific ICs (ASICs). ASIC products include fully custom designs as well as a number of new products that are "customizable" by end users to specific applications. In addition, technical improvement in computer-aided engineering (CAE) is making it possible for IC purchasers to design their own ICs. These CAE systems were initially used to test designs based on standard IC products that could be customized in a final manufacturing stage. This customization process involved the connection of predefined circuit elements on partially manufactured ICs, called *semicustom ICs,* to create a subsystem with functions desired by users. For example, these circuits were used to translate one to another set of digital codes. Further improvements in CAE systems have allowed users to assemble circuit elements, referred to as "standard cells," into a complete IC design prior to manufacture.

The market for ASIC circuits can be divided into three segments: fully custom, semicustom, and standard cell. Each segment is growing rapidly. In 1984, all three segments accounted for $2 billion in worldwide sales.[63] Fully custom circuits account for 38% of this worldwide total. Information on the U.S. share of this market is unavailable. However, if the overall share of U.S. IC merchant production in world IC production, 47%, were attributed to U.S. merchant fully custom, then U.S. producers would have sold about $350 million in custom ICs, or 3% of their total output.[64] In the other two segments of the ASIC market, Japanese producers are stronger in the semicustom market, and U.S. producers are stronger in the standard-cell market, according to ICE.[65] As a rough estimate, U.S. merchant firms may have received an additional $350 million of their revenue from these two other segments. Hence, total ASIC sales may have accounted for 6% of U.S. merchant revenue. In 1984, total world ASIC production was about 8% of the total value of IC production by all firms. Overall, then, U.S. firms may be slightly lagging in this important and growing segment. ICE estimates that 21% of world IC production will be in ASIC markets by 1990.[66]

The rapid growth and current position of U.S. firms in ASIC markets are causes for concern. ASIC markets offer closer vertical ties between systems producers and IC manufacturers. Japanese firms have made substantial direct investments in ASIC design facilities in the United States. U.S. merchants have been slow to enter this market. The leading U.S. producers include NCR in the standard-cell market and LSI Logic in gate arrays, the dominant semicustom segments. U.S. IC merchant producers may experience erosion in their vertical relationships with continued inactivity in this area. As mentioned earlier, a position of market dominance often can be used to alter the direction of technical change. It would not be surprising to find that Japanese ASIC producers used their position to favor adoption of standard products, including standard advanced-logic devices.

In summary, we have explored technical and competitive trends in two established segments and one emerging segment of the IC industry. In each area there are substantial causes for concern about the future of existing U.S. merchant IC producers. In simpler standard ICs, such as memory, U.S. firms have taken a distant second position to Japanese producers. In advanced IC designs such as microprocessors, U.S. product innovations offer some strength, but the established "standard" products show market losses. In the emerging ASIC market, U.S. firms have not fully exploited their domestic ties, and Japanese direct investment may help solve their problems with their vertical relationships with U.S. equipment producers. I now turn to the military market, which was an initial source of strength for the U.S. merchant industry. Will renewed commitment of the military services to advanced ICs again become a source of strength for U.S. IC producers?

4   Military influences in the U.S. IC industry

In addition to the differences between Japanese and U.S. industrial structures and their different historical development, the U.S. industry serves somewhat different markets than the Japanese IC industry. The history of the U.S. IC industry can be divided into three phases: the military electronics era, 1961-7, the computer-related commercial era, 1968-75, and finally the diversification-of-applications era, which began in 1976.[67]

During the military era, the IC was invented and commercialized as a means to continue the trajectory of miniaturization necessary for airborne electronics systems such as the guidance computer of the Minuteman missile.[68] Initial "integrated-circuit" designs were based on packaging innovations, rather than on the planar technology now associated with ICs. In 1961, both TI and Fairchild announced IC designs that incorporated planar techniques. These announcements, in historical retrospect, were the solution to several military programs aimed at sustaining trends in miniaturization of electronic systems.[69] Military electronics demand was extremely important immediately prior to the invention of the IC. In 1960 and 1961, military semiconductor production was 45% and 48% of total semiconductor production. In 1962, 100% of IC demand was military.[70] Military IC production as a proportion of the IC industry's total output fell as commercial applications outstripped the growth rate of military demand. By 1968, the proportion of military demand for ICs had fallen to 37% of total value of production and continued to fall in the 1970s.[71] By 1985, military demand accounted for somewhere between 11% and 14% of U.S. IC output.

The primary reason for the fall in importance of the military demand was the increasing commercial use of ICs in computers and related equipment. The demand for ICs for use in computer systems grew through the 1968-75 period, with the exception of major and damaging recessions in 1971 and 1975.[72] In the period following the 1975 recession, U.S. IC production has continued to be dominated by two demand categories: computers and industrial products. However, the breadth in both these markets has expanded dramatically.[73] IC types are proliferating to accommodate the variety of specialized applications being developed, a development closely related to the growth of the ASIC market discussed earlier. This trend has important implications for the competition between U.S. and Japanese IC producers, because it is advanced-logic and specialized devices where U.S. firms have an advantage. Many of these products also represent smaller markets and permit U.S. strengths of flexibility and design capability to be exploited.

It is important to recognize the special needs of military systems in analyzing the impact of military procurement or research support. Military semiconductors must operate with very high degrees of reliability in harsh environments. Consumers have no expectation that their products will continue to work in temperatures over 200°F while being bathed in ionizing radiation. Military systems must continue operating in such environments. This has always caused military specifications to be higher and the resulting costs of production of military-specification components to exceed those of civilian components.[74]

A principal problem facing U.S. military planners has been the "insertion" of advanced technology in military systems. The insertion problem involves choices that military-equipment producers face in meeting performance specifications for military equipment. The choice of whether or not to utilize (in military parlance, to "insert") more advanced electronics components in military systems depends on three conditions. First, military-specification components must be available to military-equipment producers. The decrease in military demand relative to commercial demand has also meant increased commercial risks in serving the military market. In many cases, to serve military demand, a firm must divert resources from commercial projects. The potential profitability and assurance of military demand are offset by uncertainties over future funding levels, by limits in demand growth even for very successful military products, and by military demands for second sourcing of components to assure availability. Another factor in military-component availability is the fact that many military systems are unable to utilize NMOS technology, which constitutes one-third of the IC industry's output.[75] These factors combine to limit the rate of advance in military-components availability.

Second, equipment specifications and cost limits must accord with IC capabilities. Military-equipment designers are in many cases performance-driven. While cost is a factor, the performance of the system must, understandably, be adequate to its mission.[76] More elementary ICs or discrete circuits offer a higher level of individual performance and greater flexibility in the design process, which reduces the risk of falling short of performance goals. Thus, in spite of higher costs, designers may opt for simpler technologies to reduce the risk of performance shortfalls that will determine the ultimate acceptance of the system by military purchasers. This factor interacts with component availability and with reliability and maintenance considerations. In some cases, peak performance of the system should be weighed against the reliability problems of incorporating discrete components. The result is that military systems are limited in their ability to use state-of-the-art IC processes or design.

Third, reliability and maintenance considerations must be highly valued, so that IC approaches are attractive. ICs offer a higher level of reliability compared with similar systems utilizing discrete components, and the simpler construction of such systems may facilitate maintenance. These advantages are offset by the potential difficulties of maintaining supplies of more complicated ICs. Encouragement of second sourcing and maintenance of production capability may be more difficult for complex ICs than for simpler ICs or discrete components.

Over the last decade, the combined influences of these factors have led to increasingly long lags in the incorporation of current IC technical developments in military technology. This development is summarized by Larry Sumney, the former director of the very high speed integrated-circuit (VHSIC) program: "A major concern of the military has been the unconscionable delay between the creation of a new technology and its application in operational systems. This 'technology insertion' gap has extended to 10 years or even longer."[77] In order to overcome these problems, the Department of Defense (DOD) initiated, with congressional approval, the VHSIC program in 1980.[78] A principal aim of this program is to accelerate the introduction of advanced IC technologies into existing and next-generation weapons systems. The VHSIC program was initially planned with four phases, with completion in 1986 and estimated costs of $313 million.[79] VHSIC project costs have been reestimated at $680 million, and a number of complementary programs have been funded, bringing anticipated total funding for this R&D program to over $1 billion.[80] Increases in funding reflect the initial success of the program in addressing the insertion problem.[81]

A principal advantage of the VHSIC program has been its focus on IC technologies that are within the main stream of IC industry technical development. This focus is deliberate. Although some research is being devoted to technologies most often associated with military systems, such as gallium arsenide (GaAs), the main stream of VHSIC research has been in areas related to technologies that have been developed for commercial applications. As Sumney reports:

> Where digital electronics are applied though, VHSIC is totally silicon-based, and VHSIC is aimed at returning DOD electronics to that mainstream. Gallium arsenide (GaAs) gates are faster than silicon ones, and GaAs microwave monolithic circuits could be used now in all military communication, early warning, and radar systems. But GaAs digital integrated-circuit technology is far less mature than silicon digital technology. Although the gap

is closing rapidly, the VHSIC program includes no plans to develop GaAs chips at this time.[82]

Hence, Sumney dismisses a major past thrust of military semiconductor research, GaAs devices, in favor of returning military electronics to the commercial main stream of IC technology.[83]

The VHSIC program has received criticism from a number of industry participants and observers.[84] A principal concern of these criticisms is whether or not the VHSIC program is inferior to the alternative policy of fundamental reform of government procurement policy and cooperation with industry. As Macaruso observes, DOD procurement policies have been based on system life cycles that far exceed the life cycles of their components.[85] Macaruso also believes that DOD testing and reliability standards are inappropriate when compared with current commercial procurement standards that result in similar reliability and dramatically lower testing costs and do not expend a significant portion of the product's expected life in grueling incoming testing procedures. Perhaps the most troubling observation made by Macaruso is that differences in military specifications and screening standards among the services and for different end uses have fragmented the already small military demand into hundreds of submarkets.[86] In the IC industry, where cost efficiencies are directly coupled to product standardization, this observation is troubling not only for costs of IC procurement but also for availability of ICs produced by profit-oriented companies.

A recent study of the VHSIC program by Leslie Brueckner and Michael Borrus criticizes the program from both practical and policy perspectives. From a practical perspective, Brueckner and Borrus conclude that the VHSIC program offers limited spillover to the commercial industry precisely because it is tightly focused on remedying the applications problems facing the military. This argument is embedded in a larger argument for U.S. commercial policy favoring the IC industry. Clearly, the VHSIC program, despite the sales pitch offered by some of its supporters, does not offer a solution for the U.S. semiconductor industry's commercial problems. Evaluation of the success of the VHSIC program should not be based on its appropriateness for civilian goals.[87] Similarly, the existence of the VHSIC program should not suffice to remove concern about Japanese government support of their *commercial* IC industry. Whether or not alternatives based on better exploitation of commercial technologies by the military is a more appropriate policy should be an issue for policy discussion. Macaruso as well as Brueckner and Borrus support such reform. Unfortunately, the history of DOD procurement policy prior to the VHSIC program indicates significant hurdles in achieving this aim.

From a policy perspective, Brueckner and Borrus are very concerned that success in attaining VHSIC program objectives of returning DOD electronics to the main stream of commercial development will further undermine the U.S. industry's commercial prospects. These concerns stem from trends toward increasing export regulation in the name of national defense. If such export restrictions apply to all of the commercial technologies having potential dual use in commercial and defense applications, U.S. firms may face a major barrier in international competition. If export controls applied only to VHSIC circuits, the VHSIC program still would represent a major diversion of U.S. companies' R&D efforts away from the internationally important commercial markets. Brueckner and Borrus's arguments, while speculative, should be considered in weighing the costs and benefits of the program to the U.S. commercial IC industry. As Brueckner and Borrus conclude, DOD interests are unlikely to directly serve the interests of commercial IC producers.[88]

Arguments about the relative influence of Japanese and U.S. government support for their domestic IC industries are likely to remain mired in problems of incommensurability. From the Japanese perspective, programs like the VLSI program and the fifth-generation computer program are necessary measures for attaining technological parity with U.S. producers. U.S. programs such as VHSIC appear as direct commercial threats to the Japanese because of potential commercial spillover from such programs and the continuing support for the industry available from military demand.[89] From the U.S. merchant semiconductor perspective, the commercial orientation of Japanese government support for the industry presents a serious threat to independent IC producers.

5   Conclusion

U.S. and Japanese firms' competition for leadership in world IC and electronics markets reveals the significance of their different industrial structures and government policies. For the last five years, Japanese firms have made major competitive gains against U.S. firms by using the advantages of vertical integration for investment in production capacity and R&D. These gains began in dynamic-memory products, where scale economies and process improvement are critical to competitiveness. As of 1985, Japanese IC producers have broadened their gains to other types of IC products. As a consequence, in 1985, NEC was, for the first time, the world leader in IC sales.[90]

The strength of Japanese IC producers in their domestic markets can be traced to three sources: First, Japanese IC producers are also the major Japanese computer and telecommunications producers, an industrial structure that encourages both captive production and close ties in product development and purchasing. Second, the Japanese government has favored domestic computer and telecommunications industries and hence increased the derived demand for ICs through both preferential procurement policies and earlier prohibition of direct investment. Third, even after direct-investment liberalization, U.S. firms have not developed a strong position in the Japanese market.

Japanese success in international markets has relied until very recently on their strength in dynamic-memory markets, where high levels of capacity investment and focused R&D expenditures provided major advantages. Both investments are facilitated by the size of the parent companies of Japanese IC producers. Gains in world-market share in nonmemory IC markets have also exploited manufacturing advantages for more mature "standard" products. These developments are a major challenge for U.S. firms because they interrupt the flow of economic returns expected from the product innovations of U.S. firms. U.S. firms can no longer rely on economic returns from the maturation of product innovations if Japanese firms continue to aggressively reduce the price of these products. Moreover, Japanese attainment of technological parity assures that Japanese producers will be able to produce close substitutes for most of these mature "standard" products. It is less certain that Japanese firms will be as successful at initiating product innovations as they have been with mature products.

For U.S. producers, Japanese competition threatens preexisting U.S. industrial structure and U.S. firm behavior. The current structure of the U.S. industry based on nonintegrated production of ICs for the open market and a large and growing captive IC output is likely to change if current trends continue. Examination of the memory, advanced-logic, and ASIC segments does not indicate that the U.S. merchant firms have a "safe haven" from Japanese competition.

No fundamental changes in U.S. government policies toward the IC industry appear likely in the near term. Military research and procurement programs are unlikely to alter commercial competition between U.S. and Japanese IC producers. Despite widespread concern over Japanese competitive gains, it seems unlikely that the U.S. government will enact an industrial policy toward specific industries. As a consequence, the most likely policies will include further easing of antitrust restrictions on future mergers or joint ventures with an international focus and trade-regulation policies aimed at specific "crisis" markets.

Industrial structure will have continuing importance. Developing innovative strength in large Japanese or U.S. system corporations may prove difficult, as indicated by the experience of many large U.S. firms. U.S. merchant producers must maintain the pace of innovation, consider alternative sources of finance, and redouble efforts to improve manufacturing efficiency.

ACKNOWLEDGMENTS

I am grateful to Mr. Yuji Masuda of the Economic Research Institute, Tokyo, who co-authored an earlier paper on this topic and made it possible to meet with Japanese company and government officials. These conclusions regarding the importance of vertical integration to the merchant IC industry were first analyzed in that paper circulated in 1981. The research underlying this chapter was partially supported by the U.S.-Northeast Asia Studies Forum at Stanford University, and I am grateful to John W. Lewis and Franklin B. Weinstein for the opportunity to participate in that program. Continuing research support from the Center for Economic Policy Research at Stanford University and NSF grant IST85-07536 have supported further research and writing of this chapter and are gratefully acknowledged. Useful comments on this or earlier drafts were provided by Timothy F. Bresnahan, Therese Flaherty, Bronwyn Hall, Karen Moffeit, David C. Mowery, Daniel I. Okimoto, Raymond T. Olszewski, James N. Rosse, and Norma H. Schroder.

NOTES

1. Since 1980, the U.S. electronics industry has been the largest source of manufacturing employment in the U.S. economy. This is readily apparent if computer and office machinery equipment is classified as an electrical rather than nonelectrical machinery industry. The same reclassification leads to an estimate of value added by the electronics industry of $100 billion in 1981, making it the second largest manufacturing industry (after nonelectrical machinery) by that measure. Bureau of the Census, *Statistical Abstract of the United States* (U.S. Department of Commerce, 1984, pp. 427–8, 768–73).
2. See Franklin B. Weinstein, Michiyuki Uenohara, and John G. Linvill, "Technological Resources," in Daniel I. Okimoto, Takuo Sugano, and Franklin B. Weinstein (eds.), *Competitive Edge: The Semiconductor Industry in the U.S. and Japan* (Stanford University Press, 1984, chap. 3).
3. William J. McClean (ed.), *Status 86* (Scottsdale, Arizona: Integrated Circuit Engineering Corporation, 1986, p. 31).
4. Internal consumption is reported for 1985, with only estimates of production value being reported. Because 1985 was a very bad year for both U.S. and Japanese producers and 1978 was more normal, 1984 figures give a more accurate reflection of recent growth in the industry.
5. *Status 1983* (Scottsdale, Arizona: Integrated Circuit Engineering, 1983, p. 64).
6. Author's estimate based on industry interviews.
7. Systematically lower estimates of internal consumption were made by the Bank of America. For 1978, Bank of America Asia Ltd. reported that only 21% of the value of production was consumed within house. Bank of America, *The Japanese Semiconductor Industry – An Overview* (Hong Kong: BOA, April 1979, p. 127). For 1982, this share was estimated to be 18% in Bank of America, *The Japanese Semiconductor Industry – 1981–1982.*
8. Bank of America Asia Ltd., *The Japanese Semiconductor Industry 1980*, p. 133, as cited in *The Effect of Government Targeting on World Semiconductor Competition* (Semiconductor Industry Association, 1983, p. 78). The qualitative nature of this conclusion would be improved by more detailed analysis of production and consumption data.

9. McClean, op. cit., p. 33.
10. Ibid. The reduced reliance on memory sales reflects not only the recession in external markets but also the growing strength of Japanese producers in other IC products.
11. Industry participants often claim that this is an important characteristic of the Japanese IC industry. They claim that particular import markets disappear as soon as a Japanese firm enters the market. This observation is not sufficient to demonstrate coordination of output decisions, although with further verification it might serve to support the case that nontariff barriers in Japan are high. See Semiconductor Industry Association, "Japanese Market Barriers in Microelectronics" (San Jose, California: SIA, June 14, 1985).
12. Confidential interview in Japan, July 1981.
13. McClean, op. cit., p. 33.
14. Paul R. Krugman, "The U.S. Response to Foreign Industrial Targeting," *Brookings Papers on Economic Activity,* 1984, pp. 77–131.
15. In the United States, an important component of knowledge transfer is the movement of skilled labor between companies. This externality is more difficult to achieve in Japan, where job transfers occur primarily within companies.
16. U.S. International Trade Commission, "Competitive Factors Influencing World Trade in Integrated Circuits." USITC Publication 1013, p. 48 (Washington, D.C.: USITC, 1979).
17. Bank of America, op. cit., pp. 30–1.
18. Nomura Research Institute, *Microchip Revolution in Japan* (Tokyo: NRI, Januaay 7, 1980, p. 50).
19. Ibid.
20. Ibid.
21. A. J. Harman, *The International Computer Industry – Innovation and Competitive Advantage* (Cambridge: Harvard University Press, 1971, chap. 6).
22. Ibid., p. 146.
23. It must be noted, however, that the profitability of Japanese computer manufacture has been low or nonexistent.
24. Congress of the United States, Office of Technology Assessment, *International Competitiveness in Electronics* (Washington, D.C.: OTA, November 1983, p. 54).
25. Carmela S. Haklisch, *Technical Alliances in the Semiconductor Industry* (New York: Center for Science and Technology Policy, Graduate School of Business Administration, New York University, February 1986, p. 97).
26. The exception is the R&D tax credit, which has been retained.
27. The appellation "North American" firms is used primarily to avoid confusion over the foreign ownership of Fairchild by Schlumberger and Signetics by Philips, both European electronics companies. Northern Telecom of Canada has a significant captive production facility located in the United States, and Canada has two merchant producers (Mitel and Linear Technology, Inc.). Mexico has little or no domestic IC manufacturing capability. McClean, op. cit., p. 8.
28. Listed in order of 1983 estimated production value; ibid., p. 55.
29. Ibid.
30. Ibid.
31. Ibid.

32. Companies are listed in order of value of 1984 production according to ICE estimates; ibid., p. 20.
33. In 1985, with severe contraction in the U.S. industry, Texas Instruments produced less than NEC.
34. Matsushita is the second largest electronics-goods producer in the world (following IBM), although not among the top five Japanese IC producers.
35. A final observation is that the other U.S. merchant IC companies are not completely out of the running as electronics producers. Six of the top 10 are among the top 35 electronics producers. They and their rankings as electronics-goods producers are Texas Instruments (12), N. A. Philips/Signetics (13), Schlumberger/Fairchild (26), Harris (29), National (33), and Intel (35). Two are already accounted for: Motorola (6) and RCA (8). The remaining two, Advanced Micro Devices and Analog Devices, like Mitsubishi, qualify for top-50 status.
36. In 1983, IBM Japan was the second largest computer company in Japan, with sales of $2.64 billion. The smaller computer companies are also IC producers: Toshiba, with sales of $759 million; Oki, with sales of $711 million; and Mitsubishi, with sales of $560 million. The dollar figures are based on an exchange rate of 232 yen per dollar. *Japan Economic Almanac* (Tokyo: Nihon Keizai Shimbun, Inc., 1985).
37. The 10 companies are, in order of size of estimated 1984 purchases, IBM, DEC, HP, AT&T, Delco, Burroughs, Sperry, Wang, Honeywell, and Xerox. Six of the 10 are among the seven largest captive producers: IBM, AT&T, DEC, HP, Delco, and Honeywell. The missing captive producer is Rockwell. McClean, op. cit., pp. 55, 70.
38. I am grateful to Charles Ferguson for this estimate.
39. Semiconductor Industry Association, *The Effect of Government Targeting on World Semiconductor Competition* (Cupertino, California: SIA, 1983, app. D, p. 7).
40. Ibid.
41. For a brief review of the controversy surrounding who invented the IC, see Ernest Braun and Stuart McDonald, *Revolution in Miniature,* second edition (Cambridge University Press, 1982, pp. 88–90). From an economic viewpoint, Robert Noyce's creation of a workable interconnection scheme for manufacturing ICs brought the invention closer to commercialization than Jack Kilby's demonstration that a circuit could be fabricated on a single substrate.
42. Braun and McDonald, op. cit., p. 8.
43. Gerald Brock, *The Telecommunications Industry* (Cambridge: Harvard University Press, pp. 191–2).
44. Ibid., p. 192.
45. McClean, op. cit., p. 57.
46. Ibid.
47. In examining the seven major captive producers, the following developments can be identified as of mid-1986. IBM has offered only a few chips from its development efforts in the VHSIC program for sale to government contractors. AT&T's activity in merchant markets has already been mentioned. Delco, a specialist in automotive electronics, sells approximately 10% of its output to overseas customers. Hughes Aircraft, recently acquired by General Motors (which owns Delco), had merchant sales in 1984 of $30 million. Hewlett-Packard has not sold ICs in the merchant market, although it continues to be

an important source of optoelectronic devices such as light-emitting diodes (LEDs). Honeywell was an active participant in the merchant market through its Synertek subsidiary, an acquisition that Honeywell closed in December 1984. Honeywell continues merchant activities in a number of specialized devices. Digital Equipment Corporation (DEC) made a brief foray into the merchant market when it announced that it might sell an advanced microprocessor in the merchant market; that offer was subsequently rescinded. The last of the seven captives listed by ICE in 1986 is Rockwell, which until recently was an active merchant firm. Rockwell has exited from merchant IC production to specialize in systems production. McClean, op. cit., pp. 28, 49, 55–64.

48. McClean, op. cit., p. 20.
49. A final alternative that has not been tested is joint venture for production. Recently, RCA and Sharp have announced such a joint venture, with a new production facility to be located in Oregon. The fate of this venture may influence the formation of joint ventures in the future.
50. Haklisch, op. cit., p. 158.
51. "IBM's $300 Million Sale of Eurobonds Is Seen As Move to Loosen Ties to Intel," *Wall Street Journal,* February 10, 1986, p. 4. Intel subsequently repurchased the shares acquired by IBM.
52. These categories are not impermeable. Products that are "custom" sometimes become released to the general market. For example, Intel's first microprocessor was originally designed as a custom product. Products that are designed as proprietary but are released to other buyers sometimes attain a larger market and are then thought of as standard.
53. For a discussion of the learning-by-using process, see "Learning by Using," in Nathan Rosenberg, *Inside the Black Box: Technology and Economics* (Cambridge University Press, 1982, pp. 120–40).
54. Basic-circuit-function chips include logic functions, multiplexing, and elementary digital-processing chips used to "glue" a system together. In fact, these chips are referred to as "glue" chips.
55. A K is a measure of memory capacity. One K is equal to 1,024 bits (electrical levels defined as 1 or 0) of binary information. Representation of an alphanumeric character using the most common coding scheme, ASCII, requires seven or eight bits, depending on whether or not error correction is desired.
56. ICE, *Status 1983,* op. cit., p. 104.
57. "World Market's Forecast," *Electronics Week,* January 1, 1985, pp. 63–4.
58. Ibid.
59. McClean, op. cit., p. 147.
60. ICE, *Status 1983,* op. cit., p. 99.
61. "Japan Semiconductors," *Electronics Week,* January 1, 1985, p. 66.
62. "NEC Vows to Stand Behind Products Hit with Intel Suit," *Electronic News,* April 1, 1985, p. 30.
63. McClean, op. cit., pp. 91–2. Captive producers are excluded, but Japanese internal use is included (p. 95).
64. McClean, op. cit., pp. 91–5.
65. Ibid.
66. McClean, op. cit., p. 90.
67. This outline of the intricate history of the IC industry is only for purposes of discussion. For a detailed history, see A. Golding, *The Semiconductor Indus-*

try in Britain and the United States (unpublished Ph.D. dissertation, University of Sussex, 1971); see also J. Tilton, *International Diffusion of Technology: The Case of Semiconductors* (Washington, D.C.: Brookings Institution, 1971) and Braun and McDonald, op. cit.

68. Kleiman, Herbert, *The Integrated Circuit: A Case Study of Product Innovation in the Electronics Industry* (unpublished D.B.A. dissertation, George Washington University, 1966, p. 123).

69. Military R&D on miniaturization was more successful in signaling the need for the IC than it was in actually producing the IC innovation as we know it today. For a detailed history of these programs, see Kleiman, op. cit.

70. Tilton, op. cit., pp. 90–1.

71. Ibid.

72. Braun and McDonald, op. cit.

73. P. Evison, "Electronics: The Market to 1982," *Financial Times,* Business Publishing Division, London, 1978.

74. Comparison of prices of military components with those of civilian components can therefore be misleading. Okimoto asserts that the higher pricing of military circuits was a means of cross-subsidizing commercial production. Okimoto et al., op. cit., p. 86. While some components that do not meet military standards are subsequently used in civilian applications, the two markets are generally separate and involve wholly different cost structures. Cross-subsidization, to the extent that it exists, involves the transferability of military technology to civilian applications, often a difficult and costly process.

75. The principal problem is that NMOS technology is radiation-sensitive.

76. A less expensive system that cannot perform its mission is of no value. However, trade-offs between cost and performance may not always be made appropriately. For an analysis of this issue, see M. Peck and F. M. Scherer, *The Weapons Acquisition Process – An Economic Analysis* (Boston: Division of Research, Graduate School of Business Administration, Harvard University, 1962, especially pp. 467–76).

77. Larry W. Sumney, "VHSIC: A Status Report," *IEEE Spectrum,* December 1982, p. 35.

78. Ibid.

79. Sumney, op. cit., p. 35.

80. Wesley R. Iverson, "VHSIC-Insertion Program Begins to Pay Dividends," *Electronics Week,* December 17, 1984, pp. 57ff.

81. For a collection of examples of retrofit and new applications of VHSIC technology, see Iverson, op. cit.

82. Sumney, op. cit., p. 35.

83. Recently, both military and commercial users have renewed their interest in GaAs technology; the military is formulating a major program in this area.

84. E. Macaruso, "DOD Vexes IC Makers," *Electronics Week,* February 4, 1985, pp. 63–8 (Macaruso is sales manager for Signetics Corporation); L. Brueckner and M. Borrus, "Assessing the Cost Impact of the VHSIC Program," Berkeley Roundtable on the International Economy, University of California, Berkeley, December 1984.

85. Ibid.

86. Ibid. Macaruso asserts that a company producing some 600 generic types of ICs may find itself listing over 100,000 military parts numbers because of screening and other differences in military specifications (p. 64).

87. Borrus's earlier work strongly advocates U.S. industrial policy favoring the semiconductor industry: "Responses to the Japanese Challenge in High Technology," Berkeley Roundtable on the International Economy, University of California, Berkeley, July 1983. Brueckner and Borrus characterize the current position as follows: "Japanese producers are hoping to combine a proven strength in semiconductor manufacturing with new development efforts in product innovation to leverage a dominant position in VLSI – and leverage U.S. producers out of the picture" op. cit., p. 1.

88. Brueckner and Borrus attempt to provide some important reservations to their argument when considering possible spillovers from the VHSIC program to the commercial sector; op. cit., p. 53.

89. According to a recent estimate, U.S. military demand for semiconductors will exceed \$2.6 billion by 1988, an estimate that will still confine the military to about 5% of the worldwide semiconductor market. Wendy Engelberg, "Military ICs Make Up for Lost Ground," *Electronics Week,* August 27, 1984, pp. 75ff.

90. "Japanese Firm Is No. 1 in Chip Sales," *San Jose Mercury News,* January 15, 1986, pp. 1ff, provides a ranking of companies by annual sales. The *Mercury* cites Dataquest, Inc., a leading market-research company serving the IC industry, as the source of these sales figures.